FRAMING
THE
GLOBAL

FRAMING
THE
GLOBAL

Entry Points for Research

Edited by
HILARY E. KAHN

Foreword by
SASKIA SASSEN

INDIANA UNIVERSITY PRESS   *Bloomington & Indianapolis*

This book is a publication of

INDIANA UNIVERSITY PRESS
Office of Scholarly Publishing
Herman B Wells Library 350
1320 East 10th Street
Bloomington, Indiana 47405 USA

iupress.indiana.edu

Telephone 800-842-6796
Fax 812-855-7931

⊖ The paper used in this publication
meets the minimum requirements of
the American National Standard for
Information Sciences—Permanence of
Paper for Printed Library Materials,
ANSI Z39.48–1992.

*Manufactured in the
United States of America*

*Library of Congress
Cataloging-in-Publication Data*

Framing the global : entry points for
research / edited by Hilary E. Kahn ;
foreword by Saskia Sassen.
    pages cm
    Includes bibliographical
references and index.
    ISBN 978-0-253-01289-0 (hardback)
— ISBN 978-0-253-01296-8 (pb) — ISBN
978-0-253-01299-9 (eb) 1. Globalization—
Research. 2. Globalization—Social
aspects. 3. Social sciences—Research.
I. Kahn, Hilary E., [date]
    JZ1318.F727 2014
    303.48'2—dc23

                              2014004005

1 2 3 4 5   19 18 17 16 15 14

To all students and scholars of the global

CONTENTS

FOREWORD

Saskia Sassen

THE GLOBAL—WHETHER AN INSTITUTION, A PROCESS, A DISCURSIVE practice, or an imaginary—simultaneously transcends the exclusive framing of the nation-state and partly inhabits national territories and institutions. Seen this way, globalization is more than its common representation as growing interdependence and the formation of self-evidently global institutions. It also comprises processes situated deep inside the national, which means that one instantiation of globalization actually is the outcome of a partial denationalizing of the national as historically constructed.

From this perspective, then, the fact that several authors in this book engage the global as regional specialists takes on a whole new meaning. Such a regional angle raises the level of difficulty of detecting the global: it is not enough to confine one's study to the self-evidently global condition. If the global also comprises processes situated deep inside the national, then the development of knowledge about the global *requires* specialized knowledge about subnational settings. Indeed, in my research I find that it is the subnational and the global scales that become strategic for developing a global analytics. It is knowledge about the nation-state as an all-encompassing formation that loses capacity to explain the global, but not knowledge about the subnational. Thus, rather than focusing on nation-states, one of my efforts has been to use the nation-state as a window into more foundational conditions—territory, authority, rights.

Such understanding brings with it methodological and theoretical challenges both to state-centric social science and to the notion of the global as that which transcends the nation-state, that which lies outside its framing. Each of these two analytic modes deploys specific instruments for discovering, conceptualizing, and interpreting its x—its object of study. Though different, they are not necessarily incompatible. But they do have different points of entry, to use one of the organizing images in this book.

While the transcending of the nation-state is a necessary part of the larger effort to theorize and research globalization, the state has continued to dominate discussion and interpretation. And in so doing it has obscured the need for research and theorization of denationalization processes, by which I do not mean privatization, but the exiting of capabilities and processes from a national framing.

From where I look at it all, one of the more important contributions this volume makes to the scholarship on globalization is its specifying of what are as yet ambiguous global conditions. As Hilary Kahn describes it so clearly: "The volume offers an approach that allows global scholars, from all disciplines and with varied interests, to investigate how our diverse lives and locales are defined by and give meaning to global processes" (2, this volume). Many of the findings and theorizations in the chapters detect and uncover what we might describe as emergent shapes in our current multi-sited global landscape. These extraordinary research projects capture foundational transformations that cannot be easily described in terms of the common categorization of global versus national. Further, these are transformations that can coexist with the ongoing presence of national states even as they can denationalize critical aspects of nations and national states.

A second feature I see in this book is that together these chapters have the effect of generating a partial, often specialized, sometimes obscure, disassembling of some of the major categories in the social sciences. This is not always made explicit, and may in some cases be far from the author's intent. It is the juxtaposition of these chapters, with their very diverse objects of study and methodologies, that produces this effect.

The issue here is not simply one of throwing out these categories. Rather, what I read in these chapters is a way of rendering them unstable. In so doing, the authors are making these categories work, analytically speaking, for their status as categories. Many of our major current categories have inherited their status from a time and place when they emerged out of analytic work. Now the challenge is to make new categories that help us theorize the current conditions. This book can then be read as an experiment in expanding the analytic terrain for understanding and representing what we have come to name globalization. Again, as Hilary Kahn puts it so clearly: "While global studies has no single master concept, there is an intellectual space in which basic epistemological concerns and critical ontological questions can be raised" (6, this volume).

Both of these features are critical for advancing research, interpretation of findings, and theorization of the global. Ours is a time when stabilized meanings have become unstable. No meaning is permanently stable. But there are periods when they can acquire a measure of stability. In the Keynesian decades that shaped much of the post–World War II period, terms such as economy, family, middle class, and national state all had a certain stability of meaning. The current global age that took off in the 1980s has unsettled many of the major social, economic, and political meanings of the Keynesian era in the West. We can see equivalent processes in other parts of the world, with their own contents and temporalities.

My concern here is particularly with some of the major categories we use in the social sciences—economy, polity, society, justice, inequality, state, globalization, immigration. These are all powerful in that they are widely used to explain the realities they represent. Yet those realities are mutants—today's concept of the economy dominated by finance and high-tech is quite different from that of the Keynesian period, which was dominated by mass manufacturing, mass consumption, and mass suburbanization.

I detect a cognate effort in some of these chapters, even though they focus on other spaces and contents. The challenge we confront as scholars is to reconstitute dominant categories so as to bring into the explanation that which is in conceptual tension with the established categories. Or to bring in that which produces a "vague" edge that unsettles the category's aspiration to clarity. For instance, when I chose the concept "global city," I was introducing one such tension, a built-in vagueness. Indeed, many responded by saying the concept was a contradiction in terms since cities are in a national hierarchy subordinate to the national state. And this is indeed part of the condition. But I found an emergent reality that needed to be named even if it entered in tension with established categories.

This brings us back to the need to actively destabilize stabilized meanings in a period of emergent formations. We need to discover what these major categories veil or obscure about our epoch precisely because they are powerful explanations. An explanation is not a description—it selects particular features and configurations and must eliminate many others or it becomes merely a description.

Thus a category such as globalization has explanatory power. But what do I not see when I invoke it? For instance, I may not see the extent to which national governments are active makers of key features of globalization, thereby overriding the standard global versus national counterpoint. Or let's take urbanization, a category full of content and much deployed nowadays. Yet invoking the urban condition on its own terms excludes a range of non-urban processes—from land grabs to environments destroyed by mining—that are part of urbanization in that they force rural peoples to seek a livelihood in cities.

At some point, experimental ruminations are what we need, and this requires the freedom to suspend, even if temporarily, method and its disciplining of the what, the how, and the why of an inquiry.[1] I need to engage in what I think of as analytic tactics—the freedom to position myself in whatever ways I want or need vis-à-vis the object of study. I think of this as the space "before method."

Engaging in such analytic tactics and what they allow us to see brings with it the need to construct conceptual instruments for using those findings to arrive at substantive interpretations. Using complex conditions that might be present both in national and in global institutional settings is one step in this effort. That is what I did with territory, authority, and rights: I have found these useful as points of entry—to use the book's image—into the national. They are complex, and their meanings are *made* through struggles and conflicts, thereby registering and capturing the specifics of a time and place. They exist in very diverse types of organizations (tribal societies, kingdoms, empires, republics). Each takes on specific formats, interdependencies, and hierarchies. It is their instantiation in the nation-state, where territory is dominant, which is still a sort of standard. And yet, there have been so many other instantiations across time and space. Today, the long-standing association of these three categories with the nation-state is becoming unstable, making visible the historicity of the latter.

I end with a thought that these chapters evoke, especially in their more ambiguous, undeclared aspects. There are analytic moments when two systems of representation intersect. Such analytic moments are easily experienced as spaces of silence, of absence. One challenge is to see what happens in those spaces, what operations (analytic, of power, of meaning) take place there. The lines that mark a difference sometimes need to be opened up into analytic borderlands. There are plenty of such in this remarkable collection.

NOTE

1. This point will be developed further in the book I am preparing for this series, *Before Method: Analytic Tactics* (Indiana University Press, forthcoming).

PREFACE AND ACKNOWLEDGMENTS

THE CONTRIBUTORS TO THIS VOLUME WRESTLE WITH VARIOUS questions. How does one empirically know when something is global? How global does the field of global studies have to be? Must one and how does one transcend disciplinary and geographic epistemologies? These questions and many others are the drivers for the Framing the Global project, an initiative of the Indiana University Center for the Study of Global Change (Global Center) and Indiana University Press, supported by a generous grant from the Andrew W. Mellon Foundation. Together, the Global Center, IU Press, and a community of scholars are currently conducting research, asking questions, seeking answers, and addressing scholarly challenges that arise in the field of global studies. By supporting and facilitating an international community of scholars, individual research projects, and book publications, the project is defining an intellectual space for the pursuit of global studies. The project aims to investigate the complexity of global phenomena, generate new knowledge, challenge traditional approaches, and provide means of exploring transnational linkages as well as the entities being linked.

In 2011, a working group of fifteen scholars from various disciplines and regions of the world, selected through an international competition, began exploring approaches to studying the global in relation to their individual research projects on an array of topics, with the ultimate aim of carving a niche for grounded global studies and publishing their work in a book series, Global Research Studies. The group posed and tried to answer critical epistemological questions about global studies. Meeting virtually and on a few occasions in person, fellows engaged in generative dialogue among themselves, with our visiting scholars, and with the greater academic community. The conversations were provocative, but it was not always easy. The essays collected in this volume are the product of those conversations.

Many people have guided and supported this scholarly dialogue. The Framing the Global fellows have been creative, candid, and collegial, and the project's success rests on their critical conversations and outstanding scholarship. Visiting scholars Matt Connelly, Michael Curtin, Carolyn Nordstrom, and Saskia Sassen were generous with their time during their campus visits and gracious when asked to give public lectures, meet with faculty and student groups, visit classes, and allow the fellows to pick their brains. From the onset, the Framing the Global Project Advisory Committee members, Alfred Aman, Matthew Auer, Eduardo Brondizio, Maria Bucur-Deckard, Bruce Jaffee, Patrick O'Meara, Radhika Parameswaran, Heidi Ross, and Richard Wilk, have shared their time and insight. The entire campus of Indiana University at Bloomington has been supportive and encouraging, and we thank Provost Lauren Robel, the School of Global and International Studies, the College of Arts and Sciences, Associate Dean of the Libraries Carolyn Walters, former provost Karen Hanson, and Vice President David Zaret for their assistance with various aspects of Framing the Global. Former IU Press director Janet Rabinowitch, who retired after nearly three years with the project as co-director, profoundly contributed to the project's intellectual direction. Her successor, Robert Sloan, continues her commitment, and IU Press sponsoring editor Rebecca Tolen has been insightful from the beginning. Rosemary Pennington has become an important voice for expanding this conversation through social media. Deborah Piston-Hatlen, project coordinator, holds the entire project together and is quite irreplaceable. The Andrew W. Mellon Foundation provided generous funding, and program officer Donald J. Waters gave input and advice from proposal to implementation. With the support from the Mellon Foundation, the project has had a significantly larger scope and impact than ever anticipated, and we are deeply appreciative for this opportunity. Lastly, we thank all our colleagues, friends, families, and co-workers who have shared ideas, provided encouragement, and allowed for occasional absences.

Readers who are engaged in asking similar questions and those who seek more context and conversations about global studies may want to visit the project's website: framing.indiana.edu. The website provides information on the project, the scholars, and books in the Global Research Studies series, as well as curricular materials to support global studies in the classroom and beyond. Together, all of the resources, portals, perspectives, scholarly voices, framings, books, readers, and areas of inquiry related to this project create an intellectual space for exploring new forms of global scholarship and publishing.

FRAMING
THE
GLOBAL

INTRODUCTION

Framing the Global

HILARY E. KAHN

WE HAVE ALWAYS LIVED IN A COMPLEX WORLD, BUT FEW DENY THAT today we live in a noticeably more interrelated world than we did even a decade ago. Multitudes of global linkages meet to form collections of meaning and materiality that affect our lives: in the things we make and use, the ways we think and feel, how and why we do what we do. They appear in our sociopolitical structures, economic systems, forms of governance, and foreign policies. We are conscious of many of these connections, oblivious to others. We know our shirts are made in Honduras and our iPads in China, and we know that we can now buy German chocolate, not long ago considered a rare treat, at every big-box store in the United States. On the other hand, we do not immediately see how personal feelings reflect transnational inequalities, how hippies and the U.S. countercultural movements of the sixties were part of the Cold War, or how southwestern Illinois and Punjab, India, are genealogically linked through activists and genetically modified seeds. Whether invisible or obvious, these connections transcend geographic, sociopolitical, and disciplinary territories, and they seamlessly slip into the everyday and the personal. The approach to global studies presented in this volume provides an empirical framework to discern how transnational interconnections like these are anchored in practices, peoples, perceptions, and policies. The volume offers an approach that allows global scholars, from all disciplines and with varied interests, to investigate how our diverse lives and locales are defined by and give meaning to global processes.

Global studies has not always provided avenues into the personal, plural, and partial, nor has it necessarily transcended geographies and disciplines. Global studies emerged in the 1980s, when intellectuals, professionals, and practitioners first took note of the rapidly increasing transnational flows of people, ideas, and products, and the social, political, economic, and cultural consequences of these trends. Economics and political science dominated this emerging field, bolstering the initial interpretations of globalization as either a faceless, singular, and neoliberal force bearing down on states and societies or, contrarily, as nothing new. By the 1990s, when undergraduate degree programs, research organizations, and academic journals began to sustain this intellectual inquiry, analytic lenses saw beyond the categorization of globalization as either an omnipresent influence or the status quo. Sociologists, geographers, and anthropologists expanded the conversation around globalization from economics and politics to include space and the social. Networks and assemblages replaced anchored geographies, and scholars began to look equally at connections and at what was being connected. Soon graduate degree programs, international conferences, and advanced scholarship were being pursued under the umbrella of global studies.

Today, interest in globalization has spread throughout the academy and entered popular awareness. Yet global studies lacks a framework of understanding and a set of empirical methods that students and researchers can apply across and within the disciplines. Global studies retains several disciplinary mindsets, and many scholars still define their global research narrowly or through binaries. While scholars may argue against simple dichotomies, or align themselves on one side, binaries such as universal/particular, global/local, and micro/macro still inform how we understand global trends. And while the field is increasingly multidisciplinary, it is far from interdisciplinary. Countless scholars focus in on singular frames of reference: culture, society, law, communication, economy, and politics retain their disciplinary significance; the humanities, though with increasing contributions from history, literary studies, and media studies, are regularly absent.

The contributors to this volume build upon previous global scholarship,[1] but in and of themselves none of the earlier approaches meets their analytic and methodological needs. While the contributors do not advocate a one-size-fits-all approach to global studies, they do recognize the need for a more rigorous global framework. Drawing on empirical knowledge to define their analytics and scholarly practices, they provide a grounded approach to global studies.

The objects of empirical inquiry, however, vary dramatically across disciplines and subject matter, from international environmental standards, financial markets, and immigration policies to the performance of aesthetics, identities, and emotions, for example. Empirical research can involve quantitative data sets and regression analysis, or it can originate in oral histories and ethnography. What the scholars contributing to this volume share is a willingness to step back in their analyses and consider the assumptions about the global implicit in disciplinary approaches and received wisdom. Each chapter is framed around an entry point or key term, with discussion of the contributor's analytical framework and empirical research. The terms and concepts that are highlighted were not chosen because of their importance in a given field or in the work of other scholars. Rather, the entry points have emerged in the course of each contributor's engagement with existing approaches to global studies, a particular research question, and ideas generated through collaboration with others in the group. They allow researchers to alter their analytics and avoid involuntarily foregrounding stubborn epistemologies and dichotomies in their scholarship. They are as much new lenses on the global as they are keywords for analysis and scholarly debate. The entry points—ranging from *Affect, Rules,* and *Rights* to *Materiality, Seascape,* and the *Particular*—offer a conceptual toolkit for global research in the twenty-first century, while the essays provide examples and insight into conducting research on a wide range of themes, from global financial gold markets and transnational labor migration to public art in China and the global significance of 1968.

FRAMING GLOBAL STUDIES

Many of the contributors were originally trained as disciplinary and regional specialists. Going *global* meant that they had to challenge epistemological assumptions and stray at times from home disciplines and geographies. They did not modify their objects of inquiry, but asked different sets of questions about them. In the end, the focus on global phenomena did not detract from disciplinary approaches or regional studies, but rather gave greater meaning to their respective objects, disciplines, and areas of inquiry, and produced deeper understandings of lived identities, communities, cultures, histories, and intimacies.

As global scholars, the contributors to this volume demand wider frames of reference, multi-scalar optics, and interdisciplinary skills in order to be aware of and continuously adjust their vantage points. Even so, understanding of the multifaceted world in which we live remains partial. As a result, there is more than one global. Just as general theories of singular society are no longer suitable for the social sciences, it is similarly unfitting to assume one way of framing global studies.[2] Rather, this collection of essays and the scholarship of their authors represent various entry points for exploring a plurality of globals that emerge and come to rest in different guises, locales, and performances. The contributors thus rupture many of the analytic and methodological cartographies that provide global certainty, and they diligently avoid an "impact model" of globalization (Hart 2002). As such, neoliberalism and capitalism are not the only drivers of globalization, nor are they normative, singular, and invincible (Ong 2007). Agency, causality, sovereignty, and power do not inevitably radiate from singular geographies or entities, even though they may cluster in particular locales, actors, and materials.

Traditional renderings of globalization tend to emphasize acceleration, rapid change, movement, and an annihilation of temporal and spatial barriers, but there are also continuities and historical structures that are in interplay with our ongoing practices and perceptions. Not everything shifts at the same rapid twenty-first-century speed. Saskia Sassen (2006) demonstrates this in her scholarship. She reveals how territory, authority, and rights merge into a conceptual framework that shifts, tips, and reorganizes through time while simultaneously maintaining its integrity as loosely assembled modular structures. By allowing for change alongside continuity, grounded global studies illustrates how transformation occurs fluidly, reliably, and at times not much at all.

This book takes a fresh look not only at global scholarship but also at what steered the authors to become global scholars. Exposing the histories, ideologies, approaches, and responsibilities that have guided them to the entry points from which they now do global scholarship, they lay bare their subjects of inquiry. They reveal the processes that led them to the global through numerous frames of reference and disciplinary points of departure. They ask essential questions and transcend the many dualisms that are regularly employed in academia and beyond to describe what is and is not global. They walk the readers through the wide-ranging methodological, ethical, and theoretical questions that bring them to far-reaching globals, anchored not only in standards, markets, media, technologies, and nations, but in identities, activisms, rights, and emotions.

If interdisciplinarity is a heightened form of disciplinarity, as Louis Menand suggests (2010), then we indeed are carving a new intellectual space for this emerging discipline. To date, global studies does not have a master concept around which theory and method can take shape, like sociology has in society, or political science has in politics. Some have suggested that globalization is the core concept (Wank 2008), but there is no consensus on this point. Other global researchers might propose *relations* or *interconnections* as a primary concept, and the authors in this volume clearly recognize the relational constructions of their global areas of inquiry. But when global studies focuses only on the connections, the specific locations and phenomena where those intersections are lodged and practiced are eclipsed, and we risk slipping back into the same dichotomies—between global and local, the general and particular, the micro and macro—that we have been working to move beyond. As Rockefeller (2011) has noted, global scholarship has too often focused on flows without a critical consideration of what is flowing. Grounded global studies must not shy away from the inequalities, anomalies, and differences that are intrinsic to global circulation.

At the core of this emerging discipline is a commitment to empirical research and a search for previously unrecognized arrangements, patterns, and productive connections and disconnections. The entry points identified in the present collection allow global scholars to scrutinize the broader relationships and particularities that intersect and emerge into visibility. They also help scholars acknowledge the power and penetration of established dichotomies or nodes of authority, while simultaneously dissecting them and exploring their mutual constitution. Rather than propose one shared formulaic framework for global research, we encourage scholars to develop their own entry points, work through series of provocations, and create their own framings for the global however and wherever it is made manifest.[3] This is our intellectual space for grounded global studies.

GLOBAL METHODOLOGIES

Our use of entry points works toward correcting various misconceptions, including the impression that global studies is not sufficiently moored in the real lives and social meanings of people and practices. Though we recognize that the global is neither all-encompassing nor linear, meaning that it has its limits, both physical and metaphoric, we are also aware that the global is found in intimate practices, personalities, and performances. The global is not only anchored in the broader regulatory frameworks, standards, and rules that structure our lives, but it is also embodied in essential aspects of our being that may seem to have nothing to do with globalization.

Like electronic web portals, entry points consolidate diverse and far-reaching ideas, people, and resources. Like entries to a citadel, they allow scholars and readers to explore halls, chambers, and secret passageways that together give structure to objects of inquiry. Similar to disciplinary frameworks, entry points give us analytic lenses through which we may pursue our research. Entry points are fallback points, creating some didactic limits and guiding structures for scholarship of global manifestations. They help us avoid branding the global or imagining the local as the origin of meaning and intellect.[4] They define units of analysis and determine our empirical paths, intellectual processes that are key challenges for research in the twenty-first century (Beck and Grande 2010, 412). Our entry points direct our gazes and guide us into the global. They slice reality differently, opening up new modes of understanding.[5]

While global studies has no single master concept, there is an intellectual space in which basic epistemological concerns and critical ontological questions can be raised. Part of defining a disciplinary space for global studies is agreeing on key characteristics that define globals. The globals in this volume are negotiated; they are processes that are created and reified relationally within hinterlands, cities, identities, economies, things, policies, and the personal. They are shaped and signified from within junctures, some of which, in fact, may not appear global at all. Globals can be partial; they need not be mega-processes but can be encountered as incomplete arrangements or even fragments. The contributors see globals as practice: they are ideologies, technologies, and habits that are structured and made legible through everyday lives. Globals are symbolic and embodied with authority and agency, always fashioned and explored within regimes of value and hierarchies of power across multiple scales.

Grounded global studies relies on the deep knowledge emerging from area specialization and the disciplines. This means that there are many potential frames of reference and patterns to discern. The essays in this volume posit no specific vantage point as an a priori starting point. The nation-state is not the primary frame of reference, but one of many used to pursue various global manifestations. There cannot be only one unit of analysis when investigating the connections between different scales (Amelina et al. 2012, 5).[6] Because scholars of the global must define their own entry points and methodological approaches, global studies avoids methodological nationalism's "bounded, static thinking while not disregarding the processes that actually construct emplacement, territorialization and the construction of ethnic, national, and diasporic identities" (ibid., 7). This approach challenges geographies while recognizing that territories and materiality do in fact still matter (Kaplan 2012).

The contributors to this volume move beyond comparative approaches to empirically probe the complex interplay among locales, practices, policies, and people (Shaw 2003). They use comparison relationally and avoid quantifying or measuring isolated cases against universal benchmarks. *Relational comparisons* (Hart 2002) emphasize how entities are formed in relation to one another as well as vis-à-vis broader contexts (ibid., 13–14). This shifts the focus from isolated units of inquiry to the transactions and relations in which they are constituted (Emirbayer 1997).

It may be an emphasis on the connections as well as on what is being connected that encourages many of these authors to embrace ethnographic methods, regardless of their own disciplinary backgrounds. One of the most pressing issues in global studies is the importance of situating understandings of the global in everyday life, in order to investigate how regulations and ideologies get lodged in people's experience. Using ethnography allows many of the authors to enter the points where globals become embodied, discussed, strategized, and performed. As a collective, however, we pursue a form of *methodological cosmopolitanism* (Beck and Sznaider 2006) that demands a plural rather than a singular approach to society and social phenomena.

ENTRY POINTS

Deborah Cohen and Lessie Jo Frazier use the concept of *Scale* as their entry point, which allows them to historicize the moment in which the world first begins to think globally. How and when did an explicit global scale emerge? Their topic is truly a global moment, the confluence of events and ideas in the late 1960s that resonated in social movements across the world, epitomized in popular imagination by the year 1968. They ask how and when Paris became connected to Chicago, Prague, Rio, Mexico City, and U.S. college campuses. As the authors pursue these questions, they provide new perspectives on the Cold War, shifting focus from competition over military prowess to a reordering of relationships of race and sexuality as well as foreign aid and geopolitics. They explore the histories that give birth to transnational ways of thinking as well as smaller optics, ultimately recognizing the role of the radical remixing of ideas and bodies in the 1960s that now allows us to seamlessly think and act through global scales.

Similarly, Prakash Kumar explores the global history of genetically modified (GM) seeds in India and the genealogy of the activism that has resisted them. These histories and genealogies are not linear or exclusive; Kumar tracks them across Euro-American, Indian, and international spaces and temporalities. In his approach, anti-GM activists become archives brimming with transnational ideologies, policies, histories, and political economies. Some activists, like Vandana Shiva, are able to discern their own global connectivities and are able to reorganize networks and genealogies, and move social and political action forward. The responsibility of a global scholar is to excavate these connections to expose the crisscrossing trajectories as well as the locales where advocacy may in fact be global mimicry.

Cohen and Frazier's and Kumar's analyses represent what Rachel Harvey calls the global particular, when research at a global scale eclipses the heterogeneity from which the global emerges. Harvey uses a grounded discussion of global financial gold markets to consider the unceasing tension between the global and the particular. She defines this friction as playing out through three analytic vantage points that define the slippage between the general and the particular and represent the relational framings often used in the field of global studies. Her shifting vantage points span the global in the particular (when the global defines the local), the particular in the global (when the local defines the global), and the global particular (when the global becomes the smallest object of inquiry and thus masks the specificity from which it emerges). All of these relationships represent a conceptual rubric that epitomizes the interplay between what are typically seen as dichotomies between local and global, the particular and the general, and the relative and universal. Harvey uses her qualitatively different moments of interconnectivity to break through the binaries that are entrenched in but yet do not adequately represent approaches in global studies. She applies her rubric to global foreign exchange, which she enters through the *Particular*, from its anchoring in a creative social movement in northeastern Nevada, the Jarbidge Shovel Brigade, to rituals surrounding the "Gold Fixing Room" in London where gold bars are priced for the world market.

As Harvey explains, global scholars must seek what is left out (of dichotomies, for example) and what gets caught between scales. In so doing, they will come face-to-face with a multiplicity of paradoxes, inequalities, and contradictions. These ruptures, frictions, or disjunctures[7] mirror what Faranak Miraftab uses as her entry point, *Displacement*. For Miraftab, displacement is as much about physical movement and distant homes as it is about neglect and inequality as practiced through international trade policies. Displacement and dispossession spring forth in a rural rust-belt town in Illinois, where multiplicities of global ruptures emerge, and where connections to faraway spaces and times define the labor force of a meat-packing plant where over eighteen thousand hogs are slaughtered each day. This is backbreaking and dangerous work that depends on immigrant labor, and Miraftab reveals how capitalist accumulation relies on harnessing the physical, social, political, and economic displacement that stretches across nations, polities, and families. The author also recognizes that her entry through displacement does not stop at the analytical. To displace the vulnerability and risk associated with conducting research within hegemonic power structures, she uses multi-sited methods. Her own shifting allows her to make sense of the lives and geopolitics colliding in and connecting Togo, Mexico, and a rural town in the United States.

Conflicts are integral parts of the global assemblages.[8] These assemblages are generative and generated, or ruly and unruly, as Tim Bartley suggests. They are governing and ignored, influential and manipulated. They are composed of capital, people, things, symbols, power, and legalities that are in constant negotiation yet quite stable and unwavering. Zsusza Gille, in her research on Hungarian food politics, emphasizes *Materiality* in her assemblage of humans and non-humans. Things like fungus, peppers, and foie gras are players as much as European Union trade policy and the world's largest processor of waterfowl. In her case, just as a meat-packing plant in Illinois is harnessing global disjunctures, all players, whether Hungarian peppers, a for-profit corporation, or a political entity, can manipulate materiality. This is a process of materializing politics, where power is not shared equally across assemblages but is clustered at certain points and within particular bodies that are able to guide and take advantage of socio-material assemblages. Hungary, according to Gille, did not just join the European Union, but rather entered into a new socio-material ordering of humans and non-humans.

Michael Mascarenhas explores the global through *Sovereignty*, as he argues that NGOs represent new contingent forms of biopolitical control and autonomy. He demonstrates that NGOs strategically harness financial and symbolic capital, authority, and actors as they develop twenty-first-century practices of humanitarianism. In so doing, sovereignty is a deterritorialized and global assemblage of knowledge, money, and crisis intervention.[9] Mascarenhas guides his readers to the technologies, donors, and politics that help NGOs craft and direct knowledge and concern about water sanitation and certain people around the world. This transnational assemblage comprises relationships between governments, citizens, NGOs, technologies, and donors, and in turn paves the way for humanitarian intervention that either succeeds or fails. That NGOs are acting more like governments than advocates for social change often leads to developmental flops, when transnational corporations and donors' demands take precedence over community interests. Akin to what Zsuzsa Gille argues, here power is not only contingent or emergent but formally embedded in materialities. As such, technologies are only effective if they are part of specific assemblages that are arranged for their efficiency and function.

Alex Perullo finds that effective development in East Africa requires not just technologies but storytellers who must delicately balance and communicate the tension between relativism and universalism. By entering the global through *Rights*, Perullo demonstrates that the strategic practice of a discourse of human rights demands insight into the inherent tension between basic human rights—clearly, one of the most "universal" foundations for human lives—and how rights are interpreted, articulated, and manipulated within collections of people, governments, cultures, neoliberal markets, and non-profit organizations. To traverse these collections of interconnectedness, individuals and organizations must utilize a lexicon of rights that allows them to communicate fluidly and globally, across institutions and governments. NGOs in East Africa are particularly skilled at using the rhetoric of rights to shift across scales of practice and power. Perullo also reminds us, as do many of the other contributors, that *development* is big business and is a practice and discourse where global connections are lodged, manipulated, and reified.

Managing an unruly phenomenon like globalization is not easy, especially as multiplicities of legalities, standards, and operations are layered and overlapping in our lives, goods, and modes of production. Exemplified by the NGOs discussed by Mascarenhas and Perullo, new rule-making projects are popping up across the various landscapes in attempts to broadly regulate environmental standards, human rights, labor conditions, and product quality and safety. Yet, as Tim Bartley demonstrates, rules are made to be broken. Globalization thus becomes a puzzle of rules that must be pursued and played to effectively practice and understand transnational governance through labor and environmental standards. Using *Rules* as an entry point, Bartley suggests that neoliberalism is the basis for this puzzle, since it represents a global marketplace as well as multiple spaces of knowledge and practice. This tension opens up opportunities for alternative rules and forms of governance. However, it also means that rules and unruliness are cut from the same cloth, such that environmental standards for forest management lead to swaths of illegal logging, and anti-sweatshop campaigns shift apparel production to countries with dreadful safety standards and feeble labor rights. This puzzling hypocrisy of tightening rules and resourceful dodging, made manifest when garment factories in Bangladesh crumble and burn, is bolstered by neoliberalism. Yet, neoliberalism is not a monolithic phenomenon. The puzzle of rules allows neoliberalism's rules and regulations not only to promulgate a global market but also to generate alternative values and orders of worth.

In a similar vein, Manuela Ciotti sees the global art market as becoming the new museum. As she carefully analyzes global exchange of modern and contemporary art from India through *Form,* she describes art institutions as global forms of aesthetic sovereignty. The institutions she examines—art fairs, galleries, auction houses, and biennales—are enterprises that are producing the new global museum, as they define exchange rates as well as aesthetics. They are global forms, both processes and outcomes of circulation, where colonial histories, market values, geopolitics, and artistic expression collide and coalesce in the construction of "Indianness," and differences are captured for capital and consumption. In many ways, these institutional art forms adhere to marketplace ideals by negotiating art as intersecting politics, histories, values, identities, cultures, materialities, and commodities.

For Stephanie DeBoer, new media, film, and technologies are arranged into patterns that forge new platforms for pursuing and defining specific globalized locations. Entering the interface of new technologies and urban landscapes in Shanghai through the concept of *Locations,* DeBoer demonstrates how social media artists, curators, and filmmakers help reinvent Shanghai as a globalized and futuristic space. In so doing they build on, and at times mask, the multivariant scales and powers that are in play in this mediated urban space, and in China more broadly. Exhibits, installations, and festivals themselves become landscapes of interactions and unevenness, as differentiated complexities of the world get performed. They are battlefields where meanings of Chinese urbanism and globalization are vying for prominence and visibility, and where technologies are strategically used to navigate urban policy, aesthetics, state mandates, and global media and industry.

Urban spaces are not the only cartographies defined as global. The scrutiny and reinterpretation of physical and political geographies are at the core of global studies. For example, even though Anne Griffiths's entry point is *Land,* she interprets land as multifaceted, metaphoric, narrative, and global. As such, she excavates the legal and cultural significance of land in Botswana, and people's relationships with it, as she fluidly switches back and forth between local, national, regional, and transnational scales. None of the scales she employs take precedence or have more authority; they are simply part of this collection of global articulations, which emerge in the life histories of two brothers. Their diverging life trajectories reveal how the navigation of legal pluralisms, global connections, and scales of meaning build individual and family access to resources and their diverse social and economic relationships with land.

For Sean Metzger, *Seascapes* are not only about histories of maritime trade and labor migration, but also about artistic inventions, new identities, and affective responses. Oceanic zones have long been spaces of global interconnectedness, but they also are heuristic metaphors for many of the goals of global scholarship. Metzger views Chineseness as performed on the island of Martinique through the optic of the seascape that frames various aesthetics, feelings, representations, and histories. He draws on cultural studies and textual and visual analysis to illustrate how spaces such as the Chinese Atlantic emerge from *roots* and *routes,* thus highlighting the relationships embedded in the flows and ripples that ultimately become localized performances of Chineseness. His privileging of sight reveals not only the visible but also the unseen that is often occluded from images, histories, and processes of identification.

Like Metzger, Katerina Teaiwa renders the global through roots and routes, and through the sea, but her roots go much deeper, not only into ancestral time but also physically into places where identities, beliefs, and practices are anchored. Teaiwa urges us to think about how geopolitical *Frames* of Oceania have shaped Pacific states and societies, and understandings of history and identity as well. The Pacific is often represented in maps of the world as a blank space between China and the United States. Reframed through the perspectives of Pacific islanders and Pacific studies scholars, Oceania becomes a sea of interlinked islands, and the ocean a highway that has connected them for millennia. Rootedness and mobility are equally important ontological frames, as ancestors, histories, authorities, and inequalities are lodged in physicalities and movements. Teaiwa demonstrates the importance of critically contextualizing not only phenomena and policies but also scholarly vantage points. She is mindful of the colonial legacies and international inequalities that structure or are challenged by practices and perceptions.

As one of her many lessons for global studies, she demonstrates how broader oceans co-produce the islands where globals are moored, performed, and studied.

Deirdre McKay approaches the global through ethnography and through a concern for *Affect,* as she shows that Filipino caregivers in the United Kingdom make sense of the global as they encounter it through formal institutions but also through emotions, imaginings, desires, and fears. Care—in the forms provided by Filipinos to their employers, and in the practice of concern and support for each other and for those at home—is re-envisioned by migrants through interactive technologies, remittances, and government welfare. Ultimately, globalization and perceptions of care define what it means to be a person in a world made up of givers and receivers of benevolence. McKay reminds us that globalization does not eclipse the cultural and the intimate, but is in fact performed and defined in acts of compassion, or the lack thereof.

Like McKay, all the contributors strive for a more nuanced understanding of the networks of people, things, practices, ideologies, and institutions. They slice up these realities differently, empirically revealing what is too often masked or ignored in global studies. The volume also raises important questions about ethics in global research, recognizing that global stories silence some voices and exclude others. From the observation that humanitarianism rests on interdependencies to the recognition that global and national interests compete on the battlefield of human rights, the contributors engage with questions about inequality as they bring to light the multiple perspectives that give meaning and substance to understanding the global. Ultimately, ethics has everything to do with global studies, from how it is taught, learned, and institutionally supported to where it is located and empirically investigated. A sense of belonging and responsibility to the world is inseparable from the intellectual space being carved out by global studies.

According to Doreen Massey (2004), responsibility derives from the same relations in which our complicated and boundless identities are created, and she urges us to think relationally about the world and our identities. When identities are conceived as concentric spheres that start with individuals and move outward through families, communities, ethnicities, states, and the world, care and responsibility are reduced to geographic units, often located in a house or in the bond between parent and child. Our most meaningful commitments are assumed to be toward those in our proximity, our family and localized communities.[10] But identities are neither concentric nor cartographic, and we must interrogate whether responsibility is truly anchored in geography. If identities are indeed developed and reified through connections extending far beyond our immediate spaces of intimacy, spilling over borders and beyond skins, then it is a simple step to confront emotional and ethical relationships to faraway geographies and communities.[11] It becomes easier to care about the world. If our identities are boundless, our responsibilities are as well.

Grounded global studies offers a critical and ethical broadening of academic pursuits that is not only beneficial but essential for the interconnected world in which we live. It examines assumptions and challenges reasoning with a number of provocations and entry points. It does not displace disciplinary ideals or regional specificity but rather strengthens and deepens their significance.[12] Global studies creates more competent and critical sociologists, anthropologists, political scientists, historians, urban scholars, scientists, area specialists, and educators. It makes us more capable of fully understanding objects of inquiry and confidently answering research questions. We become more ethical scholars, with abilities, ideas, commitments, and research that transcend academic disciplines, frames of reference, and the globe itself. The contributors to this collection map out their intellectual and empirical paths in ways that serve as examples of global scholarship for researchers of all ages. The case studies examine specific expressions and manifestations of the global, offering various routes and apertures for discerning formations of meaning. We hope that students and global scholars alike will draw liberally upon these essays, adapting these framings to ask insightful questions and discover other entry points, intersections, and vantage points for exploring the global.

NOTES

1. Scholars whose work seems particularly relevant to many of the authors include Arjun Appadurai, Stephen Collier, Gillian Hart, David Harvey, Epeli Hau'ofa, Henri Lefebvre, Doreen Massey, Aihwa Ong, Saskia Sassen, Neil Smith, and Anna Tsing. Discussions of specific works and literatures are included in each chapter.

2. See Beck and Grande (2010, 411) for their discussion of cosmopolitan methods and theories of society.

3. I thank Michael Curtin for suggesting that global studies starts with a set of provocations.

4. See Appadurai (1996), Hardt and Negri (2000), and Massey (2004) for provocative discussions of locality.

5. Thank you to Framing the Global fellow Zsuzsa Gille for suggesting that entry points are a mechanism for slicing up reality differently and ratcheting down the level of abstraction.

6. See Amelina et al. (2012), Beck and Sznaider (2006), Beck and Grande (2010), and Shaw (2003) for discussions on methodological nationalism and means to overcome these deeply entrenched approaches to scholarship.

7. Appadurai (1990) calls them disjunctures; Tsing (2005) defines this as "friction"; Sassen (2006) imagines these as "analytic borderlands."

8. For more on assemblages, see Deleuze and Guattari (1987), Latour (2005), Ong and Collier (2005), and Sassen (2006).

9. See also Hardt and Negri (2000, 37).

10. This type of thinking also reifies an anchoring of authenticity and genuineness in the local, in binary opposition to the global, which is imagined as more abstract and instrumental than profound.

11. In her argument, Massey borrows from scholarship that finds entry points with the philosophy of Spinoza.

12. Because global studies enhances disciplinary thinking, please note that authors in this volume use their preferred disciplinary referencing and citation styles. The reader may thus notice different styles across chapters.

REFERENCES

Amelina, Anna, Devrimsel D. Nergiz, Thomas Faist, and Nina Glick Schiller, eds. 2012. *Beyond Methodological Nationalism: Research Methodologies for Cross-Border Studies.* New York: Routledge.

Appadurai, Arjun. 1990. "Disjuncture and Difference in the Global Cultural Economy." *Public Culture* 2(2) (Spring 1990): 1–11, 15–24.

———. 1996. *Modernity at Large.* Minneapolis: University of Minnesota Press.

Beck, Ulrich, and Natan Sznaider. 2006. "Unpacking Cosmopolitanism for the Social Sciences: A Research Agenda." *British Journal of Sociology* 57(1): 1–23.

Beck, Ulrich, and Edgar Grande. 2010. "Varieties of Second Modernity: The Cosmopolitan Turn in Social and Political Theory and Research." *British Journal of Sociology* 61(3): 409–43.

Deleuze, Gilles, and Félix Guattari. 1987. *A Thousand Plateaus: Capitalism and Schizophrenia.* Minneapolis: University of Minnesota Press.

Emirbayer, Mustafa. 1997. "Manifesto for a Relational Sociology." *American Journal of Sociology* 103(2): 281–317.

Hardt, Michael, and Antonio Negri. 2000. *Empire.* Cambridge, MA: Harvard University Press.

Hart, Gillian. 2002. *Disabling Globalization: Places of Power in Post-Apartheid South Africa.* Berkeley: University of California Press.

Kaplan, Robert D. 2012. *The Revenge of Geography: What the Map Tells Us about Coming Conflicts and the Battle against Fate.* New York: Random House.

Latour, Bruno. 2005. *Reassembling the Social: An Introduction to Actor-Network-Theory.* Oxford University Press.

Massey, Doreen. 2004. "Geographies of Responsibility." *Geografiska Annaler: Series B, Human Geography* 86(1): 5–18.

Menand, Louis. 2010. *The Marketplace of Ideas: Reform and Resistance in the American University.* New York: W. W. Norton.

Ong, Aihwa. 2007. "Neoliberalism as a Mobile Technology." *Transactions of the Institute of British Geographers* 32(1): 3–8.

Ong, Aihwa, and Stephen Collier, eds. 2005. *Global Assemblages: Technology, Politics, and Ethics as Anthropological Problems.* Oxford, UK: Blackwell.

Rockefeller, Stuart Alexander. 2011. "Flow." *Current Anthropology* 52(4): 557–78.

Sassen, Saskia. 2006. *Territory, Authority, Rights: From Medieval to Global Assemblages.* Princeton, NJ: Princeton University Press.

Shaw, Martin. 2003. "The Global Transformation of the Social Sciences." In *The Global Civil Society Yearbook,* ed. M. Kaldor et al., 35–44. London: Sage.

Tsing, Anna. 2005. *Friction: An Ethnography of Global Connection.* Princeton, NJ: Princeton University Press.

Wank, David. 2008. "Is Global Studies a Field? (Part 1)." *global-e: A Global Studies Journal.* http://global-ejournal.org/2008/08/29/is-global-studies-a-field-part-1/

1 – AFFECT

Making the Global through Care

DEIRDRE McKAY

THE GLOBAL EMERGES NOT SIMPLY FROM THE WAYS PROCESSES, programs, and institutions intersect and form more comprehensive wholes, but also through the ways those links are understood in people's experiences, their lived and felt participation in making a global world. My take on the global in this chapter begins with affect, connection, alliance, and rule-bending, tracking what people make of the term "global"—and the ideas and networks they encounter behind it. For the Filipino migrants I work with, their global is an imaginary—a space of desire in their already-globalized lives. This global is, for them, about hope, possibility, and potential that emerge from their affective connections with other people. Affect is a valuable entry point to framing the global because thinking about the personal challenges and expands accounts of the global where people's agency is muted or lost. The global is not simply an effect of processes and networks but an object itself—something that people desire, despise, seek out, or avoid and to which they attribute experiences and ascribe meanings.

As academics, much of what we know about this kind of everyday global has been produced by mapping globalization. Studies of the global have focused on shifting sites of production for global markets and the making of these same markets, the reorganization of work and labor supply that this entails, and then the mundane bureaucratic practices and public rituals that support these movements of people and changes in work, and the public debates on citizenship and global belonging that support these changes. In my own work on the global in the Philippines, for example, the key academic work explores investment, migration, and public ritual. Philip Kelly's *Landscapes of Globalization* (2000) examines the way local elites capture the idea of globalization and redirect foreign investment to consolidate their social and economic position. Similarly, Steven McKay's *Satanic Mills or Silicon Islands* (2006) investigates the organization of Filipino workers in the global electronics industry. Rhacel Parreñas's *Servants of Globalization* (2001) charts the experiences of Filipino migrants in the global labor force, while my own *Global Filipinos* (2012) explores the ways public ritual shapes the desires of would-be migrants. Local and sectoral studies like these can then be drawn together by thinking about the shifts and changes they map in people's encounters with the everyday state, or with global products and brands—situations where economic actors and structures do things to people who are made over into the objects of their action. Such micro-level studies have then enabled other researchers to undertake meta-analyses and generate broader theoretical framings of the global. Saskia Sassen has led the way with her seminal work, *Territory, Authority, Rights* (2006). Following her lead, students of the global have both curated selected empirical data and developed their own original analyses of the ways of thinking and expressing ideas that shape the global. The combined result is an account of the global as an imagined realm being shaped and reshaped by a real-world assemblage of regulatory structures, their slippages and bureaucratic demands, and popular or institutional resistances to them. This is one very necessary and compelling kind of account of the global. But though this scholarly work is very necessary, it tends to gloss over some vital parts of the global story. It needs to be supplemented by something else, something more intimate and familiar to everyday lives, to provide the fullest possible understanding of the global.

We can also approach the global as an ethnographic object in its own
right—as a concept or category that people use in their everyday lives to
explain their circumstances, to express their desire or fear, and to give other
experiences meaning. Thus we should study the global not only in electronics
factories owned by foreign investors but also as it is being formed through
people's interpretations of news stories, and shaping their imagined futures,
hopes, and dreams. Such an approach would start with a form of words,
a ritual or practice that endorses the importance of an imagined global
realm while simultaneously bringing that realm into being. For example, we
could follow what meanings and practices would flow from exhortations to
"become a global citizen" or "think global, act local" or shared accounts of
"global terror." We can track how the global thus comes into being through
practices that condense and express globalism—the desire for the global—or
reject globalism, through global fear or moral panics. Whether people desire
or fear the global they imagine and discuss with others, the very practices
and language of discussing and imagining makes the global a space of affect.

Too often, intimate, cultural ties have been elided from accounts of the
global, not because they are unimportant, but because, as objects of research,
they are difficult to apprehend. Such ties leave behind far too few artifacts for
secondary academic analysis. These gaps in our accounts of the global have
emerged because phenomena like affect, emotions, and intimacy are usually
too obscure and language-based to be easily accessible to meta-analytical
approaches. These phenomena are difficult to represent, let alone quantify,
and seem somehow less urgent and relevant to policy than the calculations of
foreign direct investment or descriptions of the making of financial markets.
But make no mistake: affect plays a significant role in the manipulations of
identities, markets, and value that make up globalization. Neglecting affect
has meant that accounts of the global seem to hinge on the ubiquity of a
universal, Western-style individuated subject. To fill these gaps, an account
of an intimate and cultural emergence of globality requires a different sort
of methodology: an approach attuned to the different—and differentiat-
ing—forms of personhood at work in a globalizing world. Thinking about
the global through affect offers us an entry point where cultural specificities
may challenge and extend methods that apprehend the global as simply an
institutional super-object or artifact of a globalized popular culture.

FRAMING THE GLOBAL THROUGH AFFECT

Since the global is a contested and popular concept, it is something that people have strong feelings about. This global is something people understand through their everyday activities and the various ways people feel, want and make the global emerge through their relationships with others, near and far, and with the more abstract categories they appropriate to justify and explain their own dreams and desires. So the global of daily life incorporates both everyday intimacies and long-distance flows and connections, and this is where affect enters the picture. The global may be studied by academics, but it is not just an academic concept; it is constantly being reshaped by a dialogue between the popular culture of our respondents, interactions with academic colleagues and interlocutors in government and business or civil society organizations, often not in dispassionate exchanges but in heated debates. Negotiations over the shape of the global are mediated by shifting communities of practice and interpretation. Importantly, these communities do not come up with one fixed and widely accepted account of the global. Instead, the global remains a concept that is loosely defined—woolly, even. This woolliness does not stop people from feeling strongly about the global. These feelings are where affect comes in.

Here, affect names the field of communicable, manifested desire—positive or negative—that underpins people's emotions, behaviors, and actions. Affect is not simply individuated but shared or collective, working through flow and exchange and shaped by processes of mediation, and attached to the global. The global as an imaginary is something desired but not quite defined or understood, yet given substance and meaning through practices, projects, rituals, figures of speech, policies, and the like. Some people imagine the global realm they desire as a space of free movement where they may achieve economic security and be respected and recognized for their merits and talents. Their imaginary is one of round-the-world connections, increasing material security, and easy movement not just of flows of money but of migrants between nation-states, according respect and success to people who demonstrate a global awareness and build global personal connections. Affectively, their global has an expansive, positive valence—it's something to be excited about, to share, and to struggle for. Other people consider the

ways the global and its connections open spaces, routes, and links for terrorism, epidemics, and economic crises, thus creating global fear, global surveillance, and paranoid or neurotic global citizens. This global, in contrast, is
one of a diminished, fearful humanity with a negative affective valence—it's
something to struggle against, repress, or undo. Not everyone would identify
with one consistent affective orientation toward the global; people tend to
vacillate between positive and negative affective attachments.

Rather than seeking a right and a wrong way to feel about the global, it is
more useful to focus on the new ways the global as an imaginary offers us
to focus on different and interconnected sites simultaneously (Pain 2009,
468). The global does not show us whether these connections are inherently
positive or negative; instead, what the global imaginary suggests, through
our responses to it, is that affect is a social and spatial phenomenon. Being
more than purely an individuated, psychological phenomenon, affect makes
the global social and spatial because it is embodied, connected, and shared.
For example, people feel strongly about the processes and flows they know as
globalization, taking to the streets or the hustings to decry its exploitations
or praise its benefits. Globalization enacts desire for the global in a variety of
contradictory ways. Again in the Philippines, where one of the ways people
encounter their version of the global is labor migration, citizens have taken
to the streets to protest the treatment of Filipino migrant workers overseas,
but also to demand better access to those same overseas jobs for would-be
migrants. Many Filipinos imagine becoming global migrants should mean
financial security and personal success, but their shared desire for this can
lead them into real-world life experiences that fall far short of their imagined
futures. Coming up against exploitative placement agencies in the Philippines and even more exploitative workplaces abroad, many realize their own
desires are in conflict with the global visions of more powerful agents or coalitions. For individuals, apprehending something recognized as the global
opens up an epistemological trajectory of "what it means to be a person" on a
level that blurs and subverts the now-familiar modern boundaries of nation-
states, nationalities, and ethnicities (Chiang 2008, 66). Anti-globalization
protesters in the Philippines are concerned that globalization's processes
have been largely commandeered by national elites as a way of appropriat-
ing value from workers. These protesters do not contest the existence or
value of global connections themselves—indeed, the protesters use them to

organize global resistance. Behind their protests lies a vision of a more equitable, global world, populated by a new kind of globally responsible citizen:
"another world is possible." This world Filipinos imagine is one where people
are not impelled to migrate to find security and success because elite control
over land and exploitative conditions in foreign-owned factories offer little
hope. Instead, it is a place where people can move globally, if they so desire,
with freedom and ease.

Desire to be or become global or fear and anger with the very idea come out
of cathexis (an investment of feeling energy or affect) in "the global" itself.
Yet what shapes this desire is people's very intimate relationship with the
various materializations—always partial and imperfect—of the global that
make up globalization. Their experiences of globalization mean people are
resentful of, if not overtly resistant to, the structures, barriers, hierarchies,
and surveillance that come with efforts to manage migration and direct investments, restructure labor markets, or create new kinds of aspirational
citizens. Quite clearly, the outcomes of these efforts to govern the global by
shaping globalization would matter less if people could not also imagine, and
want, something else. As anthropologist Renato Rosaldo points out, via a
poem about his humiliating encounters with airport security (Rosaldo 2004,
quoted in Adey 2009, 274), the affect of the longed-for global is reshaped by
everyday experiences of global migration to become fear and anger. Rosaldo
tracks how he loses hope and has his longed-for connection refused in his
encounters with borders and immigration authorities. What Rosaldo shows
us, as he maps his loss, is how anti-globalization and the imaginary of a free
realm of the global shadow each other.

What kind of subjective orientation, experience, or understanding might
one require to become a globally responsible, globally hopeful citizen in
the face of globalization's frustrations, disappointments, and violence? How
could we construct the "we" that might enact different versions of global desire and thus a different, shared global? This is the juncture where attention to
affect comes to matter in our accounts of what the global might be or become.

Genealogies of Global Affect

Recent debates about affect, emotion, and sentiment cross anthropology,
human geography, and cultural studies, showing us three disciplines grap-

pling with the global in different ways. To date, the focus of the more general debate on affect has largely hinged on whether the notion of emotion or affect offers the best account of global experience and what those terms themselves might mean. Not surprisingly, each discipline offers an account of global affect that re-enacts its own disciplinary limitations. Cultural studies accounts of emotion tend to be popular, ahistorical, and geographically limited, capturing public sentiment and its manipulation in the contemporary moment (see Ahmed 2004) and focusing on the ways emotions are manipulated to produce hierarchies of social identity and make these orderings appear natural. The use of emotion in such work has then contributed to debates between linguists and others on the limits to universal categorizations and accounts of emotion (see Nussbaum 2001; Wierzbicka 2004). In human geography, a series of useful debates over the merits of emotion and affect have similarly drawn on psychoanalytic and feminist theories to produce an equally flattened and universal account of the feeling subject (see Pain 2009; Pile 2010), considering phenomena such as global fear and global surveillance. In anthropology, the same terrain has been explored by nuanced, detailed, and historicized accounts of emotion (see Good 2004; Beatty 2005) as well as some very useful review articles on the disciplinary history of such inquiries (see Lutz and White 1986; Lutz and Abu Lughod 1990; McElhinny 2010). Of course, the anthropological account offers less a universal sweep of useful theory than a piecemeal, historicized account of locales and, for the casual reader, far too much arcane detail. But it is this anthropological account, however partial, that seems most compelling for global studies, because it accounts for and seeks out encounters with cultural difference as fundamental to the global.

An anthropological approach shows us that, while people seem to have embodied, shared, affective responses to the idea of the global, this does not mean that any particular affective valence (positive or negative) is attached to their imaginary. Rather, people process this affect, drawing on their context, personal history, and the emotional grammars available to them (Beatty 2005), to produce interpretations that they then recognize as emotion. That emotion they experience as generated by their encounter with the global might be fear, hope, elation, panic, or a whole host of other terms that do not translate directly into English. And this intransigence in translation is a key point: while emotion is difficult to translate, affect flows across class and cultural divides. An emotion is a culturally shaped, often very culturally specific, expression of affect. Given what we know about cross-cultural emotions and emotional communications in intercultural spaces, it seems unlikely that there could be any substantive and entirely global account of emotions—happiness, sadness, anger, or frustration. Perhaps it is only in the Anglo-centric and (post)imperial West that we could have a dominant understanding of the global as homogenizing and flattening people's subjectivities, rather than as inherently emergent from its performance in and through intercultural, multilingual spaces. Yet it is clear that the global offers people an epistemological trajectory for subjectivity—a sense of being and feeling as selves in the world—that re-territorializes them on to a realm of being both local and particular but also being worldwide and expansive in their felt and shared experiences.

Anthropology has thus moved from a 1990s focus on emotions as locally bounded phenomena toward a much more mobile account of affect. Richard and Rudnyckyj (2009, 69, cited in McElhinny 2010, 4) note how an older, feminist focus on "emotion work" in anthropology has been transformed into accounts of "economies of affect" in which "subjects circulate within and are formed through affect, rather than the circulation of emotion between subjects." The advantage affect offers is that it is inherently reflexive and intersubjective, and does not carry with it the baggage of psychological individualism that comes with emotion. McElhinny (2010), meanwhile, deploys work on affect in colonial encounters to investigate the formation of globalized neoliberal economic policies. By examining manipulations of affect and the affective politics of various kinds of public debates, particularly those on terror and compassion, this growing ethnographic literature shows how global affect emerges, flows, and can be manipulated.

Recent ethnographies of affect show how governments, business, and popular movements can all be seen to manipulate global affect to their own ends. In the United States, Masco (2008) has shown how the production of negative affect and its capture, most recently as global fear, has become a central arena for American nation building since the early Cold War period, working as a tool of the national security state. In Europe, Jansen (2012) demonstrates that geopolitical affects in everyday life—affects generated by the global—emerge not only through the affective expressions in national identity politics but also through people's experiences of and practices of regulation and ranking of nations and their nationals. The vital point here is that global affect does not necessarily transcend and demolish structures and categories on which certain forms of globalization depend.

For instance, when one of my Facebook friends described herself as "a citizen of the world with a Canadian passport," my annoyance sprang from the recognition that this same sentence would be far more implausible if it ended with "a Malian passport." While it is perfectly possible to envision a Malian global citizen—just think of the many amazing musicians originating there and their reception in a global "world music" community—they would have much greater difficulty crossing national borders than someone with a Canadian passport. That is not to say that the global being created by musical connection in a shared "world music" culture does not offer subversive promise or hope. Nor does it undermine a vision of a global in which this connection forged through music forms a "we" who cares about Malian musicians as an aspect of a shared world heritage. It is just that all of that care and connection does not instantly shift hierarchies, though they may hold the promise of doing so eventually. More importantly, utopian visions of the global can be dangerous where they set out normative conditions for what this global should entail (see Chiang 2008, 61). If we start specifying from what apparent junctures a liberatory global subjectivity might arise—or not, as the case may be—we could undo its potential.

One of the paradoxes of the global is that these potentially transformatory affective connections may not always appear where we might expect. As a scholar of migration, my interest is in the ways care and global affect intertwine in the global imagined by Filipino migrants. Migrants who take on caring work, I have learned, are able to sustain the positive affective connections required to succeed as caregivers, nurses, doctors, nannies, and the like by drawing on intimate kin and social connections in the Filipino migrant community and back home, in the Philippines. For migrants, the positive, tolerant, adaptable stereotype attached to Filipino care is reproduced through caring with and about each other and having faith in a better, global future. It is this broader network of care that lets individual migrants care for employers, wards, and new consociates across intercultural difference. I would want to resist arguments about any global that suggests it would be necessarily better made by Malian musicians and their music than Filipino migrants and their labor. Likewise, we cannot accept a global entirely defined by panics about migration or global terror, nor can we exclude those affects as legitimate and understandable visions of the global based on particular experiences. The challenge is to leave the global open for further iterations. This is where affect becomes particularly useful as an entry point or framing device for studying the global in its various iterations.

ENACTING GLOBAL AFFECT THROUGH CARE

As a starting point to see how affect can work to frame the global, let's take an example of the global as an everyday object. Aida, one of my Filipino friends in London who has overstayed her tourist visa to work as a housekeeper, told me: "My employers care about me, even if I have no papers. 'Aida,' they say, 'you care; you make our lives run smoothly and thus also the UK economy. You are one in a million here in London; it's a global world and the old rules for migration don't make sense anymore.'" My own research on the global has emerged from interviews like this one with Filipino migrants in London. I am exploring their global through an ethnographic, historical, and multi-sited lens, meaning my ways of knowing globality come from classical anthropological ways of "knowing" another's language and culture. Like Aida, participants in my study are predominantly people with irregular immigration status who are doing informal, cash-in-hand caring work. They work as housekeepers, babysitters, nannies, caregivers, and private, in-home nurses, providing care for disabled people, older people, and children—all jobs that require "caring about" and "showing care" alongside skills and training. As the comments Aida reported to me, above, suggest, the employer-employee relations in these jobs are intercultural encounters that instantiate and expand broader ideas of "a global world" in a very mundane way.

In London, their employers definitely connect the care they experience with their employees' Filipino culture. Migrants doing this work agree, but suggest it is even more particular to their very local Filipino communities of origin, rather than something operating at the level of their national identity. Respondents in my study come from indigenous communities in the northern Philippines. One of the interesting features of the dialects they speak is that they do not tend to talk about emotions much in the sense of using categorical terms (McKay 2012). Instead, they speak more frequently of embodied experiences of affect—being made to feel big or small as a person, or someone feeling heavy or light inside himself or herself in response to an interpersonal encounter or experience. Exercises in translating English terms into their Filipino dialects meet with confusion. If I offer "So you felt humiliated when your employer . . . ," a respondent will typically say "umm . . . yes . . . , I felt small inside; my feeling was heavy feeling." The "umm . . . yes" means nothing much more than "I hear what you are saying, but back off with your categories, because I want to see you are sincere in learning about our experience." There is no magical act of translation that can move English terms accurately into these Filipino dialects and vice versa, and, more importantly, people do not see that they need or want one.

With Aida and other friends, I once sat around on a rainy Sunday afternoon using the iTranslate software on my iPhone to try to shift complex English emotion terms into the Filipino national language, Tagalog. The result was general hilarity at how poorly the terms matched up, and they had never heard of some of the English words. This is not the fault of the software, but the incommensurability of emotion words. Nonetheless, Aida was adamant that she and her employers held each other in positive regard; that the "care" she provided was somehow mutual. Notwithstanding a resistance to thinking about their own experiences using English emotion terms, my Filipino respondents are widely recognized as superb communicators, caring, adaptable, and excellent caregivers. While recognition of emotional categories should lead to more effective intercultural adjustment (Yoo et al. 2006), it is actually their skills in understanding and responding to affective messages, not naming English emotions, which they rely on in London's labor market. Care, particularly the expanding international market for migrants' caring labor, exemplifies the ways this kind of global increasingly shapes quotidian experience.

From my interviews, I have learned their migration experience translates Filipino concepts of *alayan* (offering, sacrifice, or assistance) and *inayan* (karma) into lives led in the United Kingdom through the actions and emotional dispositions of care. These two words are Filipino terms describing mutual exposure between self and other across human relations and are intimately related to *kalayaan*—the notion of liberty, describing a freedom that comes through a balance of gifts and obligations. Care has complex meanings for Filipinos. It underpins virtually all the social relations they inhabit—from kinship and friendships to labor and citizenship. Care shapes

Filipino migrants in East London text, Skype, and email family members and employers, building connections even on their day off.

migrants' work in London, their connections to each other, to community groups, to kin in the Philippines and their experiences of the technocratic regulatory regimes shaping migration and public rituals of national belonging such as Filipino community celebrations and embassy events.

Filipino migrants believe that a lack of perceived care from their own government undermines its legitimacy. They learn about government care because their work reveals the retreat of the British welfare state that previously provided care for many of their employers. For irregular migrants, or those breaking visa rules, the insecurity attached to their stay in the United Kingdom makes life in London particularly anxious. Migrants describe how care work produces a series of small islands of safety that link home in the Philippines to life in London through *alayan* and *inayan*. These spaces of safety depend on emotional connections established with employers within the mutual exposure required by caring work. Employers, themselves breaking employment laws and subject to fines for not checking workers' documents, feel, if not equally, then similarly exposed, dependent, and insecure. For both of these groups, recourse to the global as a shared site of justification for rule-breaking behavior and imagined realm of equality and communion assuages these feelings of insecurity. As Aida asserted, contemplating her employers' justification of her continued employment despite her irregular status, "we care for each other."

Care in these relationships and the London labor market is not simply universal disposition or a technical proficiency—a skill that can be easily mastered or a universal norm—because Filipino migrants are able to market themselves as the quintessential caring people, almost as a brand name (Manalansan 2010). Instead, care is the outcome of encounters between a group of people with a dividual subjectivity—people who carry with them a relational form of personhood and come from a non-state society—with more individuated UK residents. To see this in more detail, we can examine the biography of one of Aida's friends.

Rachel's Story

Rachel has been working in London as a housekeeper-nanny. She arrived on a tourist visa and overstayed, working in the informal, cash-in-hand economy. For the early part of her stay, she found public transit gave her a small and heavy feeling. Would she be apprehended by the transport police and turned over to the UK Border Agency? But she was only one person and chances were that she would not attract attention, or would she . . . ? Eventually, Rachel was "caught" by the authorities through her connections to other Filipino migrants. She then made a claim for humanitarian protected status (asylum).

While her asylum petition is being reviewed, she has continued to work. She is breaking the rules by working. But her employers, and those of her friends, reassure individual workers that, given the size of London's migrant population and informal workforce, they are unlikely to be caught. Since 2009, Rachel has carried a letter from the Border Agency so, if she is asked to stop and account for herself by the transport police or the police at any time, she has documents to show. Now she is in the final appeals stage. If her claim is not granted on appeal, she will be removed or take the International Organization for Migration (IOM) repatriation package.

Rachel has paid fairly steep lawyer's fees to make the claim and keep the process going while she works. She is also in debt to moneylenders back in the Philippines for a loan to support house building there, and she gives allowances to her three kids and supports other relatives on an as-needed basis. And she has recently been having difficulties with her employer, who could terminate her work without recourse at any minute. Rachel's old employer became grumpy because Rachel seemed to be distracted and was always on her iPhone, checking calls and messages (from her lawyer, her kids and her relatives in the Philippines, or her creditors).

In late 2011, Rachel told me she was also feeling small and heavy at work and wanted a change of employers. She was considering going to Australia. Her sister, Feliz, was working there, also as a housekeeper-nanny. Feliz, she thought, might be able to find her a good employer. Naively, I asked how Feliz had acquired the right to work in Australia and Rachel laughed. It turned out that Feliz had gone to Australia as a tourist and overstayed, just as Rachel had in the United Kingdom. There was no working visa or possibility of permanent residency on this new horizon either. Rachel would move, again, into the shadow economy of irregular migration and cash-in-hand, informal work. I asked her why she wanted to switch countries for no apparent gain in security or income, and she explained that immigration enforcement was comparatively lax in Australia. There, she would alleviate her heavy feeling, not having to worry as much about the authorities suddenly finding her and deporting her, disrupting her plans and networks.

Rachel eventually found a new employer in early 2012. This employer, too, was willing to risk the fine for paying cash-in-hand wages to a worker without the requisite working visa. Rachel felt much lighter in her work. She began her own fundraising initiatives for friends in the Philippines with long-term medical problems and no health insurance, feeling "big" in her ability to channel care toward home and enroll her employer as a donor. Then the Border Agency contacted her with a refusal of her claim and she was required to report every two weeks to their offices. Her employer, she explained, responded to the news with "We're willing to gamble." Rachel kept working, feeling her employer "really cared" for her welfare and valued her contribution to the household. One day, she took the employer's two daughters on an excursion, picking up McDonald's Happy Meals as a treat. When the older girl opened the McDonald's box, she looked at the french fries and asked Rachel, "What's this? Worms?," then asked for rice and fish. This family, Rachel explained to me, had recently moved to London from the United Arab Emirates for the Dutch-English father's banking job. In the UAE, they had had a Filipino nanny who cooked rice and fish. The mother, Malaysian-English, had herself grown up with Filipino nannies in Singapore. Rachel joked, "See, we're more a global brand than McDonald's."

Here in London and in these working relations, Filipino migrants exploit the disjuncture in migration regulation and labor market segmentation/demand for labor opened up by globalization. In the process of exploiting this disjuncture, they necessarily exploit themselves and open themselves up to exploitation by others. To sustain themselves in this precarious situation, assuage their anxieties, and live with hope for a better future, they rely on networks of care. Migrants' ability to care and connect brings them into relationships with a highly mobile group of employers from the "global elite" who are themselves trying to establish their own connections, however fleeting, with intersecting networks of care and support in the city.

Individuals, institutions, and networks produce and inhabit these disjunctures to make their own globals. Rachel's Facebook friends include village friends and relatives "abroad" in Cyprus, Norway, Germany, Israel, Spain, Canada, the United States, and Australia. Many of these "friends," she assures me, are similarly working in a Filipino niche of housekeeping, childcare, eldercare, and the like that lies largely outside government regulation. They are virtually all bending the visa rules, and a significant number are living entirely in the informal economy or out of sight of state authorities. The disjuncture is not simply that they are doing this, but that it is something they can consider worthwhile, profitable, and a kind of emotional and social adventure, despite the risk and sacrifices such work involves.

Regulatory regimes and institutions and implementation strategies for migration are limited or deferred by collective and collaborative intercultural action to create such social spaces. Migrant-receiving states themselves benefit from having such large shadow workforces, particularly for the care that reproduces their highly mobile, global professional elites. Both employers and employees use affective connections of various sorts—care—to sustain themselves and keep such spaces open. Some of Rachel's migrant friends have had employers support them in immigration tribunals and been granted protected status or work permits. Others, who have been deported for overstaying or breaking their visa regulations, have received termination payments when they returned to the Philippines. Both employers of migrants and migrant employees self-consciously use the global as a justificatory strategy for their practices of migration, of work, and of employment. This global that they are using to justify their non-compliance with state regulations relates to what they know of globalization and global institutions, networks, and processes. They can transform the account of the global they have acquired in, say, banking or tracking the worldwide expansion of McDonald's into the description of a space beyond migration rules where people operate by exchanging various kinds of care.

In these encounters, the global is what people make of it. The global is coming into being as an "as if" reality in people's everyday lives as they try to deal with insecurity in various forms. Framing of the global as a kind of supra-state realm does not suffice here. For Aida, the global emerges not primarily through state regulations and migration regimes, but from within the intimate connections of care in her daily life. This care consoles her, assuaging her guilt over her irregular status and, at the same time, enables her employers to find recourse in a realm of globality to justify employing her. This suggests that a very wide and varied group of people are using everyday intimacies to give shape to a global that exceeds, supplements, and calls into question the state. A fine-grained, ethnographic methodology opens up the global into a sphere of possibility and critique where cultural variations in notions of personhood are recombined and transcended through different forms of relation. This realm is being shaped by a series of cross-cultural emotional grammars (Beatty 2005) learned by participants in these relations to negotiate care. Though the global is also about regulation, synthesis, and overarching logics, it is at the same time being composed of the accretion of such intimate, intercultural connections, emerging from and through specific ethnographic contexts.

AFFECT—METHODS AND THEORIES FOR THE GLOBAL

To frame the global through affect, my methods are classic ethnographic ones, with a digital twist—participant observation, iterative interviews, focus groups, media monitoring, attending non-governmental organization (NGO) workshops, and so on. I am interested in the global as an emic category—a word that people use in daily life—not simply as the product of joining up all these programs and processes that is attached as an externally generated label to describe these experiences. I want to know what people make of the term, how they dream of it and what it means to them when they say it, how they feel about themselves as they imagine it. My approach both differs from and complements more familiar multi-sited or institution-based studies of globalization because my object of study is distinctly retro: I study globalism by expanding on traditional village and kin network studies. Right now, I am doing quite a bit of my work via Facebook, where migrants' "friends" lists show how village and kin networks are dispersed across receiving nations. I draw together participant observations, interviews, online exchanges, material objects, and documents collected in both the United Kingdom and the Philippines to interrogate conceptions of care. I trace how the ways my respondents conceive of care emerge through strategies of affective connection and exchange that Filipinos, in the absence of a strong state, have long used to turn strangers into consociates. A global imaginary then takes these cultural practices of connection building and draws employers and their networks into intimacy and exchange based on an ethic of *inayan* (reciprocal fate). Where this intimacy falters, employers are *plastik* (superficial and insincere), and, where it succeeds, they are *lenient* (supportive and generous). My respondents thus use their caring connections and manipulate global affect to both circumvent and transcend attempts by states to regulate their finances, movements, and employment.

To theorize the global as it emerges through this account of care, I apply Marilyn Strathern's (1988) account of dividual personhood and ideas of "cutting the network" (1996). With this approach, I map the ways my respondents relate to an emergent global beyond more familiar networks of kinship and village ties. They build new networks that draw in new faiths and non-Filipinos by building a variety of caring connections ranging from the exploitive to the liberatory using strategies of exchange. By giving gifts, sharing food, exchanging work and employer contacts, or even employers, migrants make themselves a new kind of safety net to cope with their irregular status. Strathern's work tells us that something called society builds up its character through repeated dissolution "into the ritual and exchange process of the main elements composing each individual" (Strathern 1992, 76, quoting De Coppet 1981, 176). Applying this theoretical formulation to the global, I am considering how the global takes on its character through its repeated dissolution into the flows of affect that make up its component processes. Thus, by tracing these exchanges and exploring how people feel within them and about them, I am gathering together signs, symbols, and performances of globalism and globalization that exemplify my respondents' experiences of global desire at work.

My migrant friends experience their migration as governed by an assemblage that produces a map of winners and losers—those who achieve, enact, and embody progress are those who care properly and those who fail its challenges are those who misdirect or fail in their care. People have feelings, good and bad, about their places on this map of global care—and about each other and those they interact with overseas, including employers. Their feelings may lead them to take action and transform themselves and their relations with others, trying to build care and closeness with new networks, distancing themselves from kin and old networks. People evaluate and enhance or diminish the affective connections these shifting positionings and relationships require during their sojourns abroad. Listening to their accounts of care in everyday lives and examining the shape of personhood and affective experiences within their working relationships gives me a different kind of purchase on the global they imagine as they make—and remake—it through care.

REFERENCES

Adey, Peter. 2009. "Facing Airport Security: Affect, Biopolitics, and the Preemptive Securitisation of the Mobile Body." *Environment and Planning D: Society and Space* 27(2): 274–95.
Ahmed, Sara. 2004. "Affective Economies." *Social Text* 22(2): 121–39.

Beatty, Andrew. 2005. "Emotions in the Field: What Are We Talking About?" *Journal of the Royal Institute of Anthropology* 11: 17–37.

Chiang, Howard. 2008. "Empire of Desires: History and Queer Theory in an Age of Global Affect." *Critical Studies in History* 1: 50–71.

De Coppet, Daniel. 1981. "The Life-Giving Death." In *Mortality and Immortality: The Anthropology and Archaeology of Death,* ed. Sarah Humphreys and Helen King, 175–204. London: Academic Press.

Good, Byron J. 2004. "Rethinking 'Emotions' in Southeast Asia." *Ethnos* 69(4): 529–33.

Jansen, Stef. 2012. "After the Red Passport: Towards an Anthropology of the Everyday Geopolitics of Entrapment in the EU's Immediate Outside." *Journal of the Royal Anthropological Institute* 15: 815–32.

Kelly, Philip. 2000. *Landscapes of Globalization.* New York: Routledge.

Lutz, Catherine, and Lila Abu Lughod, eds. 1990. *Language and the Politics of Emotion.* Cambridge: Cambridge University Press.

Lutz, Catherine, and Geoffrey White. 1986. "The Anthropology of Emotions." *Annual Review of Anthropology* 15: 405–36.

Manalansan, Martin. 2010. "Servicing the World." In *Political Emotions,* ed. J. Staiger et al., 215–28. New York: Routledge.

Masco, Joseph. 2008. "'Survival Is Your Business': Engineering Ruins and Affect in Nuclear America." *Cultural Anthropology* 23(2): 361–98.

McElhinny, Bonnie. 2010. "The Audacity of Affect: Gender, Race, and History in Linguistic Accounts of Legitimacy and Belonging." *Annual Review of Anthropology* 39: 309–28.

McKay, Deirdre. 2012. *Global Filipinos.* Bloomington: Indiana University Press.

McKay, Steven. 2006. *Satanic Mills or Silicon Islands?* Ithaca, NY: Cornell University Press.

Nussbaum, Martha. 2001. *Upheavals of Thought.* Cambridge: Cambridge University Press.

Pain, Rachel. 2009. "Globalized Fear? Towards an Emotional Geopolitics." *Progress in Human Geography* 33(4): 466–86.

Parreñas, Rhacel. 2001. *Servants of Globalization.* Stanford, CA: Stanford University Press.

Pile, Steve. 2010. "Emotions and Affect in Recent Human Geography." *Transactions of the Institute of British Geographers* 35: 5–20.

Richard, Analiese, and Daromir Rudnyckyj. 2009. "Economies of Affect." *Journal of the Royal Anthropological Institute* 15: 57–77.

Rosaldo, Renato. 2004. "Airport." In *Shock and Awe: War on Words,* ed. B. van Eekelen, J. Gonzalez, B. Stozer, and A. Tsing, 4. Santa Cruz, CA: New Pacific Books.

Sassen, Saskia. 2006. *Territory, Authority, Rights.* Stanford, CA: Stanford University Press.

Strathern, Marilyn. 1988. *The Gender of the Gift.* Berkeley: University of California Press.

———. 1992. "Parts and Wholes: Refiguring Relationships in a Post-Plural World." In *Conceptualizing Society,* ed. A. Kuper, 75–104. London: Routledge.

———. 1996. "Cutting the Network." *Journal of the Royal Anthropological Institute* 2: 517–35.

Wierzbicka, Anna. 2004. "Emotion and Culture: Arguing with Martha Nussbaum." *Ethos* 31(4): 577–600.

Yoo, Seung Hee, David Matsumoto, and Jeffrey LeRoux. 2006. "The Influence of Emotion Recognition and Emotion Regulation on Intercultural Adjustment." *International Journal of Intercultural Relations* 30: 345–63.

2 – DISPLACEMENT

Framing the Global Relationally

FARANAK MIRAFTAB

HISTORICALLY, IT WAS COLONIALISM AND SLAVERY THAT INTRO-
duced the large-scale displacement of labor forces around the globe. While
white colonial settlers relocated to explore and exploit new territories, slaves
were captured, uprooted, and forced to work for free for European masters.
In the contemporary global order of free-market capitalism, complex movements of people across territories, some through voluntary relocation, others through systematic displacement, have continued. However distinct in
their incentives and trajectories, these population movements are commonly
referred to as (im)migration—a term that often conflates the varied stories
behind people's movements within and across political, social, and cultural
borders. In this chapter, I retell a narrative that is often told as one of immigration by uncovering the systematic dispossessions that make it a story of
a displaced labor force.

America's heartland in the last four decades has seen a significant transformation. Once capital moved overseas or south and west, many rust-belt

towns struggled with depopulation. In the last two decades, however, many rural counties of the rust belt that did not have much, if any, foreign-born population have seen the end or even the reversal of their population shrinkage, thanks to the arrival of a new and growing foreign-born labor force (Massey and Capoferro 2008; Durand, Massey, and Capoferro 2005). Since the 1990s in particular, the percentage of foreign-born population has been decreasing in gateway metropolitan areas while increasing in non-gateway areas.[1] Apart from the lower cost of living, immigrants arrive in these towns for employment. Often, these are jobs in manufacturing sectors that need to stay closer to their raw material—namely agriculture and animals—but to maintain profitability in the face of global competition they offer depressed wages unattractive to the local labor force. These rust-belt towns are saved by the arrival of an immigrant labor force and their families (Grey and Woodrick 2005). Immigrants in many cases "solve" the problem of urban shrinkage—a common reality for many dying towns of the heartland. They revitalize the towns by fixing up houses, registering their children in the local schools, and spending their wages at local shops and other facilities.

One example is a town I have studied in the rural rust belt since 2005: a small town in Illinois that lost many of its local manufacturing jobs in the 1970s and 1980s. A meatpacking plant which remained in the area saw a transition in ownership during the mid-1980s, lowering wages by $2 per hour. As many local residents sought opportunities elsewhere, an immigrant labor force was recruited by the plant, transforming the town and its diminishing population. Adjacent small towns struggled to keep their schools open and their downtowns became filled with boarded-up businesses and houses, while in this packing town a new elementary school and library were built and there were steady markets for home ownership and rentals and a functioning downtown business area.

In this case, which some describe as a success story for immigration, I grapple with two questions: What is the global cost of the revitalization of rust-belt towns like this? What kinds of globally constituted relationships and practices make meatpacking jobs more viable for immigrant workers and less so for their native-born counterparts? To answer these questions, I conducted ethnographic fieldwork in the Illinois meatpacking town and also visited the home communities of immigrant workers in Mexico and Togo. I spoke with their children, parents, relatives, friends, and neighbors back home to understand the set of social, political, and economic processes in communities of origin that not only motivated their move to the United States, but contributed to their willingness to accept and stay in meatpacking jobs in the Midwest. Conducting ethnographic research in multiple global sites that are intimately, albeit not so obviously, connected allowed me to see the series of systematic dispossessions that produce the workforce that shows up at my study site in Illinois. It made clear the need to speak about immigration in close conjunction with displacement.

To frame the story of this meatpacking Illinois town as one of immigration, without exposing the dispossessions and displacements that have produced such population movements, suggests that it is a natural and inevitable occurrence and assumes a certain innocence in the process of globalization. To leave displacement out of the picture assumes and suggests that international migration is similar to the laws of physics or nature: water flows to the lower plain; people move to places with higher likelihood of jobs. To avoid such simplification, in my study of the revitalized midwestern town I also study the transformation processes in immigrants' communities of origin. This helps us to better understand the processes that send populations to relocate in faraway places and why they take on backbreaking jobs that many native-born workers walked away from at the end of the 1980s.

FRAMING RELATIONALLY

How we tell the story of globalization matters. Our framings of the global determine what we reveal and what we obscure; what we place at the center and what remains at the margin; what defines the structure or becomes a marginal element in the construction of the story. The story of revitalizing packing towns framed merely through the processes of immigration to the heartland reveals some and obscures other aspects of the global processes. It reveals how the international migration of the labor force transforms local communities which, despite their geographic isolation, are intimately involved in the production of global capital and its processes of accumulation. But it renders invisible the stories of dispossession and displacement that produce a migrant labor force in the first place. Dispossession and displacement are important conditions that produce migration by laborers. Telling the story of migration without its interwoven stories of displacement offers a picture that is not only incomplete but inaccurate. As the saying goes, "Half the truth is a lie."

In this chapter I stress the importance of telling the story of immigration, an important inroad into the story of globalization, *relationally*. I use a multi-scalar analysis developed through a multi-sited methodology to see not only the node but the web, not only the processes that capture and consume immigration and the labor force of migrants, but also those that produce them. Multi-scalar analyses and multi-sited ethnographic approaches reveal the indivisible processes of dispossession and displacement that create the contemporary processes of migration and globalization.

What drives me in my global research is to see communities relationally—that is, to detect points of junction and disjunction, and to expose the inequalities required to make up the "global village" that is celebrated today. This urge arises from an acute awareness of the points of disconnection, disjunction, and friction (Tsing 2000) as well as the stoppages and decelerations (Sassen 2000) through which globalization takes place. My approach to framing such global processes strives for a multi-scalar and multi-directional analysis that scholars before me have explored (see Gille 2001; Burawoy et al. 2000; Guarnizo and Smith 1998). While anchored in specific locations, my analysis of the global spans local, national, and global boundaries, and recognizes the multiple directions through which globalization is constituted. Such a framework allows me to see the complex and multiple spatialities and temporalities of globalization (Miraftab 2011). It accounts for the non-linear zigzags that shape global policies and human migration, and recognizes the structures that selectively include and exclude nations in the imagination of a global community.

Following Gillian Hart (2006), I argue we must eschew an "impact model of globalization," whereby localities are mere sites in the global restructuring of capital. Our scholarly optics must allow us to recognize the interconnections and multi-directionality of these relationships. The methodology Michael Burawoy and colleagues (2000, 2001) label "global ethnography" is very helpful in this regard. It allows us to see how "[w]hat we understand to be 'global' is itself constituted within the local; it emanates from very specific agencies, institutions and organizations whose processes can be observed first-hand" (Burawoy 2001, 150). Hart contributes to this approach a Lefebvrian concept of place that stresses the relational constitution of a specific place in the production of global processes. According to Hart, this constitutes a critical ethnography capable of unearthing the local production of globalization that is not "a bounded enclosure," but rather highlights "nodal point[s] of connection in wider networks of socially-produced space . . . Places are always formed through relations with wider arenas and other places; boundaries are always socially constructed and contested; and the specificity of a place—however defined—arises from the particularity of interrelations with what lies beyond it, that come into conjuncture in specific ways." Critical ethnography, Hart argues, builds "directly on this conception of the production of space and place" (2006, 994–95).

To see the interconnected relationships that shape the story of globalization and international migration, we need a shift in modes of seeing. Such a shift requires that we examine the phenomenon at several scales—local, regional, and global—and examine the inter-scalar relationships. It also requires that we utilize a multi-sited mode of inquiry that not only follows objects and people across locations but, more than that, is able to reveal how each of these seemingly independent processes and locations is intimately connected with the others through hierarchically structured relationships.

To this end, I undertook a multi-sited ethnographic inquiry (Marcus 1995). I expanded the physical sites of my ethnographic study beyond the town in Illinois to other locations across the globe intimately connected with this town. But unlike Marcus's methodological intervention, I did not follow and stay with the movements of a particular group of initial subjects. I started with the relatives of Illinois immigrants in their communities of origin but moved beyond the specific practices connecting these transnational families and networks of support to include those who have not emigrated or have returned after migration, and beyond them to the broader processes and relationships that shape power structures connecting these three sites.

In the spirit of multi-sited global ethnography I studied historical, political, economic, and cultural forces, as well as immigrants' everyday practices and imaginations (Burawoy et al. 2000) that connect these communities to each other to construct the global. I combined several years of fieldwork in Illinois (beginning in 2005) with visits to Michoacán, Mexico, in 2008 (followed up by my research assistant in 2010); and to Lomé, the capital city of Togo, in 2010. In the Midwest, I focused on one specific town in Illinois. I interviewed residents, including the native-born and new immigrants, authorities, and members of non-profit groups and civic associations and conducted focus groups among recent immigrants through their English as a second language (ESL) community college classes. In Mexico and Togo I interviewed the relatives of Illinois immigrants, returned immigrants, future immigrants, and other key informants.

Using a multi-sited ethnographic approach unveils the interrelated global realities that shape new immigration to the rust belt. These transnational processes are not merely a global restructuring of production. They are also restructurings that occur in the sphere of social reproduction and through simultaneous place-based and translocal strategies. The countervailing processes rely on local communities, neighbors, and households and yet draw on translocal and transnational networks of families, friends, and remittances. Thus, the processes of local development in this packing town need to be understood in conjunction with processes of dispossession and displacement taking place in other global locations.

Multi-sited ethnography, in particular, proved helpful for working on contentious issues and in communities that are politically constrained. In this modern-day company town, everyone and every institution are tied to the company. If you do not work at the plant, you probably have a wife or a husband, a son or a daughter, a niece or a nephew who does. One way or the other, "all roads end at the plant," as one local resident said. As a small town with a single employer, the situation introduces a different set of concerns for field-based research. As one respondent explained: "If you get into an altercation with the police or you get drunk and get into a fight in the local bar this Saturday night, you are called to the management office at the plant on Monday and risk being dismissed depending on what the issue has been." There is not much one can do in town without the plant management knowing, or for that matter without the whole town knowing. "Think about it: even your traffic violation is listed in the local weekly newspaper," observed a new arrival from Detroit. The implication of this for research into potentially contentious issues can be grave. The difficulty of researching and breaking into the closed circle of a company town is a matter not only of gaining trust, but also of the risk your questions may impose on your respondent.

In such a context there were many questions I did not readily pose to my interviewees. For example, much of my information regarding labor practices of the company when it comes to the injuries of undocumented workers had to come from my fieldwork outside of the packing town and among returned immigrant workers. Conducting research in the communities of the workers' origin or among workers who had returned home was liberating in that these respondents were not subject to the same pressure as their counterparts back in Illinois. They openly shared their stories and their observations. I also felt free to participate in conversations about the company's labor practices, injuries, and bonuses, since I knew they posed little or no risk to my respondents. The advantages of multi-sited ethnography are therefore important when working with vulnerable populations and highly contentious contexts: namely, you can avoid an omnipresent power structure by conducting the interview in another context.

ACCUMULATION BY DISPLACEMENT AND GLOBAL RESTRUCTURING OF SOCIAL REPRODUCTION

A vast body of literature on the global restructuring of the meat industry has long established the logic of capital in this process (Broadway 1995; Warren 2007). In relocating to rural areas, industry moves away from urban centers where unions have a stronghold and closer to raw materials (in this case hog farms). It also is better able to integrate vertically (production of animals and their feed, slaughtering of animals, processing and packing of meat) and take advantage of economically distressed rural municipalities offering tax abatements along with lax labor and environmental regulation. In the last two decades, the recruitment of immigrants and minorities to plants in small towns has further enhanced a rural industrialization strategy by creating a segmented labor market, pitting one group of workers against the other. Such processes and dynamics are extensively documented and discussed in a broad body of labor literature (Bonacich 1972; Farley 2005; Edwards 1973).

While an analytical focus on the global restructuring of production helps explain some aspects of the rapid social and demographic transformation taking place in rural towns, parts of this complex process remain murky. The restructuring of production analysis offers insights into the logic of capital in relocating production sites and wooing an immigrant labor force. But this approach falls short in explaining the logic of laborers and what kind of practices motivate them to keep these jobs.

My research brings to light two key conditions for understanding the story of rural revitalization: (1) processes of accumulation by displacement; and (2) the global restructuring of social reproduction.

The developments that take place in heartland Illinois, in Michoacán, Mexico, and in Lomé, Togo, form intricate parts of the conditions Marxian analysts articulate as accumulation by dispossession (Harvey 2006). Using a relational comparison approach (Hart 2006) we uncover how the diminishing agricultural livelihoods in Mexico and rising unemployment and political instability in Togo contribute to the vitality of this midwestern packing town, its sustained population growth, healthy housing market, and flourishing school system. A relational analysis helps us see how the meat industry's crisis of accumulation in the 1970s and '80s benefited from a series of dispossessions around the world resulting from political and economic adjustment policies.

In Mexico, for example, the advance of free trade policies, particularly the North American Free Trade Agreement (NAFTA), undermined agricultural production by Mexican farmers and contributed to their being dispossessed of viable rural livelihoods—processes that ultimately catalyzed the supply of cheap labor to the plant in Illinois. The privatization of *ejidos* (or communal lands)[2] and the subsequent passage of NAFTA and other neoliberal policies facilitated the dispossession of Mexican farmers of their limited resources. The story of Mr. Fernández, the father of two Illinois immigrant workers, whom I interviewed in Michoacán, is a case in point. Mr. Fernández had formerly been involved in domestic milk production. He explained his decision to sell his *ejido* share and send his sons to the United States as migrant workers when he could no longer compete with the price of imported milk brought in under NAFTA. "We have no other way to support ourselves," he told me. His experience testifies to the logic that has dispossessed and displaced his sons, who are now workers at the Illinois meatpacking plant.

Similarly, the end of the Cold War and the implementation of structural adjustment policies in Togo created the economic conditions leading to a brain drain and the uprooting of educated youth and civil servants. The fall of the Berlin Wall shifted the geopolitics of West Africa. No longer would Togo receive international aid, as it was not an asset as a pro-capitalist ally against other Soviet-leaning governments of the region (see Piot 2010). This shift removed both political and economic support for the corrupt Togolese government from Europe, the United States, and international development agencies. The post–Cold War geopolitical shifts that reduced the position of Togo within the hierarchy of priorities of global institutions, combined with globally implemented structural adjustment policies, shrank the Togolese public sector and its social service activities, creating massive unemployment. Educated youth found a way out of this unemployment by obtaining diversity visas through the U.S. government's Diversity Visa lottery. This facilitated the displacement of educated Togolese to the Global North and their transformation into inexpensive labor.

In more recent recruitment strategies, the company has turned to yet another group of migrant workers, which I refer to as an "internally displaced" labor force. This group of workers includes African Americans recruited from Detroit. What attracts the employer to this labor force is their legal citizenship, but in the imagination of local white residents they are nearly as foreign as the immigrants. While the Togolese and Mexicans cross national borders, African Americans displaced from their urban neighborhoods, lifestyle, and culture in Detroit are equally "out of place" in towns that before this recent wave of immigrant labor force recruitment did not have any nonwhite residents. Here I will not go into the violent racism African Americans experience when imported as workers. Nor will I discuss the dynamics among the diverse groups of workers and how identities are constructed inside and outside the plant.[3] I mention the African American workers recruited from Detroit to highlight the parallels that exist between their experiences and those of the international immigrant workers. Both groups represent a displaced labor force, one constituted internationally and the other internally displaced. In the last two decades de-industrialized cities of the rust belt such as Detroit have been subject to free-market policies similar to those that have produced dispossessed and displaced populations in Mexico and Togo.

While dispossession and displacement are forces that motivate the labor force to relocate and accept high-risk, low-paying jobs, they do not explain why and how these jobs are not filled adequately by the native-born workforce. What are the practices and processes that make meatpacking wages "viable" for a foreign-born workforce, but less so for their native-born counterparts?

Transnational reorganizations of familial and community care, what I call "the global restructuring of social reproduction," are critical to answering this question. I use the term "social reproduction" in a broad sense, one that extends beyond biological reproduction or childcare to include the reproduction of place, cultural identities, traditions, and sense of pride. Important to

the ability of the foreign-born workforce to accept the high-risk, low-paid
jobs of the meat industry are the possibilities for "outsourcing" reproduction
and care work for segments of the workers' life cycle to their home communities. Many immigrants leave their children behind in the care of relatives
and spouses; others return home to their relatives and families when they are
old or injured. Hence, responsibility for such care work rests elsewhere. This
includes childhood, old age, and periods when they are unable to work due
to health considerations. Social reproduction during these periods of "down
time" is carried out in communities of origin. To realize the social reproduction of immigrant workers in Illinois, an army of people, with women at the
center, are at work elsewhere in their support.

A range of factors moves immigrants to and keeps them in places of destination: from remittances that they can send home to pay for daily bread, for
paving roads and infrastructure development, or for education and health
care; to the hope that motivates immigrants to embark on risky journeys
and perform hazardous jobs out of a sense of obligation; to honor and pride
that drives immigrants to tolerate disillusionment and meet cultural expectations. All of these factors keep immigrant workers in jobs that otherwise
would not be viable. The imagination of an "elsewhere" to which one could
retire or retreat is yet another important consideration in determining what
wages workers are willing to work for. The promise of a home where a person
would "be set for life" has a material power and exchange value. Moderate
savings in the United States offer a source of capital which can be combined
with the labor of family members at home to create a comfortable retirement
or to finance a business which would constitute another sort of promise. But
this is not always a possibility. Immigrants put down "roots" in towns they
move to; they do not want to move away from their children and grandchildren in communities of destination; their connections to home weaken; or
their U.S. savings are lost in bad business deals. Multiple factors might make
this promise of "elsewhere" only an imagined one. Nevertheless, this imagination has the material power to make a wage untenable for one worker but
acceptable for another. Imagined or real, home community as an alternative
place that workers create or dream of creating becomes an asset that distin-
guishes the viability of wages across groups of workers.

The African American workers recruited from Detroit are also displaced
migrant workers who are dispossessed through previous cycles of capital

accumulation in the rust belt. While this population moved to Illinois attracted by the promise of a full-time job at the packing plant, they are not able to outsource segments of their social reproduction to communities of origin or to networks of support elsewhere with a lower cost of living. Nor can they enjoy the imagination of the elsewhere as a resource the way internationally displaced migrant workers can. The former Detroit residents do not rely on the kinds of social reproduction strategies that Togolese or Mexican workers employ. As one of them said, "I cannot leave my child to be raised by my mother in Detroit, it will cost her as much as it will cost me here." The ability to take part in global restructuring of social reproduction for oneself and one's family makes a difference in workers' ability to make the wages of the company worthwhile. Workers who do not take part in transnational practices for social reproduction cannot restructure their care work in ways that their internationally displaced counterparts do. So while displaced migrant workers from Detroit and Togo and Mexico are similar in that they are all displaced and are considered as foreign in the imagination of the white locals, they are distinct in how they can strategize the challenge of social reproduction.

A multi-scalar and multi-sited ethnographic approach to the complex transformation of this rust-belt town makes visible the series of connected dispossessions that have created the crisis of social reproduction and hence have displaced workers from their communities of origin to join the army of cheap labor in communities of destination. It also makes visible how an internationally displaced labor force deals with the crisis of social reproduction through their transnational families and practices. If white native-born workers earn the "wages of whiteness" (Roediger 1991) and the internationally displaced migrant workers earn wages subsidized by their families and home institutions in their communities of origin, African American workers are displaced only to remain at the bottom of the stack. Displaced from their home communities and often experiencing a history of discrimination, they do not take part in transnational practices for their social reproduction.

FRAMING FOR GLOBAL JUSTICE

When framing global processes, what we place inside or outside the frame, at the center or margin, is key to the silences we create or the voices we amplify.

Telling the story of revitalized Midwest towns as a story of immigration creates many silences. Immigration studies, by framing the phenomenon within one singular location, either captures the story of towns receiving immigrants and hence the challenges and perks that come with them, or focuses on locations that have sent immigrants. Those focused on immigrants' communities of origin often focus on remittances or the kinds of policies that displace rural or native populations. Seldom, however, has immigration studies connected these nodes to see them relationally and understand the relationships between displacement on the one hand and revitalization and economic prosperity on the other.

Looking through a multi-scalar analytic lens and a multi-sited ethnographic approach, we discover local developments and transformations of the rust-belt town in relation to processes taking place in other communities—some far away, as in Togo and Mexico, and others closer by, as in rust-belt cities like Detroit. A multi-scalar analysis indicates that two sets of interconnected relationships are crucial to understanding contemporary global processes: the interconnected processes of dispossession and displacement and the global restructuring taking place within the realm of production and reproduction.

Framing the global relationally is critical in bringing to light the injustices that shape it. As my research makes visible, the hard work of the dispossessed peasants in Michoacán and the pain of parents who left their children behind in Lomé are integral to the economic revitalization and repopulation of the Illinois packing town. Scholarship with a deep commitment to social justice frames global processes such that connections between faraway yet intimately related contexts are exposed, explained, and integrated into the core of our work.

NOTES

1. Traditional gateway metropolitan areas are Los Angeles, Miami, Chicago, New York, and Houston (Gozdziak and Martin 2005; Frey 2006; Portes and Rumbaut 2006). The percentage of the total foreign-born population in the United States living in these traditional gateway metro areas shrank from 43 percent in 1990 to 33 percent in 2010, while the percentage of foreign-born residents living in non-gateway destinations grew from 56 to 66 percent (calculated from IPUMS data [Ruggles et al. 2010]).

2. *Ejido* is an Aztec system of communal landownership reintroduced and institutionalized as a component of the Mexican land reform programs of the revolutionary governments 1911–1934. *Ejidos* were by and large dismantled by the neoliberal privatization policies of Pres-

ident Salinas in the 1990s, which amended Article 27 of the constitution to allow privatization of communally owned *ejidos*.

3. For that see my forthcoming book with Indiana University Press, *Making a Home in the Heartland: Immigration and Global Labor Mobility*.

REFERENCES

Bonacich, Edna. 1972. "A Theory of Ethnic Antagonism: The Split Labor Market." *American Sociological Review* 37(5): 547–59.

Broadway, Michael. 1995. "From City to Countryside: Recent Changes in the Structure and Location of the Meat- and Fish-Processing Industries." In *Any Way You Cut It: Meat Processing and Small-Town America,* ed. Donald Stull, Michael Broadway, and David Griffith, 17–40. Lawrence: University Press of Kansas.

Burawoy, Michael. 2001. "Manufacturing the Global." *Ethnography* 2(2): 147–59.

Burawoy, Michael, et al. 2000. *Global Ethnography: Forces, Connections and Imaginations in a Postmodern World*. Berkeley: University of California Press..

Durand, Jorge, Douglas Massey, and Chiara Capoferro. 2005. "The New Geography of Mexican Immigration." In *New Destinations: Mexican Immigration in the United States,* ed. Victor Zúñiga and Rubén Hernández-León, 1–20. New York: Russell Sage Foundation.

Edwards, Richard. 1973. "The Labor Process." In *Labor Market Segmentation*, ed. Richard Edwards, Michael Reich, and David M Gordon. Lexington, MA: D. C. Heath.

Farley, John E. 2005. *Majority-Minority Relations*. 6th ed. Upper Saddle River, NJ: Prentice Hall. First published in 1982.

Frey, William H. 2006. *Diversity Spreads Out: Metropolitan Shifts in the Hispanic, Asian, and Black Populations since 2000*. Washington, DC: Brookings.

Gille, Zsuzsa. 2001. "Critical Ethnography in the Time of Globalization: Toward a New Concept of Site." *Cultural Studies Critical Methodologies* 1(3): 319–33.

Gozdziak, Elzbieta M., and Susan F. Martin, eds. 2005. *Beyond the Gateway: Immigrants in a Changing America*. Lanham, MD: Lexington Books.

Grey, Mark, and Anne Woodrick. 2005. "Latinos Have Revitalized Our Community: Mexican Migration and Anglo Responses in Marshalltown, Iowa." In *New Destinations: Mexican Immigration in the United States,* ed. Victor Zúñiga and Rubén Hernández-León, 133–54. New York: Russell Sage Foundation.

Guarnizo, Luis, and Michael Peter Smith. 1998. "The Locations of Transnationalism." In *Transnationalism from Below,* ed. Michael Peter Smith and Luis Guarnizo, 3–34. New Brunswick, NJ: Transaction.

Hart, Gillian. 2006. "Denaturalizing Dispossession: Critical Ethnography in the Age of Resurgent Imperialism." *Antipode* 38(5): 977–1004.

Harvey, David. 2006. *Spaces of Global Capitalism: A Theory of Uneven Geographical Development*. New York: Verso.

Marcus, George. 1995. "Ethnography in/of the World System: The Emergence of Multi-Sited Ethnography." *Annual Review of Anthropology* 24: 95–117.

Massey, Douglas, and Chiara Capoferro. 2008. "The Geographic Diversification of American Immigration." In *New Faces in New Places: The Changing Geography of American Immigration,* ed. Douglas Massey, 25–51. New York: Russell Sage Foundation.

Miraftab, Faranak. 2011. "Faraway Intimate Developments: Global Restructuring of Social Reproduction." *Journal of Planning Education and Research* 31(4): 392–405.

Piot, Charles. 2010. *Nostalgia for the Future: West Africa after the Cold War.* Chicago: University of Chicago Press.

Portes, Alejandro, and Ruben Rumbaut. 2006. *Immigrant America: A Portrait.* Berkeley: University of California Press.

Roediger, David. 1991. *The Wages of Whiteness: Race and the Making of the American Working Class.* London, New York: Verso.

Ruggles, Steven, J. Trent Alexander, Katie Genadek, Ronald Goeken, Matthew B. Schroeder, and Matthew Sobek. 2010. *Integrated Public Use Microdata Series: Version 5.0.* Minneapolis: University of Minnesota. Machine-readable database.

Sassen, Saskia. 2000. "Spatialities and Temporalities of the Global: Elements for a Theorization." *Public Culture* 12(1): 215–32.

Tsing, Anna. 2000. "The Global Situation." *Cultural Anthropology* 15(3): 327–60.

Warren, Wilson. 2007. *Tied to the Great Packing Machine: The Midwest and Meatpacking.* Iowa City: University of Iowa Press.

3 — FORMS

Art Institutions as Global Forms in India and Beyond

Cultural Production, Temporality, and Place

MANUELA CIOTTI

AN ART WORLD MADE OF GLOBAL FORMS

In December 2012, the Kochi-Muziris Biennale, the very first in India, was inaugurated in the southern state of Kerala.[1] A biennale is a large-scale exhibition held every two years in a fixed urban location.[2] The very first biennale in the world opened in Venice in 1895: there is now a biennale circuit with over one hundred such events.[3] With hardly any infrastructure and few actors from the art world present in Kochi-Muziris when it took place, this biennale can be considered a laboratory for observing the processes of circulation which have given meaning and value to the biennale "form" as it is embedded in diverse locations. Kochi-Muziris was a coalescence of local and non-local objects, histories, and peoples through the display of artworks by artists from India and beyond—which all blended with the city and its architecture. A lively website and Facebook page provided the platform for the many activities planned throughout the exhibition period. The first biennale had an unprecedented number of visitors for such an art event in India and an impressive level of attendance for these events globally.

But it is not just the biennale form which has been appropriated in India—and in many other geographic locations before that: since the 1990s, the globalization of the art world has led to the spread of an entire arsenal of art institutions and actors—together with the circulation, display, and purchase of art—to India as well as the Middle East, Brazil, and China among others. This has resulted in the multiplication of institutions such as biennales, auction houses, museums, galleries, and art fairs. This increase has turned the visual and material consumption of art into a global practice as well as a catalyst for a myriad of individual, national, and transnational sensibilities, cultural statements, and politics.

In this chapter, I conceptualize the art institutions which have experienced such a geographical expansion as "global forms" and the art world as an ensemble of such circulating forms. (Hence the chapter is not concerned with art forms per se.) As forms travel and are appropriated in specific contexts, they acquire new features and meanings and engender novel identities and practices while redesigning the space around them. Over the past two decades, art institutions have traveled to regions historically situated outside the historical western centers of the art world: thus, "the art world, once a western phenomenon, has gone global" (Buddensieg 2009, 10). However, the circulation of a number of forms such as the biennale, the art fair, and the auction house connects to broader questions concerning globalization and cultural production. As Adams puts it, "We need to ask why cultural forms are increasingly similar across the globe, whether content follows form, and if not, does the homogenization of form itself produce new opportunities for diversifying and localizing culture, or does the new container simply reproduce traditional cultural meanings?" (2008, 616). In this chapter, "global" is conceived both as circulation and as its *outcome* (encompassing both form and content). Understanding art institutions as forms interrogates the meanings of global as cultural production not solely through a "from the west to the rest" lens but by thinking of art institutions as emanating contents, engendering new conversations, and producing novel circulation trajectories as they settle in new locations. This understanding allows us to conceive the art world itself as *global*—and beyond movement and flows.

The embedding of art institutions in new geographic regions has multiple genealogies that unfold under different historical eras and conditions; for example, the career of the museum in the Indian subcontinent during the colonial era is an example of this form's past trajectories.[4] However, the circulation of global forms examined here is situated in a specific historical period: the neoliberal era. For the art world, this era is marked by a partnership between the art market and the finance industry through which artwork was gradually transformed into an asset class and hence deemed worthy of investment. With reference to a Global South location such as India, the increasing visibility of Indian art parallels the liberalization of the Indian economy since the early 1990s, the country's economic growth, and the emergence of the new middle classes and their expanding consumption horizons. The phenomenon of the renaissance of modern and contemporary Indian art under these conditions has resignified the relations between art and sections of these classes (in terms of viewing, knowing, and collecting art). Harnessing these trends, artworks become an aesthetics of social and economic change (Ciotti 2012, 638).

Conceptually, the current phase of the globalization of the art world has engendered important shifts, one of which is the distinction between world art and global art. According to Buddensieg, "[W]orld art [is] the world heritage of art from all ages and countries, and global art . . . denotes a contemporary development. Contemporary, rather than modern, has also become a new buzzword on the international market, as it signifies an *art without boundaries and without history*" (Buddensieg 2009, 10; emphasis mine). Further, Buddensieg contends that "global art may also be identified as a manifestation of a post-colonial world" (ibid., 11). The shift from world to global art needs to be placed in relation to the paradigmatic institution of the museum. On this matter, Belting has argued, "World art encompasses most cultures beyond the West whose heritage was preserved in empire type museums. In fact, world art for a long time was primarily owned by Western museums, where it existed as an expatriated and contested treasure from colonial times. . . . Universal museums, as an idea, are a legacy from modernity's claim to offer universal models. Globalism, on the other hand, is a response to universalism and serves to propagate the symbolic capital of difference on the market" (Belting 2009, 44).

If globalism serves as a "platform" for the propagation of the symbolic capital of difference and to defy the hegemonic and universalizing trends arising out of the West, such capital is produced not only in the art market but also through broader circuits of display and visual consumption in sites for contemporary art production. Art emerging from India bears the marks of national and local histories, identities, and contemporary society. The production of the symbolic capital of difference can be observed, for example, in the different ways of representing "Indianness" which have been key to the success of contemporary art in India and beyond.[5] The presence of "Indianness" in art objects from India is not striking per se. Rather, what is worth deciphering is what this Indianness is the vehicle for in times of globalization and neoliberal capital (Ciotti 2012, 638).[6] Although a great deal of the contemporary dynamics between capital investment and culture that have emerged from India's postcolonial context takes place under the rubric of "Indianness," this rubric should not be understood as exhausting all possibilities for indexing artistic production. Precisely because of being woven into globally scaled practices, artistic expressions out of India have destabilized and complicated art taxonomies around the "national," the "native," and the "folk," and have often recast the above expressions in ways that transcend fixed notions of place and identity.

The marks of national and local history, identities, and contemporary society and the relevance of the geopolitics of art-making and "art's identity" are also visible in the establishment of new art institutions. Deeply imbricated with local concerns, the Kochi-Muziris Biennale introduced above aimed to bring back to light the past of the ancient Muziris port and the biennale city of Kochi, evoking notions of cosmopolitanism and heritage and combining the images of old trading networks and cultural exchanges with the new images engendered by art-related flows of people and objects. To understand the climate in which its appropriation in South India has occurred, it should be mentioned that the Kochi-Muziris Biennale was the result of both public and private support. In the context of contemporary art in India, many trends are driven by private enterprise over state initiative. Singh has contended that "[i]n the absence of public institutions that could form the repositories of the art of the time, or a developed academy that could build the archives or write the books about the period, today in India . . . the art market itself has begun to take on some of the museum's role. It is the market that is producing the discourse, through web-resources, auction catalogues and books; it is the market that is re-writing our art history by conducting research and bringing old and new artists to new prominence; it is the market that is building the archive of modern and contemporary art" (2010, 32). What is more, private contemporary Indian art museums and galleries are enlisted as prominent actors which are contributing to the development of such art to the extent that "[i]n recent years, critics in Europe and America have bemoaned the increasing infiltration of market forces into their museums. In India today, we seem to stand in an altogether different place, where the market is making the museum" (ibid., 33). Needless to say, the appropriation of the museum's role by market institutions, and the influence which the market exercises in other art domains—at a historical juncture marked by neoliberalism, global-ization and mass consumption, and the intensification of commodification trends in the art world—is highly relevant for an analysis of art institutions as global forms.

RETHINKING GLOBAL FORMS

The appropriation of art institutions as global forms in India appears as the material and symbolic site for the play of the simultaneous forgoing, recap-turing, and mobilizing of place, history, identities, and contemporary society. A situated account of art institutions would have as its focus multiple private and public forces juxtaposed with a map of the transnational ones which link institutions to the global art world.

Taken together, the issues arising from the effects of the globalization of the art world in India have provided the context for an articulation of "global form" which might best capture the circulation of art institutions around the world more broadly. Such circulation accounts for "what is explicitly global in scale" (Sassen 2007, 7). However, as pointed out earlier, placing the attention solely on circulation—resting, as in this instance, on a west-to-the-rest directionality and not on its outcome—would be limiting. Thus, the investigation of global forms involves a twofold task: the examination, first, of their circulation and second, of the outcome, in this case the career of the newly established art institutions. Looking at both circulation and outcome would take the investigation of the globalization of the art world beyond its most explicit aspects and spectacular claims. To this end, Tsing's problematization of globalization theories is helpful. In these theories, she argues, "we have confused what should be *questions* about the global ramifications of new technologies and social processes into *answers* about global change" (2000, 351; italics in original). Hence, she attempts "to reverse this globalist thinking [in order] to turn concerns about the global back into researchable questions" (ibid., 351).

Global forms are understood here as both archetypical models and historical formations with multiple genealogies and histories. In the process of circulation, forms experience a continuous *palingenesis*—and this is inflected by the nature of the form itself, the different temporalities at stake in this process, and the place where this occurs. To think of a suitable formulation of global forms, I start with a discussion of Appadurai's analytical grid consisting of "circulation of forms" and "forms of circulation." According to Appadurai, forms are "a family of phenomena, including styles, techniques, or genres, which can be inhabited by specific voices, contents, messages, and materials" (2010, 9), while the forms of circulation are linked with the circuits, speed and scale through which they take place (11). More broadly, Appadurai argues that "[t]oday, global cultural flows, whether religious, political or market produced, have entered into the manufacture of local subjectivities, thus changing both the machineries for the manufacture of local meaning and the materials that are processed by these machineries" (7). To what appears to be a "genetic" restructuring of the subject's cultural and intellectual resources and repertoire, Appadurai adds that the period since the 1970s "is characterized by the flows not just of cultural substances [types of identity, for example], but also of cultural forms, such as the novel, the ballet, the political constitution, and divorce" (7).

When we think of circulation of forms Appadurai suggests that a "first step to escape the conundrum of the local and the global that many scholars are facing may be to accept that the global is not merely the accidental site of the fusion or confusion of circulating global elements. It is the site of the mutual transformation of circulating forms, such as the nation and the novel" (10). Concerning the forms of circulation, that is the level of circuit, speed, and scale, it is their various effects on the circulation of forms which produce blocks, disjunctures, and differences as well as determining the level of traffic of such forms (11–12). While Appadurai says a theory which builds the relation between forms of circulation and circulation of forms does not yet exist, he suggests that forms of circulation and circulation of forms "create the conditions for the production of locality. . . . Localities—in this world and in this argument—are temporary negotiations between various globally circulating forms. They are not subordinate instances of the global, but in fact the main evidence of its reality" (12).

Appadurai's grid provides a framework to understand the interplay between form and movement. Regarding the outcome of circulation, Appadurai focuses on the production of locality not as the global's epiphenomenon but rather as the ontological proof of its existence. In this respect, Appadurai appears to be deriving the life of locality from "global." To his view—and to the emphasis on circulation which undergirds "global"—I juxtapose Sassen's view of the role of locality emerging from her examination of the subnational "as a site for the global and the translocal" (2007, 7). Sassen contends, "Localities are productive in that they make possible processes and conditions that situate them in often complex scalar interactions and translocal networks. They are not simply sites for the extraction of value by national and global actors" (7–8). In addition to this more functional (rather than ontological) and "active" role of locality, further analytics are needed with regard to the examination of art institutions as global forms and their instantiation within (and hence production of) a locality—which take materiality into account—which an examination of art institutions undoubtedly calls for.[7] Further, different dimensions of materiality must be evoked for the explanation of a "transient" global form (such as the one-off event of a biennale) or of a more permanent one (such as the museum). Moreover, analytical tools are also required to examine the career of newly established institutions, that is, the specific outcome of circulation (besides the production of locality).

Materiality appears to be similarly absent in Collier and Ong's conceptualization of global forms; nevertheless it provides a deeper sense of the nature and functioning of forms and their relation with the broader terrains from which they emerge. In Collier and Ong's book *Global Assemblages,* the focus of the analysis is not on capturing globalization as

> broad structural transformations or new configurations of society and culture. Rather, [the volume] examines a specific range of phenomena that articulate such shifts: technoscience, circuits of licit and illicit exchange, systems of administration or governance, and regimes of ethics or values. These phenomena are distinguished by a particular quality we refer to as *global.* They are abstractable, mobile, dynamic, moving across and reconstituting

"society," "culture," and "economy," those classic social scientific abstractions that, as a
range of observers have recently noted, today seem over-vague and under question. As
global forms are articulated in specific situations—or territorialized in *assemblages*—they
define new material, collective, and discursive relationships. (2005, 4; italics in original)

The concept of assemblage pins down "technoscience" (the exemplary global
form) (Collier and Ong, 11), to a set of recognizable features without evading
the analysis of context. The examination of macro phenomena through assemblages is combined with the global form's nature of extreme malleability
vis-à-vis context:

> Global phenomena are not unrelated to social and cultural problems. But they have a
> distinctive capacity for decontextualization and recontextualization, abstractability and
> movement, across diverse social and cultural situations and spheres of life. Global forms
> are able to assimilate themselves to new environments, to code heterogeneous contexts
> and objects in terms that are amenable to control and valuation. At the same time, the con-
> ditions of possibility of this movement are complex. Global forms are limited or delimited
> by specific technical infrastructures, administrative apparatuses, or value regimes, not by
> the vagaries of a social and cultural field. (Collier and Ong 2005, 11)

The applicability of this idea of global forms to the investigation of art institutions raises a number of issues: Collier and Ong's forms are portrayed as
highly abstractable, movable, almost "viral" entities whose life is regimented
by the above elements. The total abstractability of their global forms, however, contrasts with the materiality with which global forms, such as art
institutions, are almost synonymous (if we think of the museum form, for
example). They are also sensitive to the above "vagaries of a social and cultural field"—given the above-mentioned imbrications of art institutions to
national and local histories, identities, and society. While territorialization
is a process well suited to the idea of the establishment of an art institution
in a given context, the importance of materiality to the study of global forms
is found also in the relation between art objects and subjects within the
space of a given territorialized form—and in how this contributes to their
co-constitution.

Further, Collier and Ong's forms fall within the rubric of governmentality:
if this might be an aspect of art institutions' field of signification too, institutions as global forms need to be read against a larger interpretive framework
for understanding contemporary social life. Making sense of global phenomena only in terms of governmentality (however constitutive of social life this
can be), again, does not account for the above-mentioned "vagaries of a social

and cultural field," whose importance Collier and Ong's conceptualization of global forms actually displaces and which need to be brought back into the picture. Thus global cultural forms such as art institutions are shaped by social and cultural fields and, if they play the active role of reconstituting "society," "culture," and "economy" in the place where they occur, they are also *constituted* by them. In other words, both processes are important.

CATCHING THE FORM

Art institutions appear to be less volatile (but not necessarily less global), than other global forms, be they technoscience or the novel, so different ways of "grounding" them in context might be required—by including elements of materiality not found in existing conceptualizations of global form. Three main analytical lines of inquiry are useful in conceptualizing and situating global forms. The first problematizes the nature of the specific form which is being circulated, re-embedded, or territorialized—that is, the nature of the cultural form under analysis. The difference among art institutions matters, and this difference affects the forms of their circulation (for example, a museum versus an art fair—that is, a permanent versus a temporary manifestation of materiality). As suggested earlier, a paradigmatic form for the art world is the museum. While much has been written on the museum in India, the same cannot be said for the "new" temporary art institutions such as the biennale—the youngest form to be appropriated in South India. The nature of the form is also relevant in terms of its role in the globalization of the art world. For example, that of the auction house has been remarked upon by Belting: "Auction houses, with their new branches, have become the most important agent of the global turn. They today attract a clientele even from countries where art collecting has had no tradition at all" (2009, 62–63).[8] While histories of the western art market and collecting exist, what remains largely unknown is a comparative history of the creation of new auction houses in India (and elsewhere), the ways in which these auction houses have been appropriated and rewritten locally, and the collecting practices and identities which have emerged over the past two decades.

Four points of analysis make up the second line of inquiry, which focuses on the temporality of both the circulation of forms and the forms of circulation. The first point concerns the pace of circulation. What is striking in the contemporary art world is the unprecedented spread of art world institutions—i.e., the circulation of forms—which is taking place at a very fast pace. Commenting on the ubiquity of the biennale phenomenon, for example, de Duve remarks: "Their number increases at a crazy pace, and though Europe still houses the majority of them, the so-called periphery, Asia in the first place, is quickly catching up" (2007, 681). What is this pace the product of? Neoliberal capital, public foundations, or a combination of both? And where do these driving forces reside? Moreover, the narrative of the globalization of the art world through the spread of art institutions introduces a degree of historical linearity: however, how should the slowing down of this pace, the interruption of flow, and "disruptions" to the pace of circulation (for example, "failed" biennales) be accounted for? Further, the pace of appropriation of art institutions has important implications as far as a new body of knowledge and practices are generated around them. This is to be combined with the analysis of place where the process of re-embedding occurs (see below)—as there might well be no historical precedents for a particular art institution in the context under analysis (as in the case of the Kochi-Muziris Biennale). The second point about temporality emphasizes the historical terrain of a global form's embedding into context: how do the last two decades of the circulation of art world institutions compare with other such phases in history? In other words, how does one incorporate historical analysis in the examination of rapidly shifting contemporary global phenomena? For example, how do the early twenty-first-century liberalizing economy, capital, consumer society, and art as asset class compare—in the case of India—with the pre-colonial and colonial economy, society, and art commodity form in those historical periods? The third point concerns the "production of the new" in relation to the process of the establishment of art institutions as a result of the globalization of the art world. There is the need to examine "the global now and then"—for example, by thinking of accounts of the nineteenth-century world expositions (Breckenridge 1989), collecting, and the history of the art market. The production of the new should also be assessed against the increasing standardization of global forms: for example, the similarities across mega-museums designed by star architects in both established and emerging centers of the global art world evoke the similarities across global cities which scholars have remarked upon. Conversely, the embedding of an art institution brings about a resignification of space in terms of its redesigning. The creation of gallery districts as separate spaces for art is one such spatial redesign. But there is more to it: the planned construction of the Kolkata Museum of Modern Art (KMoMA), a mega-museum in India, will have a different impact on "place," if compared with other cities where such museums are an established presence. The fourth point on temporality concerns art and time and, in particular, how the circulation of art institutions is tied to the simultaneous exploration of competing labels of time, such as "classic," "ancient," "modern," "contemporary," and "heritage," and how these are differently mobilized—singularly or as a meaningful network—within a new art institution.

Considering that contemporary art is defined as having no history or boundaries, the third line of inquiry focuses on place and the establishment of forms. This is where the globalization of the art world has served, according to Belting, "to propagate the symbolic capital of difference" conveyed by art produced in specific locations; the geopolitics of circulation of global forms and their re-embedding is inflected by the particular place in which this occurs. Thus, if scholars have investigated the nexus between the world of materiality and thought vis-à-vis "place" (see Clunas 1991 and Chakrabarty 2000, respectively), the encounter between a circulated global form (as the confluence of both materiality and thought) *and* place calls for attention. Thus, it is important to investigate how "India" affects the appropriation of art institutions as a global form. With this investigation in view, the analysis of place is not exclusively appended to nation but also includes the wider cartographies of belonging evoked by it, in particular through the role of diasporas: in this respect, the analysis needs to draw on process geographies rather than just trait ones (Appadurai 2000, 6–7).

The ensemble of analytical directions provided here informs the investigation of art institutions in their territorialized manifestations—whether permanent or impermanent. Multi-sited ethnography can capture both these and the globally scaled dynamics which articulate with the former, as this approach not only "investigates and ethnographically constructs the lifeworlds of variously situated subjects, it also ethnographically constructs aspects of the system itself through the associations and connections it suggests among sites" (Marcus 1995, 96). Elaborating on these connections from the standpoint of his ethnography of Mumbai advertising agencies (which might be viewed as akin to art institutions insofar they both perform the role of creators of meanings, value, and marketing strategies), William Mazzarella has cogently argued that "the question of the dynamic relationship between these various sites [participant observation, interviews with company representatives, and archival research] remained open." He observes that "increasingly, I found myself exploring a kind of force-field, a space of circulation comprising sites that were public, private, and ambiguously located along the continuum. I imagined myself following images and discourses as they moved through this field . . . Always, I had the sense that I was trying to inhabit and understand (not 'overview') a kind of totality, but one that was open-ended and part of larger networks that reached out far beyond Bombay. Obviously, I could not describe or record everything; my aim instead became to look for telling juxtapositions . . . , critical 'nodes,' as it were" (2003, 31–32). A multi-sited ethnography of art institutions could be combined with a single or "multi-form" investigation where art institutions are identified as critical nodes to be explored through a number of sites. In other words, investigating global forms might not entail moving just geographically but also across art institutions. In turn, this would enable one to grasp the "kind of totality" of the art world from the standpoint of a given context. This multi-form ethnography would have to bring to the fore the material dimensions of art institutions (for example, the exploration of the built environment through visual and textual documentation) as well as their lives in archives and, in the present, their organizational structures. Such an approach would examine the people inhabiting institutions, policy regimes, market forces, and transactions, and the sense of networks across institutions. The sense of totality of the art world—from the standpoint of a particular institution—would also imply tracing Indian art in critical sites of display and consumption (for example, major exhibitions organized globally) as these function as conceptual landmarks on the wider map where institutions are situated. Equally important, ethnography would require an attention to objects: it is in fact around them that art institutions operating at several geocultural nodal points function so that the institutions' relations with them and the paths of these objects' virtual and physical circulation are of critical importance. Thus, a multi-sited/multi-form exploration of art institutions would have to include an "object-graphy" of the artworks—reinforcing the importance of materiality in the study of the global form itself. Objects are being circulated, bought, and sold within the realm of auction houses, international exhibitions, biennales, and art fairs: these flows are relevant to the territorialization (temporary or permanent) of the art institutions insofar as the institutions function as their "repositories," value-makers, and "distributors" among others. However, an investigation of art institutions or global forms does not necessarily require one to "follow objects" in and out of institutions—as a different arsenal of analytical and methodological tools is required to investigate art institutions for the different agency, regimes of mobility, and commodity status involved. The online and offline "life" of art institutions would also be an important site where both locality and connections with globally scaled dynamics are produced. More importantly, this would lead to the analysis of the role of mediation as "a constitutive process in social life" (Mazzarella 2004, 345), and one largely responsible for producing relations across objects, subjects, and India as a conceptual entity. Thus, art websites, blogs, and social networks constitute additional research sites whose study provides an understanding of the work of mediation on cultural forms and of how relations with the art world and art objects are constructed.

FUTURE AVENUES OF INVESTIGATION

Kavita Singh has argued that "[i]n the past ten years or so, contemporary art from India has 'gone global'" (2010).⁹ She remarks on the rise of international star artists who have transcended their "Indian" identity, art objects commanding high prices on the market, and artists being sought after by important collectors. Singh then proceeds to ask: "Has this shift in Indian art's place in the world affected the art? Does the expansion of the viewership change the way the artist addresses audiences? Has the need to stand out in an ever-larger crowd affected the scale and look of the art? What forms does an engagement with local contexts take? In short, what has globalization meant for the world of contemporary Indian art?" (ibid.).

Singh's question on the effects of globalization on the world of contemporary Indian art—with art-making, artists, and their audiences in view—invokes a double optic: one from *within* India and one from *outside* it. What is more, tackling her question through the presence of art institutions as global forms—as territorialized assemblages once they are established in India—provides different, but surely complementary, answers to an analysis centered on art-making, artists, and audiences. Further, the investigation of how institutions partake in the circuits of the global art world—and become one with them—would also shed light on the resulting accumulation of cultural and symbolic capital and the possibilities for new institutions to challenge both historical institutions and established hierarchies of power—and their ability to influence wider conceptual apparatuses and value systems and add new meanings to "global."

If contemporary art has been defined as having no boundaries and no history, I have shown how art institutions as global forms call instead for a situated account of multiple intentionalities which are partially embedded in particular histories, cultures, and societies. Thus, answers to the question of how globalization has affected the world of contemporary art and the spread of art institutions would also shed light on the question of how difference itself is produced through a global form in a postcolonial context. The production of "difference" has been at the heart of postcolonial claims vis-à-vis narratives of western modernity (Chakrabarty 2000). An investigation of global forms would reveal whether the "search for difference" still constitutes a salient line of inquiry to be pursued in the analysis of phenomena of cultural production outside a postcolonial context, or whether other lines are more productive in capturing the global form and the conditions which inform it in the context of neoliberalism, globalization, and mass consumerism. Further, the investigation will also probe whether the argument for the existence of postcolonial historical difference can be extended to a "present difference." To return to the example of the art world in India, the circulation of the symbolic capital of difference as "Indianness" in contemporary art from India might well not result in a statement about "difference" itself, but rather one about the combined practices of producing, staging, and circulating it. Answers to the question of the production of "Indian difference" in the life of newly established institutions—that is, the relation between forms and belonging—will be as indebted to local cultural logics as to those of broader circulation.

What goes under a global form in a specific context might vary (for example, the biennale form has experienced a great deal of diversity historically and across geographical contexts), drawing attention to the relation between the *resilience* of form and the extreme *variety* of content—with the latter almost eclipsing the former. This is in line with the culturalist approach to globalization which claims that "as culture globalizes, it both homogenizes on the dimension of form and diversifies on the dimension of content" (Adams 2008, 616). The effort to make sense of a (limited) repertoire of global forms/art institutions vis-à-vis the immense variety of what is included in them as content remains as important as the question of the absence of *new* forms—as a limit of, or better, a central feature of, cultural production itself.

NOTES

I wish to thank the Framing the Global fellows for their feedback on an earlier version of this chapter, and Stephanie DeBoer, Zsuzsa Gille, Hilary Kahn, Rebecca Tolen, and an anonymous reviewer for Indiana University Press for taking the time to provide detailed comments, suggestions, and encouragement. This has been of invaluable help.

1. http://kochimuzirisbiennale.org/.

2. See Filipovic, Van Hal, and Øvstebø (2010) for multiple accounts of this circuit.

3. http://www.biennialfoundation.org/about/.

4. Studies have been carried out that identify the historical milieu which led to the building of fifty museums in British India by 1900 (Cohn 1998, 35), the role of the museum vis-à-vis imperial projects (Singh 2009), the nature of museums in the colony, and the construction of new ones in the wake of independence (Guha-Thakurta 2004).

5. While the nexus of art and nation has long been a concern in the history of Indian art (Guha-Thakurta 2004), the production of "Indianness" through art today is suggestive of a new wave of "artistic nationalism." At a broader level, anxieties about "self-ethnologizing" in contemporary art (Singh 2010) raise questions about art's global features vis-à-vis its need to be culturally "locate-able" through the identity label in the global art world.

6. Interestingly, institutions in India have also adopted "Indianness" as identification: the largest online auction house founded in India is called Saffronart, one of the most important art foundations is the Devi Art Foundation, and the websites of many galleries and art markets feature labels connected to India.

7. Appadurai's conceptualization of form as "styles, techniques, or genres" does not seem to require materiality.

8. As far as Indian art is concerned, it is Indian-owned capital—at home and in diaspora—which has played a crucial role, and hence I have argued that Indian collectors are "buying themselves" (Ciotti 2012, 637).

9. http://www.globalartmuseum.de/site/guest_author/163.

REFERENCES

Adams, Laura L. 2008. "Globalization, Universalism, and Cultural Form." *Comparative Studies in Society and History* 50(3): 614–40.

Appadurai, Arjun. 2000. "Grassroots Globalization and the Research Imagination." *Public Culture* 12(1): 1–19.

———. 2010. "How Histories Make Geographies: Circulation and Context in a Global Perspective." *Transcultural Studies* 1: 4–13.

Belting, Hans. 2009. "Contemporary Art as Global Art: A Critical Estimate." In *The Global Art World: Audiences, Markets and Museums*, ed. H. Belting and A. Buddensieg, 38–73. Ostfildern: Hatje Cantz Verlag.

Breckenridge, Carol. 1989. "The Aesthetics and Politics of Colonial Collecting: India at World Fairs." *Comparative Studies in Society and History* 31(2): 195–216.

Buddensieg, Andrea. 2009. Editorial. In *The Global Art World: Audiences, Markets and Museums*, ed. H. Belting and A. Buddensieg, 10–35. Ostfildern: Hatje Cantz Verlag.

Chakrabarty, Dipesh. 2000. *Provincializing Europe: Postcolonial Thought and Historical Difference*. Princeton, NJ: Princeton University Press.

Ciotti, Manuela. 2012. "Post-Colonial Renaissance: 'Indianness,' Contemporary Art and the Market in the Age of Neoliberal Capital." *Third World Quarterly* 33(4): 633–51.

Clunas, Craig. 1991. *Superfluous Things: Material Culture and Social Status in Early Modern China*. Cambridge, UK: Polity Press.

Cohn, Bernard S. 1998. "The Past in the Present: India as Museum of Mankind." *History and Anthropology* 11(1): 1–38.

Collier, Stephen, and Aihwa Ong. 2005. "Global Assemblages, Anthropological Problems." In *Global Assemblages: Technology, Politics, and Ethics as Anthropological Problems*, ed. A. Ong and S. Collier, 3–21. Malden, MA: Blackwell.

de Duve, Thierry. 2007. "The Glocal and the Singuniversal." *Third Text* 21(6): 681–88.

Filipovic, Elena, Marieke Van Hal, and Solveig Øvstebø, eds. 2010. *The Biennal Reader*. Ostfildern: Hatje Cantz Verlag and Bergen Kunsthall.

Guha-Thakurta, Tapati. 2004. *Monuments, Objects, Histories: Institutions of Art in Colonial and Postcolonial India*. New York: Columbia University Press.

Marcus, George E. 1995. "Ethnography in/of the World System: The Emergence of Multi-Sited Ethnography." *Annual Review of Anthropology* 24: 95–117.

Mazzarella, William T. S. 2003. *Shoveling Smoke: Advertising and Globalization in Contemporary India*. New Delhi: Oxford University Press.

———. 2004. "Culture, Globalization, Mediation." *Annual Review of Anthropology* 33: 345–67.

Sassen, Saskia. 2007. "Introduction: Deciphering the Global." In *Deciphering the Global: Its Scales, Spaces, and Subjects*, ed. S. Sassen, 1–18. New York: Routledge.

Singh, Kavita. 2009. "Material Fantasy: The Museum in Colonial India." In *India: Art and Visual Culture, 1857–2007*, ed. G. Sinha. Mumbai: Marg Publications and Bodhi Art Gallery.

———. 2010. "A History of Now." *Art India* 15: 26–33.

Tsing, Anna. 2000. "The Global Situation." *Cultural Anthropology* 15(3): 327–60.

4 – FRAMES

Reframing Oceania

Lessons from Pacific Studies

KATERINA MARTINA TEAIWA

The Pacific Islands region is full of contradictions.
Vast yet small; weak, yet influential; important, yet frequently ignored.
—*Richard Herr and Anthony Bergin 2012*

You have lived long and time has passed
The buzzard added
Don't call the wind that will carry you away
The gull counseled
Don't talk to the rain that will drown you
And the turtledove concluded
Do not confine to the hut those who inhabit the world.
—*Dewe Gorodey, in Waddell, Naidu, and Hau'ofa 1993*

FRAMING

If global studies is about critically engaging and understanding issues and processes across an interconnected world through multiple disciplinary and interdisciplinary lenses, then research in Pacific studies provides a particularly interesting series of histories, rationales, and approaches (T. Teaiwa 2010). The Pacific, or Oceania as it is commonly called, encompasses twenty-eight nation-states and territories of diverse geographic, demographic, cultural, and economic scales, from the independent atoll nation of Tuvalu with ten thousand citizens at the forefront of the climate change debate, to the continent of Australia with over twenty-two million people in one of the world's most affluent countries.

My global is Oceania and my research is shaped by Pacific studies as it has been developed from scholarly centers in Hawai'i, New Zealand, Fiji, and Australia with interdisciplinary, comparative, multi-sited, and indigenous tools and frameworks for scholarship, art, and activism (T. Teaiwa 2010). This chapter focuses on key aspects of the field because most of my academic career has been spent not teaching courses in established disciplines, but rather developing new courses and a new teaching program in transdisciplinary Pacific studies. For the last six years this has been in Australia, which has a significant neocolonial political and economic relationship with the region, but where there is little interest in teaching about or, more specifically, *learning from* Pacific peoples and islands at any level of national education (see Herr and Bergin 2012). My research, therefore, is motivated by a sense of concern that geopolitical powers such as Australia and the United States need to be as interested in what they can learn from the Pacific as in what they can gain from dominating it.

In thinking about how geopolitical framings in this part of the world have profoundly shaped Pacific states and societies, political scientist Greg Fry wrote of a long-standing Australian practice of "framing" Pacific Island peoples in three senses: "First, drawing geographical boundaries around them for purposes of making generalizations; second, intending to shape the lives of the people so bounded; and third, in the colloquial sense, setting them up for outcomes not of their making" (Fry 1997, 307). This diverse region is regularly reduced to a set of simplistic frames with their origins in European imperial imaginations and cross-cultural island encounters, and powerful contemporary expression through the discourses of underdevelopment that dominate national planning, priorities in tertiary education, regional cooperation, and policy-making. Edward Said's (1978) critique of Orientalism and its attendant negative representations of the Middle East and East Asia are regularly cited in Pacific studies as reflecting similar processes in Oceania as the result of Spanish, French, British, German, Australian, New Zealand, American, Japanese, and Dutch colonialism.

Since the eighteenth century such framings have taken form in the sometimes contradictory representations of the islands as a paradise inhabited
by both noble and ignoble savages; infantilized natives in need of colonial
rule and missionary conversion; small, insignificant islands and populations;
relatively new independent, underdeveloped, corrupt nation-states; islands
of violence, instability, and crisis; sinking nations in the context of global
warming—and the list goes on (Jolly 2007; Finin and Wesley-Smith 2001;
Wallis 2012). At the end of the twentieth century in particular, after violent
clashes between pro- and anti-independence groups in New Caledonia, a
civil war in Bougainville, one civilian and three military coups in Fiji, anti-
nuclear protests in French Polynesia, a coup and civilian conflict in the Solomon Islands, and riots in Tonga, a series of dramatic images of the whole
island region became popular in which it was depicted as on the brink of a
"Doomsday Scenario" (Callick 1993); on an "Arc of Instability" or an "Arc of
Crisis," or an "Arc of Responsibility" and an "Arc of Opportunity" (Wallis
2012); as "the Hole in the Asia-Pacific Doughnut" and "the Eye in the Asia-
Pacific Cyclone" (Fry 1997). Greg Fry argues that this framing is created by
"the heartland of 'rational' thinking—the intersecting worlds of the bureau-
crat, the politician, the foreign affairs journalist and the academic economist"
(1997, 305). In the meantime, representations still abound of Pacific islands as
pristine, sun-drenched havens for tourists. The mundane or creative reality
in the middle is rarely visible in popular media or in the foreign affairs and
development policies of Pacific powers such as Australia, which dominates
the most populous, largest, and well-endowed islands in the southwestern
Pacific (K. M. Teaiwa 2009, 2012b).

In the twenty-first century, combining older historical visions and contemporary anxieties, Pacific journalists and travel writers, from the Australian
Broadcasting Corporation (ABC) to American writer Paul Theroux, still
delight in the juxtaposition of a palm-fringed paradise and laid-back natives, against a perceived reality of coups, conflicts, and crises (Finin and
Wesley-Smith 2001). Scholars and activists across the region have countered
such framings by arguing for Pacific Islanders to construct their own representations and articulate their own knowledge approaches, especially with
respect to place-based claims of cultural identity, political sovereignty, and
self-determination (see, for example, Smith 1999). What is interesting about
emplaced resistance is that it is shaped by Islanders' connections to both land

and sea, and predicated not on static but rather on mobile and dynamic identities and networks that extend across time and space (Jolly 2007; Hau'ofa 2008; Clifford 2009).

The process of framing by deficit, and dominant assumptions about power, scale, and the things that matter globally, feeds these views of the Pacific, with real consequences for Islanders' sense of agency, efficacy, and sovereignty. These are most explicit in the southwestern Pacific, defined and racialized in 1832 by Jules Dumont d'Urville as Melanesia ("black islands" in Greek) as distinct from Polynesia ("many islands") and Micronesia ("small islands"). Pacific studies research in Australia, the former colonial authority in Papua New Guinea (PNG) and Nauru, is driven primarily by a pragmatic and strategic rationale and funding system shaped by the federal government's foreign affairs and aid and development interests and priorities. These often wane in times of creativity and stability, are most engaged, patronizing, and interventionist in times of crisis, and are inclined to reward policy-relevant research that is of direct Australian "national benefit." Enabling this rationalist approach to Pacific research are two terrestrial-centric optical illusions, the first of which brings the islands into relief against a massive blue space, and the second of which focuses only on the blue, and usually presumed empty, space between the three important shores of Asia, Australia, and the Americas. The latter is reflected in the Asia-Pacific Economic Cooperation (APEC) logo below; APEC is a regional economic forum dedicated to enhancing growth and prosperity in the Asia-Pacific region, and regularly highlighted in Australian media and foreign affairs.

Such depictions of Oceania as an empty blue space are not confined to Pacific Rim imaginations. They are a regular feature of visual representations of the globe based on Mercator projection maps, which present continental spaces north of the equator as larger, thus amplifying their geopolitical importance. Margaret Jolly, in her exploration of historical cartographies of Oceania, also draws on Greg Fry's approach, stating that "in any image of Oceania there is always a 'frame,' an 'edge' . . . and . . . as with photography, the point of view is crucial" (Jolly 2007, 524–25). She critiques discourse that views the Pacific Rim as "the high ground of strategic economic and geopolitical interest and of moral presumption" (ibid., 525).

Pacific studies scholars such as the late Professor Epeli Hau'ofa have challenged discourses of belittlement and absence that regularly frame regional

Asia-Pacific
Economic Cooperation

The APEC logo is reproduced with the permission of the APEC
Secretariat, Singapore. For more information, visit www.apec.org.

and international views of Oceania. Hauʻofa argued that the Pacific was not
constituted by tiny "islands in a far sea," but was rather a "sea of islands" and
the ocean a highway, long traversed by ancient mariners (1993; and see Wendt
1976). He acknowledged that Europeans did not invent the practice of belittlement but stressed that contemporary international discourses depicting
island states and territories as too small, too poorly endowed, and too isolated
from metropolitan centers to rise above conditions of dependence on wealthy
nations erase histories of imperialism, innovation, and resilience, and inflict
lasting damage on Islanders' images of themselves (1993, 4).

Hauʻofa further identified the literary, visual, musical, and performing arts
as arenas in which Pacific Islanders could express a powerful regionalism
and weave their creative ideas drawing upon local and introduced materials
and concepts (see also Metzger, chapter 13, this volume). Directly addressing histories of colonialism, (under)development, dependence, and globalization, he challenged the logics of territorial scale, demographic size, and
geopolitical might to reframe dominant perspectives of Pacific peoples and
islands, thus inspiring countless artists, scholars, and students who now trace

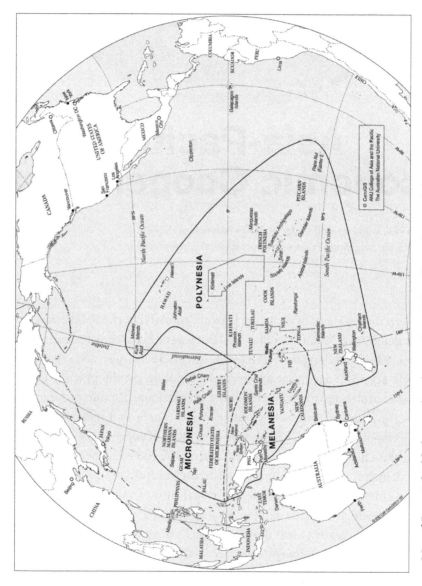

Map of Oceania highlighting cultural areas. CartoGIS, College of Asia and the Pacific, Australian National University.

their intellectual activism to his 1993 essay "Our Sea of Islands." The title of a collection of his works, *We Are the Ocean* (2008), sums up the philosophy of Pacific autonomy, resistance, and creativity he applied while building the Oceania Centre for Arts and Culture at the University of the South Pacific (USP) in Fiji.

Both indigenous Pacific Islander and Pacific studies scholarly frameworks and motivations thus offer some productive insights for the field of global studies. Here I understand global studies, in distinction to international studies or international relations focused primarily on the interactions between states, as a field concerned with exploring globally shared issues and the nature and effects of globalization. These are not assumed to be all-encompassing or linear but rather as involving subjects that are multi-scalar, partial, emergent, and relational. Furthermore, as argued by Arif Dirlik, the global we speak of today is more than a world dominated by U.S. corporations. Rather it involves alternate cultural and political claims on the modern, thus reconfiguring the temporalities and spatialities of capitalist modernity (2005, 158). The geographically large, diverse, deeply connected, and yet often invisible region of Oceania offers one such compelling alternative.

THE BIG PACIFIC

In an unprecedented speech at the 2012 post-forum talks of the Pacific Islands Forum in Rarotonga, Cook Islands, U.S. secretary of state Hillary Clinton announced an expanded role for the U.S. Navy and renewed American engagement in the Pacific. Clinton led the largest and highest-level U.S. delegation in the event's forty-one-year history, with fifty officials, including Navy admiral Samuel Locklear, the head of the U.S. Pacific Command, and Coast Guard rear admiral Charles W. Ray.

The Pacific Islands Forum (PIF), created in 1971 as a vehicle for dialogue and cooperation between members, comprises fifteen Pacific states: Palau, Papua New Guinea, Marshall Islands, Vanuatu, Solomon Islands, Tonga, Tuvalu, Australia, Cook Islands, Federated States of Micronesia, Niue, Kiribati, Nauru, New Zealand, and Samoa. A sixteenth member, Fiji, was suspended from the forum in 2009 after Commander Frank Bainimarama overthrew the elected government in a 2006 military coup. The forum has become the primary vehicle for discussing shared regional political and economic challenges and strategies with powerful donor states such as Australia regularly using the gathering to introduce and implement their own visions for the region.

Several international media stories on the 2012 meeting emphasized the remote and insignificant nature of the Pacific Islands, reporting that just 11,000 people lived in the Cook Islands (a parliamentary democracy in free association with New Zealand), a population roughly the size of the U.S. Foreign Service, as one reporter pointed out. Shaun Tandon of Agence France-Presse (AFP) wrote about the "Island welcome for America's rock-star diplomat":

> Wherever the US secretary of state goes, certain things inevitably follow: super-serious security guards with earpieces, secure communications from top-tier hotels, and a punishing pace of stuffy meetings and formal dinners. But for two-and-a-half days Hillary Clinton's universe was forced to adapt to a tiny and remote island in the middle of the South Pacific, with sometimes curious results . . . The Cook Islands offer misty vistas and pristine beaches galore, but for an entourage accustomed to luxury hotels, a clear lifestyle-change was in store. Clinton's aides, security guards and accompanying press were spread out to locations across the main island of Rarotonga, including rented-out private homes. Officials used to the ultra-sleek rooms found themselves taking outdoor showers under the sun. (Tandon 2012)

The visiting reporters were not the only observers baffled by the significant U.S. presence in the Cook Islands. Fergus Hanson of the Lowy Institute, an Australian think tank, stated to the *Christian Science Monitor* that it was "serious overkill to send the world's most senior diplomat to the after-party of an obscure regional meeting" (Ford 2012). But "obscure" from whose perspective and by what definition?

Hanson's statement and the amused tenor of much of the reporting on the U.S. participation in these regional talks reflect that dominant concept of power predicated on framings of size, scale, and global relevance from a Euro-American and North Atlantic perspective. So this large U.S. delegation had to explain to the world why the "small" Pacific was so relevant.

Clinton told the Pacific Islands Forum that the United States considered the region strategically and economically vital and becoming more so. Admiral Locklear reinforced the point, saying that "[f]ive trillion dollars of commerce rides on the (Asia-Pacific) sea lanes each year, and you people are sitting right in the middle of it . . . We will enhance the US Navy and coastguard Ship Rider program so that we can more effectively combat the illegal activity and enforce conservation measures and build nation capacity to do the same." Clinton added: "I know there are those who see America's renewed engagement in the Pacific perhaps as a hedge against particular countries . . . The Pacific is big enough for all of us . . . We all have important contributions and stakes in this region's success, to advance your security, your opportunity and your prosperity" (Flitton 2012).

The United States has actually dominated naval and military affairs, foreign policy, culture, and education in parts of the Pacific for several decades through its incorporation of Hawai'i as the fiftieth state; its territories of Guam, the Commonwealth of the Northern Marianas, and American Samoa; and the former trust territories of Palau, the Federated States of Micronesia (FSM), and the Marshall Islands. Citizens of those islands would not find American interest or indeed dominance in a political and military context surprising at all. A "Compact of Free Association" between Palau, the FSM, the Marshall Islands, and the United States guarantees U.S. naval and military dominance over the region in exchange for economic assistance and the right of its citizens to travel freely to and reside in United States, accessing educational and health services (also see Shigematsu and Camacho 2010).

While the Pacific is regularly viewed as the home of small, insignificant states, the Pacific Ocean, which is what Secretary Clinton referred to, covers about one-third of the whole planet and is larger than all land masses combined. The "us" in her speech referred to the superpowers of the United States and China. The latter is increasingly viewed by Western countries as undermining their interests and their vision for a sea of democratic, neoliberal Pacific states: these states are now being tempted by China's untied aid and increased business and diplomacy (Wesley-Smith and Porter 2010). In January 2013 the Australian Department of Defence released a draft white paper which *The Australian* reported as raising the specter of competition between China and Australia for the hearts and minds of small and "impoverished Pacific nations" (Stewart 2013). China is now the third largest donor in the region after Australia and the United States.

While such geopolitical duels are of great interest to those rationalist groups highlighted by Fry, they privilege the Pacific as a space that continues to be a field for playing out foreign interests and representations rather than one that generates its own knowledge and integrity, or one that might have a very different relationship with Asia outside of "international relations." The

dynamic nature of Pacific Island cultures and societies in both deep time and
the present does not just offer examples and strategies for balancing ancient
values and beliefs with modernity; it also highlights the consequences and
opportunities of globalization, especially where indigenous cultural identities, together with land and sea, are at stake. Taiwan, for example, increasingly, and strategically, highlights its indigenous rather than its geopolitical
relations with the Pacific Islands, foregrounding the fact that indigenous
Taiwanese and all Pacific populations (except for the Papuans) belong to the
linguistic Austronesian family and diaspora.

Furthermore, the view of the Pacific region as "small" ignores both the
span and depth of the ocean, a space viewed by Islanders not as marking
the borders and boundaries of their inhabited worlds, but rather as a highway connecting a much larger zone of spiritual, environmental, cultural,
economic, and political interaction and exchange prior to and beyond the
establishment of colonial nation-state boundaries (Jolly 2007). In a volume
dedicated to reimagining and reinvigorating area studies, Dirlik argued:

> We are quite aware by now that there is nothing innocent about our spatializations of the
> world. The Pacific has played a significant part over the last two decades in the production
> of discourses of globalization. Conflicts over the Pacific in turn offer clues to grasping
> ideological conflicts within these discourses. How we view the Pacific, and regionalize
> it, is not just an academic question but a political one as well. They may all refer to more
> or less the same location, but terms such as East and Southeast Asia, Asia Pacific, Pacific
> Asia, Pacific Rim and the Pacific have different, and conflicting, referents that remain to
> be sorted out. (Dirlik 2005, 159)

Within this variously labeled and framed zone—called "the South Pacific"
by the Spanish and "Oceania" by the French, and collapsed into the "Asia-
Pacific" by most today—there are also groups who are not indigenous to their
current home islands, such as the descendants of indentured Indian laborers
in Fiji; a growing number of Chinese, Japanese, and Filipino migrants (especially in Hawai'i, Micronesia, and Fiji); displaced or migrant communities;
and Islanders living in metropolitan centers in the Pacific Rim and beyond.
All Pacific Islanders, regardless of their origins, are deeply shaped by indigenous Islander values and ways of seeing and being in the world. Institutionally, these are reflected in the development of indigenous programs such as
Hawaiian studies, Maori studies, Fijian studies, Papua New Guinea studies,
Samoan studies, and so forth. In his reflections on area studies, Dirlik also

discusses indigenous studies as challenging Euro-American modernity and, moreover, as questioning modernity's ways of knowing. Islander scholars, educators, and artists are increasingly using the terms "Oceania" (to foreground the ocean), "Moana" ("the sea" in most Polynesian languages), and "Pasifika" (a pan-Pacific way of pronouncing the word) to counter hegemonic framings by what some call, with tongue in cheek, "outlanders" (Borofsky 2000; Jolly 2007).

Pacific Islands studies has evolved out of three related and sometimes overlapping rationales for area studies. The first involves those pragmatic and strategic motivations for states to understand their immediate region and the geopolitical spaces between their allies and enemies. Language studies have been a big feature of this work. Second, linking area studies to intellectual and scientific pursuits is what Terence Wesley-Smith (1995) called "the laboratory rationale" involving fields such as anthropology, linguistics, archaeology, and history mapping and illuminating human historical, sociocultural, and political characteristics and events. The Pacific, with its perceived isolated islands and societies, is seen to constitute ecological and human laboratories for studying a wide range of phenomena (Deloughrey 2001). And finally, Wesley-Smith describes a more recent "empowerment rationale" reflecting Pacific Islander decolonization, resistance, and transformation of the impacts of colonialism, development, and globalization in scholarship, activism, and the arts.

ROUTES AND ROOTS

Much of my research has explored how a reframing of concepts about small islands through ethnographic work and deeper engagement with Pacific histories can illuminate our assumptions about size and scale in a regional and global context. My research on Banaba, also known as Ocean Island and the home island of my great-grandfather, for example, reflected on how a two-and-a-half-square-mile raised coral atoll in the central Pacific, just eighty meters above sea level at its highest point, was of critical significance to the British Empire and its outposts of Australia and New Zealand for most of the twentieth century (K. M. Teaiwa 2005). The entire island was made of high-grade phosphate rock, a key ingredient in fertilizer and at the time a crucial input for developing and sustaining global industrial agriculture.

Mining Banaba, therefore, was seen to be for "the good of mankind," and the renowned Australian photojournalist and travel writer Thomas McMahon described it as "Let's-all-be-thankful-island: a little spot in the Pacific that multiplies the world's food" (McMahon 1919).

But Banaba was inhabited and the mining resulted in a clash of worldviews, the decimation of a landscape that had taken tens of thousands of years to form, and the displacement of indigenous peoples whose ancestors had arrived two thousand years before Europeans came to the Pacific. The island was reframed by prospectors, mining companies, superphosphate manufacturers, and farmers as a critical agricultural resource, overwriting the Banaban concept of the island as *te aba,* a term that incorporates and links both land and people in embodied, conceptual, and spiritual ways. In the Banaban language you do not say "my land" or "our land," you say "me/land" or "we/land." It is similar across the region whether you're Maori in New Zealand and talking about *whenua, fenua* in French Polynesia, or *vanua* in Fiji. In 1945 the Banabans were removed to Rabi Island in Fiji, where most of them have lived ever since, and by 1980, twenty-two million tons of *te aba* had been mined and shipped to fertilize other landscapes and fuel a vast chain of global agricultural commodities.

So the second lesson for global studies from Pacific studies is that place always matters, and it matters with a deep sense of kinship and history. Land and sea are specific materially, culturally, and spiritually grounded and often animated spaces. The Banabans protested and challenged the British Empire for decades, a challenge that culminated in a decade-long court case in the British High Court where they sued the Crown and the mining company, which was co-owned by the British, Australian, and New Zealand governments. Young male and female warriors of the Banaban Dancing Group led their cause, representing both old and new cultural identities and, in their minds, evidence of their critical survival and creative existence. They lost their case but gained global attention and their dancing is now iconic across the Pacific Islands (K. M. Teaiwa 2012a).

As Chris Ballard has argued, it is often hard for people whose "ties to land consist of casual contacts with . . . infrequently tended suburban gardens" to conceive of the relationship between Pacific communities and the lands and resources they consider theirs (2013, 47). There is a similar lack of understanding of how time might be experienced less as chronological but rather as relational and genealogical with contemporary Pacific societies feeling as connected to their ancestors and ancestral atua, akua or gods, as your average Americans might feel to their grandparents. While parts of the region are increasingly urbanizing, the genealogically animated landscape, both terrestrial and marine, still grounds cultural identities. Across the region, the authority and capacity of the state are limited, and customary rights, especially to land, continue to complicate national and foreign desires to exploit abundant natural resources.

These ties to place, however, do not fix or lock Pacific peoples in static cultural realities. Mobility actually constitutes a primary ontological and epistemological condition for people who regularly move between villages, towns, regions, and islands and across national borders. James Clifford, in reflecting on old and new forms of mobility in New Caledonia, for example, asked: "[H]ow is 'indigeneity' both rooted in and routed through particular places?" and "[A]re there specifically indigenous kinds of diasporism"? (Clifford 2001, 469; and see Harvey and Thompson 2005).

The Pacific has been profoundly shaped by both travel and emplacement. Cluny Macpherson aptly described the settlement of the entire Pacific from Southeast Asia across to the far-flung islands of Polynesia over a period of about six thousand years as the "Pacific Diaspora" (Lal and Fortune 2000). Archaeologist Matthew Spriggs, for example, writes of how navigators in eastern Polynesia had a very clear sense of the other islands in their sphere across 2,600 miles, the width of the Atlantic, long before European sailing and technology entered the region. But before humans arrived in the east, in the western Pacific there was a significant degree of interaction between societies that had been there for much longer.

Spriggs writes that the first evidence in the world of a human "blind crossing" happens in the Pacific between the north coast of the former continent of Sahul (what is now New Guinea, Australia, the Aru Islands in eastern Indonesia, and Tasmania) and the islands of Manus around twenty-six thousand years ago:

[W]hen people set off on that 200–230 km journey they could not see where they were heading to, and for about 60–90 km in the middle of the journey they could no longer see where they had come from . . . that Ice-Age episode of human voyaging is of greater significance than humans landing on the Moon. We have always been able to see the Moon, but these early voyagers were truly alone for that 60–90 km or so. (Spriggs 2009, 10–11)

The next blind crossing happens twenty-three thousand years later, when bearers of the Lapita culture, rising out of a mixture of Papuan and Austronesian cultures and identified by the specially designed clay pots they carried, colonize 4,500 kilometers of the Pacific Ocean within eight to ten generations (Kirch 1997). Spriggs writes that during this period you might have met the same man or woman one year in Tonga, and the next on New Britain or in Vanuatu. Thus, three thousand years ago people from the New Guinea islands and out as far as Tonga and Samoa were more interconnected than at any time until the age of mass transportation began some two centuries ago. The Lapita culture is the cultural heritage of almost all Pacific Islanders today, and thus provides a powerful evidence base for shared values and connections (Spriggs 2009, 14).

So why should we think that any of these activities and ideas spanning tens of thousands of years are relevant today? Because they still are for Pacific Islanders, not as vestiges of primitive traditions but as an ontological aspect of contemporary life and cultural expression. Indeed, shared heritage and shared ancestors *are* recorded and archived in Pacific oral traditions, and many communities today can trace their ancestry with cultures across vast oceanic distances—between, for example, Tonga, Samoa and Fiji, the Cook Islands, and New Zealand, between Hawai'i and Tahiti, and so on. And Islanders still invoke origin stories in their daily lives that link them not just to ancient traveling ancestors, but to the origins of the cosmos and the birth of land, sea, plants, and animals that constitute kin, what Roberts and colleagues call a "metaphysical gestalt" (Roberts et al. 2004; and see, for example, Jolly 2007 and Meyer 2001). Even more interesting to anthropologists is how all this goes on in one form or another even after the conversion to Christianity of the majority of Islander populations over the last hundred years. Rather than substitute one religious system for another, Pacific Islanders incorporated and indigenized Christianity, expanding their range of spiritual, political, and economic choices and tools.

Over 20 percent of the world's languages are spoken in Oceania so the shared heritage is also marked by real linguistic and sociopolitical diversity. The region is thus shaped by cultural forces both unifying and divergent that continue to influence identity, action, and discourse. Politically, these include the formation of regional subgroupings, such as the Melanesian Spearhead Group and the newly established Polynesian Leaders Group in addition to the Pacific Islands Forum. But at the base of regionalism is a very real shared sense of kinship, what Fiji's late president Ratu Sir Kamisese Mara called "the Pacific Way." Under this Pacific Way, there is generally a shared understanding of the importance and nature of dialogue in the process of decision making, of a shared sense of temporality, of the place of ancestors, relations to land and sea, and of the centrality of culture to people's sense of identity and belonging. The Pacific Way has been critiqued from within and outside the region as elitist and ignorant of increasing class and gender issues on the ground, but the idea persists (Lawson 2010).

In the 1980s, the fifteenth Pacific Science Congress met in Dunedin, New Zealand, to address issues of multi-sited indigenous Pacific mobility and identity (Chapman 1985). Among other things, scholars discussed how human identification and activity across the region was marked by both the rooted and stable, as well as the traveling and dynamic. The apparent binary was not oppositional or paradoxical but simultaneously at work in shaping identity and fueling and sustaining social life. Pacific identities were maps connecting specific places and traversing vast oceanic spaces. With respect to current anti-essentialist sentiments amongst postmodern, postcolonial, and cultural studies scholars, the Pacific offers histories that recognize both autochthony and movement, roots and routes, emplacement and flow. Matt Matsuda, in speaking recently about "the world ocean" at the Australian National University (ANU), characterized this mobile Pacific reality as "translocality" and as constituting "translocal assemblages" (Matsuda 2012).

So the third lesson from Pacific studies for global studies is that while place matters, multiple places can be connected via people in a dynamic network of meaningful relations that extend across deep time and vast space. But despite all this movement, scientists, artists, and other scholars have traditionally approached the islands as insular cultural and ecological laboratories. The focus on travel and migration is a relatively recent scholarly move that emerges out of archaeology, linguistics, geography, sociology, postcolonial literature, and Pacific cultural studies (Diaz and Kauanui 2001). Nevertheless, those discourses of boundedness, smallness, peripherality, instability, and the helplessness of small island states and their peoples still persist (Fry 1997, 2004; Cole 1993; Wallis 2012).

The language of development "experts," aid agencies, and good governance projects coming out of countries like Australia in particular often ahistorically conflates powerlessness with peripherality. It is conveniently forgotten that half of World War II was fought across the lands of Papua New Guinea, the Solomon Islands, the Gilbert Islands (now Kiribati), and the islands of Micronesia; that the United States and France needed the Marshall Islands and French Polynesia to test their nuclear weapons; that Australia and New Zealand desperately needed phosphate from Nauru and Banaba to develop their agricultural industries; and that the fortunes of many a British, Australian, Dutch, German, French, New Zealand, and American company were made on copra, cotton, sugarcane, sandalwood, bèche-de-mer, whales' teeth, copper, gold, guano, and other Pacific island resources, including labor. Today, former colonial states still use the Pacific to extract key resources and as a buffer zone between geopolitical powers. The Australian government also uses Papua New Guinea and Nauru as detention and processing centers for refugees it does not want on its own shores. The region of West Papua is still under an often brutal, contemporary Indonesian colonial rule, a reality some Oceanic states choose to ignore. Pacific islands are central, not peripheral, to colonialism, globalization, development, and capitalist expansion (also see Lockwood 2004).

It was in response to all this that Epeli Hau'ofa wrote his now famous piece on critical and creative Pacific regionalism as resistance to imperialism, neocoloniaism, and globalization. Partially inspired by Caribbean poet Derek Walcott, by a revelation Hau'ofa had in Hawai'i encountering the majestic Mouna Kea on the big island of Hawai'i, and by the faces of his disenchanted USP students, he reframed the Pacific to inspire and empower Islanders (Hau'ofa 1993). Like Walcott he affirmed the sea as "history," reminding everyone that the ancestors traversed a tremendous expanse of water long before the Spanish arrived and named it "Pacific." Hau'ofa's vision was to recognize what he called the ancient and contemporary processes of "world enlargement," carried out by thousands of ordinary Pacific Islanders, "crisscrossing an ocean that had been boundless for ages before Captain Cook's apotheosis" (ibid., 6; and see Wilson and Connery 2007).

CULTURE AND INDIGENEITY

There are many island regions, but the Pacific, I argue, is unique in a number of ways, not least because of its geographic expanse. The majority of its people are "indigenous," but not always in the "Fourth World" sense where "indigenous" is assumed to mark minorities among a majority, settler context and within a bounded nation-state. In her quest to unpack indigeneity as a contingent, interactive, and historical product, Francesca Merlan discusses a "criterial" definition of indigeneity as referring to first-order, small-scale connections between group and locality connoting belonging and originariness, and deeply felt processes of attachment and identification. She writes: "Indigeneity as it has expanded in its meaning to define an international category is taken to refer to peoples who have great moral claims on nation-states and on international society, often because of inhumane, unequal, and exclusionary treatment" (Merlan 2009, 304).

She then discusses Martínez Cobo's definition for the United Nations, presenting indigenous communities, peoples, and nations as "those which have a historical continuity with preinvasion and precolonial societies . . . consider themselves as distinct from other sectors of societies now prevailing in those territories . . . and are determined to preserve and transmit to future generations their ancestral territories, and their ethnic identity, as the basis of their continued existence as peoples" (ibid., 305). This definition is also reflected in the International Labour Organization's 1989 description of indigenous peoples as tribal and distinct from other sections of society, descended from precolonial populations, and retaining some or all of their own institutions (ibid., 305).

Merlan also talks of another, "relational" definition of indigeneity characterized by relations between particular groups and the state, especially with respect to historical tensions between indigenous and settler groups and the power imbalances ensuing. Under this schema indigeneity is defined against that which is considered not indigenous, an approach that characterizes, for example, Dyck's term "Fourth World" (ibid., 305). Most of these definitions and understandings focus on the moral and ethical relations between minority indigenous populations and the state within a sea of settler and dominant populations. Merlan only discusses Aboriginal Australian, Hawaiian, and Maori examples because most of the rest of the Pacific would not fit those international definitions of indigeneity that presuppose a tension and set of ethical issues between indigenous peoples and their respective, usually liberal democratic, nation-states.

The problem here includes one of optics and framing with the nation-state as the major unit of analysis. While contemporary state boundaries have often been drawn around and straight through pre-existing linguistic and cultural spaces, it is also the case that most Pacific states and territories have what would qualify in terms of precolonial continuity and attachment to place, as predominantly indigenous populations and governments. They may not always be minorities in their own home countries, but as a regional whole, the Pacific suffers from structural challenges and invisibility, similar to indigenous minorities. As a bloc, for example, the Pacific Islands could be framed as a "Fourth World" against the Pacific Rim countries of East and Southeast Asia, Australia, New Zealand and the Americas, particularly North America.

A fourth lesson for global studies then, is that the Pacific allows us to explore how structures of imperialism and inequality might be experienced by entire regions with small formerly or currently colonized, indigenous, interconnected populations and governments. Furthermore, unlike many populous countries whose citizens have been displaced and disconnected from their historical lands, the Pacific allows us to imagine what kinds of creative survival strategies are developed by Island peoples with strong, extended kinship structures who also still have that deep connection to and knowledge of their environments. In countries such as New Zealand and Hawai'i where there are majority settler populations, these strategies are particularly well articulated in scholarship, activism, education, and the arts.

Antony Hooper (2005) argues that it is culture that sets Pacific Islanders apart from most other populations. He says that what is construed as culture in the Pacific is constructed in ways that are distinct from the kinds of construction prevalent in, for example, larger Asian countries. Culture for him impinges on the "harder" structures of political and economic organization much more directly and effectively. There is, for example, in every Pacific country, a large and vigorous traditional sector. It does not consist, as is the case in many other regions, of minorities or a few rural groups with little influence on national economic and political affairs. In most cases 80 to 90 percent of land resources are under customary tenure, and the traditional sector accounts for a significant percentage of national GDP.

Furthermore, Hooper writes that the systems of customary tenure are commonly entrenched in constitutional or other legal structures which attempt to insulate them, either absolutely or in large degree, from the operation of market forces and state coercion. While this is changing and the

market has figured out ways around customary tenure in countries such as
PNG, Vanuatu, and Fiji, custom, or *kastom* in Melanesia, still controls a large
proportion of the economic resources that are "basic for development in any
of its conventional senses" (Hooper 2005, 2). In these circumstances development is not, argues Hooper, simply a matter of engineering a transition from
subsistence to dynamic monetary economies:

> The economic mode of Pacific traditional sectors is not "subsistence" if by that is meant
> "mere subsistence"—nor has it ever been. There is instead a wide variety of reciprocal
> exchanges and redistributions that integrate whole districts in networks of mutual obliga-
> tion and concern going far beyond "mere subsistence." Such transactions are more than
> "mere economics." They are, in the well-worn phrase, "embedded in the society," carrying
> within them a large moral and ideological force. (ibid., 2–3)

Hooper then discusses how culture also impinges on national politics.
Most Pacific countries are democratic and politicians are elected by people
whose livelihoods depend primarily on traditional sectors. Matters of custom
and tradition thus carry considerable political weight. He writes, "Pacific
countries have constitutions which assert national legitimacy in terms of
their distinctive culture and traditions, and these are given at least as much
attention as universal notions of democracy and individual rights. In these
ways, culture in one form or another is right at the heart of national economic
and political life" (ibid., 3). Combining all this with how significantly connected Islanders are via kinship, cultural, and other exchanges over hundreds
of years (thousands in the western Pacific), this sense of "unity" lends itself
to a particular mode of regionalism and expressions of decolonization and
resistance based not primarily on shared experiences of class, as they might
be in industrialized countries or former settler colonies, but on indigenous
values and worldviews (see Bargh 2007).

Of course there are specific exceptions to this generalized overview, and
you can only take the argument of "Pacific exceptionalism" so far. Some
Pacific experiences are not at all unique, and there are critical differences
between Pacific societies. Furthermore, the layers of intersecting political,
social, and economic interests can complicate and hinder systems of justice
and governance. However, as a counter-framing exercise, and given the relative invisibility of this region in global studies, it is worth highlighting what
is indeed distinctive and similar across Oceania.

THE OCEANIA CENTRE

One of the most powerful expressions of Pacific regionalism is embodied in the University of the South Pacific (USP), modeled on the University of the West Indies (UWI). It is a multinational university owned by the Cook Islands, Fiji, Kiribati, the Marshall Islands, Nauru, Niue, Samoa, the Solomon Islands, Tokelau, Tonga, Tuvalu, and Vanuatu. The main campus in Suva, Fiji, educates the largest number of Pacific students in the region, and satellite centers in member countries provide extension services for an even larger number of students. USP's mandate has always been to train students in key disciplines for filling the civil service ranks of its member states, such as business, accounting, management, communications, the natural sciences, development, sociology, English, literature, history, and politics. Disciplines like anthropology, cultural studies, or the arts have not been considered as pragmatic or as urgent as the technical training required to run developing states. While USP hosted an Institute of Pacific Studies for many years and literary expression, at least, thrived, Pacific studies was not converted into a teaching program until 2006. This is in stark contrast with Caribbean studies, which has been popular and central to the scholarship of UWI faculty.

I was born and raised in Fiji and grew up on the USP campus as both my mother and elder sister worked there for a number of years. Professor Epeli Hau'ofa had been the head of the School of Social and Economic Development at USP and was initially accepting of a fatalistic, geopolitical approach to island nations. This transformed after he began to pay attention to the reactions of his students to his lectures on the dependency and smallness of island states. He wrote in his now famous essay, "Their faces crumbled visibly, they asked for solutions, I could offer none." He began to ask himself: "What kind of teaching is it to stand in front of young people from your own region, people you claim as your own, who have come to university with high hopes for the future, and you tell them that our countries are hopeless? Is this not what neocolonialism is about? To make people believe that they have no choice but to depend" (1993, 5)?

Throughout his essay, Hau'ofa reimagines the Pacific not as small isolated islands, but as a sea of islands in a vast and ever-expanding Oceania. He cites indigenous cosmologies which include worlds far above, beyond, and below the surface of land and sea as evidence of a vast and ever expanding indigenous worldview, boldly displayed in Pacific oral, visual, and performing arts. This worldview was ever expanding, he said, until Islanders arrived in universities to be told that their islands and cultures were small and dependent. He then declared that "[s]mallness is a state of mind" (1993, 7) and urged Islanders to move beyond the individuality of islands or states to a perspective in which Oceania was seen in terms of a totality of human, environmental, and historical relationships. He boldly (and controversially) imagined Pacific cultures at their most positive and impressive, where contemporary travels and migration were on a continuum with ancient mobility and exchange (ibid.; and see Lee and Tupai 2009). If the world of Oceania today did not always include the heavens and the underworlds, it did now include cities in Australia, New Zealand, Canada, and the United States, where large numbers of Polynesians, in particular, now reside. The essay became a work of such scholarly and popular discussion that USP published a series of nineteen responses that examined "Our Sea of Islands" from every conceivable angle, some of which strongly critiqued it as fanciful and impractical (Waddell, Naidu, and Hauʻofa 1993).

In 1985 Hauʻofa petitioned the vice chancellor of USP for a building that "creative people could call home" (personal communication 2004; K. M. Teaiwa 2011). This was viewed as a request for some kind of "Bohemia" and denied. When other ideas surfaced for a formal program in Pacific arts, Hauʻofa resisted, believing that such a space would not be autonomous if linked to formal studies. Although a successful writer, he felt that writing was a personal and solitary kind of activity tied too much to the self or ego. Moreover, writing, at least on paper, was not a feature of Oceanic culture until the arrival of missionaries, and he wanted to support forms of expression that were "our own" (ibid.). His aim was to create a space for collaboration and for the production of creative arts among a community of artists.

In 1997 Hauʻofa established the Oceania Centre for Arts and Culture (OCAC), which took a specifically grassroots, informal, anti-global, and pro-Pacific stance. In the South Pacific, as many Islander scholars joke, culture was not something one studied in a university but lived, danced, or sang on a daily basis, and so the OCAC offered no formal classes. Hauʻofa had written *Tales of the Tikongs* (1983), a satire in which the institutions and forces of native government, the church, tradition, colonialism, aid, and development

were skillfully mocked. One of his central characters, aptly named Ole Pa-
sifikiwei (Old Pacific Way), symbolized the vast array of creative strategies
that Islanders had developed over centuries, now hastily discarded for money
and shortcuts to Western-style progress. Hauʻofa considered the arts (from
sculpture and architecture to tattooing, music, and dance) to represent the
archives of Pacific knowledge and philosophy, the pinnacle of their creativity, and he imagined the arts center as an open space for reconnecting with
those roots (Hauʻofa 2008).

What began as four small rooms and a veranda, in 2013 comprises over ten
offices, a metal workshop, an open-air painting and carving studio, a record-
ing studio, a display stage, two galleries, a replica of a traditional Fijian *bure*
(house), a reception area, and an open-air performance space. Permanent
staff includes a director, two administrators, three lecturers, several teaching assistants, technical support, performing arts director, artistic director,
choreographer, music coordinator, and visual arts coordinator. In addition,
the community of artists has expanded to include a large number of painters,
carvers, musicians, and the dancers of the Oceania Dance Theatre (ODT).
In any given year, the OCAC runs public art and dance workshops; puts on
several exhibitions, dance, and theater productions in Fiji and overseas; and
hosts visiting artists and choreographers from across the region. For a fee,
performances by the ODT have become a standard feature of university
social events, and while this commercialization departs from Hauʻofa's vision, it has professionalized the artists and dramatically raised their profile.

Dancers at the ODT are exposed to choreography from a wide variety
of Pacific genres, which they have blended under the direction of Samoan
director Allan Alo from 1999 to 2011 and Hawaiian-Samoan choreographer
Peter Rockford Espiritu most recently. The aim has always been to create
a new, remixed, unifying, and contemporary "Oceanic" style drawing on
ancient values and motifs, rather than to re-present traditional dance genres
or reinforce ethnic and national cultures. When the dance program began in
1998, it relied on the abilities of existing performers in Suva, many of whom,
like myself, had basic training in ballet and gymnastics and had danced in
the tourism industry. I eventually became a founding member of the theater
and collaborated with Alo on two productions: *The Boiling Ocean I* and *The
Boiling Ocean II*. In the early 2000s, the ODT struggled to attract versatile

Sorpapelu Tipo Fatiaki and performers of the Oceania Dance Theatre (University of the South Pacific) and Pasifika Voices in *Ta'aroa: Pacific Ballet of Creation,* directed by Allan Alo, choreography by Katalina Fotofili. Photo by Jeremy Duxbury.

dancers and had a rather eclectic company with varying performance skills. Today, however, young people with dance potential are trained in several Pacific styles with a strong emphasis on ballet, Pilates, and modern dance technique, and the program has become highly disciplined. ODT performances are supported by all resident artists, including visual artists and musicians, all of whom contribute to the calendar of Pacific-themed productions (K. M. Teaiwa 2011).

In Hau'ofa's original vision, the Oceania Centre embodied a resistance to multiple pressures—institutional, ethnic, national, and international—and at the regional level it resisted the term "Pacific." He said: "When the powers that be use the term Pacific they usually refer to the Pacific Rim and islanders are excluded. Oceania, the word itself, means the sea ... The notion of Oceania cannot be contained. Metaphorically, for creative purposes, it's tremendous. For the mind it is a liberating concept, the idea of limitlessness

... we can at least dream into eternity" (personal communication 2004). His Oceania thus aspired to be global, a world almost 70 percent covered by ocean which has hitherto focused mainly on terrestrial needs and activities or simply used the ocean as resource. He maintained that this imagination and aspiration in actuality is a practical exercise: "creativity is what keeps us alive" (ibid.).

James Clifford described Hauʻofa's legacy as an "alter-globalization" concerned with reinventing the Pacific in the face of neocolonialism and globalization, rejecting the narrow confines of ethnic politics, and projecting a vision of "indigenous cosmopolitanism" (2009, 239; and also see Forte 2010). In 2010, a year after Hauʻofa's passing, Pacific Worlds, the first-ever undergraduate Pacific studies course, was established at USP; it is now a required course for every single one of the university's twenty thousand students, regardless of degree or discipline. It is taught by the staff of the renamed Oceania Centre for Arts, Culture and Pacific Studies.

CODA

In 2011 President Obama announced that the twenty-first century would be America's "Pacific Century," and for the first time there was an emphasis on the "Pacific" half of the "Asia-Pacific" region implicated in the title. Hillary Clinton's 2012 visit to the post-forum dialogue was viewed by journalists as specifically addressing China's rising interest in the region and indeed the rising interests of more than a few other nations. There were sixty observer countries at that year's post-forum talks, including Britain, Canada, China, Japan, and France.

The space between the United States and China has become the pivot around which geopolitical power will be expressed and cemented this millennium with the largest, albeit oceanic, region on the planet providing the potential not just for political and economic maneuvers but, with the vast improvement in extractive technology, for natural resources from oil to minerals to natural gas. While Pacific countries are terrestrially small, they have large oceanic exclusive economic zones (extending for two hundred nautical miles offshore) that are teeming with fish and other maritime resources. The rush to secure friendship and cooperation from Pacific nations, especially

Sign advertising a night market in Avarua on the island of Rarotonga in the
Cook Islands on August 30, 2012. Photo by Mary Melville/AFP/GettyImages.
Used by permission.

those independent nations with a UN vote, raises many eyebrows because of
the sheer imbalance of demographic, economic, and political power between
the small island states and almost every other interested party.

On the ground in the Cook Islands, however, Secretary Clinton's presence was cause for much fanfare and excitement. In true Pacific fashion she
was laden with colorful and sweet-smelling garlands and quickly incorporated affectionately into daily vocabulary as "Aunty Hillary." Echoing the
observations of countless travel writers who have visited the Pacific since the
eighteenth century, the experience of Agence France-Presse reporter Shaun
Tandon in Clinton's entourage is worth sharing here in his own entertaining
prose:

> In other countries on assignments with Clinton, I've found myself in vast suites and
> regretted that I barely had the time to sleep-test their king-size beds. In the Cook Islands,
> I shared a room with another reporter for three nights in an inn usually frequented by
> budget travelers from New Zealand, with a menagerie of cats, dogs, and the occasional
> chicken showing up at the front door.

In a nod to local sensitivities in a country that—unlike the United States—tightly controls firearms, Clinton's security guards eschewed their usual suits and exposed hand-guns in favor of loose-fitting aloha shirts . . . Not that there was an obvious security threat in Rarotonga, where the (only) main road rings the island's coast, and there are two bus routes: "clockwise" and "anti-clockwise." A travelers' guide stated that the leading risk on the Cook Islands is falling coconuts, as can attest those who have had the misfortune to be underneath a tree when the Pacific winds picked up. Another friendly warning in the travel advice read, "Roosters on the island are on their own time zone."

Hillary Clinton is clearly used to rock-star receptions. At her next stop in Jakarta, some staff members of the Association of Southeast Asian Nations literally screamed as they snapped pictures of her. But the excitement in the Cook Islands was as omnipresent as the coconuts . . . Such light moments of "public diplomacy" in such a small island state may not be as consequential as Clinton's talks with China's top leadership, her policy prescriptions for staunching Syria's bloodshed or, for that matter, the U.S. stance on climate change, which poses an existential threat to all low-lying island nations. But there's surely some hard-to-measure positive impact for the United States and its reputation when one of the world's most powerful individuals takes the time to mingle with folks in one of the world's remotest corners. (Tandon 2012)

Nic Maclellan, long-term Pacific journalist and researcher, wrote rather differently of the gathering. He reminded everyone that the 2012 meeting was themed "Large Ocean Island States—the Pacific Challenge," a very deliberate play on Epeli Hau'ofa's concept that had now moved from the realm of scholarly activism and art to policy, motivating a strategic political and economic reframing of the region by Pacific leaders (Maclellan 2012). The following year, the largest gathering of Pacific Islanders at the University of Hawai'i's Manoa campus occurred to mark Nuclear Survivors Day, promote political and cultural solidarity, and work toward a just and peaceful Oceania (Verán 2013).

Oceania is vast, Oceania is expanding, Oceania is hospitable and generous, Oceania is humanity rising from the depths of brine and regions of fire deeper still, Oceania is us. We are the sea, we are the ocean, we must wake up to this ancient truth . . . We must not allow anyone to belittle us again, and take away our freedom.

—Epeli Hau'ofa, 1993

Poster advertising the Oceania Rising event held on March 1, 2013, at the University of Hawai'i at Manoa. Designed by 'Ilima Long and used with permission from the Oceania Rising student organization.

REFERENCES

Ballard, Chris. 2013. "It's the Land, Stupid!: The Moral Economy of Resource Ownership in Papua New Guinea." In *The Governance of Common Property in the Pacific Islands*, ed. Peter Larmour. Canberra: ANU E Press. First published 1997.

Bargh, Maria, ed. 2007. *Resistance: An Indigenous Response to Neoliberalism*. Wellington, NZ: Huia Publishers.

Borofsky, Robert, ed. 2000. *Remembrance of Pacific Pasts: An Invitation to Remake History*. Honolulu: University of Hawai'i Press.

Callick, Rowan. 1993. "Pacific 2010: A Doomsday Scenario?" In *Pacific 2010: Challenging the Future*, ed. Rodney V. Cole. Canberra: National Centre for Development Studies, ANU.

Chapman, Murray, ed. 1985. *Mobility and Identity in the Island Pacific*. Wellington, NZ: Victoria University Press.

Clifford, James. 2001. "Indigenous Articulations." *The Contemporary Pacific* 13(2): 467–90.

———. 2009. "Hau'ofa's Hope for Social Anthropology in Oceania." *Oceania* 79(3): 238–49.

Cole, Rodney V., ed. 1993. *Pacific 2010: Challenging the Future*. Canberra: National Centre for Development Studies. Canberra: National Centre for Development Studies, ANU.

Deloughrey, Elizabeth. 2001. "The Litany of Islands, the Rosary of Archipelagos: Caribbean and Pacific Archipelagraphy." *ARIEL* 32(1) (January): 21–51.

Diaz, Vince, and J. Kehaulani Kauanui, eds. 2001. "Native Pacific Cultural Studies on the Edge." Special issue, *The Contemporary Pacific* 13(2): 315–491.

Dirlik, Arif. 2005. "Asia Pacific Studies in an Age of Global Modernity." *Inter-Asia Cultural Studies* 6(2): 158–70.

Finin, Gerard, and Terence Wesley-Smith. 2001. "Coups, Conflicts and Crises: The New Pacific Way?" *Race and Class* 42(1): 1–16.

Flitton, Daniel. 2012. "Pacific Is Big Enough for Us All, Insists Clinton." *Sydney Morning Herald*. September 2. http://www.smh.com.au/world/pacific-is-big-enough-for-all-insists-clinton-20120901-2573m.html.

Ford, Peter. 2012. "Clinton to the Cook Islands: US Cares (More Than China)." *Christian Science Monitor*. August 31. http://www.csmonitor.com/World/Asia-Pacific/2012/0831/Clinton-to-Cook-Islands-US-cares-more-than-China.

Forte, Maximilian C., ed. 2010. *Indigenous Cosmopolitans: Transnational and Transcultural Identities in the Twenty-First Century*. New York: Peter Lang.

Fry, Gregory. 1997. "Framing the Islands: Knowledge and Power in Changing Australian Images of the South Pacific." *The Contemporary Pacific* 9(2): 305–44.

———. 2004. "The War against Terror and Australia's New Interventionism in the Pacific." In *Governance Challenges for PNG and the Pacific Islands*, ed. Nancy Sullivan. Madang, Papua New Guinea: Divine Word University Press.

Harvey, Graham, and Charles D. Thompson Jr., eds. 2005. *Indigenous Diasporas and Dislocations*. London: Ashgate.

Hau'ofa, Epeli. 1983. *Tales of the Tikongs*. Auckland: Longman Paul.

———. 1993. "Our Sea of Islands." In *A New Oceania : Rediscovering Our Sea of Islands*, ed. Eric Waddell, Vijay Naidu, and Epeli Hau'ofa. Suva, Fiji: School of Social and Economic Development, University of the South Pacific, in association with Beake House.

———. 2008. *We Are the Ocean: Selected Works*. Honolulu: University of Hawai'i Press.

Herr, Richard, and Anthony Bergin. 2012. "White Paper Must Revive Pacific Studies." *The Australian: Higher Education Supplement*. March 14. http://www.theaustra-

lian.com.au/higher-education/opinion/white-paper-must-revive-pacific-studies/
story-e6frgcko-1226298542206.

Hooper, Antony, ed. 2005. *Culture and Sustainable Development in the Pacific*. Canberra: ANU
E Press. http://epress.anu.edu.au/titles/culture_citation.

Jolly, Margaret. 2007. "Imagining Oceania: Indigenous and Foreign Representations of a Sea
of Islands." *The Contemporary Pacific* 19(2) (August 13): 508–45.

Kirch, Patrick V. 1997. *The Lapita Peoples: Ancestors of the Oceanic World*. Oxford, UK:
Blackwell.

Lal, Brij, and Kate Fortune, eds. 2000. *The Pacific Islands: An Encyclopedia*. Honolulu: University of Hawai'i Press.

Lawson, Stephanie. 2010. "Postcolonialism, Neo-colonialism and the 'Pacific Way': A Critique of (Un)critical Approaches." State, Society and Governance in Melanesia Discussion
Paper, ANU. 2010/4.

Lee, Helen, and Steve Tupai Francis, eds. 2009. *Migration and Transnationalism:
Pacific Perspectives*. Canberra: ANU E Press. http://epress.anu.edu.au/titles/
migration-and-transnationalism.

Lockwood, Victoria S., ed. 2004. *Globalization and Culture Change in the Pacific Islands*. Upper Saddle River, NJ: Pearson/Prentice Hall.

Maclellan, Nic. 2012. "Our Sea of Islands to Pose Serious Policy Challenges." *Crikey*. August
31. http://www.crikey.com.au/2012/08/31/our-sea-of-islands-to-pose-serious-policy
-challenges/.

Matsuda, Matt. 2012. "The World Ocean: Writing Pacific Histories as Translocal Assemblages." Paper presented at the Research School of Asia and Pacific Symposium, Re-experienc-
ing Asia and the Pacific: New Visions of Region across Disciplinary Boundaries, College of
Asia and the Pacific. November 28–30.

McMahon, Thomas. 1919. *The Penny Pictorial*. September 20.

Merlan, Francesca. 2009. "Indigeneity: Global and Local." *Current Anthropology* 50(3):
303–33.

Meyer, Manulani Aluli. 2001. "Our Own Liberation: Reflections on Hawaiian Epistemology."
Contemporary Pacific 13(1): 124–48.

Roberts, Mere, et al. 2004. "Whakapapa as a Maori Mental Construct: Some Implications for
the Debate over the Genetic Modification of Organisms." *The Contemporary Pacific* 16(1):
1–28.

Said, Edward. 1978. *Orientalism*. New York: Pantheon Books.

Shigematsu, Setsu, and Keith Camacho, eds. 2010. *Militarized Currents: Toward a Decolonized
Future in Asia and the Pacific*. Minneapolis: University of Minnesota Press, 2010.

Smith, Linda Tuhiwai. 1999. *Decolonizing Methodologies: Research and Indigenous Peoples*.
London: Zed Books, 1999.

Spriggs, Matthew. 2009. "Oceanic Connections in Deep Time." *PacifiCurrents: eJournal of the
Australian Association for the Advancement of Pacific Studies* 1(1): 7–27.

Stewart, Cameron. 2013. "White Paper Draft Warns of China Influence in the Pacific." *The
Australian*. January 25. http://www.theaustralian.com.au/national-affairs/defence/
white-paper-draft-warns-of-china-influence-in-pacific/story-e6frg8yo-1226561297330.

Tandon, Shaun. 2012. "An Island Welcome for America's Rock-Star Diplomat."
Agence France-Presse. http://blogs.afp.com/correspondent/?post/2012/09/05/
An-island-welcome-for-America-s-rock-star-diplomat.

Teaiwa, Katerina Martina. 2005. "Our Sea of Phosphate." In *Indigenous Diasporas and Dislocations: Unsettling Western Fixations,* ed. Graham Harvey and Charles D. Thompson Jr. London: Ashgate.

———. 2009. "Paradise in Crisis." *The Drum.* Australian Broadcasting Corporation. November 6. http://www.abc.net.au/unleashed/27296.html.

———. 2011. "Choreographing Oceania." In *Islands as Crossroads: Sustaining Cultural Diversity in Small Island Developing States,* ed. Tim Curtis. 138–51. Paris: UNESCO Publications.

———. 2012a. "Choreographing Difference: The (Body) Politics of Banaban Dance." *The Contemporary Pacific* 24(1): 65–95.

———. 2012b. "Cultural Development and Cultural Observatories in the African, Caribbean and Pacific Group of States (ACP)." In *The Atlantic World in the Antipodes: Effects and Transformation since the Eighteenth Century,* ed. Kate Fullagar. Newcastle upon Tyne: Cambridge Scholars Publishing.

Teaiwa, Teresia K. 2010. "Specifying Pacific Studies: For or Before an Asia-Pacific Studies Agenda." In *Remaking Area Studies: Teaching and Learning across Asia and the Pacific,* ed. Terence Wesley-Smith and Jon Goss, 110–24. Honolulu: University of Hawai'i Press.

Verán, Cristina. 2013. "Oceania Rising." *Cultural Survival Quarterly,* no. 37–2. May 28. http:// www.culturalsurvival.org/publications/cultural-survival-quarterly/oceania-rising.

Waddell, Eric, Vijay Naidu, and Epeli Hau'ofa, eds. 1993. *A New Oceania: Rediscovering Our Sea of Islands.* Suva, Fiji: School of Social and Economic Development, University of the South Pacific, in association with Beake House.

Wallis, Joanne. 2012. "The Pacific: From 'Arc of Instability' to 'Arc of Responsibility' and then to 'Arc of Opportunity'?" *Security Challenges* 8(4): 1–12.

Wendt, Albert. 1976. "Towards a New Oceania." *Mana Review* 1(1): 49–60.

Wesley-Smith, Terence. 1995. "Rethinking Pacific Islands Studies." *Pacific Studies* 18(2) (115–137).

Wesley-Smith, Terence, and Edgar Porter, eds. 2010. *China in Oceania: Towards a New Regional Order?* London: Berghahn Books.

Wilson, Rob, and Christopher Leigh Connery, eds. 2007. *The Worlding Project: Doing Cultural Studies in the Era of Globalization.* Berkeley, CA: North Atlantic Books, 2007.

5 – GENEALOGIES

Connecting Spaces in Historical Studies of the Global

PRAKASH KUMAR

THE 1980S AND 1990S WERE A PERIOD OF TRANSITION IN THE WORLD
of seeds. The decades were marked by the arrival of agricultural biotechnology which made it possible to harvest plants with desirable physical and
physiological characteristics by changing their genetic structure at the cel-
lular level. These technologies appeared in the Euro-American arena and
were quickly appropriated by a handful of private companies in the West.
The backers of agricultural biotechnology soon began trying to disseminate
their new biotech crops globally. This endeavor had the potential to alter
global farming in a fundamental way, including radically transforming the
nature of agriculture in many parts of the "developing" world. The latter had
been dominated by the "Green Revolution" since the middle decades of the
twentieth century.[1] The Green Revolution, focused as it was on the cultivation of high-yielding "hybrid" varieties of seeds, was bound to crumble if the
expansion of biotech seeds gained momentum.

The same transitional decades in India were marked by wide-ranging social
movements opposing the technological changes unfolding in Indian agricul-

ture. Ecological sensibilities in India in the seventies and eighties opposed
the order of hybrid seeds and the so-called Green Revolution that required
high-cost inputs of irrigation, fertilizers, and pesticides, and a facilitating
social environment of domestic policies and global science. These movements set the stage in the 1990s for the next round of oppositional movements
against genetically modified (GM) seeds; these movements also targeted the
new global arrangements of the World Trade Organization (WTO), which
sanctioned the commodification and globalization of patent-protected biotech seeds. As one set of social movements melded into another, remarkable
continuities were evident in the common resolve of social and political forces
in India to protect what were believed to be foundational and desirable characteristics of agriculture.

The conflicts in the world of seeds in the era of transition from a horticul-
tural to a biotechnological paradigm tell a rich history that pivots on developments unfolding in disparate physical spaces that seem remote only on the
surface. The biotechnological revolution in agriculture was marked by two
watershed moments: in the United States, the first planting of genetically
modified plants in 1996; and in India, the approval for planting GM cotton
in July 2002. It is indeed possible to tell a history of biotech seeds that links
developments in the United States (and the West generally) and in India
with a global approach. But how might historians hone their tools in order to
recount this history based on these two sites? What analytical frames might
historians deploy to bind the rise of GM crops in the West with the resistance
to forces of change in Indian agriculture? Recounting the GM revolution
across the United States and India requires establishing causal connections
across large distances and tracking influences along multiple channels. In
theoretical terms it invites a willingness to move away from explanations involving a single, hegemonic "core," as is commonly prevalent in theories like
the world-systems approach.[2] It also involves bypassing nation-dominated
modernist frames of analysis.[3] In addition, it requires exploration of spaces
beyond the "local." This global analytic for discerning connections rests on
Foucauldian genealogies, which are non-linear trajectories that while situated in specific spaces and times are definitively interrelated and collectively
give rise to histories in multiple locations.

While historical events are a product of their local circumstances, it is
difficult to think of the local spaces as self-contained "local wholes."[4] The

"local" has come to be associated with a certain mystic legitimacy that induces an unwillingness to interrogate it further. More useful for our analysis is the notion of "locale" as a point traversed by multiple forces originating from multiple sources.[5] The self-conscious act of disprivileging the "metropolitan," the "national," or the "local" makes it possible to acknowledge that genealogies may be located at multiple locations in dispersed territories. Exploring unobvious spaces, including spaces and actors in the "cores" whose multilateralism has remained unanalyzed, may lead us to the multiple loci of the history of GM crops. In many ways, thus, the "global" history of GM embraces analytical stances that are antithetical to strictly local, national, and regional approaches.

The task of finding the hidden connections in this global history also requires developing appropriate analytical strategies. These must include a willingness to move back and forth between temporalities in order to track genealogies of resistance. The stable and sustained structures of resistance endure over time even though they take on different forms. This is particularly relevant in a "global" world where different arenas may exist at different temporal points and yet be intimately connected to each other in meaningful ways. Any methodological insistence on a linear narrative history makes it hard if not impossible to see such connections and thus forecloses the option of writing a history based on them.

CONNECTING DEVELOPMENTS IN DISTANT SPACES

The GM history incorporating developments in the United States and India unfolded in distinct spaces. These spaces are somewhat difficult to characterize because their outer boundaries were often fuzzy as well as shifting. Yet, for purposes of analysis, the three relevant spaces could be identified as Euro-American, Indian, and international.

The Development of GM Crops in the Euro-American Arena

The science of GM crops incorporating a reductive understanding of life forms developed in the space that could be broadly characterized as Euro-American. The emerging science of molecular biology and genetics embarked on a quest to understand and manipulate life by intervening at the most basic structural and functional levels. The development of very precise techniques to intervene at the subcellular level heralded the birth of industrial biotechnology in the 1970s. Such techniques made it feasible for scientists to break and rejoin DNA and to splice sequences of DNA with unit "genetic code" into a cell. This meant that protein synthesis in cells could be controlled at will and thus physiological processes and physical characteristics of life forms could be organically transformed.

Commercial enterprises rushed to take advantage of the possibilities opened up by biotechnology to develop products for the market, both in industry[6] and in agriculture. Efforts were made on both sides of the Atlantic to extend the science of bioengineering to plants in order to enhance specific characteristics of crops and plant products. The task at the level of technology development for agricultural biotechnology was fourfold: identify a desirable sequence of genes; load it onto a vector that might carry it to the host plant cell or develop a process to transfer the new gene into the host cell; ensure that the host genome accepts the new gene; and finally activate the new gene sequence to synthesize protein in the new environment. The science was meritorious, cutting-edge, and exciting. Its commercial prospects were immense. If changes to genotype could transform the physical characteristics of specific plants in a beneficial way, this science could potentially rationalize and cheapen farming, fortify crops in the field against pests, and enhance the nutritional value of their produce.[7]

American corporations, venture startups, and seed companies noticeably took the lead as agricultural biotechnology moved from technology development to product development. An "industrial ideal" seemed to be driving these efforts.[8] Scientists at the industrial and university laboratories pursued several directions in their research. But the major effort of plant biotechnologists was invested in developing crops that would limit the need for herbicides and insecticides. Synthetic anti-weed herbicides were mostly used prior to the emergence of seedlings. Once the plant germinated, only herbicides of weaker potency could be employed because of the high sensitivity of young plants to herbicides. Inserting a gene to enhance the plant's tolerance for the chemicals could simplify the process of indiscriminate spraying with minimal labor input. Agrochemical companies also hoped to insert a specific gene into the plant that would be sensitive to the particular brand of herbicide that they were selling in the market. This way they could ensure a monopoly in the market for both the patented seed and the herbicide with which it was coupled. Similarly, scientists also searched for a gene to insert into a crop to make it pest-resistant.

Scientists at Monsanto, based in St. Louis, achieved the most stellar success in developing herbicide-resistant and pest-resistant plants. Monsanto scientists searched for a gene that would make plants resist Roundup, a Monsanto weedicide that was both a market leader and Monsanto's highest-grossing product. Such a gene could help Monsanto corner the seed and weedicide market in combination. By the mid-1980s they were ready with a commercial version of a Roundup-resistant soybean and a GM tomato plant with a fully functioning Bt gene[9] that resisted its primary pest, the American bollworm. On June 2, 1987, Monsanto accomplished the historical feat of sowing the first truly genetically altered plants in Jersey County in southwestern Illinois. A large collection of tomato plants with the Bt gene for insect resistance and Roundup resistance were planted after approval was obtained from the United States Department of Agriculture (USDA).[10]

The first corporations ready to launch GM plants into the market in the early 1990s were American. Calgene, a California-based biotech company, first got approval from the U.S. Food and Drug Administration (FDA) on May 18, 1994, to launch its GM tomato into the market. The tomato contained a gene that slowed its softening and loss of solid content. Although approved, Calgene's GM tomatoes lasted only briefly in the market as they were outcompeted by a tomato developed by breeders that had similar characteristics.[11] In contrast, Monsanto's food crops did spectacularly well after vetting by the regulatory agencies. During the Clinton administration, the Environmental Protection Agency (EPA) insisted on a case-by-case government review of GM crops, as opposed to the FDA's prior system of blanket approval,[12] but nonetheless it approved Monsanto's seeds for sale in the United States. The first large-scale planting of Monsanto's GM crops transpired in 1996; these seeds were ready for export the same year, and for domestic consumption the following year.

India: Government Response versus Apathy of Social Movements

The Indian government braced itself early to receive and appropriate the rDNA technology of bioengineering as it was developed at numerous sites in

the West. Government officials were well aware of this technology's development and also conscious of the benefits it might offer. To explore the potential
of biotech, the Indian government set up a separate Department of Biotechnology (DBT), which was duly carved out from the Government of India's
Ministry of Science and Technology in 1986. The new department aimed to
bring the advantages of biotech to "the broad areas of agriculture, health care,
environment and industry."[13] The charter of the DBT emphasized that it was
committed to "promote biotech industry" and derive "societal benefits" from
it. It reflected the Indian state's vision for facilitating a biotechnology-based
industry and promoting social welfare through biotechnology. In 1989, the
state also crafted a new set of guidelines for handling genetic material and
genetic-engineering-related experiments and field trials. The Recombinant
DNA Advisory Committee (RDAC) was constituted to regulate import,
handling, experiments, and field trials of genetic materials and products.
Through an executive order the central government created a multi-tiered
structure for enforcing the government's guidelines. An interministerial
Genetic Engineering Approvals Committee (GEAC) within the Ministry
of Environment and Forests would award final approval for large-scale trials
and commercial releases based on scientific advice offered by a committee
of experts, the Review Committee on Genetic Manipulation (RCGM).[14]

In contrast, the civic actors in India in the 1980s were not curious about
the surge of biotechnology in the West, a development which was still at
a distance from them. Those engaged with agricultural questions did not
discuss the implications of transgenic seeds and did not agitate over the
possibility of their entry into India, even though this prospect was being
actively considered by multinational biotech corporations. The implications
of transgenic seed for agriculture in India were at this point unrecognized
and unarticulated.

What was the cause of this lack of attention? It seems that social movements invested in agricultural questions in India were primarily focused on
pushing back the still expanding Green Revolution. The dominant politics of
social movements in India in the 1980s has been characterized as "post-devel-
opment" in orientation. This resonated with movements in Asia, Africa, and
Latin America all of which sought to break away from the model of "development" that had been embraced earlier as an ideology of progress.[15] Within
such larger critiques of development, the insurgent, oppositional politics in

agriculture during the 1980s was directed against the high-yielding-variety seeds of the Green Revolution. Hybrid seed strains from Mexico had been introduced into India for the first time in 1964. Later a hybrid variety of rice developed in the Philippines was added. In the 1980s, the Indian government was committed to cultivating more land in the country using hybrid seeds. It would seem that civic actors were invested in opposing the current realities of agriculture in India. They had to fight what was at hand and what seemed immediately objectionable. Thus the lack of attention to biotechnology actually reflected these activists' focus on other priorities.

The Third Space: A New International Structure for Regulating Trade

During the same time frame, a new structure for international trade was negotiated and put in place. This reflected the emergence of a new institutional structure of a neoliberal global trade order. As part of broader arrangements, it cast the United States and India in a new relationship and paved the way for the journey of GM cotton from the United States to India. This was a specific outcome of what that order ordained. In that sense, the new trade order in all of its implied physicality was the third space that impinged upon the history of GM crops.

The Uruguay Round of negotiations under the General Agreement on Tariffs and Trade (GATT) from 1986 to 1994 radically transformed the statutory basis for conduct of international trade in agriculture. Since the 1940s the subject of agricultural trade had had a somewhat special and even uneasy status within GATT compared to trade in manufacturing. Many elements of international trade in agricultural commodities were left undefined. The GATT also tolerated subsidies and quantitative restrictions imposed by several member countries. In a major break from the past, the Uruguay Round took a bold step toward regulating international trade in agriculture. This was done in two ways. First, it clearly established procedures for new plant varieties to be protected in world markets either through a system of patents or by a system created especially for this purpose, that is, a sui generis system. Second, in a move that had direct implications for agricultural biotechnology and GM crops, it allowed the patenting of the microorganisms and microbiological processes that lay at the core of commercial agricultural biotechnology.

The renegotiated norms of the Agreement on Trade-Related Aspects of Intellectual Property Rights (TRIPS) under the implementing authority of the WTO started a new era of patent protection and trade in agricultural commodities. The Indian government was now under mandate to complete implementing legislation as required under the GATT/TRIPS treaty it had signed in December 1993 and April 1994. This meant introducing legislation to amend existing patent laws. This also meant introducing "seed patents" or a sui generis system for affording protection to plant varieties separately. TRIPS allowed a transition period, allowing member nations either ten years to complete patent changes or five years to set up a mechanism for protecting plant varieties.

The salience of TRIPS to the transformation of U.S.-India linkages and GM history is too apparent to miss. Monsanto, the U.S. GM company, approached the Indian regulatory body for approval of its GM cotton in 1993, thus showing its clear desire to enter the Indian market. As part of its strategy to move into India, Monsanto acquired a controlling stake of 26 percent in India's largest seed company, Mahyco (Maharashtra Hybrid Seed Company) in 1998. Clearly these moves were made in the shadow of the unfolding TRIPS regime.

Connections with TRIPS could also be found in the budding social opposition to what came to be construed as "external" efforts to control Indian agriculture. This was most apparent in the founding of an anti-GM organization, the Gene Campaign, in India. In December 1991 Arthur Dunkel, the director-general of GATT, presented a comprehensive draft final act after the conclusion of negotiations in the Uruguay Round. The "Dunkel Draft," as it came to be known, was the most prominent document that laid down the major elements of TRIPS publicly for the first time. The Gene Campaign was set up a few weeks after the presentation of the Dunkel Draft at GATT.[16] Its founder, Suman Sahai, a geneticist, had earlier received a PhD in genetics from the Indian Agricultural Research Institute in New Delhi. She was completing a postdoctoral degree at the Institute of Human Genetics, University of Heidelberg, when she learned of the Dunkel proposal. She had been following the GATT debates relating to intellectual property in plants. As a trained geneticist she had a nuanced understanding of the scientific issues in the trade discussions. Sahai was convinced that if formalized the impending trade structure under TRIPS would establish control of external forces on Indian agriculture and compromise Indian farmers' rights. Dunkel's proposals prompted Sahai to return to India, the country of her birth, and start the Gene Campaign.[17]

CONNECTIONS ACROSS TEMPORALITIES

Moment of Contact and Genealogies

The journey of GM seeds into India brought face-to-face two separate political economies and two sets of social and cultural values. But even before this moment of contact these distinct political economies and value systems were part of two histories that were distant and distinct but not completely unconnected. To understand how these two histories connected and eventually came into alignment, historians must develop analytical strategies and categories that allow for studying genealogical patterns. A narrative based on the "present" of GM seeds by itself does not capture this complex connection or the history that needs to be told based on it.[18]

Connecting the development of transgenic seeds in the West in the 1980s with contemporary developments in India, one immediately becomes aware of the distinct temporalities of the two contexts. In the late 1970s and 1980s, when corporations based or headquartered in the United States were developing transgenic seeds, the activists on the ground in India and local ecological movements were arrayed against hybrid seeds of the Green Revolution variety. But the activists opposed to Green Revolution agriculture had much in common with the later civic actors and movements opposing GM seeds. Some of the leading activists and movements opposing hybrid seeds of the Green Revolution variety later became the most trenchant adversaries of transgenic seeds, even though in the 1980s they ignored the threat from GM seeds. Exploring the relationship between movements against hybrid seeds and movements against GM seeds allows us to spotlight the long-term connections between India and an external arena focused on Indian agriculture generally and seeds specifically. Thus activists of long standing in India are both our cue and our source for studying these movements of resistance in a longer historical perspective.

Vandana Shiva as Ecological and Social Critic: 1970s and 1980s

The important Indian activist Vandana Shiva entered ecological debates through a study of social forestry and Green Revolution agriculture in select regions of India. It is through this lens that Shiva launched a critique of the policies of development and their impact in India. At the broadest level Shiva's advocacy was a rejection of the notion that a combination of capital, state action, expertise, and technology would essentially improve lives. She initially critiqued social forestry as a major plank both of the national planning process and of development activity in India supported by international aid. She studied the impact of a state-initiated project to plant eucalyptus trees in the southern Indian state of Karnataka. The government's step was declaredly to create productive assets by taking cognizance of market forces. But in reality the project was impoverishing those at the lower ends of society. Shiva criticized state efforts for ignoring the complex relationships between forest communities, plant life, and natural resources. Using the example of social forestry she offered a critique of national and international development planning.[19] Vandana Shiva took a conceptual leap with her subsequent critique of the agriculture around resource-intensive high-yielding-variety seeds (HYVs) that had been promoted in India since the launch of the Green Revolution. Punjab was one of the states where HYVs were most intensively cultivated. The state of Punjab in the 1980s was also in the throes of terrorism, separatism, and communal violence. Shiva argued that the violence in Punjab was ultimately a by-product of social and ecological imbalances wrought by the Green Revolution.[20]

Shiva also started to explicitly identify an external determinant of the process of ecological and community disruption in India. She called the Green Revolution agriculture an "American" model and identified American backers and aid agencies as drivers of this model.[21] She saw the local "hard national-scientific state" as a cohort of external aid agents. Development was in her opinion but "a continuation of the process of [prior] colonization."[22]

Getting Back to the "Present" of Vandana Shiva: 1990s and 2000s

The ten years from the middle of the 1980s to the middle of the 1990s saw the transformation of Shiva from a scholar-critic to the leader of an institutionalized movement and a global activist. Shiva's activism played out in two arcs. On the one hand, Vandana Shiva framed opposition to the granting of patents in the West to traditional Indian products in terms of the frame of "biopiracy." Shiva actively networked with partners in the North to get a European patent on *neem* (*Azadirachta indica*), a tree of Indian origin, revoked after a sustained battle at the European Patent Office in Munich.[23] At the U.S. Patent and Trademark Office (USPTO), Shiva won another battle, against an American holding a patent on the basmati rice of the Indian subcontinent.[24]

The second arc of Shiva's activism was a sustained campaign against changes to India's patent regime under mandate from TRIPS and the launch of GM cotton by Monsanto. In 1998, when the government of India gave permission to Monsanto-Mahyco to conduct large-scale field trials of Bt cotton at forty locations in nine states across India, Shiva went to the courts to stall testing on procedural grounds. In 1999 legislators passed the first of the amendments to domestic patents mandated by the new regulatory regime of WTO. In response, Shiva prominently led the *Bija yatra,* or March for Seeds, in New Delhi, which was followed by similar rallies all over India. The first march in Delhi was deliberately launched on March 5, the anniversary of the 1930 Dandi March by Gandhi to break the colonial salt laws that had launched the famous civil disobedience movement against British rule. The *bija yatras* throughout the country were to constitute the *bija satygraha.* As Shiva's organization, Research Foundation for Science, Technology, and Ecology (RFSTE) explained, "The Bija Satyagraha is the refusal to accept the colonization of life through patents and perverse technologies, and the destruction of the food security by free-trade rules of W.T.O."[25] The movement embodied the same urge for political, economic, and cultural autonomy as Gandhi's nationalism. Increasingly, from this period, Shiva turned toward constructive programs of Gandhian vintage by focusing on the organization of communities and the preservation of common genetic resources as commons. Shiva's movement called for saving and using indigenous seeds while boycotting the seeds of multinational corporations. Her movement, Shiva claimed, would "promote social resistance through constructive and creative action."

In comparing Shiva's earlier movements against Green Revolution agriculture with her movement against GM cotton, one is struck by the parallels. In the 1970s and 1980s, Shiva critiqued HYV-based agriculture as a resource-intensive and labor-displacing production form while blaming external forces for bringing it to India. In line with Gandhi's views, she called for building an alternative civilizational grid defined by restraint in resource use, ecological stability, and social justice, while citing his famous lines from the magazine *Young India:* "Earth provides enough to satisfy every man's need but not for every man's greed."[26] In the post-Dunkel phase of patent reforms and GM launch, Shiva again turned to deploying Gandhian imagery to protect the autonomy of Indian agriculture.

Activists as Archives of "Connection"

Anti-GM activism demands our attention for exploring the long-term history of opposition to "global" seeds or seeds of external origin in India. The activists become in some ways our archives, embodying long-term trajectories of opposition. These activists' programs and activities provide cues about where to look for the past of such resistance and to find sources of stable narratives. And a consideration of such narratives illuminates the deeper history of such movements.

The incuriosity of civic actors in the 1970s and 1980s about bioengineered seeds does not mean that they cannot help us connect Indian movements of the 1970s and 1980s with the politics of biotech seeds in the West. The activists and movements against HYVs still serve as a useful archive for establishing connections between Indian agriculture and the ascendant world of transgenic seeds in the West. It is true that the civic actors were invested in the current realities of the Green Revolution in India. But an analysis of their response to Green Revolution agriculture shows that there already existed a platform and a political alignment in India with the wherewithal and willingness to oppose GM seeds and its facilitating apparatus when they arrived in India. The study of such elements in the activist response in 1980s India makes it seem as if the opposition to GM crops in India was suspended, something waiting to happen. Thus, regardless of the information gap or the apparent disjuncture in the nature of politics in different eras, activists still afford us an opportunity to reflect on the states of connectedness between voices in India and the agricultural biotechnology regime in the United States even if our analytical focus must keep shifting across temporalities to tease out such connections.

This global approach to the history of agricultural modernization and new social movements in India offers a more rounded understanding. Such an approach requires studying history in breadth as well as depth. Historians invested in interrogating this field need to scout for nodes of influence beyond India's frontiers and look for genealogies of resistance in India's agrarian sector. Such an exercise offers more fruitful insights than what a national focus or a straightforward linear account of agricultural change in India might provide.

NOTES

1. These seeds were developed using specific breeding techniques at international crop research centers, and a network of private foundations, governments, development professionals, and extension workers had worked to expand their reach.

2. For the basic positions of the world-systems approach, see Immanuel Wallerstein, *World Systems Analysis: An Introduction* (Durham, NC: Duke University Press, 2005); Janet L. Abu-Lughod, *Before European Hegemony: The World System A.D. 1250–1350* (New York: Oxford University Press, 1991).

3. An acknowledgment of the relevance of "national" without an exclusive commitment to a seamless "nation" brings its own advantages. The historians of the Subaltern School in South Asia have made seminal contributions in pointing out the limitations and erasures of nationalist approaches in historiography. See Partha Chatterjee, *Nationalist Thought and the Colonial World: A Derivative Discourse* (Minneapolis: University of Minnesota Press, 1986); *The Nation and Its Fragments: Colonial and Postcolonial Histories* (Princeton, NJ: Princeton University Press, 1993); Dipesh Chakrabarty, *Provincializing Europe: Postcolonial Thought and Historical Difference* (Princeton, NJ: Princeton University Press, 2000).

4. William F. Fisher, "Doing Good? The Politics and Antipolitics of NGO Practices," *Annual Review of Anthropology* 26 (1997): 439–64; quote on 450.

5. Here my debt is to Arjun Appadurai's notion of locality within the disjunctive and overlapping layers of the global order that cannot be explained by reference to a simple core and periphery. See Arjun Appadurai, "The Production of Locality," in *Counterworks: Managing the Diversity of Knowledge*, ed. Richard Fardon (New York: Routledge, 1995), pp. 204–25; and *Modernity at Large: Cultural Dimensions of Globalization* (Minneapolis: University of Minnesota Press, 1996).

6. The application of rDNA technology for manufacturing rare health- and life-saving products came in the 1970s, with human health-care products such as insulin, human growth hormone, and interferon materializing between 1976 and 1980.

7. In many ongoing projects scientists tried to enhance specific characteristics in plants such as photosynthetic efficiency, nitrogen fixation, and resistance to frost, or to impart specific characteristics to their produce. Paul Lurquin, *The Green Phoenix: A History of Genetically Modified Plants* (New York: Columbia University Press, 2001).

8. Deborah Fitzgerald has used the concept of "industrial ideal" to interpret changes in American agriculture in the earlier part of twentieth century. Deborah Fitzgerald, *Every Farm a Factory: The Industrial Ideal in American Agriculture*. London and New Haven: Yale University Press, 2003.

9. Farmers were known to commonly spray their crops with the soil bacterium *Bacillus thuringiensis* (Bt) to kill pests. Scientists knew that Bt contained prototoxins that broke down into toxins on ingestion by the insects and that is when it turned fatal. It was also known that Bt prototoxins did not break down into toxins within the human intestine. Thus the Bt gene could be assumed to be absolutely safe for human consumption. Many experts in Europe and the United States identified the prototoxin-producing gene in Bt and then devised a way to splice that gene into the DNA of specific crops, which came to be known as Bt cotton, Bt corn, and so on.

10. For the history of development of GM seeds at Monsanto, see Daniel Charles, *Lords of the Harvest: Biotech, Big Money, and the Future of Food* (Cambridge, MA: Perseus Books, 2001); federal regulators in the United States determined that transgenic seeds were not a special technology requiring a distinct regulatory net. In coming to this conclusion, they focused on the product rather than the process through which seeds were developed. Thus in 1985 the Reagan administration announced the "Coordinated Framework for Regulation of Biotechnology," which involved using the existing agencies to regulate field trials for GM seeds. The same minimalist approach in federal monitoring continued under the George H. W. Bush administration, which issued a document in 1990, *Four Principles of Regulatory Review for Biotechnology,* that fleshed out the Reagan administration's declaration. By and large federal institutions, specifically the Food and Drug Administration, continued to believe that rDNA technology did not cause increased risk in testing, end use, and general dissemination and thus should be regulated like any other food product. Henry I. Miller, *Policy Controversy in Biotechnology: An Insider's View* (Austin, TX: R. G. Landes and Academic Press, 1997), 106–16.

11. Charles, *Lords of the Harvest,* 133–39.

12. Miller, *Policy Controversy in Biotechnology,* 106–16.

13. "Introduction: About DBT," Department of Biotechnology, Ministry of Science and Technology, http://www.dbtindia.nic.in.

14. "Rules for the Manufacture, Use, Import, Export and Storage of Hazardous Microorganisms/Genetically Engineered Organisms or Cells, Union Ministry of Environment and Forest, Government of India," dated December 5, 1989; *Recombinant DNA Safety Guidelines,* Department of Biotechnology, Union Ministry of Science and Technology, 1990. A description of the regulatory structure has been provided in P. K. Ghosh and T. V. Ramanaiah, "Indian Rules, Regulations and Procedures for Handling Transgenic Plants," *Journal of Scientific & Industrial Research* 59 (2000): 114–20.

15. Arturo Escobar has most elegantly spoken of this moment of departure. He contrasted the willingness of new social movements in the 1980s and 1990s "to shake off the meanings imposed on them by the Development discourse, to open up in a more explicit manner the possibility for a different regime of truth and perception within which a new practice of concern and action would be possible." This constituted a new phase as " . . . until recently, it seemed impossible to get away from Development and to conceptualize social reality differently." Arturo Escobar, "Reflections on 'Development': Grassroots Approaches and Alternative Politics in the Third World," *Futures* (June 1992): 412, 414.

16. "Campaign Update" (New Delhi: Gene Campaign, undated); *Gene Campaign: A Profile* (New Delhi: Gene Campaign, undated). The papers of the Gene Campaign are located at the organization's office in New Delhi. Henceforth, these are cited as "Gene Campaign papers."

17. Interview with the author, New Delhi, August 27, 2005.

18. The non-linear narrative in this paper reflects in part an effort to engage both history and theory. Also, without attempting a Foucault-like analysis in terms of genealogy, the approach nonetheless shows the influence of Foucault's conviction in his later writings of treating "discourse" as a "series of events," rather than as a completely autonomous, non-contextualized entity, appearing almost sui generis. See Eric Paras, *Foucault 2.0: Beyond Power and Knowledge* (New York: Other Press, 2006), 67; especially see chapter 4, "Restructuring: Foucault and the Genealogical Turn."

19. Vandana Shiva, H. C. Sharatchandra, and J. Bandopadhyay, *Social, Economic and Ecological Impact of Social Forestry in Kolar* (Bangalore: Indian Institute of Management, 1981); Vandana Shiva and J. Bandopadhyay, *Ecological Audit of Eucalyptus Cultivation* (Dehra Dun: Research Foundation, 1985).

20. Vandana Shiva, *The Violence of Green Revolution: Third World Agriculture, Ecology and Politics* (Dehra Dun: Research Foundation of Science and Ecology, 1989).

21. "There were three groups of international agencies involved in transferring the American model of agriculture to India—the private American foundations, the American Government and the World Bank." Vandana Shiva, *The Violence of Green Revolution*, 29.

22. Vandana Shiva, *Staying Alive: Women, Ecology, and Development* (London: Zed Books, 1988), 2.

23. *Bija* 27 & 28 (2002): 88; *Bija* 35 & 36 (2005): 16–17.

24. "RiceTec Inc. a Texas-Based US Corporation Has Lost the Basmati Battle," http://www.navdanya.org/articles/chronology_basmati_battle.htm, accessed on October 27, 2007 (the link is no longer active); Vandana Shiva and Radha Holla-Bhar, *Intellectual Piracy & the Neem Patents: The Neem Campaign* (New Delhi: RFSTE, 1993).

25. "A Call for a New Freedom Movement: The Bija Satyagraha," *Bija*, nos. 23 & 24 (1999): 1–3.

26. Vandana Shiva, "Ecological Movements in India," *Alternatives* 11 (1986): 256.

6 – LAND

Engaging with the Global

Perspectives on Land from Botswana

ANNE GRIFFITHS

GLOBAL DIMENSIONS OF LAND

My entry point to the *Framing the Global* project is land. It has been the subject of my research in Botswana, southern Africa, over a number of decades.[1] I have chosen land because it not only forms a crucial component of macro-perspectives that center on national, international, and transnational engagement with trade and commerce in the global marketplace, both economically and symbolically, but is also at the heart of micro-processes connected to the well-being of individuals, families, and households. For these reasons land features prominently on international agency agendas for promoting state economies (particularly in the Global South), as well as in discussions concerning empowerment of the poor and alleviation of poverty. In its 2008 report, the Commission on the Legal Empowerment of the Poor[2] identified land as one of the four pillars of legal empowerment that address not only material deprivation but also the powerlessness that stems from a lack of access to justice. In these processes "traditional" or "informal justice" (generally associated with oral, unwritten forms of ordering derived from customary law) plays an important role. For it is now acknowledged to be an important phenomenon worldwide; in sub-Saharan Africa it deals with around 80 percent of disputes (Piron 2005).

IMPORTANCE OF LAND FOR BOTSWANA

In Botswana, land is significant as it is a vital resource for families' and households' livelihoods and capital accumulation. It provides crops for a family's subsistence, and in cases of surplus, income from agriculture. It is also used to support livestock, especially cattle, both for the subsistence of poor, rural households and for wealthy elites who maintain cattle for prestige and commercial purposes. It underpins households and is also highly sought after to develop multi-residential plots for rent in high density areas. In addition, it is central to the socio-politico-administrative structure of a Tswana polity (tribe) that is formed around the physical location of households, grouped into *dikgotla*[3] and wards on a tenurial basis, at the apex of which is the *kgosi*'s (chief's) ward, Kgosing, where the chief's *kgotla* is located. At a national level, land forms an important part of the government's strategy for development, as embodied in the draft National Plan 2011, which is related to the government's agreement to pursue the millennium goals through its signing of the Millennium Declaration in 2002. These goals overlap considerably with Botswana's overall development goals as contained in its Vision 2016,[4] which represents the framework guiding all national policies and programs in the country. Part of this strategy includes making land available for the development of foreign investment, for example in the pursuit of tourism, through organizations such as the Botswana Export Development and Investment Authority.

In pursuing these goals the government of Botswana recognizes that "poverty remains one of the major development challenges for Botswana" (Botswana NDP9, 25). It also acknowledges that "studies worldwide have shown that the impact of population growth on poverty is strongest at the micro-level, that is, at the level of households and communities" (ibid.) and that women bear the brunt of poverty, especially among the female-headed households that are prevalent in the country (Botswana 1981, 21; UNICEF 1993).[5] Thus land embodies a nexus of relations that takes shape between families, community, city, state, and world.

Law forms an important part of these processes because it regulates the framework within which land is distributed, allocated, transferred, or inherited.[6] For many years there have been debates on the question of customary land tenure in Africa and its effects.[7] Part of this discussion has involved assertions about the need to move to a system of individual, registered title to land because communal land tenure was perceived as lacking the necessary "security" to ensure agricultural investment and the productive use of land in the quest for improved economic growth and reduction of poverty. Such views informed the thinking of international agencies, like the International Monetary Fund and the World Bank, that have been influential in exerting pressure on African governments which are dependent on aid to introduce or extend registration of land. The move towards registration of title and privatization of land has not gone unchallenged. Scholars engaging in empirical field research (Peters 2006; Berry 1975, 2002; Moore 1986; Bikaako and Ssenkumba 2003; Musembi 2007) have questioned the underlying assumptions on which such moves are predicated, especially the validity of framing economic development on a paradigm derived from western European experience.

ADOPTING A RELATIONAL APPROACH: EXPLORING CONNECTIVITY

Rather than posing abstract propositions against empirical observations in a way that treats them as being in opposition to one another, I, like many of my colleagues in this volume, approach studying the global in relational terms. I adopt a connective perspective linking domains so that what is "local" and what is "global" become hard to disentangle as these categories acquire more flexible dimensions that cannot simply be set apart from, or against, one another, but come to be seen as sets of relations that connect and reconnect, or rupture, in a variety of ways in a number of different places. Thus it runs counter to those perspectives that approach discussions of the global in terms of clearly defined, bounded entities that are juxtaposed against one another, such as local/global, national/international, state/non-state, and so on.[8] While these terms can be, and are, used to designate certain spaces, what is key is the way in which they are viewed in relation to one another without predetermining the nature of that relationship.

FIELD RESEARCH IN BOTSWANA

My perspective on land derives from field research carried out in Botswana (1981–1989, 2009–2010, and ongoing). A variety of methods were employed in the data collection, including archival research, examination of formal laws, and court and land board records, as well as fieldwork on unwritten, oral customary law; participant observation of disputes; and interviews with government personnel, members of NGOs, and local people. Extended oral life histories were taken of families from Molepolole village, updating earlier research to cover five generations within two family groups.

In 2009 a new dimension was added: a study of Kweneng Land Board and of the Land Tribunal that deals with appeals from land boards. Under the formal legal system of Botswana there are three types of land tenure: state tenure,[9] freehold tenure (which reflects individual registered tenure),[10] and customary tenure, where the land is vested in land boards under the Tribal Land Act of 1968. Kweneng Land Board (KLB) is responsible for dealing with the allocation, use, and cancellation of land rights that fall within its jurisdiction.[11] My research on land focused primarily on customary land tenure because it covers 70 percent of land in the country. It was located in Molepolole village, in Kweneng district (where I carried out my earlier research), because it not only functions as a regional center where Kweneng Land Board operates, but is also the center of the Kwena polity where the chief's kgotla is situated.

RE-ENVISAGING THE LOCAL:
LIFE HISTORIES AND ETHNOGRAPHY

My diverse sources of data draw on a range of academic disciplines including history, law, and anthropology/social science. The focus in this chapter, however, is on the ethnographic aspect of my research embodied in my study of life histories from Mosotho kgotla in Molepolole. It centers on the two sons of Koosimile, Makokwe and Radipati, and their descendants. These histories are based on field notes provided by anthropologist Isaac Schapera up to 1937, as well as fieldwork carried out in 1984, 1989, and 2010; oral testimonies extend them into the nineteenth century so that my research to date covers five generations. This enables me to document continuities and differences among individuals, families, and households across a precolonial, colonial, and postcolonial landscape.

Studying the local has long been part of anthropological inquiry. It has been subject to critique on the basis of its self-contained remit (both territorial and conceptual), which raises questions about its claims to knowledge and representation.[12] The practice of ethnography based on fieldwork that represents "the key method of social anthropology" (Moore 1994a, 1) has been taken to task, in some cases, for its lack of self-reflexivity (Stocking 1992, 12–59) or for removing selected parts of the social context from its social formation, leading to a form of cultural essentialism (Wilmsen 1989).[13] However, this need not always be so, and as Moore (1994a, 2) has observed, "the anthropologist cannot but be intensely and constantly conscious of the larger world that surrounds the field site." My study re-envisages the local through an examination of the links between persons and land derived from these life histories extended over several generations.[14] Thus it not only takes account of a specific site in which social relations are bounded and locally constituted but also incorporates how perceptions of what is local are discursively and historically constructed.

The importance of this approach is that the life histories highlight the ways in which individuals, who form part of a local community, in terms of genealogical and spatial relationships, find their life courses shaped by wider geographic processes that have an impact on their everyday lives. In engaging with these life histories micro- and macro-perspectives become interwoven in ways that demonstrate how experiences of contemporary land tenure link back to the past and forward to the future in ways that undermine any notion of a linear development or concept of progress. In my study the trajectories that emerge for individuals' and families' relationships with land underline the differing dynamics that connective threads to the past embody, creating varying access to and control over land. Such an approach reveals disparities between the sexes and among individuals; and families' experiences of social networks reflect diverging patterns of human, social, and economic capital that promote or hinder processes of accumulation and control over land. What emerges are the uneven ways in which resources, such as land, are apportioned. These are not simply produced through local conditions but connect to wider processes of political, economic, and social disbursement. This has implications for the ways in which upward mobility may become open to some individuals and families, while constraining others in ways that perpetuate social stratification and inequality. These concrete effects are not the product of random chance, but derive from particular conditions that may challenge the more general and abstract propositions on which prescriptions about land and its development are based.

DIVERGING LIVES: THE MAKOKWES AND RADIPATIS

Makokwe and Radipati were brothers who shared a father, Koosimile, but had different mothers because their father was a polygamist and had three wives. They were the founding members of Mosotho *kgotla* in 1937, which forms part of the chief's ward, Kgosing. In 2010 I focused on updating the genealogies of these particular families because, although related, they demonstrate very different life trajectories. The Makokwes had access to a resource base that revolved around subsistence agriculture, raising livestock, and migrant labor of an unskilled nature on an intermittent or contract basis. These characteristics, shared by many other families in Botswana, associated them with what Parson (1981) termed "the peasantariat." The members of this kin group were increasingly distanced from the elite cattle owners and higher-income wage earners (Botswana NDP6, 8). In contrast the other family group, the Radipatis, has focused on attaining education and the acquisition of skilled and secure employment, which among the younger generation was predominantly government based but has now branched out to include more commercial and corporate activities. This has set them apart from other families and placed them among those whom Cooper (1982) has referred to as "the salariat." They represent a growing middle class in Botswana that no longer engages in subsistence agriculture or insecure migrant labor. It is not possible for me to replicate the life histories in detail here, so what follows is an overview that highlights their distinguishing characteristics.[15]

MAKOKWE FAMILY GROUP

Ramojaki (aged 73 in 2010)[16] is the youngest son of Makokwe and has been living in Lekgwapheng ward in Molepolole for many years. He is the only one of six brothers who is still alive. Ramojaki moved from Mosotho *kgotla* to Lekgwapheng with four of his brothers because of lack of space. They got land there from relatives, but this has come under the administration of Kweneng Land Board, which is responsible for dealing with tribal land in the area today. Under the Tribal Land Act passed in 1968, shortly after Botswana received its independence in 1966, land boards[17] replaced chiefs in the allocation of land under customary law. This was the first piece of legislation to propose substantial changes to the dominant Tswana tribal systems of land tenure, which had been left intact after the proclamation of the tribal reserves during the colonial era (Ng'ong'ola 1997, 14). It was deemed necessary to accommodate "more modern practices of land use, such as more exclusive allocation and utilisation of tribal grazing ranges" (Morolong and Ng'ong'ola 2007, 146). These developments were perceived as being in keeping with more modern notions of governance, enabling a young country to provide for a more just system of land administration that would be more accountable to the newly elected politicians than to the chiefs, whose authority for dealing with land was stripped away and vested in land boards established for each tribal area.[18] It was in keeping with a move toward a Westminster model of government that many former African colonies adopted when they acquired their independence in the 1960s. It formed part of a nation-building exercise that was intended to leave "tribal factionalism" behind in the creation of a modern state whose forms and institutions were modeled on those of their former colonial rulers.

When he was interviewed in his home in 2010, Ramojaki was attempting to earn a living as a subsistence farmer, having spent most of his adult life at the South African mines before returning to work as a borehole mechanic for the district council in Molepolole prior to his retirement. His protracted employment at the mines (thirty-three years) was common to many of his generation, including his brothers.[19] It took place at a time that embraced colonial rule (1885–1966), when Botswana was known as the British Protectorate of Bechuanaland. During this period, it was subject to indirect rule by a resident commissioner whose levying of taxes forced many men to seek employment beyond the protectorate's borders, principally at the mines in the Union of South Africa (now the Republic of South Africa). Dependence on European imports, ecological constraints (vulnerability to drought and diseases, especially those decimating cattle, such as rinderpest), and the need to meet the cash obligations newly imposed by colonial administrators contributed to the escalation in migration that set the context in which Kweneng, like many other African regions, became a labor reserve.

Thus ordinary people's lives became entangled with regional and global patterns of consumption and labor relations that created a dependence on a cash economy (Schapera 1947; Kerven 1982). This set the context in which social relations, regulated through kinship and *mafisa*[20] (representing the class ranking inherent in Tswana society), came to be played out within the broader context of political and economic change. Colonial rule and the new labor relations nonetheless favored the continued position of powerful elites, such as *dikgosi* (chiefs), who were able to manipulate this situation to their advantage (Ramsay 1991).[21] As we shall see, maintaining good connections to those in power, as Radipati did, contributed to a situation in which his descendants were able to pursue a life trajectory different from that of the Makokwe family.

Caught up in migrant labor like many in his generation, Ramojaki remitted money home to pay taxes, provide support, and pay for the substitute labor required for subsistence agricultural activities on which families left behind depended for their existence. Under these conditions, when Ramojaki's sons and those of his brothers were old enough, they went to the mines and their fathers retired home to work the land and at the cattle post. This pattern, passed down from one generation to another, became associated with Parson's (1981) term the peasantariat. Among this group it reflects a lifestyle based on fluctuations in income and the instabilities that derive from temporary, contract labor, linked with the diminishing returns from subsistence agriculture and small-scale livestock production.

In 2010 Ramojaki lamented the position he found himself in, observing that sickness[22] had deprived him of "a good lifestyle." This had affected his ability to engage in subsistence activities, and he bemoaned the fact that "only two children and grandchildren are keen to take care of livestock." This marks a departure from earlier times when families worked cooperatively across households, pooling their labor. For when Sechele I (c. 1833–1892) transformed the Kwena into a regional power, land formed a central feature of a settlement pattern that was based on agro-pastoral activities requiring families to move between three locations: the village, where they pursued their social and political life; the land, where they pursued their agricultural activities; and the cattle posts, where they herded their cattle.[23] In this environment, the need for labor and for access to resources beyond those of individual families led to a situation where Kwena society was bound together in a system of mutual if somewhat unequal series of exchange relationships (Griffiths 1989, 62–105). Today, however, this is no longer the case. As Ramojaki's sister-in-law explained in 2010: "Nkadikang [her deceased husband] and his brothers used to help each other plough their fields using their livestock." This no longer happens due, in part, to the "advent of modern technology." For when "the brothers resorted to the use of tractors . . . they stopped helping each other." According to Nkadikang's son, Ranko (52), now "everyone fends for his [own] family."

Yet times are hard. For land, which is central to providing shelter and a resource for individuals' and families' livelihoods, is becoming harder to acquire. Ranko worries for his children's and grandchildren's future because "it is not an easy thing to acquire plots within the area as it used to be." This is because of the great demand for land in certain areas that has resulted in land boards being subject to intense pressure to provide land. While there is no shortage of land in Botswana as a whole, most is in the waterless Kalahari Desert and suitable only for seasonal grazing of livestock.[24] Around Gaborone (the capital) and its catchment area, which extends to Molepolole (only around sixty kilometers from the capital), there is acute pressure on land as this is where a third of Botswana's 1.9 million people live.

The situation has been exacerbated by a 1993 amendment to the Tribal Land Act that permits all citizens to apply to land boards anywhere in the country, regardless of tribal affiliation. By January 8, 2010, there was a waiting list of 149,500 people who had applied for land in Mogoditshane,[25] the peri-urban area adjacent to the capital, and a waiting list of 37,354 people who had applied for land in Molepolole[26] itself. Such pressure has come about because, as the government acknowledges, the economy is no longer based predominantly on agriculture.[27] The result is that the majority of Batswana[28] seek to make a living in urban areas and are now classified as urban dwellers.[29]

In developing an economic strategy for the country the government is involved in negotiating bi- and multilateral treaties with other international states and transnational organizations like the European Union and exploring development agendas associated with the United Nations or the World

Bank. In this process it is recognized that there needs to be a national policy on land, one that will take account of changing attitudes to land and of the need for tribal land management to be based on principles of efficiency and equity and to be responsive to market forces.[30] Such market forces include the development of wildlife reserves and tourism that form an important part of Botswana's development strategy. Both Botswana's development strategy and its National Land Policy have had to deal with the fact that while agriculture represented 40 percent of GDP in 1966, it only represented 2 percent in 2005, although it is still important for people like the Makokwes who engage with a rural economy.

Thus the administration of land, as outlined in the draft National Land Policy of 2011, aims to be in line with the country's overall development goals contained in the Vision 2016 document.[31] What these policies seek to take account of is the fact that land-based activities are no longer the dominant source of income for most of the country's population. While land remains important, the nature of its importance has shifted. Urban dwellers' access to rural land for retirement is not as vital as it once was, but access to urban land and safe, secure housing has become very important.

Thus land, especially in Kweneng district with its proximity to both the capital and the South African border, is an extremely valuable resource.[32] While tribal land cannot be sold as it is vested in the land board "for the benefit of citizens of Botswana,"[33] it can be transferred and developments on it can be "sold" to a transferee. Where residential plots are allocated by the land board, they are free. Thus selling developments on them, such as houses and other buildings, can yield a substantial sum, particularly where these are in peri-urban areas or areas such as Molepolole that are close to the capital. This has led to a market in land that has fostered speculation and illegal dealings, which have been the subject of public inquiries and commissions[34] as well as court cases[35] over the years, as the government acknowledges that land has acquired a capital value that has led to its commodification through the sale of developments on it.[36] This in turn has fostered a notion of individual control and ownership of land, in keeping with Western notions of individual, registered title, one that is completely alien to customary law. Nonetheless, these notions can be seen to fit in with government approaches to home ownership and public-private partnerships in pursuit of this goal, which is in keeping with many international agencies' approaches to development.

However, many families, like the Makokwes, find it hard to enter this market because they lack the resources to pursue or benefit from these developments. Lack of education has meant they have been unable to pursue higher-income employment. Ramojaki and his brothers never went to school; as young boys they herded cattle until they left for work at the mines. Among men of the younger generation who have had the opportunity to go to school, poor educational attainment has limited their opportunities at a time when jobs even for those with a postsecondary education are hard to come by.

While female members of the family generally have a higher level of education, because as girls they were able to attend primary school in the village while their brothers were herding cattle, they have had difficulty acquiring remunerative employment. The women in Ramojaki's generation focused on domestic and agricultural activities that provided little surplus income. Among the younger generation of women, attempts have been made to expand their income-generating activities. Ramojaki's daughter, Akohang (47), for example, has found work from time to time as a cook or a cleaner, when not engaged in agricultural activities. Her cousins, Koketso (age not known) and Mmopi (51), have also worked briefly, as a domestic and a shop assistant, when they were younger. Where women in this family group have found employment, it tends to be low paid and generally of an insecure and intermittent nature.

The same is true for their male siblings, who have suffered from retrenchment at the South African mines (following the end of the apartheid era) and who have had to shift from external to internal migration. Where they find work—like Rammutla (43), who is employed in construction in Jwaneng (a mining center in Botswana); or Kgangwana (36), who works at a grocery in Gaborone; or Tumelo (29), who works for a bakery—it continues to be contract based and lacking in stability. While the informal sector provides work for many in Botswana, especially women, who, for example, make a living selling food at kiosks along the road, only Ranko's daughter, Malebogo (25), has managed to find work in this sector, selling air time for mobile phone companies. As a result, many of the younger generation, both female and male, remain unemployed, which leads them to remain living at home in the natal household or with relatives.

This situation puts pressure on land as adults who would normally be absent continue to live at home with their siblings, along with their own and their siblings' children. In the past marriage provided an impetus for establishing new households. Although a couple might live for some time with one spouse's family, they were expected to create their own household over time. Makokwe's sons did this, acquiring land through their father's maternal relatives, which enabled them to establish new households in Lekgwapeng, at the other end of the village from Mosotho *kgotla*.[37] However, the postponement of marriage due to prolonged labor migration meant that many unmarried women with children remained in their natal household, extending its life cycle and its generational composition. A feature of colonial life, this pattern has continued into the post-independence period (Kocken and Uhlenbeck 1980, 53; Molenaar 1980, 12; Griffiths 1988, 295; Gulbrandsen 1986, 29–30). As a result many women in Botswana today have children but remain unmarried. It is among this group, consisting of female-headed households, that the government of Botswana acknowledges that poverty is most prevalent.[38]

Among Makokwe's family group, out of the thirteen women in the younger generation (ages 20 to 34), only one (32) is married although seven others have children. Some have several children with different fathers. Ompatile (33), who is unmarried, for example, had her first daughter when she was 20, her second child when she was 25, and her third at the age of 29. Similarly, Onkgopotse (25), who is also unmarried, had her first daughter at 18, her second daughter at 22, and is currently expecting her third child. Accommodating all these children within existing households is not easy and can lead to conflict.

Such a situation often leads to overcrowding, which local headmen who deal with disputes in the village acknowledged at public meetings in 2010 was a serious problem. Headmen from Ntoloolengwae ward attributed these problems to "daughters [who] have children out of marriage . . . as parents we have to support these children . . . because we can't chase them away." All too often, however, other siblings put pressure on them. In these cases, where younger siblings are chasing away other siblings, headmen usually "advise them that all children as family members are equal [in rights]"[39] and if they are uncomfortable with this they "should look for their own plot to stay [by] applying to the Land Board." The problem is that not many plots are available unless one is prepared to pay for developments on a plot of land that is being transferred. In its Draft National Land Policy of 2011,[40] the government proposes restricting applicants to a maximum of two free residential plots, one at his or her home village and another "elsewhere in Botswana."[41] There will, however, be no restriction if parties are prepared to pay for tribal land that has already been allocated and that is the subject of a transfer.[42] Such a situation benefits those who have the resources to purchase such plots and does nothing for those who lack these resources.

While some, such as Ramojaki's unmarried niece, Mmupi (51), have managed to acquire a residential plot and to raise children despite lack of support from their fathers, Mmupi believes that her children are facing an even greater uphill struggle than she did because "the youth of this generation [face] a very big challenge of finding both residential and plough field plots due to the land shortage that has affected most of the big villages in Botswana." This is compounded by the fact that they face another "major challenge" in "the lack of employment."[43]

The two together create problems for families like the Makokwes because even where a plot of land is allocated free of charge, substantial costs may be incurred in connecting it to services such as water and electricity. In addition, the plot must be developed within a certain period of time from its allocation (five years in Kweneng in 2010) or it will be repossessed by the land board, a policy that is actively being enforced in recent years, thereby dispossessing those who fail to meet the deadline.

Under these conditions, the Makokwes resource base places them at a disadvantage when it comes to acquiring and developing land. The returns on their investment in subsistence agriculture have always been unpredictable due to diseases affecting animals, climatic constraints including drought, and poor soils that produce variable results. While government subsidies exist to assist with farming at this level, through providing free seeds and free plowing for up to five hectares, this does little to lift the Makokwes out of poverty. The United Nations System in Botswana notes "the chronic weakness of agriculture as a source of income" (2007, 8) and observes that "there was no evidence that poverty-focused agricultural support schemes such as ALDEP [Arable Land Development Programme] and ARAP [Accelerated Rainfed Arable Programme] had ever succeeded in raising anybody out of poverty, and . . . were unlikely ever to do so" due to "problems of diminishing agricultural income and activity related to, and compounded by, environmental degradation" (2007, 8).[44] The Makokwes also face a problem because, as the government acknowledges, Kweneng district spans an area "where only 5 percent of the total land is suitable for arable agriculture" (Botswana NDP9, 19). It observes that the implications of this are that "increases in population will result in more industrial and residential construction as well as construction of physical infrastructure" (ibid.). Unfortunately, the attempts of the younger generation of Makokwes to alter their livelihoods and move out of farming have not met with much success, given their limited resource base, low educational attainment, and constrained opportunities for enhancing their livelihoods.

RADIPATI'S FAMILY GROUP

The descendants of Radipati's family group are in a very different position. Although born into the third house, Radipati regarded himself as more senior in status to Makokwe because his mother's connections to the Kwena ruling family led to his being adopted as "a kind of nephew" to *Kgosi* Kgari Sechele II (1911–1918). As a result he received an education, which was unusual among men of his generation. He sought to educate all his children, including his daughters, and after his death his widow, Mhudi, continued to fund their education by selling cattle acquired through her labor. Cooper (1982, 18) has noted that having cattle to sell which had been inherited or bought was crucial to a family's ability to finance education. As a result all Radipati's sons and daughters acquired an education. This was uncommon at that time. Two of his sons, David (67) and Moses (55), acquired university degrees in law and agriculture from outside the country because there were no facilities for higher education in Botswana.

Their education enabled them to follow a different career path from most of their contemporaries. David set up his own business, a bar/bottle store and disco, before moving to Boputhatswana to work as a law lecturer. In 1989 he came back to Molepolole to work as a freelance lawyer. He pursues an entrepreneurial lifestyle, taking an active interest in local and national politics. His brother Moses, however, went straight into government employment as an agricultural officer in the Ministry of Agriculture, where he continues to work to this day and uses his expertise to build up his cattle post. Their brother, Pelonomi (60), did poorly at school so he did not have the options that were open to his brothers. Like many of his generation, he went to work at the mines, then came back to the village to find work as a hospital orderly.

He is fortunate because he has been consistently employed and could live and work in Molepolole. He retired at 60 and now lives in a residential plot in Goo-Thato ward that he acquired from the land board.

Radipati's daughters are also unusual. They have all been formally employed for most of their lives, and that has given them a degree of independence, making them less dependent on male networks for support. Goitsemang (72), the eldest daughter, recalls that her mother's contemporaries were very surprised by her mother's attitude: "[M]any people asked her why she spent money from ploughing on education when tomorrow you may have nothing and your children may do nothing for you." As a result of her education Goitsemang was able to train as a nurse and work in South Africa "because there were no jobs in Botswana before Independence." She left nursing in 1969 to return home to help look after her sick sister, Salalenna. She then found employment in Gaborone with a construction company during the construction boom taking place in post-independence Botswana. She was promoted by the company from store worker, to wages clerk, to personnel officer, a position she held until leaving in 1984 to look after her mother in Molepolole. By this time she had acquired two plots of land in Gaborone. One of them was acquired through the company. It provided housing for her daughter Eva and her husband in 1989, when Eva was working as a teacher there. The other was acquired through the Self Help Housing Association (SHHA) and was and continues to be rented out.

Like many of her generation, including her two sisters, she has children but has never married. Unlike many other female-headed households, however, she and her sisters do not find themselves in impoverished circumstances. Through her position with the company Goitsemang was able to get a job for her younger sister, Olebogeng (66), who has also been able to purchase a SHHA plot, which she rents out.

Of the sisters' four daughters, all have been employed as teachers, in government service—for example, as a court clerk in Tribal Administration—or in business, for example, as an executive in Barclay's Bank. Their children are pursuing postsecondary education at the University of Botswana, predominantly in business studies. They have all been successful in acquiring residential plots from Kweneng Land Board, as well as land in urban areas that they have developed.

The Radipatis very much fit the profile of those whom Cooper (1982) refers to as the salariat, and none more so than Olebogeng's eldest son, Bongi (42), who exemplifies upward social mobility. Like his uncle David he did a law degree but at the University of Botswana (UB) and then completed an LLM at the University of Witwatersrand in South Africa in 1994. After working in private practice he went to Columbia University in 1999 to study for a doctorate. He left after acquiring an LLM and spent a year at Harvard as a visiting researcher. He returned to Botswana and was appointed a law lecturer at UB in 1997. From there he went on to become a legal adviser to the Office of the President in 2007, where he was working in 2010. In 2011 he moved to the Attorney General's Office. He has consistently been in professional, pensionable employment throughout his adult life.

As a result he has been able to invest in land. He and his wife, Adelaide, bought a residential plot in Phakhalane, a highly sought after and expensive suburb of Gaborone,[45] where they have been living since 2002. Aware of the problems facing the younger generation with regard to land, he and his wife have acquired land from land boards for all three of their daughters, the eldest of whom was in her first year at UB in 2010. They have been able to take advantage of the amended Tribal Land Act, which no longer links allocation to tribal affiliation, to acquire two plots outside Kweneng district, in Ramotswa and Mmankgodi, both desirable locations close to the capital. The third plot is in Molepolole. They also have land about ten kilometers from Letlhakeng, gateway to the Central Kalahari Game Reserve, where tourism is actively being promoted. While it is a field and they "have not done anything with it [yet]," it has the potential for future development, especially if tourism is successfully established there.

MAKING THE INVISIBLE VISIBLE:
VIEWING THE GLOBAL FROM BELOW

In approaching the "global" through a study of land focused on families' life histories, my research makes visible what has often been rendered invisible in previous discourses on globalization, where the focus has been on the bigger picture that it represents.[46] Yet what happens at a local level is equally important for deciphering how transnational forces and their impact are shaped by local actors in particular contexts. For in order to move away from a homogenizing narrative on globalization, it is necessary to pursue an understanding of how "external" interventions become embedded with diverse and localized sets of meaning and practices.

My study forms part of a move in studies on globalization and law[47] to re-engage with the local and the particularities it presents in order to promote a better understanding of what gives rise to the uneven and diverse effects of globalization. Such studies also explore processes of "internalization" and "relocalization" of global conditions that may allow for the emergence of new identities, alliances, and struggles for space and power within specific populations.

In adopting a relational approach to globalization my study provides perspectives on the transnational from below, revealing how the "global" is produced and practiced in terms of everyday lives. Such visibility is critical for acquiring a proper knowledge of processes of globalization that, among other things, are "taking place inside the national to a far larger extent than is usually recognized" (Sassen 2008, 1). For the capacity of individuals, families, and households to engage with land depends not only on particular kinds of networks to promote their interests, but also on state administration and regulation of land. This has an impact on local populations, connecting them to wider realms of policy-making derived from regional, international, and global arenas.

In this context, Botswana has long been dependent on first South Africa and then Europe as markets for its cattle, as well as on global market prices for the diamonds that have underpinned its economic prosperity to date.[48] All of these markets have been subject to the vicissitudes of fluctuating world demand and wars (Parson 1981; Parsons 1977; Wilmsen 1989, 105–29). The government of Botswana (NDP7, xxi, 95, 145) itself acknowledges the ways in which the country's development is inextricably tied to decisions, processes, and events that take place at regional and international levels beyond its borders. Indeed, publication of its most recent development plan was postponed beyond its normal six-year cycle so that government ministries could recalculate their forecasts for growth and development in the light of "the effects of the just ended global financial and economic crisis."[49]

As the life histories of Makokwe's and Radipati's descendants demonstrate, their life courses have been linked into and shaped by wider geographic processes that have had a differential impact on their everyday lives. For families such as the Radipatis, this has created the conditions for upward mobility, equipping them to diversify their livelihoods in ways that have given them access to and control over land. The Makokwes, however, have not been so fortunate. They lack the resources (financial and skills-based) that would enable them to move away from the peasantariat by investing in more commercial ventures, such as raising crops for sale to large chains like the South African company Pick 'N Pay, or developing an agribusiness or extending production of livestock to sell cattle to the European Union. Such activities are in keeping with the government's drive toward development of "globally competitive enterprises that produce goods and services that comply with local and international standards," thus creating an "entrepreneurship culture."[50]

The value of these life histories, based on an ethnographic approach, is their capacity to "contribute to an understanding of how tightly or loosely the compound parts of the large-scale composites are glued together at this particular historical moment" (Moore 1994b, 372). For they highlight the multiple ways in which international, transnational, national, and local domains intersect with one another in a whole variety of ways that undermine any grand narrative of globalization and attendant vision of law. Such an approach reframes the discussion of institutions and specific practices—both public and private—"away from historically shaped national logics" (Sassen 2008, 2) based on notions of sovereignty and territoriality, through engagement with all these multiple dimensions that shape people's experiences of the global.

NOTES

1. I am indebted to the Leverhulme Trust for funding my research in 2009–2010. I would also like to thank the government of Botswana and all those who have participated in my research over the years, especially my research assistants Phidelia Dintwe, Kawina Power, and Boineelo Baakile, who worked with me in 2009–2010.

2. Commission on Legal Empowerment of the Poor and the United Nations Development Programme (2008).

3. This is a plural form; the singular form is *kgotla*. A *kgotla* is the assembly center (both the physical location and the body of members) of a group of households presided over by a male headman or ward head; in the past, but no longer, all household heads were related through the male line. It forms part of the organization of Tswana society that revolves around the construction of a *morafe* or polity. *Dikgotla* are structured through a tightly organized hierarchy of progressively more inclusive administrative groupings, beginning with the households that make up a *kgotla* and extending through wards, which are the major units of political and legal organization of the *morafe* as a whole.

4. Approved by Parliament in 1997.

5. In 2002–2003, 30 percent of the population lived below the national poverty line. Among this group nearly two out of three were rural and most of them were women, with

female-headed households the most vulnerable in both rural and urban areas (van Klaveren et al. 2009, 31–32).

6. For a more detailed account of land tenure in Botswana see Griffiths (2011, 2012a, 2012b).

7. For a more detailed discussion of these debates see Griffiths (2007).

8. The difficulties inherent in such an approach are exemplified by debates on human rights that have been framed in terms of universalist/relativist positions. For a critique of this see Cowan, Dembour, and Wilson (2001) and Goodale and Merry (2007). See also Baxi (2006), who interrogates the ideological dimensions of these debates revolving round an Orientalist perspective that is founded in notions of "self" and "other" and predicated on characteristics associated with western and non-western domains. See also Benda-Beckmann (2009), who makes the case for a comparative analysis of human rights that would lead us towards a more two-dimensional debate.

9. Used to develop cities and commercial urban activities.

10. That represents a minuscule portion of land and is really an historical development recognizing nineteenth-century grants to South African Boers in the Ghanzi farms and Tuli Block.

11. S.10(1) of the Tribal Land Act 1968 (as amended).

12. See Clifford and Marcus (1986), Clifford (1988), and Marcus and Fischer (1989).

13. Other critiques of cultural essentialism include Abu-Lughod (1998), Mani (1990), Mohanty (1989), Narayan (1997), and Ong (1996).

14. For a detailed account of my research and these life histories prior to 2009 see Griffiths (1997).

15. For a detailed discussion of the life histories of all members of Mosotho *kgotla* (including the Makokwes and Radipatis) up to 1989, see Griffiths (1997). For a more detailed discussion of the updated life histories of the Makokwe and Radipati descendants see Griffiths (2013).

16. All ages in parentheses represent a person's age in 2010.

17. At the date of my research the composition of these land boards involved local elections at the chief's *kgotla,* as well as appointees from the Ministry of Lands and Housing, and the Ministries of Agriculture and of Commerce and Industry. When I carried out my research of KLB there were nine members, four of whom were women.

18. There are twelve land boards in Botswana.

19. His brother Nkadikang, for example, worked at the mines for forty-two years and his brother Ntlogelang for thirty-five years.

20. Under a *mafisa* arrangement cattle are lent out in a patronage arrangement to individuals who become clients under obligatory conditions which include mortgaging the clients' assets against the safety of the patron's property and interests.

21. Note that chiefs were able to continue to consolidate their power through the accumulation of wealth acquired through their collection of taxes on behalf of the British (Wylie 1991).

22. Many who return from working at the mines become sick because of the poor working conditions that they were subject to.

23. This was at the time when Tswana groups such as the Kwena and Ngwato transformed themselves from the small mobile units that existed in the mid-eighteenth century into regional powers located in large settlements that characterize Tswana *merafe* (tribes) today (Okihiro 1976, 13; Parsons 1977, 115; Tlou 1985, 32).

24. Botswana is about the size of France or Texas, covering an area of 581,730 square kilometers.

25. It now has a population of 56,139, making it the second largest village in Botswana after Molepolole. See 2011 Population & Housing Census, Preliminary Brief, para 2.4, downloaded from http://ecastats.uneca.org/aicmd/Portals/0/Census%202011%20Preliminary%20%20 Brief%20Sept%2029%202011.pdf (downloaded on April 18, 2013).

26. Molepolole has an estimated population of 63,128 according to the 2011 Population Census, para 2.4.

27. While the Report of the Presidential Commission on Land Tenure in 1983 noted that the economy of Botswana was still largely agricultural (para 1.06, 3) by 2002 it was recognized that this was no longer the case, according to the Botswana National Land Policy, Issues Report (Revised), vol. 1 (2002, para 1.01, 1). Indeed, it has been observed that "agriculture which was the largest sector in the 1960s contributed only 2 percent of GDP in 2005/06" (African Economic Outlook 2007, 13).

28. In Setswana, the official language of Botswana, the prefix "Ba" is the plural modifier of a noun designating persons, so "Batswana" is the plural form of Tswana.

29. See Botswana National Land Policy, Issues Report 2002 (para 1.01, 1).

30. See the Draft Land Policy issued in June 2011, which attempts to frame policy in these terms.

31. These policies include a National Conservation Strategy (1990), to increase the effectiveness with which natural resources are used; the National Policy on Agricultural Development (1991); the National Master Plan for Arable Agriculture and Dairy Development (2002); and the Revised National Policy for Rural Development (2002), to improve food security and lead to diversification of the agricultural product base; Botswana National Settlement Policy (1998), to provide guidelines and long-term strategy for the development of human settlements; and the National Policy on Housing (2000), to foster a partnership with the private sector and all major employers in facilitating homeownership.

32. The jurisdiction of Kweneng Land Board covers 35,683 square kilometers (*Kweneng District Development Plan 6, 2003–2009*, 1). In its jurisdiction it administers the entire spectrum of land allocation from rural cattle posts to peri-urban and urban residential and industrial areas.

33. S.10(1) of the 1968 Act.

34. See, for example, the *Report of the Commission of Inquiry into Nkgwaketse Development Area Ranches and Government Decision on the Recommendations of the Commission* (Botswana 1981); see also the *Report of the Presidential Commission of Enquiry into Land Problems in Mogoditshane and Other Peri-Urban Villages* (Botswana 1992).

35. *Kweneng Land Board (KLB) v. Matlho and Another* [1992] BLR 292; *KLB v. Mpofu and Another* [2005] 1 BLR 3; *KLB v. Selaki [and Sekgome]* [2004] 1BLR 154(HC); *KLB v. Molefhe and Another* [2005] 2 BLR 155; *KLB v. Murima* (08) (CA) CACLB-034–07.

36. Botswana (2002, 2003). See also the Draft Land Policy of 2011, which refers to a land values market and capitalization of land (2011, para 4.1, 20).

37. This was due to lack of space for building new households in the *kgotla*.

38. See earlier discussion in the introduction and footnote 5.

39. Note this is a statement of the position under customary law where no one person should have absolute title to the natal compound but should hold it for the family as a whole.

40. The draft policy is aspirational in nature and seeks to protect disadvantaged groups, such as widows and orphans, youth, people with disabilities, and those who dwell in remoter

areas, along with making land available for foreign and domestic investment (Botswana 2011, 13–15). However, it is exceptionally vague in its outline, leaving the details which are crucial to policy implementation to be formulated elsewhere.

41. Botswana 2011, para 2.1, 1 and 2.1.2, 8.

42. There has been debate about whether such "sales" should be permitted. While some land board members are in favor of this, others are not. One government official who has worked for a long time on land issues and was interviewed in 2012 (and wishes to remain anonymous) considered this approach to be unacceptable because it "helps to perpetuate inequality." This is because those with resources will benefit at the expense of those without. Attitudes vary according to differing views of what development entails and how it might best be achieved.

43. The government of Botswana recognizes that this is a big challenge. See Botswana 2012, para 34, 12. See also Botswana NDP10 (para 2.14, 19), which notes that according to the Demographic Survey of 2006, 66% of those aged 15–19 were unemployed, along with 55% of those aged 20–24. In their presentation to the 64th Session of the United Nations General Assembly on October 6, 2009, the Botswana youth delegates, Bogolo Kenewendo and Yolisa Modise, observed: "Youth unemployment is a big challenge in Botswana." They observed as well that "[p]overty also remains a problem especially in rural areas, affecting particularly women, youth and the elderly."

44. See United Nations 2007.

45. This is on state land that had to be purchased.

46. See Dezelay and Garth 1995, 2010, and 2012; Likosky 2002; and McBarnet, Voiculescu, and Campbell 2007. The emphasis in these studies has been on international relations as manipulated by multinational corporations seeking to bypass states in the regulation of their affairs.

47. F. and K. von Benda-Beckmann and Griffiths 2005; Drummond 2006; Griffiths 2009a and 2009b; Griffiths and Kandel 2005, 2009, and 2011.

48. See African Economic Outlook (2007, 137). Note that there is concern over the need for economic diversification given "the declining per capita earnings from diamonds and slow growth of non-mining exports of goods (Botswana 2012, para 8, 4).

49. Botswana 2012, para 2, 2.

50. Ibid., para 28, 10.

REFERENCES

Abu-Lughod, Lila. 1998. "Introduction: Feminist Longings and Postcolonial Conditions." In *Remaking Women: Feminism and Modernity in the Middle East,* ed. Lila Abu-Lughod. Princeton, NJ: Princeton University Press.

African Economic Outlook. 2007. *Botswana:* 136–46, AIDBH/OECD. Available online at www.africaneconomicoutlook.org/en.

Baxi, Upendra. 2006. *The Future of Human Rights.* New Delhi: Oxford University Press.

Benda-Beckmann, Franz von. 2009. "Human Rights, Cultural Relativism and Legal Pluralism: Towards a Two-dimensional Debate." In *The Power of Law in a Transnational World: Anthropological Enquiries,* ed. F. and K. von Benda-Beckmann and A. Griffiths. New York: Berghahn Press.

Benda-Beckmann, Franz and Keebet von, and Anne Griffiths, eds. 2005. *Mobile People, Mobile Law: Expanding Legal Relations in a Contracting World.* Aldershot, UK: Ashgate Publishing.

Berry, Sara. 1975. *Cocoa, Custom and Socio-economic Change in Rural Western Nigeria*. Oxford, UK: Clarendon Press.

———. 2002. "Debating the Land Question in Africa." *Comparative Studies in Society and History* 44(4) (October): 638–68.

Bikaako, Winnie, and John Ssenkumba. 2003. "Gender, Land and Rights: Contemporary Contestations in Law, Policy and Practice in Uganda." In *Women and Land in Africa: Culture, religion and realizing women's rights*, ed. L. Muthoni Wanyeki, 232–78. London: Zed Books.

Botswana Gazette. 2009. "Unemployment, a Big Challenge to Botswana: Graduates Settle for Lesser Jobs." January 20. Online.

Botswana, Government of. 1981. *Report of the Commission of Inquiry into Nkgwaketse Development Area Ranches and Government Decision on the Recommendations of the Commission*. Gaborone: Gaborone Printer.

———. 1983. *Report of the Presidential Commission on Land Tenure*. Gaborone: Government Printer.

———. 1990. *National Conservation Strategy*. Gaborone: Government Printer.

———. 1991. *National Policy on Agricultural Development*. Gaborone: Government Printer.

———. 1991. *Report of the Presidential Commission of Enquiry into Land Problems in Mogoditshane and Other Peri-Urban Villages*. Gaborone: Government Printer.

———. 1992. *Land Problems in Mogoditshane and Other Peri-Urban Villages*. Gaborone: Government Printer.

———. 2000. *National Policy on Housing in Botswana*. Gaborone: Government Printer.

———. 2002. *National Master Plan for Arable Agriculture and Dairy Development*. Gaborone: Government Printer.

———. 2002. *Revised National Policy on Rural Development*. Gaborone: Government Printer.

———. 2002. *Botswana National Land Policy, Issues Report (Revised), Volume 1*. Ministry of Lands and Housing Department of Lands. Gaborone: Government Printer

———. 2003. *Review of Botswana National Land Policy. Final Report. Volume 1*. January 31. By National Resources Services (Pty) Ltd and in association with LANDflow Solutions (Pty) Ltd. Ministry of Lands and Housing. Department of Land. Gaborone: Government Printer.

———. 2003. *Ministry of Lands and Housing, B. M. Mathuba. Botswana Land Policy*. Unpublished paper presented at an International Workshop on Land Policies in Southern Africa, Berlin, May 26–27.

———. 2009. *Long Term Vision for Botswana. Vision 2016, Botswana Performance Report. A Report on the Progress Being Achieved against the Vision 2016 Goals*. Vision Council. Gaborone: Government Printer.

———. 2009. Presentation to the 64th Session of the United Nations General Assembly on the 6th of October, by Botswana Youth Delegates, Bogolo Kenewendo and Yolise Modise.

———. 2011. *Draft National Land Policy*, Ministry of Lands and Housing. June. Gaborone: Government Printing and Publishing Services.

———. 2012. *Keynote Policy Paper for Mid-Term Review of NDP 10*. Ministry of Finance and Development Planning. June. Gaborone: Government Printer.

———. NDP6. *National Development Plan 1985–1990*. Ministry of Finance and Development Planning. Central Statistics Office. Gaborone: Government Printer.

———. NDP7. *National Development Plan 1991–1997*. Ministry of Finance and Development Planning. Central Statistics Office. Gaborone: Government Printer.

————. NDP9. *National Development Plan 2003/04–2008/09.* Ministry of Finance and Development Planning. Central Statistics Office. Gaborone: Government Printer.

————. NDP10. *National Development Plan 2010–2016.* Ministry of Finance and Development Planning. Central Statistics Office. Gaborone: Government Printer.

Clifford, James. 1988. *The Predicament of Culture: Twentieth Century Ethnography, Literature, and Arts.* Cambridge, MA: Harvard University Press.

Clifford, James, and George Marcus, eds. 1986. *Writing Culture.* Berkeley: University of California Press.

Commission on Legal Empowerment of the Poor. 2008. Volume 1, Report of the Commission on the Legal Empowerment of the Poor: Making the Law Work for Everyone. Commission on the Legal Empowerment of the Poor and United Nations Development Programme.

Cooper, David M. 1982. *An Overview of the Botswana Class Structure and Its Articulation with the Rural Mode of Production: Insights from Selebi-Pikwe.* (Dated 1980.) Cape Town: Center for African Studies, University of Cape Town.

Cowan, Jane, Marie-Bénédicte Dembour, and Richard A. Wilson, eds. 2001. *Culture and Rights: Anthropological Perspectives.* Cambridge: Cambridge University Press.

Dezelay, Yves, and Bryant Garth. 1995. "Merchants of Law as Moral Entrepreneurs: Constructing International Justice from the Competition for Transnational Business Disputes." *Law & Society Review* 29(1): 27–64.

————. 2010. "Marketing and Selling Transnational 'Judges' and Global 'Experts' Building the Credibility of (Quasi) Judicial Regulation." *Socio-Economic Review* 8(1): 113–30.

————. 2012. *Lawyers and the Construction of Transnational Justice: Law, Development and Globalization.* Oxford: Routledge.

Drummond, Susan G. 2006. *Mapping Marriage Law in Spanish Gitano Communities.* Vancouver: University of British Columbia Press.

Goodale, Mark, and Sally Engle Merry, eds. 2007. *The Practice of Human Rights: Tracking Law Between the Global and the Local.* Cambridge: Cambridge University Press.

Griffiths, Anne. 1988. "Support among Bakwena." in *Between Kinship and the State,* ed. F. von Benda-Beckmann et al., 289–316. Dordrecht: Foris Publications.

————. 1989. "The Legal Heritage of Colonialism: Family Law in a Former British Protectorate." In Law and Anthropology, *International Yearbook for Legal Anthropology,* 75–107. Netherlands: Martinus Nijhoff.

————. 1997. *In the Shadow of Marriage: Gender and Justice in an African Community.* Chicago: University of Chicago Press.

————. 2007. "Making Gender Visible in Law: Kwena Women's Access to Power and Resources." In *Human Rights, Plural Legalities and Gendered Realities: Paths Are Made by Walking,* ed. A. Hellum, J.Stewart, S. S. Ali, and A. Tsanga. Harare: Weaver Press.

————. 2009a. "Anthropological Perspectives on Legal Pluralism and Governance in a Transnational World." In *Law and Anthropology: Current Legal Issues,* vol. 12. Oxford: Oxford University Press.

————. 2009b. "Law, Space and Place: Reframing Comparative Law and Legal Anthropology." *Law & Social Inquiry* 34(2): 495–507.

————. 2011. "The Gendered Dynamics of Land Tenure in Botswana." Special issue on International Development Interventions, *Journal of Legal Pluralism and Unofficial Law* 63: 231–62.

————. 2012a. "The Changing Dynamics of Customary Land Tenure: Women's Access to and Control over Land in Botswana." *Acta Juridica* 11: 65–96.

———. 2012b. "Managing Expectations; Negotiating Succession under Plural Legal Orders in Botswana." In *Managing Family Justice in Diverse Societies,* ed. M. Maclean and J. Eekelaar, 221–46. Oxford: Hart Publishing.

———. 2013. "Re-envisaging the Local: Spatiaility, Land and Law in Botswana." *International Journal of Law in Context* 9(2): 213–38.

Griffiths, Anne, and Kandel, Randy F. 2005. "Localising the Global: Rights of Participation in the Scottish Children's Hearings System." In *Mobile People, Mobile Law: Expanding Legal Relations in a Contracting World,* ed. F. and K. von Benda-Beckmann and A. Griffiths, 482–514. Aldershot, UK: Ashgate Publishing.

———. 2009. "The Myth of the Transparent Table: Reconstructing Space and Legal Interventions in Scottish Children's Hearings." In *Spatializing Law: An Anthropological Geography of Law in Society,* ed. F. and K. von Benda-Beckmann and A. Griffiths, 157–75. Aldershot, UK: Ashgate Publishing.

———. 2011. "Local Responses to National and Transnational Law: A View from the Scottish Children's Hearings System." In *From Transnational Relations to Transnational Laws: Northern European Laws at the Crossroads,* ed. A. Hellum, S. S. Ali, and A. Griffiths, 189–207. Aldershot, UK: Ashgate Publishing.

Gulbrandsen, Ornulf. 1986. "To Marry—or Not to Marry." *Ethnos* 51: 7–28.

Kerven, Carol. 1982. "The Effects of Migration on Agricultural Production." In *Migration in Botswana: Patterns, Causes and Consequences; Final Report of the National Migration Study* 3, 526–622. Gaborone: Government Printer.

Kocken, E. M., and G. C. Uhlenbeck. 1980. *Tlokweng, A Village near Town.* ICA Publication no. 39. Leiden University, Institute of Cultural and Social Studies.

Kweneng District Development Plan 6, 2003–2009. Kweneng District Council, Kweneng District Development Committee, Ministry of Local Government. Gaborone.

Likosky, Michael, ed. 2002. *Transnational Legal Processes: Globalization and Power Disparities.* London: Butterworths.

McBarnet, Doreen, A. Voiculescu, and Thomas Campbell. 2007. *New Corporate Accountability: Corporate Social Responsibility and Law.* Cambridge: Cambridge University Press.

Mani, Lata. 1990. "Multiple Mediations: Feminist Scholarship in the Age of Multinational Reception." *Feminist Review* 35: 24–41.

Marcus, George, and M. Fisher, eds. 1989. *Anthropology as Cultural Critique.* Chicago: University of Chicago Press.

Mmegi Online. 2011. "Graduate Unemployment Passes 3,000 Threshold." October 18.

Mohanty, Satya P. 1989. "Us and Them: On the Philosophical Bases of Political Criticism." *New Formations* 8: 55–80.

Molenaar, Marja. 1980. "Social Change within a Traditional Pattern: A Case Study of a Tswana Ward." M.A. thesis, University of Leiden.

Moore, Sally Falk. 1986. *Social Facts and Fabrications: "Customary Law" on Kilimanjaro, 1880–1980.* Cambridge: Cambridge University Press.

———. 1994a. *Anthropology and Africa: Changing Perspectives on a Changing Scene.* Charlottesville: University of Virginia Press.

———. 1994b. "The Ethnography of the Present and the Analysis of Process." In *Assessing Cultural Anthropology,* ed. Robert Borofsky, 362–76. New York: McGraw-Hill.

Morolong, Siamisung Thoki, and Clement Ng'ong'ola. 2007. "Revisiting the Notion of Tribal Land." In *Essays on the Law of Botswana,* ed. C. M. Fombad, 142–75. Cape Town: Juta Law.

Musembi, Celestine N. 2007. "De Soto and Land Relations in Rural Africa: Breathing Life into Dead Theories about Property Rights." *Third World Quarterly* 28(8): 1457–78.

Narayan, Kirin. 1997. "How Native Is the 'Native' Anthropologist?" In *Situated Lives: Gender and Culture in Everyday Life,* ed. Louise Lamphere, H. Ragone, and P. Zavella. New York and London: Routledge.

Ng'ong'ola, Clement. 1997. "Land Rights for Marginalized Ethnic Groups in Botswana, with Special Reference to Basarwa." *Journal of African Law* 41: 1–26.

Okihiro, Gary Y. 1976. "Hunters, Herders, Cultivators and Traders: Interaction and Change in the Kgalagadi, Nineteenth Century." PhD diss., University of California, Los Angeles.

Ong, Aihwa. 1996. "Anthropology, China and Modernities: The Geopolitics of Cultural Knowledge." In *The Future of Anthropological Knowledge,* ed. H. L. Moore. London: Routledge.

Parson, Jack. 1981. "Cattle, Class, and State in Rural Botswana." *Journal of Southern African Studies* 7: 236–55.

Parsons, Neil. 1977. "The Economic History of Khama's Country in Botswana, 1844–1930." In *The Roots of Rural Poverty in Central and Southern Africa,* ed. N. Parsons and R. Palmer, 113–43. Berkeley: University of California Press.

Peters, Pauline. 2006. "Beyond Embeddedness: A Challenge Raised by a Comparison of the Struggles over Land in African and Post-Socialist countries" In *Changing Properties of Property,* ed. F. and K. von Benda-Beckmann and M. Wiber, 84–105. New York: Berghahn Press.

Piron, Laure-Hélène. 2005. "Donor Assistance to Justice Sector Reform in Africa." *Open Society Justice Initiative.* Online at http://www.odi.org.uk/sites/odi.org.uk/files/odi-assets/publications-opinion-files/2309.pdf.

Ramsay, Jeff. 1991. "The Rise and Fall of the Bakwena Dynasty of South Central Botswana." PhD diss., Boston University.

Sassen, Saskia. 2008. *Territory, Authority and Rights: From Medieval to Global Assemblages.* Princeton, NJ: Princeton University Press.

Schapera, Isaac. 1947. *Migrant Labour and Tribal Life: A Study of the Conditions of the Bechuanaland Protectorate.* London: Oxford University Press.

Stocking, George W. 1992. *The Ethnographer's Magic and Other Essays in the History of Anthropology.* Madison: University of Wisconsin Press.

Tlou, Thomas. 1985. *A History of Ngamiland, 1750–1906.* Madison: University of Wisconsin Press.

UNICEF. 1993. *Children,Women and Development in Botswana: A Situational Analysis.* Report prepared by Maendeleo (Botswana) for the Government of Botswana and UNICEF.

United Nations. 2007. *Second Common Country Assessment for Botswana, Final Report.* United Nations System in Botswana, December 2007.

Van Klaveren, Maarten, Kea Tijdens, Melanie Hughie-Williams, and Nuria R. Martin. 2009. *An Overview of Women's Work and Employment in Botswana.* Working paper 09–81. Amsterdam Institute for Advanced Labour Studies, University of Amsterdam.

Wilmsen, Edwin N. 1989. *Land Filled with Flies: A Political Economy of the Kalahari.* Chicago: University of Chicago Press.

Wylie, Diana. 1991. *A Little God: The Twilight of Patriarchy in a Southern African Chiefdom.* Hanover, NH: Wesleyan University Press.

7 – LOCATION

Film and Media Location

Toward a Dynamic and Scaled Sense of Global Place

STEPHANIE DeBOER

We need "to think through what might be an adequately progressive sense
of place, one which would fit in with the current global-local times and
the feeling and relations they give rise to, *and* which would be useful in
what are, after all, political struggles often inevitably based on place."
—*Doreen Massey, "A Global Sense of Place"*

FILM AND MEDIA ARE OFTEN USED TO PROMOTE LOCATIONS TOWARD
developmental futures and global vistas. These mediated locations are
equally sites of struggle, as they are produced across a fraught and differentiated geometry of film and media technologies, cultural geographies, and
transnational processes. The poster for the 2007 Shanghai eArts Festival
(Shanghai dianzi yishu jie) featured a panorama of future-oriented Shanghai
architecture configured into a circular globe. Here, the gleaming span of
the latest skyscrapers to transform the Shanghai cityscape extended out in
all directions—Jing'an district's Plaza 66, the then new CITIC building, for
example—against an encircling horizon of bright blue sky and streaming
white clouds. Advertising a week-long transformation of Shanghai through
site-specific new media art installations, outdoor performances, and gallery
showings produced and curated by figures both in the People's Republic of

China (PRC) and from around the globe, this promotion underscores the promise that the eArts Festival was to enable for the city. For its organizers and curators, commissioned by the Shanghai Municipal Government, the festival was to present "important methods in the development of Shanghai's new culture."[1] As it "enabled Shanghai to become a center for twenty-first century electronic and new media arts," it constructed new urban spaces, globally networked to technological and creative initiatives in other new media capitals—among them, London, Linz, New York, Tokyo, and Seoul.[2] "Globalisms," as Anna Tsing has underscored, indicate "endorsements" toward an aspirational globe—future-oriented visions that hail the possibilities of global connectivity and the even exchanges and converging interests they engender.[3] As the eArts Festival here worked to forge new geographies and thereby new experiences for Shanghai, new media arts and their locations were to transform the city into a platform for addressing twenty-first-century technological and creative imperatives.

No mere sites of millennial promise, the locations produced in the eArts Festival's engagement with such developing Shanghai districts as Pudong, Yangpu, or Xuhui are better understood as sites of intense struggle over the meanings of place—here within the limits and possibilities of China's uneven openness to transnational incursions in creative, cultural, technological, and monetary capital following its entry into the World Trade Organization (WTO). Such struggle is a reminder of the ways in which locations linked to film and media have long stood at the heart of much debate regarding how best to evaluate the experiences and productions engendered against the intensities of late capitalism. Arjun Appadurai's often-cited assertion, made in the early 1990s, that there is "nothing mere about the local," echoed contemporary calls across a wide range of disciplines for better interrogating the visions of utopian possibility or dystopian despair that all too often colored accounts of the places and experiences engendered by new global processes.[4] Place and the local, as considered by scholars in such fields as anthropology, cultural geography, and cultural and media studies, were not mere affirmations of the onslaught of globalization. For many, film and media had been harbingers of the time-space compressions that rob publics of "emplaced" or "authentic" local experience, homogenizing the globe into one Western imperialist (for some) or global capitalist (for others) façade. Yet, for Appadurai, as for others, the travel of popular and image culture across the globe was an impetus for interrogating how such locations are constructed within a dynamic of uneven and competing global/local flows. Flash forward over two decades later, and Elena Gorfinkel and John David Rhodes underscore the imperatives of continued examination of the places of film and media. For their recent collection on location and the moving image, "a stubborn insistence on place might serve as a tactic . . . with which to resist the forces" that threaten our apprehension of "the uniqueness, the power, and the political potential of both place and the moving image."[5] Indeed, any sustained look at film and media locations demands an adequate accounting of place as it is produced within competing material, discursive, and social practices, and over a geometry of competing claims.

This chapter attends to the methods by which "location," as a term situating place and the local against the dynamics of film and media, might be adequately articulated in relation to the competing scales of new media arts in its transnationally urban frame—here as both mobilized by and expressed within the Shanghai eArts Festival, which was held annually from 2007 to 2009. Place-based and site-specific video and media arts have long been produced and interrogated for their "situatedness"—that "inextricable, indivisible relationship between the work and its site."[6] Speaking to the context of the gallery, Ji-hoon Kim has argued for the ways in which "various artistic approaches to film and video installation inside the black box are understood to render the gallery space an arena for the overlapping, even competing, material, sociocultural, and discursive claims of locations"—for him, an experience "bound up with media technologies crossing the boundary between the virtual and the material, or between the represented space and the site, as part of the surrounding structure framing them."[7] As city-, state-, and corporate-sponsored events such as the Shanghai eArts Festival extend such new media screens and experiences further out into the architectural structures of the city, these boundary crossings are radically reconfigured, demanding an expanded account of the locations that can be produced at the interface of new urban geographies and transnationally circulating modes of media arts exhibition. On the one hand, events such as the Shanghai eArts Festival speak to the ascendance of what Audrey Yue has termed "spatial regeneration developments" in urban centers around the globe. As metropolitan cultural industry initiatives emplace video and new media screens for their locales, thereby working to "cultivate new national pride, fast tracked tourism and engineered new communities," they connect up with a seemingly serialized set of initiatives in other urban centers also concerned with the use of public screens and new media arts in the processes of urban renewal. To be sure, however, as Yue further underscores, "different modes [and contexts] of urban regeneration produce significantly different outcomes."[8]

To adequately address the production of these different outcomes for particular urban and media contexts, and thereby not to acquiesce in the seeming global seriality of it all, requires interrogation of the competing practices at work in producing the locations engendered at this interface between site-specific new media arts and the regenerated spaces of the city. Doreen Massey has argued for the importance of understanding place as constructed in a "global sense"—across a geometry of power relations among local and global practices, identities, and processes.[9] To be sure, the Shanghai eArts Festival was mandated by state and municipal creative industry initiatives intent on transforming Shanghai toward new "global city" status. So-called new media and new media arts have been a particularly salient hub within these initiatives, as digital technologies are often endorsed as platforms for entering into the transnational processes deemed necessary for engendering twenty-first-century lifestyles. To attend to the "competing material, sociocultural, and discursive claims of locations" within this context, however, is to also situate these creative industry aspirations against the practices of curation and exhibition for the festival as they both colluded with and at other times competed against these aims—all against the backdrop of a Shanghai landscape, and a public within it, contending with dramatic cycles of architectural demolition and urban renewal. The video and media arts curated throughout Shanghai over the three years of the annual festival were culled from a global network of media arts practitioners, inclusive of China, but primarily from North America, western Europe, and new media capitals in the Asia Pacific such as Tokyo, Melbourne, and Seoul. Exhibited and emplaced within the most prominently developed districts of new Shanghai, these video and media artworks were often resituated in a new Shanghai matrix of media, architectural, and social practices. Not insignificant in influencing this was Shanghai's participation in what has widely been called the PRC's recent "culture of demolition," wherein its landscapes are kept in "a state of perpetual destruction and disruption" in the service of the city's constant redevelopment.[10] Indeed, though emerging in particular from the

1990s, such processes of dramatic urban transformation are not exclusive to the PRC's more contemporary market and state embrace of transformations in real estate. The Shanghai eArts Festival, for example, is only one nodal moment within a contingent trajectory of film and media's forging of the new Chinese city as it was transformed, at differing moments, as a semi-colonial, communist, socialist, or capitalist gateway for the world.

To concern ourselves with the struggles that construct such new and globally aspiring locations, we need a set of frames by which to interrogate the practices through which they are reconstituted among competing claims of media technologies, urban geographies, and social and transnational processes. The Shanghai eArts Festival is one arena for examining these frames, and for considering the methods for best interrogating such aspirational global geographies—in other words, for considering what particular approaches might disallow or enable us to see the competing practices that make up location within a Shanghai developed at the interface of new media technologies and the city's aspirations for status as a global media capital. The two sections of this chapter thus offer two approaches for doing so. The first section sets its sights upon culture and creative industry designs on Shanghai's development into a global city through the Shanghai eArts Festival and on the discourses that surrounded these aspirations. The second section expands its frame on the eArts Festival to examine a wider geometry of claims that were made regarding the locations engendered in this festival. What sets these two approaches apart is not only their differing location of significance here (in industry practice, in social practice, or in the practices of film and media curation and production, for example). Also setting these two approaches apart are their differing understandings of scale. On the one hand, the mobilization of scale is one means for cultural industries to move "up" along a perceived hierarchy—in this instance, as local urban contexts aspire toward participation in global urban and arts networks. Yet this is not the only use of scale available to us. Scale, as Neil Smith has powerfully argued, denotes a site of difference. Differences across scale define "the boundaries ... around which control is exerted *and* contested."[11] It is thus a term across which we can productively attend to the competing claims to and struggles over locations at play in this interface between new media arts and the new city engendered by the eArts Festival. Here, artists and curators, urban planners, and a bifurcated urban public have also participated in their production

across a range of material, discursive, and imaginary practices.[12] Against the
ideal globalisms often endorsed to stand at the interface of new technologies
and new urban landscapes, the multiple frames of this essay are offered as a
means for laying bare the struggle through which "location" can be produced
against the competing scales of film and media.

LOCATION, TAKE ONE:

SCALED ASPIRATIONS AND NEW MEDIA CAPITAL

The interface between new technologies and new geographies is thus a central platform from which urban planners and creative cultural workers have
promoted film and media locations. For Shanghai, events such as the annual
2007–2009 eArts Festival, municipal aspirations toward developing particular districts of the city for "global city" status were entwined with creative
industry efforts to link up with a network of established culture and media
initiatives in other media capitals of the globe. This phenomenon underscores Xiangming Chen's observation, in her assessment of the megacity's
remarkable economic and infrastructural transformations since the 1990s,
that Shanghai is "a timely urban laboratory for understanding how local
transformations occur in global or globalizing cities as a combined function
of global impact and state power."[13] The work of cultural planning often mediates this consideration of global impact and state power. "Coming out of
the fields of cultural policy studies as a concept that aims to nurture cultural
activities to suit economic arts and social life," cultural planning here has
been widely taken up, as Audrey Yue underscores, "as the 'best practice' in
urban renewal."[14] Indeed, in attending to Shanghai's municipal aspirations,
organizers of the eArts Festival garnered input and advice from established
creative and media initiatives linked, for example, to London, where "culture" and cultural policy had been advocated as central to economic and
spatial regeneration since at least the late 1990s.[15] For the Shanghai festival to
focus on the curation of new media arts for the city, in this instance, in consultation with Ars Electronica, the premier Linz-based new media arts collective, was to dovetail with state municipal policy since the 1990s "of turning
Shanghai into the kind of global city characterized by strong service and
high tech industries."[16] As new media arts brought together disparate media
forms and experiences—video, photography, public performance—all under

the rubric of digital technology, cultural and creative industries deemed it perfectly suited for the developmental designs, both discursive and material, for advancing new infrastructures and cultural experiences for the city.

With regard to such events as the Shanghai eArts Festival, it is worth noting the particular structures and logics whereby locations are showcased, promoted, and produced as visible in the context of the interface of new urban geographies and new media forms. Promoted as "today's largest-scaled and highest level of international art festivals," the 2007 eArts Festival organized the city around seven arenas of outdoor performance, site-based installation, and interactive exhibition, each designated as a distinct but networked "tectonic plate."[17] Highlights included, for example, the New Visions Electronic Music Hall, the Prix Ars Electronica exhibition, the New Futures Interactive Forum, and the Interactive Art Gathering. Saskia Sassen has observed that the contours of the global city do not correspond to the whole of an urban space per se, but rather to the particular urban arenas where global capital accumulates, classed (in this instance, creative) workers gather, and supportive infrastructures are concentrated.[18] The exhibition sites of the festival were located in districts throughout Shanghai that had been targeted for particular development. As Tingwei Zhang has described, the municipal government had adjusted district boundaries in the city since the 1990s "as an administrative tool to empower and reinforce some districts [Yangpu, Huangpu, and Pudong among them] to be 'global players.'"[19] Capitalizing upon this nodal structure of the city, the installations, exhibits, and performances of each of the eArts Festival's tectonic plates were to constitute an especially "heightened" locus of interaction between new media, new urban geographies, and transnational incursions of creative and monetary capital. To be sure, the organizers of the festival were cognizant of how these arenas of Shanghai could, if only for the few weeks of the annual event, serve as platforms from which its inhabitants could envision themselves within the future of this city. New media arts, for these planners, were to provide ways for the inhabitants to "look forward to and yearn for a heartfelt dream, giving to Shanghai an energy for bringing forth new ideas," as one periodical report put it.[20]

In such contexts, the production of film and media location is often a matter of scaled aspiration, engendered across an assemblage of media, cultural, and creative industry initiatives intended to situate the city—and the city's inhabitants—within the advancement of a perceived "international" or "global" culture. An assessment of the 2007 eArts Festival published in a prominent city magazine suggested how the progress of new media arts was essential to the development of the city; Shanghai's ongoing development, moreover, was to be necessarily apparent against a sliding and uneven scale of global advancement. "Electronic arts," asserted the reporter, reflecting on his conversations with municipal and state cultural workers, constitute "a completely new and independent set of ideas" that are "essential to bringing forth new domains... to contemporary culture throughout the globe." New media arts, in other words, were a crucial component of the "blazing [of] new trails in the development... and rising competitiveness of the contemporary city." They were notably central, moreover, to bringing Shanghai to a level where it could "no longer be looked down upon from the advanced heights of globalization."[21] For these urban planners and cultural workers, new media arts were a portal to the modes of "innovative" ideas central to securing Shanghai's place within the scales and "heights" upon which global media capitals were perceived to be networked. The planned accumulation of new media art spaces, industries, expression, and education throughout the city was thus a central means of transforming and reinventing Shanghai into a globally resonant center of media and creative production.

Film and media's entwining with developmental aspiration is certainly not new or exclusive to Shanghai. Henri Lefebvre's 1971 well-cited articulation of the "production of space," for example, underscored the ways in which such artist practices had long colluded with what he termed the "conceived" and totalizing space of the planned city.[22] What is particular to the contemporary interface between media and urban space is its frequent mobilization toward the establishment of "creative" media capital. For Shanghai, such aspirations toward the accumulation of "new media capital" have been closely linked to the development of creative industry initiatives. Promoted widely as the most prescient form of urban development, creative industries, as they have most generally been articulated around the globe, work to link "creative personality" with "organized production" for the purpose of engendering profit and prestige for the city.[23] Asked about the reasoning for the 2007 theme of the Shanghai eArts Festival, its central organizer replied, "Electronic arts express the 'Wisdom of the Crowd' and not just a minority of elite positions." Not simply engendered to "vindicate the self of the crowd," he further emphasized, such "unending interaction between ... technology and arts" was for festival organizers to "bring about the majority of ordinary people's knowledge." Simultaneously, it was also to enable "culture's vigorous industrialization" and innovation.[24] China's tenth Five-Year Plan (2001–2005), as Michael Keane has underscored, "signalled the prominence of the information society (represented as a pillar industry) with an emphasis on raising productivity through the use of information technology." Alongside China's accession to the World Trade Organization, culture thus "emerged as a major development issue." In 2004, the "new 'foreign' idea . . . of the creative industries" brought to the foreground widely held linkages between personal creativity, infrastructural upgrade, and the ascendance of multinational capital.[25] Indeed, Shanghai's own launching in 2005 of "extensive creative industries plans,"[26] including a creative industries research institute, stood on the shoulders of a longer trajectory of so-called international multimedia initiatives that had begun in the early 2000s. By 2007, city and cultural planners had integrated "all of Shanghai's digital exhibition industries." They had done so, moreover, to develop the skills, practices, and infrastructures in "spatial and conceptual planning" necessary to produce the interactive, multimedia, and digital exhibitions that would launch Shanghai as a global city, as it hosted the upcoming 2010 Shanghai World Expo.[27]

For promoters of the eArts Festival and other creative industry initiatives, new media arts have thus been a central conduit for transforming not only the "traditional art conditions" of the city, but also the very possibilities of its "cultural life and economic development."[28] Shanghai's status as a locus for the creation of achievements in Chinese "modern" and "new culture" have here, as is often the case, relied upon a selective genealogy of the city's repeated and close interface with various global circulations of culture and capital. In this rendering, the "advanced" image cultures of 1930s and 1940s Shanghai, for example, were to have vitalized new cosmopolitan lifestyles for China. By extension, the city's long-standing centrality to the development of an inherently "international" and capitalist film culture was a platform that could bolster Shanghai's contemporary status as a location of globally creative innovation. Such leapfrog narratives of the city, we should note, have significantly sidestepped a range of other, less capitalist-oriented techno-urban dynamics for China since at least the early twentieth century. Leftist image cultures of the 1930s—the often-cited film *New Women*, for example—set warning images of cosmopolitan decadence against the progressive female figure leading the factory workers toward a bright future of socialism—and decidedly away from the semi-colonial status that had brought such global capitalist possibilities to Shanghai. From the 1950s, as Yomi Braester has starkly described, filmmaking was at the forefront of the reinvention of Shanghai as a newly Communist industrialized city, as "the Communist government had to show a yet newer Shanghai, in which technological advancement went hand in hand with [socialist and] ideological progress." Following capitalist reforms of the 1980s and over the course of the 1990s, Shanghai was reinvented again, in new policies and perceptions that "saw new construction as a miraculous leap over current [and past] urban troubles."[29] The 2007 eArts Festival's feature of new media arts installations and performances within the gleaming district of Pudong—a premier district of this new urban development—emplaced digital and creative media squarely within state and urban planners' endorsements of Shanghai's immanent and future "global" status. Echoing a long history of "leaps forward" in Chinese urban and rural space, such festival endorsements incorporated a common discourse on the inherent power of technologies for engaging the globe—one that, as Wise and Slack underscore, equates "the development of new technology with progress," both cultural and economic.[30]

In this endorsement of the technologized city, Shanghai is made "global" in its linkup to a network of established transnational media capitals. For city planners, the large and heightened scale of the eArts Festival was a means by which even access to already established creative and media initiatives in such urban centers as London, Linz, Sydney, or Tokyo could be engendered. It is important to note here, however, that significant debate continued regarding the transformations actually engendered by these new technologies, as interrelations were felt on a sliding hierarchical scale of uneven global development. Debates surrounding the function of Ars Electronica in the 2007 eArts Festival provide a telling illustration. Based in Linz, Austria, Ars Electronica has since its establishment in 1979 articulated a range of initiatives that focus on issues at the interface of media art, new technologies, and social development. Ars Electronica's recognition as the "world's leading media arts festival," as well as its status as a celebrated site of new media arts production and practice, rendered it the premier organization with which to consult.[31] For Shanghai-based popular and journalistic reviews of the 2007 festival, however, Ars Electronica did not actually serve to bring Shanghai to the techno-urban levels and competencies toward which it had aspired.

Its presence in the festival was instead cited as evidence of Shanghai's having "not yet arrived," evidence even of its failed place within the worldwide networks and standards of new media arts, and thereby along the hierarchies of global media capital. "The Shanghai eArts Festival did not exhibit an adequately global sense here," argued one such critic. Such global status was only engendered, for such commentators, in its tenuous proximity to, and exhibition alongside, already developed media arts initiatives like Ars Electronica. Against this, Shanghai's status as a new media capital was instead deferred to a future of global proximities. Given that contact with other creative and industry initiatives was to have "great influence on the future development and yielding of electronic arts," the eArts Festival's Austrian Ars Electronica exhibition was "one aspect that [would] cause people to expectedly await the future."[32]

Within the realms of state promotion and industry endorsement, "location," and in particular the formation of specifically "global" locations for the city, is a matter of aspired scale. Scale   large scale, heightened scale   here becomes the means through which urban and cultural initiatives aspire to link up with a network of perceived global standards and initiatives in urban and media arts production. Michael Curtin's term "media capital" explains why media industries develop in one location of the globe instead of another—how creative and monetary capital accumulates here rather than there, and how such accumulation is articulated within particular sociohistorical contexts.[33] As the Shanghai eArts Festival suggests, media capital status can be planned and endorsed in the assertion of one's presence in a global network of other competing media capitals. In this transnational interface of the new media city, particular aspirational notions of place are starkly legitimized, to be sure. Scale, in its developmental sense, thus serves to endorse the production of certain types of location, while at the same time obscuring others. This is not the only use of place and scale available to us, however.

LOCATION, TAKE TWO:

TECHNO-URBAN ASSEMBLAGES AND INTERACTIVE PRACTICE

Such endorsement of film and media's central role in enabling Shanghai's access to the perceived heightened scales of the global are, of course, only one mode of approaching location at the interface of new media arts and emerging urban geographies. Approached from another perspective, film and media locations are also produced in practices that do not *promote* ideal "globalisms." Rather, they engage in negotiation, even struggle, over the competing media technologies and the urban and transnational processes that lay claim to them. Yomi Braester has underscored the ways in which, for Beijing, alongside other contemporary cities of the PRC, "filmmakers act as intermediaries in the process of forging the city" in what he terms the "post spatial," virtual and pointedly "non material" façade of the Chinese metropolis as it is reinvented into a global site. Such is a common critique of what Braester has further termed the contemporary "contract" between urban geographies and film and media for a wide range of transnational contexts, as "urban space turns into a commodity marketed through iconic landmarks, brand name architecture and theme parks."[34] Certainly, my analysis of the terms through which the Shanghai eArts Festival was promoted in the previous section of this essay would simultaneously collude with and critique such an endorsement. Yet film and media locations in the context of media globalization are not simply sites of promotion toward "globalized" space. They are not, in other words, mere markers of space devoid of authentic or located meaning. With their foregrounding of the embeddedness of film and media in urban sites, new media arts bring to the fore the struggle for significance that characterizes their locations. They thus enable us to consider how such senses of place are produced across a competing range of media, architectural, and social practices.

Location, in this context, is less a platform for entry into a progressing globe than an arena constructed over the differently scaled practices and competing powers that make up the Chinese city as it is engendered through such transnational new media arts events as the Shanghai eArts Festival. Attention to the competing practices through which locations linked to film and media are produced is therefore imperative. Such practices are, as Neil Smith has also argued in his definition of scale, the arena and "language" through which "spatial difference" can be articulated.[35] Attention to the valences of new media practice can help us to understand the ways in which artists and curators not only promote a globalized sense of place, but can also intensely grapple with the competing material, sociocultural, and discursive claims through which film and media locations are produced in this context.

"Interactivity" has become a central term through which new media arts have been widely understood. The theme of the 2008 iteration of the Shanghai eArts Festival, for example, conceived by the festival's guest curator Richard Castelli, was "urbanized landscape." This theme set the stage for the development and redeployment of art projects throughout the city concerned with the fraught interactions between "city" and "landscape" engendered by new media technologies.[36] "Interactivity" was thus here mobilized as a preeminent practice for addressing the interface between new media arts and its urban locations.

In her discussion of the use of large-scaled screens within spatial regeneration developments in urban centers in Australia and elsewhere, Audrey Yue writes: "Interactivity can be defined as a kind of feedback that provides the means to control and change information." As a "form of 'suture' between ourselves and our machines, it creates an immersive environment that enhances the participants' sense of embodied interaction." For the spatial and urban regeneration projects she addresses, "[t]his urban circulation of bodies and technologies enables a new level of communication that enhances public expression and transforms spaces into social places of shared use. . . . At once social, audio, visual, tactile and affective, this experience shapes the material conditions of the event to produce an embodied interaction that actively engages place, technology and the body in the performance of cultural citizenship."[37] Indeed, a similar linking across social space, new media arts environments, and encouraged senses of citizenship—here conjoined to the possibilities of new and more creative lifestyles to be encouraged by such transnational events—can also be found in the cultural planning involved in the Shanghai eArts Festival. The 2008 iteration of the festival expanded upon its 2007 foregrounding of "outdoor interactive" installations and performances. "To execute the [2008] theme 'urbanized landscape,'" advocated a Shanghai-based assistant curator, "the Shanghai eArts Festival has extended electronic arts to the parks and wide avenue spaces" of the developed districts of Xuhui, Yangpu, and Pudong. These areas, this curator made a point of saying, were no mere backdrop for the activity of curators and artists; they were no static canvas against which to set film and media images. As foregrounded sites of outdoor "interactivity," they were sites for negotiating, as other curators further argued, not only "the interface between creator and new media," but also "the interface between new media and the public at large." All of this was established in the service of creating more symbiotic paths between "the environment and a new and future 'artistic' way of life."[38] In this linking of a public to an "artistic" (read "creative") way of life, interactivity was deemed an integral part of the creative industry imperatives so central to the Shanghai municipal government's support of the eArts Festival. For city planners, this techno-urban interaction between new media and new geographies was the very means through which global city status could be achieved for Shanghai.

Brought more squarely to the level of cultural analysis, however, "interactivity" is also a mode for parsing the differentiated scales and thereby powers through which locations are produced at this interface. Media scholars and cultural geographers concerned with the production of place in a "global sense" have long approached place as constructed in a "struggle" over "geometries" of competing practices, identities, and infrastructures of power.[39] Divorced from the discourses of creative and media policy, interactivity can instead become for us—as scholars, critics, and cultural workers—a rubric for recognizing the uneven and differentiated scales that make up the locations produced in this context. Take, for example, the "Outdoor Transnational Exhibition" that was set in Plaza No. 10 of the Pudong New Area, a particularly celebrated festival platform that was to enable Shanghai inhabitants to "better comprehend the 2008 eArts Festival's theme of 'urbanized landscape.'"[40] The Pudong district was first established as a site of intense planned construction in 1993, as part of urban initiatives set forth under the slogan "Developing a New Shanghai." By 2007, its future-oriented architecture most prominently featured the Oriental Pearl Tower, with its heights signaling the city's inclusion within a network of other global cities in the region and beyond. Dai Jinhua has explicated the ways in which the valences of *guangchang*/plaza shifted over the course of the 1990s, such that "a new marketplace rhetoric" came to imbue the heretofore revolutionary twentieth-century public square. Significant to her analysis is how the *guangchang*/plaza came to reflect the spatial differences between "apparent economic prosperity and the increasingly widening gap between rich and poor."[41] Here, the dramatic demolition and relocation of urban inhabitants that constitute the recent incursions of construction for the Chinese city has rendered the new marketplace inaccessible to many. The "outdoor transnational exhibition" of the Shanghai eArts Festival thus intersects with an urban space constructed over stark differentiation of scale—not only of rich and poor, but also of rural and urban, local and global—that, as Neil Smith has also argued, "defines the boundaries . . . around which control is exerted *and* contested."[42]

Once emplaced in Shanghai, new media arts projects linked to the 2008 eArts Festival, as they were curated under the themed concerns of the interface of new media and new urban geographies, were also entwined with the claims, controls, and contestations that constitute the city's intense cycles of architectural demolition and urban renewal. In her discussion of television and public space, Anna McCarthy underscores how a recognition of television as "a spatial instrument that is at once a physical object . . . and a source of enunciations originating in, and displaying, other places, suggests that the screen not only exists in more than one place, but also on more than one scale; it is the space where local processes meet 'global' determinations of the image."[43] These dynamics over distance, and over place and scale, are the stuff of interactive media arts practice; these are the terms that are often negotiated by subjects within site-embedded arts projects. Once exhibited and emplaced in Shanghai, the new media arts projects curated from both Shanghai and other locales of new media arts production from across the globe for the 2008 eArts Festival theme, "Urbanized Landscape," were emplaced within a particular matrix of media, architectural, and social concerns; they also became entwined with the powers and practices that constitute the Chinese city's locally infected cycles and disruptions of renewal, construction, and demolition.

In the commercial district of Xuhui, 2008 Shanghai eArts Festival curators replaced the commercial content of outdoor LED advertising screens with artist videos from around the world. Once a site of factories in postrevolutionary China, Xuhui was one of several districts targeted by municipal authorities from the early 1990s to be a hub within Shanghai transformed for commercial use. This transformation has more recently manifested in a proliferation, within its central business district, of public advertising screens of a dizzying array of scales and heights—a development that similarly has transformed the façades of many of Shanghai's commercial districts. The emplacement of "40+4," a multimedia screen installation collaboratively produced by Davide Quatro, Lothar Sprec, and Zhu Xiaowan, is an example of one such artwork that was emplaced on these commercial screens. "40+4" consists of a series of framed video interviews, scrolled side to side, all simultaneously commenting on the interface between the artwork, the artist, and the "product." In the eArts Festival exhibition of Xuhui, it was displayed on an enormous screen set atop a tall building. Curated within (and indeed produced for) the Shanghai eArts Festival, intermingling voice commentaries are highlighted by English and Chinese captions that underscore what it might mean for the artist to consider her work to be a commercial product. The ironic tone of this dialogue—"if responsibility exists, it is nothing but a by-product," for example—suggests a worldwide class of artistic and cultural workers, collectively encountering a globalized regime whereby "urban space turns into a commodity marketed through iconic landmarks, brand name architecture and theme parks."[44] Displayed on a wide screen set high above the streets of Xuwei, "4+40" certainly speaks to the generic and strategic structures of the global city—structures that a wide range of cultural critics have critiqued as simply being reproduced within the new Chinese city. Reading this exclusively through the lens of a globalized virtuality, however, would ignore the Shanghai materialities and scaled claims into which this installation was simultaneously embedded. Here, Shanghai sits in interface with larger structuring processes and discourses whereby culture is subsumed within the globalizing needs of networked connectivity. Such a critique and reading ignores, moreover, from another perspective, the workings and differentiations engendered across scale here, which would otherwise enable us to attend more to differentiated and tactical possibilities within Shanghai's cycles of urban renewal.

As it speaks to the competing claims and interests across them, the urban emplacement of new media arts practices and works curated by the 2008 eArts Festival is also indicative of more tactical possibilities within Shanghai's cycles of urban renewal. Moreover, it is suggestive of the demolition/reconstruction cycle that constitutes its contemporary urban experience. Against the heightened display of the "40+4" video project, for instance, Brooklyn-based Michael Bell-Smith's "On the Grind" addressed the Shanghai inhabitant as an everyday walker. Originally produced for gallery exhibition, Bell-Smith's digital video was blown up to fit the large public and architectural screens to populate the Xuhui commercial district. This time, however, the screen was set at the height of an overpass walkway, as passersby walk past it in nighttime silhouette against the light of the video, some pausing to look, others simply passing by. The content of this video arts project displayed an abstracted urban landscape. Buildings are boxes, chimneys are rectangles, and the gray scales of the piece render it reminiscent of a declining North American industrialized city. "On the Grind" also works with a disjointed aesthetic of varying velocities, as its grayscale landscape variously speeds by and slows down, even to a halt, to then disappear below the bottom of the screen, only to rise up again to speed horizontally, if disjointedly, on. As this landscape scrolled by Shanghai passersby in randomly timed and horizontal velocities, "On the Grind" rendered a precarious and unstable urban geography.

With this media arts landscape scrolling by Shanghai urban passersby, "On the Grind" demands that we consider the differences and collusions—and "exertions and contestations" of control—that emerge as the more "global" determinations of the image meet local processes. Robin Visser has underscored what it means for Chinese cities such as Shanghai to remain caught in what is now widely called a "culture of demolition." Here, its inhabitants are kept in "a state of perpetual destruction and disruption" as their lived and built environments are continually transformed in the service of the (official) imperatives of urban development—and urban development over which they have little individual control. As "On the Grind" is emplaced across different scales, and even as it references differently empowered landscapes and North American contexts of arts production, demolition nonetheless becomes the experience across which interactivity here occurs between new media and new Shanghai geographies within the context of the transnationally circulating practices of new media arts exhibition.[45] In his discussion of the history and development of public screens in Shanghai, Chris Berry has argued for the ways in which attention to the local situatedness of such urban screens enables understanding of how "they manifest not so much 'glocal' adaptations of an established Western or metropolitan usage but rather coeval development of the usage of new media under conditions of rapid global uptake."[46] What "On the Grind"'s emplacement within Xuhui and curation by the eArts Festival suggests is the significance of scale to understanding the dynamics of this coevalness. Referencing differently empowered landscapes, here between Brooklyn and Shanghai, demolition nonetheless becomes the experience across which interactivity here occurs between new media and new Shanghai geographies. Set within the rapidly developing and transforming façade of the contemporary Chinese city, "On the Grind" thus offers not only a disjunctured image, produced as it was for a different sociocultural context; it also offers an uncanny image, a landscape against which Shanghai's own unstable grounding—its demolition and rebuilding—might be differently experienced, once again.

This once-again-but-different ethos constitutes a "geography of the new," in David Morley's sense of geographies endorsed as such in their close proximity to new technologies. Within the impetus of Morley's critique, an examination of the interface between new technologies and new geographies is an opportunity for interrogating what he further terms the "globalisms of our age."[47] In the context of interactive media arts practice, the "geographies of the new" so valorized as indicative of the "globalisms of our age" are accessed across differentiated articulations of scale and place. Not simply an idealized field of global aspiration—though certainly this, also—the arenas of such events as the Shanghai eArts Festival also constitute, viewed from another lens, a contested field for addressing how local Shanghai contexts do not simply acquiesce in the promises held by the global city, both here and elsewhere. To consider location as a site of uneven and competing practice is not to consider its "lack" of meaning or materiality per se; it is rather to recognize the possibilities of contingency, and with this perhaps even change, across its scales.

The Shanghai eArts Festival, itself lasting at most a month each time, was produced for only three years. This premier new media arts event for promoting the city was cut short following a change in high-level Shanghai municipal government personnel and policy in 2009. This is not to say, of course, that the dynamics of place and scale addressed throughout this chapter no longer hold for Shanghai. They have simply been emplaced elsewhere—in even larger events such as the 2010 Shanghai World Expo, for example. Such events offer not simply shiny façades of global aspiration. They moreover offer locations and locales that are dynamically constructed over competing media, architectural, and social practices. To refuse to see as much is to acquiesce in the ideal globalisms and productions of global advancement toward which they are so often promoted.

NOTES

1. Promotional and curatorial comments on the 2007 Shanghai eArts Festival are digitally archived, in Chinese, at http://www.artlinkart.com/cn/exhibition/overview/518cryn.

2. Ibid.

3. Anna Tsing, "The Global Situation," *Cultural Anthropology* 15(3) (2000): 327–60.

4. Arjun Appadurai, "Disjuncture and Difference in the Global Cultural Economy," *Public Culture* 2(2) (1990): 1–24.

5. Elena Gorfinkel and John-David Rhodes, "Introduction: The Matter of Places," in *Taking Place: Location and the Moving Image,* ed. John-David Rhodes and Elena Gorfinkel (Minneapolis: University of Minnesota Press, 2009), xii.

6. Miwon Kwon, "One Place after Another: Notes on Site Specificity," in *Space, Site, Intervention: Situating Installation Art,* ed. Erika Suderburg (Minneapolis: University of Minnesota Press, 2000), 252–62.

7. Ji-hoon Kim, "Into the 'Imaginary' and 'Real' Place: Stan Douglas's Site-Specific Film and Video Projection," in *Taking Place: Location and the Moving Image,* ed. John-David Rhodes and Elena Gorfinkel (Minneapolis: University of Minnesota Press, 2009), 257.

8. Audrey Yue, "Urban Screens, Spatial Regeneration and Cultural Citizenship: The Embodied Interaction of Cultural Participation," *Urban Screens Reader,* ed. Scott McQuire, Meredith Martin, and Sabine Niederer (Amsterdam: Institute of Networked Cultures, 2009), 262, 263.

9. Doreen Massey, "A Global Sense of Place," *Space, Place, and Gender* (Minneapolis: University of Minnesota Press, 1994): 146–56.

10. Robin Visser, *Cities Surround the Countryside: Urban Aesthetics in Post-Socialist China* (Durham, NC: Duke University Press, 2010), 146.

11. Neil Smith, "Contours of a Spatialized Politics: Homeless Vehicles and the Production of Geographic Scale," *Social Text* 33 (1992): 66. I am concerned here with what an analytics of scale might enable for scholarship and criticism in these contexts.

12. Yomi Braester, *Painting the City Red: Chinese Cinema and the Urban Contract* (Durham, NC: Duke University Press, 2010).

13. Xiangming Chen, "Introduction: Globalizing City on the Rise: Shanghai's Transformation in Comparative Perspective," in *Shanghai Rising: State Power and Local Transformations in a Global Megacity,* ed. Xiangming Chen (Minneapolis: University of Minnesota Press, 2009), xx.

14. Yue, "Urban Screens," 266.

15. Ibid., 265.

16. Chen, "Introduction," xxi.

17. Liu Ying, "Tiyan meili keji, fengxiang yishu shenghuo—2007 Shanghai dianzi yishujie yishu ditu [Experiencing Beautiful Technology, Sharing Artful Life—Landscape of the 2007 Shanghai eArts Festival]," *Da meishu [Great Arts],* Oct. 15, 2007, 26. In Chinese.

18. Saskia Sassen, *The Global City: New York, Tokyo, London* (Princeton, NJ: Princeton University Press, 2001).

19. Tingwei Zhang, "Striving to Be a Global City from Below: The Restructuring of Shanghai's Urban Districts," in *Shanghai Rising: State Power and Local Transformations in a Global Megacity,* ed. Xiangming Chen (Minneapolis: University of Minnesota Press, 2009), 170.

20. Cao Can, "Pengpidu de yanjing: ganshou 2007 Shanghai yishujie [The Eyes of Pompidou: Experiencing the 2007 Shanghai eArts Festival]," *Jianshang-jia [The Connoisseur]* 23 (2007): 76. In Chinese.

21. Ibid.

22. Henri Lefebvre, *The Production of Space,* trans. Donald Nicholson-Smith (Malden, MA: Blackwell, 1991).

23. Chris Bilton, as quoted in and discussed by Michael Keane in *Created in China: The Great New Leap Forward* (New York: Routledge, 2007), 4.

24. Cao Can, "The Eyes of Pompidou," 76.

25. Keane, *Created in China,* 60–61, and also for more on China's creative industries.

26. Ibid., 2.

27. Ming Haoxia, "Shuzi yishu gaibian women chuantong de chengshi yishu xingtai [Digital Arts Will Change the Traditional Art Configuration of the City]," *Da meishu* [*Great Arts*], Dec. 15, 2007, 30. In Chinese.

28. Ibid.

29. Braester, *Painting the City Red,* 57.

30. Jennifer Daryl Slack and J. Macgregor Wise, *Culture and Technology: A Primer* (New York: Peter Lang, 2005), 23.

31. Ars Electronica may be found here: www.aec.at/about/en/.

32. Li Fengming, "Xia yizhan xin meiti yishu jidi? Cexie 2008 nian Shanghai dianzi yishujie 'Chengshihua fengjing [The Next New Media Arts Base? Portrait of the 2008 Shanghai eArts Festival, 'Urbanized Landscape],'" *Zhonghua wenhua jiaoliu* [*Chinese Cultural Exchange*], Feb. 1, 2009, 33. In Chinese.

33. For an introduction of Michael Curtin's notion of media capital, see the introduction and conclusion to Michael Curtin, *Playing to the World's Biggest Audience: The Globalization of Chinese Film and TV* (Berkeley: University of California Press, 2007).

34. Braester, *Painting the City Red,* 283.

35. Smith, "Contours of a Spatialized Politics," 62.

36. Promotional and curatorial comments on the 2008 Shanghai eArts Festival are digitally archived, in Chinese, at http://www.artlinkart.com/cn/exhibition/overview/8e3gsto.

37. Yue, "Urban Screens," 269.

38. Liu Ying, "Experiencing Beautiful Technology, Sharing Artful Life," 26.

39. Massey, "A Global Sense of Place," 146–56.

40. Qiu Jiahe, "Yi 'Chengshihua fengjing' huying 2010 nian shibohui: 2008 Shanghai dianzi yishujie simian kaihua [Calling Forth 2010 World Expo with 'Urbanized Landscape': 2008 Shanghai eArts Festival Blooms from Wall-to-Wall]," *Shanghai Zhengquan bao,* Oct. 18, 2008, T01. In Chinese.

41. Dai Jinhua, "Invisible Writing: The Politics of Mass Culture in the 1990s," in *Cinema and Desire: Feminist Marxism and Cultural Politics in the Work of Dai Jinhua,* ed. Jing Wang and Tani E. Barlow, trans. Jingyuan Zhang (London: Verso, 2002): 213–34.

42. Smith, "Contours of a Spatialized Politics," 66.

43. Anna McCarthy, *Ambient Television: Visual Culture and Public Space* (Durham, NC: Duke University Press, 2001), 15.

44. Braester, *Painting the City Red,* 283.

45. Visser, *Cities Surround the Countryside,* 19.

46. Chris Berry, "Shanghai's Public Screen Culture: Local and Coeval," *Communication and Society* 21 (2012): 28.

47. David Morley, *Media, Modernity and Technology: The Geography of the New* (London: Routledge, 2007), 3.

8 – MATERIALITY

Transnational Materiality

ZSUZSA GILLE

IN RECENT YEARS IT SEEMS MORE AND MORE OF THE NEWS AND OUR political discourse is about nonhumans: dams that fail in a hurricane, sodas that kill teenagers, bacteria that become resistant to antibiotics, oil rigs that explode, cows that go mad, sleeping pills that make you eat in your sleep. As these negative examples suggest, nature and the object world seem to us riskier than ever.[1] At the same time, we also increasingly wonder about our ability to become political in ways that are more about our relationships with the object world than about our relationships with other humans; for example when we opt for purchasing local food or commodities with various certificates, such as organic or fair trade labels, or when we install energy or carbon meters or solar panels on our homes. My purpose in this chapter is not to answer whether we actually have more and more things surrounding and connecting us, or whether we simply perceive it that way for some reason. Instead, I wish to explore what such experiences—whether they are really new or they are just imagined as novel—say about globalization and about the types of connections that are proliferating across the globe. To that end

I will provide an overview of how scholars have conceptualized the relationship between humans and nonhumans, then I will analyze what that relationship has to do with globalization through two case studies, both taken from Hungarian food politics. In conclusion I will suggest that global capitalism and the European Union are not purely social entities but rather are sociomaterial assemblages, and understanding them as such will let us see power inequalities in new ways, ultimately making new types of politics possible.

What does materiality mean? It does not mean materialism—either in the colloquial sense of "being into" material possessions and being concerned with money, or in the philosophical sense, namely believing that it is being that determines consciousness and not the other way around. Rather it refers to the physical world that surrounds us: nature, manmade objects, our bodies, and even more broadly, the way space is organized around us, and the concrete practices and technologies we employ in our everyday lives. While this seems like a rather general term, outside philosophy and the natural sciences we have not given much thought to the relationship between society and materiality, or to be more precise, we have tended to assume that especially with the advance of modern science and technology, we can fully master the object world, including nature, and thus that the nature of this materiality is, well, immaterial.

In the last couple of decades, there has been a growing acknowledgment by humanities and social science scholars that consideration of this physical world's role in creating societies and institutions cannot be limited to Marxism, which found that nature is either enabling or constraining for capital (Rudy 2005). That formulation still assumed that there is a purely social logic that runs up against a distinct and purely material or natural logic and that, with proper social institutions (collective ownership of the means of production, workers' control over the state and science, and so on), the two logics can be brought into harmony. Instead more recent views argue that there will always be some aspect of the nonhuman world that will not entirely mold to human and social intentions. Some people call this the phenomenon of "things biting back" (Tenner 1996); others argue that there is a certain dance of agency between humans and nonhumans, as each tries to assert itself in a particular context, whether of laboratory experiments, production, or the reorganization of space (Pickering 1995). Most radically, sociologists associated with Actor Network Theory (ANT) say that our reality has always been hybrid, that is, simultaneously social and material, human and nonhuman (Latour 1993a, 1993b, 2005). Two concepts have been used to describe this hybrid nature of reality: actor networks and socio-material assemblages.[2] Both suggest that humans and nonhumans are linked in particular and quite temporary ways, and thus that things, technologies, animals, plants, will have political effects that are not determined by society alone but by how they are inserted into arrangements with each other and with human individuals and collectives.

Others, however, disagree with this view of politics as always unpredictable and of power as always facing uncertainties. I count myself among these skeptics. My interest has actually been in showing the different ways in which materiality has been sutured with power, that is, in analyzing the relationships between social inequality or disenfranchisement and the organization of materiality.

Langdon Winner (1986), in his pathbreaking work on the relationship between technology and democracy, has argued that sometimes a certain technology is explicitly implemented in the interest of producing certain, often anti-democratic, political effects; at other times, such an outcome is a mere "unintended consequence." An example of the former is Noble's (1984) study of technological innovation in industry that he found often to be motivated by managers' need to decrease workers' control over the production process—which would weaken the power of labor unions—rather than by a short-term interest in increasing efficiency and profitability. More recently, Timothy Mitchell (2009) has argued that the shift from coal to oil as a main source of energy in postwar Europe, encouraged and subsidized by the United States, was similarly aimed at breaking the power of coal workers and socialists. An example of the latter, unintended political consequences, comes from the historian Karl Wittfogel and later from environmental historian Donald Worster (1985), who showed that hydraulic societies, such as ancient Egypt, are heavily dependent on tapping into and then distributing scarce water resources. Since irrigation channels require major efforts of planning and cooperation, these societies all tend to develop highly centralized and stratified structures. That is, in order for rivers to flow where they are needed, social power must flow upward to install and operate the complex materiality of irrigation. A similar centralizing and even despotizing effect has been attributed to nuclear power plants (Winner 1986).

Chandra Mukerji (2010), also relying on an infrastructural example, however, shows that even when political actors are initially successful in achieving their political goals by manipulating, changing, or reorganizing the material world, they may in the end find that they cannot stay fully in control. Her
historical case study shows how the Canal du Midi, which was constructed
in the seventeenth century in the south of France to connect the Mediterranean Sea with the Atlantic Ocean, decreased the power of local nobility
vis-à-vis the king, Louis XIV. The nobility could not benefit from the canal
(since they had been banned from engaging in trade), and also had their
power eroded over local craftsmen, farmers, traders, and village women, who
now found new sources of economic livelihood facilitated by water transport
and the reliable availability of water for various economic activities such as
laundering, irrigation, and weaving. At the same time, due to their lack of
scientific understanding, local nobility could not interfere with the location,
the size, or other physical aspects of the canal; they appeared to have been
simply determined by technical rationality and thus it came to embody an
impersonal power. Mukerji calls this *logistical* power. The nobility found that
their traditional political tools (such as making and breaking alliances, using
ideology, cajoling, intimidation, or coercion—modes of domination Mukerji
calls *strategic* power) could not match logistical power. The Sun King not
only increased his tax revenues from the novel economic activities along the
Canal du Midi but also extended his power over territories that previously
he could control only through and with the help of local nobility. Eventually,
however, Louis XIV realized that this new type of power resided not in his
person—as is the case with traditional, strategic power—but in his administration, and thus lessened his individual influence as well. Ultimately, he
solved this problem by disgracing the key architects of the project, that is,
resorting to the traditional political tools of strategic power. The point is not
that logistical power always wins out over strategic power—after all, those
holding only logistical power, the architects and the other experts working
for them, lost out in the end—but that historically logistical power became
more important so that those who could engage in both held an upper hand.
Mukerji argues that infrastructures—not only canals, but roads, and later,
dams, railroads, electric grids, and phone lines as well—facilitated the cen-
tralization of power that was less and less strategic and more and more logis-

tical, ultimately laying down the socio-material foundations of the modern territorial nation-state. But if logistical power was crucial for the formation and endurance of the territorial nation-state, it is no less important today when that state finds its scope of authority curtailed due to global economic relations and due to supranational organizations, such as the United Nations—including two of its financial organizations, the World Bank and the International Monetary Fund—the European Union, or the World Trade Organization. How materiality matters at the global and transnational level is what I turn to next.

MATERIALITY AND GLOBALIZATION

Why do we need to pay attention to materiality when we study globalization and transnational social relations? A key reason is that in mainstream interpretations of globalization and in the early globalization scholarship, there is an assumption that goods, people, and money can now circulate with such speed that material and spatial obstacles have been transcended. One way in which this belief is expressed is the argument that meaning has evaporated from place (Castells 1997, 1989) because the enabling and limiting physical, geographical, and social characteristics of any given locality no longer matter: capital and people can always move elsewhere or insert that place in networks in such a way that its previously limiting features no longer matter. Another argument is the one advanced by geographer David Harvey (1990), who argued that time and space have been compressed by new technologies and by new economic arrangements, thus making it easier for capital to search out the places on the globe where it can be invested with the greatest profit margins. Other scholars have also emphasized the unprecedented mobility and connectedness of places and called for using new concepts, such as flows and networks, to describe society.

Contrary to this assumption, we now have a great deal of empirical evidence that the speed of circulation and connectedness around the globe is uneven. Moreover, this unevenness is strategically employed by states and corporations to extract value from the juxtaposition of slow and fast flows, connection and disconnection. Saskia Sassen (2000), for example, shows that divergence in the temporalities of the financial sector (in which returns are realized very quickly, if not instantaneously) and of the auto industry (where returns take months or years) opens up new possibilities for profit-making and allows finance capital to subject other economic sectors and forms of capital to its own rhythms. New sources of profit can also emerge from connecting places with some circuits and not others. For example, inserting a fishery in Mexico into global circuits of free trade but simultaneously not applying international laws on sustainable fishing or labor regulation reaps benefits for producers and traders at the expense of nature and workers. Cases such as these suggest that whether globalization is beneficial to a certain group of people depends on concrete practices and the way in which the object world is organized and brought into relation with humans in a particular economic activity.

It is for this reason that many scholars now advocate what we might call a grounded view of globalization: a perspective of transnational social relations that sees local materialities as consequential for how globalization is experienced. This is a very important step in the right direction, in my view. However, we need to go even further. You might think, for example, that how Mexican fisheries go about catching fish (what nets they use, how they vary the location of fishing to avoid overfishing, how much they fish from one location, what size fish they throw back in the water, and so on) is determined not only by local tradition or the technologies available to local fishermen. More and more these practices and technologies are influenced, if not put in place, by transnational actors, such as big multinational fish-processing companies or retailers that contract with local fishermen. In a different scenario, they might also reflect the standards of global environmental or animal rights organizations that are increasingly successful in getting the biggest corporations to adopt their sustainability and ethical principles and "best practices." Whatever the source of these practices—corporations or international nongovernmental organizations (INGOs)—the interaction between the human and nonhuman world is less and less locally determined. This means that we have to start understanding materiality not just as something that resides in and is limited to a particular place, but also as something that transcends the boundaries of the local. We used to think that in order to understand the role the nonhuman world plays in the human world we had to stay in one place and study the local manifestations of materiality. In contrast, I suggest that we have to understand materiality as simultaneously local, translocal, and transnational.

THE HISTORICAL CONTEXT OF THE CASE STUDIES

To demonstrate how this might be done, I use two case studies, both taken from my research on Hungarian food politics. One is the case of a 2004 scandal involving paprika; the other is a 2008 boycott of Hungarian foie gras. In order to properly understand what these stories are about, I need to provide some background information about Hungarian agriculture and food consumption. Hungary was under Communist rule until 1989, when, along with many other countries in the East European Soviet bloc, it ended state socialism—the sociological term we use to describe the type of society that had dominated that part of the world since 1947. Agricultural land that under state socialism was mostly owned by large state farms or cooperatives was privatized, that is, handed back to individual owners. The year 1989 also inserted Hungary into new trading networks, mostly opening towards the West, to which the country exported agricultural products and from which it primarily bought high-value-added commodities, such as cars, electronics, or computers. Initially import duties were imposed on goods from the West, which made them expensive, and thus favored Hungarian products which did not have the duty added to their prices. Soon after 1989, however, Hungary began to eliminate tariffs imposed on import goods, and in return the countries to which it exported Hungarian produce also did away with their import duties; this trade liberalization was also one of the conditions for joining the European Union. Free trade was beneficial for consumers of Western goods because those now became more affordable, but at the same time producers of Hungarian goods were no longer shielded from foreign competition through import tariffs. This had especially dire consequences for farmers, who had just reasserted their ownership over land, domestic animals, and machinery. The reason is that western Europe already had such an oversupply of food that it had been paying its farmers to limit their output. Clearly, the last thing Western farmers needed was cheap competition from eastern Europe. That is why the condition on which they allowed Hungary to enter the European Union was that Hungary also limit its output. The key agricultural products for which they implemented quotas were dairy, sugar, beef, and grain. There were no quotas for garden vegetables and fruits. The quotas were determined in such a way that Hungary could not end up with much of a surplus—above its domestic consumption—to export. Meeting such quotas required, for example, that farmers who had previously raised cattle for dairy or meat now had to shift to new produce. This created a hardship, because these new investments (in technology, seeds, storage facilities, and the like) could only be made by taking out loans, but these were hard to get since the new farmers had no credit history, nor much collateral, nor the required business expertise to convince banks of the soundness of their plans. Nevertheless, provided that Hungary did not exceed its production quotas and could thus export food to EU markets, it was still at an economic advantage because its labor costs were considerably lower than those of western European farmers.

What eliminated even this advantage was the imposition of new standards. Some of these standards had to do with quality (such as how knobby carrots could be, how big apples should be), some with environmental safety (such as the type of pesticides used), others with hygiene (such as the requirement that animals can be slaughtered only in rooms that are tiled wall to wall), and yet others with animal rights (such as that animals had to be sedated before slaughter). Some of these are imposed by the European Union itself, such as the food hygienic standard, HACCP,[3] or EC Regulation 2257/94, which required that all bananas sold in the EU be at least fourteen centimeters in length and be "free of abnormal curvature." Bananas that were too short or too bent could only be sold in lower quality categories that fetched lower prices.[4] Others are designed and imposed by corporations, such as food processing and retail chains or NGOs, such as the Sustainable Forestry Initiative or the Marine Stewardship Council, both of which certify that producers, processors, and retailers source their products from sustainable forests and fisheries, respectively. What is important to note about these divergent standards is that they all have to do with how humans engage the nonhuman world, that is, they profoundly affect materiality. Changing the materiality of production, storage, and retail, of course, also requires new investments, and these tended to create new economic uncertainties and dependencies for Hungarian producers.

Two circumstances were supposed to ease such hardships. One was the allocation of the farm subsidies that had been in place in western Europe for decades.[5] As my interviews with farmers and their associations revealed on the eve of Hungary's joining the EU in 2004, applying for and then documenting the use of such funds requires a certain know-how that they did not have, and as a result, most could not take advantage of these subsidies. Another way the European Union protects domestic producers from competition is the elaborate legal framework by which producers of traditional food and drink, especially those from regions famous for such commodities, could claim an exclusive right to use the name or geographical designation to guarantee the authenticity and alleged highest quality of the product in question. The legal regimes of "protected designations of origin" (PDO) and "protected geographical indications" (PGI) reserve the right to use these quasi-brand names for products that are certifiably from that particular geographic location and/or are produced according to strictly defined rules, and embodying regional cultural know-how and traditions, as is the case with the label "Traditional Specialty Guaranteed" (TSG). Parmesan cheese, for example, enjoys the EU's PDO label as "Parmigiano-Reggiano," that is, from the region near Parma and Reggio Emilia, Italy.

While Hungarian farmers, their associations, and officials in the agricultural ministry wanted to take advantage of these EU-sanctioned certificates and quickly initiated the process for securing such protections for domestic farmers, the circle of products that can receive them is quite limited, so the vast majority of farmers could not claim such exceptions. Hungary, for example, received PDO designations for the paprika of Szeged and Kalocsa, for the onion of Makó, for the spicy horseradish of Hajdúság, and for camomile from the Alföld (Great Plains). It received PGI for a few brands of sausage and salami but currently has no TSG designations (European Commission Directorate-General for Agricultural and Rural Development, 2012). These legal categories can apply only to regional or local specialties and not national ones, which further restricts the kinds of products and thus the circle of farmers and food processors that can benefit from them.

In short, after accession most Hungarian farmers found themselves facing shrinking markets, increasing regulation via standards, and limited protection from the world market. In this environment, there were only a handful of commodities through which the country could retain or increase its market share. Not surprisingly, such commodities were also those that could be claimed to embody Hungarian national tradition and local or regional know-how. I will attend to two such goods: paprika and foie gras.

THE 2004 PAPRIKA BAN

Paprika is the key spice used in Hungarian cuisine, and Hungarian paprika is probably the best-known export product of the country. Paprika is essentially dried and finely ground red peppers, whether mild or hot. Because of its unique taste as well as its image as old, authentic, and traditional, it has been more expensive than spice peppers from elsewhere. This difference between the price of Hungarian paprika and other paprika is what we call "value-added." Large retailers, such as those in Germany, however, tried to increase their profit margins by changing the materiality of the product they sell as Hungarian paprika. They mixed Hungarian paprika with paprika from other sources, but they still sold the resulting product at the higher price. Until Hungary joined the European Union, there had been an import duty on imported spice peppers, which made them expensive relative to Hungarian paprika. When on May 1, 2004, this duty went from 94 percent to a 5 percent rate overnight, Hungarian paprika-processing factories could suddenly afford to buy imported peppers, which made it possible for them to reap the same economic benefits their German counterparts had been enjoying for many years from mixing paprika from different sources.

Had it not been for the nonhuman world, no one would have known that the famous Szeged and Kalocsa paprika sold all over the world as a Hungarian product was actually only partly Hungarian. But, as in many other cases, things bit back. To be precise, a fungus bit back. In October 2004—that is, within five months of EU accession—Hungarian health authorities found a carcinogenic mycotoxin in various paprika products.[6] The toxin they found was aflatoxin B1, which is produced by mold. The concentration was as much as sixteen times higher than the threshold permitted by the European Union (5mg/kg). To extend the testing to all products containing paprika, their sale was banned. The testing and thus the ban lasted three days, during which ÁNTSZ—the chief Hungarian public health authority—gradually released the list of products found to be safe. Ultimately, forty-eight products tested positive for contamination, though it is not clear how many of these were legally toxic as well, that is, above the EU limits, the sale of which would thus constitute a criminal act. Aflatoxin, which in public discourse had been primarily linked to repeated EU bans on African or Brazilian nuts, can only grow in peppers that are produced in Mediterranean or tropical climates. Indeed, the Hungarian paprika processors had to admit they had added Brazilian and Spanish spice peppers to paprika from domestic sources.

THE EUROPEAN UNION AS A TRANSNATIONAL SOCIO-MATERIAL ASSEMBLAGE

The importance of materiality in this case, however, is not limited to betraying hidden human intentions. Equally important is the role nonhuman agents, plants and fungi, played in creating a particular experience of globalization, or in this case, Europeanization, and to understand this we must reveal their nonlocal and transnational character. I suggest therefore that we view the new European Union not simply as an economic or political arrangement, that is, as a purely social entity, but as a hybrid one: a particular assemblage of humans and nonhumans. Relying on Latour (2005), and Ong and Collier (2005), I call this hybrid arrangement an assemblage rather than an institution to signal that this whole is not entirely intentional or strategic.

The European Union prior to Hungary's entrance implemented a particular set of practices by which certain undesirable nonhuman actors could be kept under control. For example, when peppers crossed its borders, most likely at the Rotterdam port, food safety agencies tested these peppers for a variety of harmful substances. One of these was ochratoxin. If the import product tested positive, that is, proved to contain contaminants above a certain concentration, they denied entry to it. However, they were not required, or in fact allowed, to test for aflatoxin. They tested other products, such as peanuts, for aflatoxin but not peppers. The reason for this is most likely that, unlike Hungarians, western Europeans do not consume enough paprika for aflatoxin to be considered a serious threat to public health. Another reason could be that, unlike for Hungary, paprika was not a significant source of economic gain for these countries, so spending money on testing was unjustified in monetary terms. When Hungary joined the European Union, it also eliminated its customs borders vis-à-vis other EU member states, so that national authorities and customs officials no longer checked people and goods entering the country. This meant that once a product was within the European Union, it was, legally speaking, in Hungary as well. Prior to accession Hungarian authorities tested imported peppers for aflatoxin, and thus could effectively protect the population from this mycotoxin. After May 1, 2004, however, there was no longer such a test in place at the national border, and since aflatoxin was not on the list of tests to be performed at the EU borders (the port of Rotterdam), spice peppers contaminated with aflatoxin could enter Hungary and reach grocery stores unimpeded. To sum it up: Hungary didn't simply join the European Union as a purely social supranational actor but it entered into the EU's specific socio-material assemblage as well. By opening the doors to cheap peppers, it also allowed a fungus to enter, and this single material event had social consequences that would not have occurred had entering the European Union simply been a matter of humans and societies.

What were these consequences? First of all, without the discovery of contamination, paprika processors would have continued mixing peppers. Before the scandal, these processors tried to convince Hungarian paprika producers (farmers) to lower their prices by threatening them with buying less from them and more from external sources, whose prices, thanks to the radically lowered import duties, were now comparable or lower. Because of the scandal, however, the Hungarian regulatory agencies tightened rules on misrepresenting the geographical sources of a product, and this ultimately increased the leverage of Hungarian paprika producers vis-à-vis the processors.

Because of the scandal, some countries no longer accepted Hungarian laboratory test results in declaring a product safe, even though it was a Hungarian authority that found the contamination. Performing tests abroad, of course, increased the costs of exporting paprika to these countries, further eroding the gains Hungarians hoped to make from their agricultural exports.

Prior to the scandal Western buyers had attempted to buy the Szeged Paprika Company. They had been unsuccessful. The scandal, however, damaged the image and cheapened the assets of the company so that it could no longer resist such a takeover. In 2006 a competitor bought the company for two-thirds of what the company's assets were valued at (Vitéz 2006). This

competitor is fully Hungarian-owned, but some of my informants know this
company to act on behalf of a western food conglomeration.

Hungary requested that the European Food Safety Authority require aflatoxin tests on spice peppers at its customs borders, but this request was
turned down. If Hungary wanted to keep protecting itself from this toxin, it
was now on its own: it had to implement its own testing (that is, returning
to the pre-accession practice) at its own expense. In effect, while the scandal
weakened the power of the processors in relation to the producers within
Hungary, the European Union's power remained unshaken and its authority
uncontested in relation to Hungary. The paprika case thus made it clear for
all whose agricultural products deserved community-level and collectively
funded protection, and whose did not. This is important because the European Union advances and cherishes an image of itself as "capitalism with a
human face," that is, an economic order in which the market is curtailed in
the interest of the environment and of consumers, workers, and farmers.
This case, however, reveals that when it comes to protecting the agriculture
of a smaller and weaker country from pressures of ever-freer trade, naked
market interests prevail. To put this in another way, in the European Union,
economic and political goals, such as maintaining the market advantage of
the oldest and most powerful member states, can be achieved not only by
purely social, political, and legal measures such as quotas, but by changing or
leaving unchanged the socio-material assemblage that makes up this union.
This is what I call the materialization of politics.

Going even further, I argue that capitalism itself is far from being a simply social arrangement—such as the relationship between capitalists, who
own the means of production, and those who do not and therefore have to
sell their labor—or a purely social and economic logic, such as the logic of
supply and demand or the imperative of profit. It is also an arrangement that
entangles humans and nonhumans in particular ways.[7] Realizing a profit
requires not simply private ownership and relatively unfettered markets,
but also a certain way of organizing space and a certain way of using nonhumans. For example, one cannot own privately a certain brand of rice, unless
we materially separate the gene from the plant species, and say that we own
the gene. This separation in turn necessitates particular material practices,
such as using experts and devices with which one can identify genes or gene
sequences with some measure of regularity and reliability. One also cannot

hope to increase one's profit margins without technological innovation, but as we know, not all new materials and new technologies will have this effect, and even the same materials and technologies do not have the same effect unless they are coupled with social institutions in a particular way. It is, for example, in vain that a manufacturer in Gabon invests in faster trucks if the roads and highways are of low density and of relatively poor quality. Technological innovations result in monetary gain if only the socio-material assemblages they require for smooth and efficient functioning are in place.

Global capitalism is no different: it is now faced with the task of organizing or taking for granted socio-material assemblages that cross not just borders but also scales. A key question of power, especially under conditions of globalization, is how to scale up or scale down one's capacity to control humans and nonhumans. In my paprika case, we see how western European economies reproduced their local or national socio-material assemblages, that is, their practice of not testing for aflatoxins in spice peppers at the supranational—EU—level, and how Hungary, in contrast, was not able to carry out such an upscaling. This case refutes Actor Network Theory's argument that because maintaining power requires constant effort at managing humans, nonhumans, and their interaction, power always emerges anew. I agree with the first part of the ANT proponents' argument: there are usually so-called unintended consequences that arise from marrying humans with nonhumans, "things bite back," or the sheer complexity of these assemblages is what creates new challenges (Perrow 1984). However, humans and their collectives have also developed and routinized practices to minimize these "unintended consequences." Routinized practices are what institutions engage in. Institutions, however, also have another goal, and that is to preserve themselves. They do this by developing routinized practices that in addition to dealing with human and nonhuman contingencies also maintain or increase the institutions' power in society. For example, for a retail chain to minimize food safety risks in raw meat, it would be sufficient to demand that its suppliers slaughter animals in clean facilities—for example, by obliging them to wash all surfaces with a chlorine-based detergent three times a day. This requirement is based on its experience that such a routinized practice has proven sufficient to prevent contamination and that it is easily accomplished so employees do not need to figure out whether it is already time to do the cleaning or what solvent to use, thus reducing the possibility of error.

However, when this same corporation also demands that suppliers use its own brand of cleaning agent, it has insinuated itself just a little further into the world of the supplier, no matter how geographically distant that is. To put it another way, it has increased its power over the supplier. Of course suppliers can always leave this chain, but they are likely to find that they will have to implement a whole set of other technologies and monitoring systems required by the new chain, and thus they are better off staying with their previous business partner.

From this simplified, though not entirely hypothetical, example, one can see that, far from Latour's argument above, institutions' power can be and often is fossilized in the material world. It is also for this reason that we have to agree with Castree (2002), who in his critique of ANT demonstrated that certain actors have accumulated—or, I would add, upscaled—power, so that they do not have to fight this battle every day, or they do not do not have to start from scratch, so to speak. The reason why the European Union can refuse to change its testing practices, for example, is because it has suc cessfully upscaled and solidified its power, which was rooted in a particular socio-material assemblage.

THE 2008 BOYCOTT OF HUNGARIAN FOIE GRAS

Hungarian foie gras was subjected to an international boycott orchestrated by an Austrian animal rights organization in 2008.[8] This organization, called Vier Pfoten (Four Paws [FP]), joined the ranks of many celebrities and organizations in declaring foie gras, fattened goose or duck liver, an unethical product, because, they claim, it results from animal torture, primarily from force-feeding the birds. In the 1980s, animal rights activists started targeting foie gras production as inhumane, and the campaign grew wider and louder in the early 2000s.

Their campaign has been remarkably successful, partly because of the star quality of their spokespersons. The anti-foie gras campaign has enjoyed the support of such diverse actors as the pope, liberal NGOs, the Chicago City Council, Arnold Schwarzenegger, Roger Moore, and Dutch and British royalty, exemplifying the relative independence of such ethical projects from political and cultural identity. Today there is a ban on foie gras production in fourteen European countries and Israel.[9] Israel decided in 2003 to cease production, partly because of animal rights concerns, partly because of concerns about observing kosher principles, and, as Caro (2009) argues, former Israeli producers left for Hungary. Among these countries, only Israel had significant foie gras production before the ban (300 tons). France, in contrast, as the greatest producer of foie gras, managed to convince its consumers that no torture is involved, and even passed legislation in 2006 that claimed foie gras as part of French cultural heritage, which thus deserves protection;[10] what's more, in 2010 UNESCO added "the gastronomic meal of the French" to the world's "intangible cultural heritage" (UNESCO 2012).

Foie gras is one of a few agricultural products in which Hungary has managed to increase its market share since joining the European Union. This is in part because of the ban on production in Israel and elsewhere. But foie gras is not a new product in Hungary: it is part of traditional cuisine. For two hundred years Hungarians served foie gras around November 11, the feast day of Saint Márton, but these days it is a more common and less seasonal delicacy. While not an everyday item on the Hungarian menu, it is also not the luxury item it is considered to be in the United States and elsewhere. As an entrée it is rather expensive, but as an ingredient in other dishes or various pâtés, it is affordable and is eaten regularly.

At the time of the boycott, in 2008, Hungary was the second-largest producer of duck and goose liver (2,000 tons annually), after France, which produces an annual 16,000 tons, out of a world total that on the average is around 20,000 tons. However, Bulgaria's production was growing faster, so that by 2009 it was the second-largest producer with 2,200 tons.[11] Since the French consume almost all of their own goose and duck liver, Hungary is the biggest exporter of foie gras. In contrast to the French, who export a diverse array of luxury pâté products, Hungarians tend to export goose liver unprocessed. China has been steadily increasing its output as well. Its foie gras production was projected to reach an annual 1,000 tons by 2011.

Foie gras, like paprika, is not only a so-called *Hungaricum*—that is, a unique product of Hungarian tradition and know-how, in itself a fuzzy legal category that does not have a lot of tangible implications other than image building—but it now enjoys protection under the EU's PDO designation. Both scandals have to do with the materiality of these products, to be precise, with certain undesirable aspects of the production process. There are, however, also differences between the two products and thus the two cases. The source of the scandal in the paprika case was contamination, that is, it was a scandal about food safety, while in the case of foie gras, the source of outrage was primarily ethical.[12]

We usually readily admit that what is ethical is in the eye of the beholder, that different cultures disagree about what constitutes ethical behavior. We are, however, more reluctant to admit that ethical norms arise from certain material practices, and that therefore societies with different practices will disagree about what practice meets local ethical norms. Latour (2002) argued that certain bans, taboos, or ethical norms are put in place "to slow us down on our way" to a certain desired outcome. In other words, it is not so much the outcome of a certain practice, but rather the way and ease with which we get there that needs to be regulated by ethical surveillance. For example, in the case of anti-foie gras activists, it is not eating birds' liver in itself (the outcome) that is morally reprehensible, but rather the way in which we acquire this product. These activists therefore raise quite specific objections to the organization of materiality in foie gras production. Let me attend to these one by one.

First, the unique and highly coveted taste of fattened duck or goose liver results from the force-feeding of the birds, which the French call *gavage*. This practice enlarges the size and intensifies the flavor of the birds' livers. Geese and ducks possess a natural tendency to overeat in preparation for their fall migration, which is why foie gras was originally a seasonal product. With *gavage* this seasonality is avoided. Anti-foie gras activists argue that force-feeding causes pain, gagging, and injuries to the birds' esophagi, and that an enlarged liver is a symptom of a disease that causes suffering and untimely death.[13]

Second, because male ducklings are not fattenable, they are culled in an especially brutal way: as a clandestinely recorded video exposes, they are ground alive. The third issue concerns the conditions within the barns, more specifically overcrowding and metal bars in cage floors that cut into and injure the birds' legs. Finally, the activists also argue that the slaughtering technology is itself inhumane, because the birds are not always unconscious by the time they reach the killing station, even though European Union rules demand this.

Anti-foie gras activists condemn not the consumption of ducks or geese or their livers but the practices that currently yield foie gras.[14] An American anti-foie gras chef, for example, argued in a no less spectacular venue than Ted.com that it is possible to make foie gras without force-feeding and with an ecologically sustainable open ranch method that he encountered and personally tested in Spain (Barber 2008). It is therefore clear that what constitutes ethical foie gras is foie gras produced in a particular way.

When the anti-foie gras campaign reached Hungary it was assumed that foie gras was produced the same way it was in the countries where the boycott and movement had originated. This was not the case. In Hungary, only geese are fattened, and in their case both sexes are fattenable, thus there is no need to cull the male goslings. Hungarian feeding techniques are also different. In France, a rigid metal tube is used, while in Hungary, at the recommendation of the Veterinary Association (which functions both as a trade association and as an advisory agent) farmers use rubber tubes, a Hungarian innovation. This tube is much more flexible and if used properly prevents injury to the birds' esophagi. While I saw cages with metal bars for floors—to prevent the accumulation of feces in the cages—I also saw a barn in which the floor was made of cement and was covered with hay that was changed regularly. The animal rights organization FP, however, did not investigate the local practices and continued using the campaign video animal rights activists used elsewhere. On a Hungarian TV talk show, the leader of FP's campaign was ridiculed for not being able to tell the difference between a duck and a goose.

FP drew up a blacklist of Hungarian meat-processing plants that produced fattened poultry products[15] and started a media campaign, concentrating on Germany and Austria, where most Hungarian poultry is exported. As a result, several supermarket chains removed not only Hungarian foie gras but also all Hungarian poultry products from their shelves. According to industry representatives the damage has been tremendous: an estimated 4–4.5 billion forints (about 19 million USD) in lost exports. The target of the campaign was ultimately consumers in Germany and Austria, who were ideally to put pressure on Hungarian producers, primarily the biggest producer, Hungerit, by withholding their money. The Hungarian response to this campaign, from farmers, from Hungerit, from the government, and from consumers and citizens in general, has been unequivocally negative. Even a major Hungarian animal rights organization eventually condemned it.

MATERIALITY AND POLITICS

As in the paprika case, we see how the differences in existing socio-material assemblages between western Europe and Hungary are ignored to the detriment of the latter. In neither case did the authorities of the European Union step in to protect the interests of Hungarian farmers. As in the paprika case, it is quite likely that there are economic interests behind the respective scandals or behind the ways in which the scandal is resolved. Most Hungarian experts and government representatives I interviewed found it curious that FP did not target France, the biggest producer and consumer of foie gras, but picked a country where farmers had been politically weak. The main Hungarian competitor of Hungerit was Hunent, which fell under the sphere of interest of the German Wiesenhof, the world's largest processor of waterfowl. The fact that Pannon Lúd, a foie gras-producing subsidiary of Hunent, was missing from the first version of the blacklist gave rise to suspicions that FP was acting on behalf of this competitor and perhaps even funded by it.[16] FP representatives never explicitly denied this. To this day, Hungerit and the Hungarian Poultry Product Committee suspect an unsuccessful buyout attempt behind the Four Paws' campaign.

Such interests are of course very hard to find convincing evidence for, and I am well aware that corporations everywhere can use such accusations to discredit the movements or activists who bring environmental or ethical charges against them. My goal is not to provide excuses for them. What I do hope to have demonstrated is that calls for changing material practices or leaving them unchanged can be used to advance political or economic interests quite independently of what the goals of, for example, the animal rights activists are. While some economic or political objectives may be achievable by usual political, legal, or economic means, there is a distinct advantage to achieving them by manipulating materiality, or in what I call materializing politics. Technological or material changes in production can be seen as rational exigencies, as things that have to do only with technology and efficiency; as such, they are seen as apolitical. As mentioned above, Chandra Mukerji (2010) calls the capacity to exercise political control via manipulating the nonhuman world "logistical power." It is logistical because the logic that governs humans and their collectivities in such cases is seemingly nonhuman: it is not the explicit demand of a political authority but simply the consequence of applying or using a certain socio-material assemblage. In our foie gras case, weakening the market position of the Hungarian poultry industry is never stated as an explicit goal, and yet it may be the outcome simply by demanding that force-feeding be stopped. Material means simply tend to be less visible and thus harder to contest than plain political or economic means, such as implementing quotas or imposing tariffs on the exports of a particular country. As the foie gras case proves, however, it is possible to expose the social effects of such attempts, and thus it is possible to politicize materiality rather than going along with the currently dominant strategy in the EU, which is materializing politics. For every such case, however, there are many others that succeed in shielding the political intent or outcome of a particular socio-material assemblage, and at present we do not have a sufficiently nimble theoretical framework, or the scientific expertise, to study them.

What is particularly cumbersome in our approaches to materiality is that we have a very simplistic and even one-dimensional understanding of how nonhumans matter. Much of our debate has strived to answer the question of whether or not humans matter "once and for all" (Marres 2012). With Noortje Marres (2012), I suggest that we shift our discussion from "whether" to "how." The way and extent to which materiality matters depends on the ways in which nonhumans are inserted into human-nonhuman relationships, but to Marres, I would add that the scales at which these relationships operate also have a bearing on the "agency" of nonhumans. In the paprika case, a previously nationally scaled socio-material assemblage that is the Hungarian paprika industry aims to go transnational, but at that higher scale it runs up against an already existing or, better said, previously upscaled socio-material assemblage, the European Union, which allows a new nonhuman agent, a fungus, to enter it. In the foie gras case, an animal rights organization brings in ethical demands that emerged from the particular socio-material assemblage of foie gras production in France. It reduces ethics to particular aspects of this assemblage. For FP the key aspect of this assemblage is the interaction between the human (the farmer) and the nonhuman (the bird). The hand of the farmer seems to commit an act of violence pushing food down the throat of the bird. But as I witnessed in Kiskunfélegyháza, a small town in the Hungarian Great Plains, the hand of the farmer also pets and cuddles the bird before, during, and after the few seconds it takes for him to administer the batch of grains. The hand of the farmer also checks for signs of injury or disease regularly, diagnoses problems, and applies cure if necessary. I am not idealizing the goose farmer as some kind of a noble savage, I am simply pointing out that there is more to the human-bird interaction than what is implied in the propaganda materials of the anti-foie gras campaign, which, for good reasons, attends only to some aspects of this contact. We could also extend our gaze to outer reaches of this socio-material assemblage, namely the livelihoods that goose raising affords. The hand that interacts with the birds, to wit, is also a hand that shops, cooks, tidies, and in numerous other ways sustains a family and a community. To sever the few seconds of interaction between goose and farmer during feeding times from this larger assemblage is once again to make possible a certain social, legal, and political interpretation of foie gras production.

A key feature of the relationship between politics and materiality is which aspects of the socio-material assemblage are ignored and which are highlighted in order to yield the desired political results. Choosing how far and to what scale to follow the chains, or, better said, the entangled webs of human and nonhuman assemblages, is itself an act of political framing. Because issues of concern in global policy arenas, such as environmental protection, animal rights, and food safety, are made political exactly by framing global socio-material assemblages in particular ways, we as scholars also have to be explicit about how we frame "our" global. That is, we need to be up front about our reasons for following certain entanglements and not others, and about the political implications of our frames. But we should no longer exclude materiality from those frames.

NOTES

I am grateful to Rachel Harvey, Prakash Kumar, peer reviewers of this volume, and Rebecca Tolen of Indiana University Press for their constructive comments. I wish to express my thanks to the many people who, in conversations with me over the years, have greatly enhanced my understanding of the empirical and theoretical issues this chapter addresses: Diana Mincyte, Martha Lampland, Gyula Kasza, Jakob Klein, Harry West, Yuson Jung, Saskia Sassen, Andrew Szasz, Peter Jackson, Richard Wilk, Chandra Mukerji, Rebecca Gresh, Jose Peralta, Grant Shoffstall, Jeremiah Bohr, and my fellow Fellows from the Mellon-funded Framing the Global Project, especially Hilary Kahn. I also wish to thank for their valuable feedback audiences at the University of California at San Diego, New York University, the University of Michigan at Ann Arbor, University of Wisconsin at Madison, Johns Hopkins University, Illinois State University, Sheffield University, Bowdoin College, Central European University in Budapest, and the Unit for Criticism at the University of Illinois. Research on which this chapter is based was funded by the Focal Point Initiative of the University of Illinois' Graduate College (2009) and the Campus Research Board of the University of Illinois (2007).

 1. See Ulrich Beck (1992) on what is new about today's risks.

 2. Latour and other scholars associated with actor-network theory (ANT) initially used the metaphor of network to talk about the relationships between human and nonhuman

actors. Recently, however, most of these scholars have argued that network may not be the best concept and instead started using the term "socio-material assemblages" (see especially Latour 2005 and Law 2007). It is this concept, somewhat inflected by Deleuze's concept of assemblage (translated from the French *agencement*), that Aihwa Ong and Stephen Collier apply in their edited volume *Global Assemblages* (2005). Saskia Sassen's (2006) use of the concept of assemblage is quite different. Her task in *Territory, Authority, Rights: From Medieval to Global Assemblages* is to hold the sociological categories of nation and state fixed enough, through the categories of territory, authority, and rights, to demonstrate change and continuity while showing that the meaning of those bundles of functions and logics have also been transformed. So assemblages here are more about functions bundled together than about a more direct joining of human and nonhuman actors.

3. HACCP stands for the Hazard Analysis Critical Control Point system; it is a risk-management tool based on the identification and monitoring of critical points in food production and services where biological, chemical, or physical risks arise. Though designed by a United Nations organization, the Food and Agriculture Organization (FAO), the European Union required that all former Communist countries adopt it into their own national food legislation prior to accession. Note that existing members of the EU faced no such obligation.

4. This regulation was finally eliminated in 2009, but many similar ones on apples, citrus fruit, kiwi fruit, lettuces, peaches and nectarines, pears, strawberries, sweet peppers, table grapes, and tomatoes are still in place.

5. Such subsidies are part of the Common Agricultural Policy of the European Union, and of its legal predecessors, and their main goal was to protect farmers from low market prices whether domestically or internationally. They were also used as incentive to limit output, as mentioned, and more recently to encourage and reward farmers who implement environmentally more sustainable practices.

6. I have analyzed this case in greater detail in a book chapter (Gille 2009). I have also used this case as my key case study for a methodological model of transnationalizing ethnography in Gille (2012).

7. Michel Callon has written the most about the kinds of entanglements and disentanglements required for the market to function, ultimately arguing that there is no capitalism as such. See Callon (1998), Callon, Méadel, and Rabeharisoa (2002), and Barry and Slater (2002), but also see his critics, such as Miller (2002) and Mirowski and Nik-Khah (2007).

8. I have analyzed this case in greater detail in an article (Gille 2011).

9. According to Farm Sanctuary, Turkey also has a ban on force-feeding. http://www .nofoiegras.org/legal.html. Accessed March 28, 2012.

10. DeSoucey (2010) calls this a case of gastronationalism.

11. The U.S. produces 420 tons a year, and imports foie gras primarily from France and Canada.

12. Though, as I explained in the article mentioned, FP tried to convince consumers that not only was foie gras unethical but it was also unhealthy; after all, it argued, an enlarged liver is a sign of disease.

13. The video used in the campaign can be viewed on YouTube: http://www.youtube .com/watch?v=a7su4qPZKL8. The campaign's protest letter can be signed at https://www .secureconnect.at/4pfoten.org/protest/0801/index.php. Both accessed December 27, 2012.

14. PETA (People for the Ethical Treatment of Animals) is an exception. In 2009 PETA issued the "foie gras challenge," which will award $10,000 to anyone "that can produce a purely vegetarian faux foie gras comparable in taste and texture to the real thing" (Sun 2009).

15. Fattened poultry products include more than just foie gras: duck and goose breast and thighs are also among these delicacies.

16. Indeed, Wiesenhof had attempted to buy Hungerit a few months before FP's blacklist was published. Hungerit not only was and is a major foie gras producer in Hungary but it also owns the country's most high-tech poultry processing plant. Wiesenhof is part of a group that is not only the largest poultry processor in Germany but also operates that country's largest supermarket chain, but it has a much smaller share of fattened poultry production in Hungary. If Wiesenhof had crippled a key product line of Hungerit, it would have exerted significant control over the entire Hungarian poultry market.

REFERENCES

Barber, Dan. 2008. "Dan Barber's Foie Gras Parable." Talk at Taste3 conference, filmed July. TED video, 20:19. Posted November. http://www.ted.com/talks/lang/en/dan_barber_s _surprising_foie_gras_parable.html.

Barry, Andrew, and Don Slater. 2002. "Technology, Politics and the Market: An Interview with Michel Callon." *Economy and Society* 31(2): 285–306.

Beck, Ulrich. 1992. *Risk Society: Towards a New Modernity.* London: Sage.

Callon, Michel. 1998. *The Laws of the Markets.* Oxford: Oxford University Press.

Callon, Michel, Cécile Méadel, and Vololona Rabeharisoa. 2002. "The Economy of Qualities." *Economy and Society* 31(2): 194–217.

Caro, Mark. 2009. *The Foie Gras Wars: How a 5,000-Year-Old Delicacy Inspired the World's Fiercest Food Fight.* New York: Simon & Schuster.

Castells, Manuel. 1989. "Conclusion: The Reconstruction of Social Meaning in the Space of Flows." In *The Informational City: Information Technology, Economic Restructuring, and the Urban-Regional Process,* 348–53. Oxford, UK: Blackwell.

———. 1997. *The Information Age: Economy, Society and Culture.* 3 vols. Oxford, UK: Blackwell.

Castree, Noel. 2002. "False Antitheses? Marxism, Nature and Actor-Networks." *Antipode* 34: 119–48.

DeSoucey, Michaela. 2010. "Gastronationalism: Food Traditions and Authenticity Politics in the European Union." *American Sociological Review* 75(3): 432–55.

European Commission Directorate-General for Agricultural and Rural Development. 2012. DOOR (Database of Origin and Registration) (for HU—Hungary, PDI—Protected Designation of Origin). Accessed December 27. http://ec.europa.eu/agriculture/quality/door /list.html?recordStart=0&recordPerPage=10&recordEnd=10&sort.milestone=desc&filter .dossierNumber=&filter.comboName=&filterMin.milestone__mask=&filterMin .milestone=&filterMax.milestone__mask=&filterMax.milestone=&filter.country =HU&filter.category=&filter.type=PDO&filter.status=REGISTERED

Gille, Zsuzsa. 2009. "The Tale of the Toxic Paprika: The Hungarian Taste of Euro-Globalization." In *Food and Everyday Life in Postsocialist Eurasia,* ed. Melissa Caldwell, 97–128. Bloomington: Indiana University Press.

———. 2011. "The Hungarian Foie Gras Boycott: Struggles for Moral Sovereignty in Postsocialist Europe." *Eastern European Politics and Societies* 25: 114–28.

———. 2012. "Global Ethnography 2.0: Materializing the Transnational." In *Beyond Methodological Nationalism: Research Methodologies for Cross-Border Studies,* ed. Anna Amelina, Devrimsel D. Nergiz, Thomas Faist, and Nina Glick Schiller, 93–110. Oxford, UK: Routledge.

Harvey, David. 1990. *The Condition of Postmodernity: An Inquiry into the Origins of Cultural Change.* Oxford, UK: Blackwell.

Latour, Bruno. 1993a. *We Have Never Been Modern.* Trans. Catherine Porter. Cambridge, MA: Harvard University Press.

———. 1993b. *The Pasteurization of France.* Trans. Alan Sheridan and John Law. Cambridge, MA: Harvard University Press.

———. 2002. "Morality and Technology: The End of the Means." *Theory, Culture & Society* 19(5/6): 247–60.

———. 2005. *Reassembling the Social: An Introduction to Actor-Network Theory.* Oxford: Oxford University Press.

Law, John. 2007. "Actor Network Theory and Material Semiotics." Version of April 25, 2007; available at http://www.heterogeneities.net/publications/Law2007ANTandMaterialSemiotics.pdf (accessed May 18, 2007).

Marres, Noortje. 2012. *Material Participation: Technology, the Environment and Everyday Publics.* Basingstoke, UK: Palgrave Macmillan.

Miller, Daniel. 2002. "Turning Callon the Right Way Up." *Economy and Society* 31(2): 218–33.

Mirowski, Philip. E., and Eddie Nik-Khah. 2007. "Markets Made Flesh: Callon, Performativity, and a Problem in Science Studies, Augmented with Consideration of the FCC Auctions." In *Do Economists Make Markets? On the Performativity of Economic,* ed. Donald MacKenzie, Fabien Muniesa, and Lucia Siu, 190–224. Princeton, NJ: Princeton University Press.

Mitchell, Timothy. 2009. "Carbon Democracy." *Economy and Society* 38(3): 399–432.

Mukerji, Chandra. 2010. "The Territorial State as a Figured World of Power: Strategics, Logistics, and Impersonal Rule." *Sociological Theory* 28(4): 402–24.

Noble, David. F. 1984. *Forces of Production: A Social History of Machine Tool Automation.* New York: Alfred A. Knopf.

Ong, Aihwa, and Stephen J. Collier, eds. 2005. *Global Assemblages: Technology, Politics, and Ethics as Anthropological Problems.* Malden, MA: Blackwell Publishing.

Perrow, Charles. 1984. *Normal Accidents: Living with High-Risk Technologies.* New York: Basic Books.

Pickering, Andrew. 1995. *The Mangle of Practice: Time, Agency, and Science.* Chicago: University of Chicago Press.

Rudy, Alan. 2005. "On ANT and Relational Materialisms." *Capitalism, Nature, Socialism* 16(4): 109–25.

Sassen, Saskia. 2000. "Spatialities and Temporalities of the Global: Elements for a Theorization." *Public Culture* 12(1): 215–32.

———. 2006. *Territory, Authority, Rights: From Medieval to Global Assemblages.* Princeton, NJ: Princeton University Press.

Sun, Andrew. 2009. "Animal Rights Group Targets Restaurant Serving Up Foie Gras Burgers." *South China Morning Post,* April 28, 2.

Tenner, E. 1996. *Why Things Bite Back: Technology and the Revenge of Unintended Consequences.* New York: Alfred A. Knopf.

UNESCO (United Nations Educational, Scientific and Cultural Organization). 2012. Culture Sector. Intangible Cultural Heritage List. Accessed March 28, 2012. http://www.unesco.org/culture/ich/index.php?lg=en&pg=00011&RL=00437.

Vitéz, Ibolya F. 2006. "A fűszerpaprikaügy utóélete: porrá lett." [The afterlife of the paprika case: It became powder.] 2006/10 (March 8). http://hvg.hu/hvgfriss/2006.10/200610HVG Friss186/print.

Winner, Langdon. 1986. *The Whale and the Reactor: A Search for Limits in an Age of High Technology.* Chicago: University of Chicago Press.

Worster, Donald. 1985. *Rivers of Empire: Water, Aridity and the Growth of the American West.* New York: Pantheon.

9 — THE PARTICULAR

The Persistence of the Particular in the Global

RACHEL HARVEY

MOST DEFINITIONS OF "GLOBALIZATION" REFER TO THE GROWING ecological, social, institutional, and cultural connectedness of the world. Beyond this basic consensus, analyses of the core characteristics and implications of this increased interdependency diverge. Hyperglobalists proclaim the power of global processes to undermine local and national economies, polities, and culture. Others contend that such sweeping propositions are strong overstatements. One line of argument focuses on the resilience and continued distinctiveness of local and national sociocultural processes in the face of globalization. Building on this point, a third framework contends that the global is produced by the very processes and formations it is thought to overrun.[1] Together these three perspectives result in globalization being simultaneously identified as a contemporary condition, an unfolding process, an eventual endpoint, a universalizing trend, and multidimensional phenomena (Van Der Bly 2005). The existence of these strongly contrasting viewpoints, and the difficulty in resolving their differences, is not solely attributed to divergent theoretical points of departure, objects of study, methods, and data. Rather it is grounded in a critical dimension and dynamic—the particular.

The particular refers to the irreducible specificity of all sociocultural processes in terms of, at the very least, their time-space location (Wrong 2005). The objects and dynamics associated with globalization are not exempt from this condition. Processes seen to be the most globalized bear the imprint of the particular in their emergence and development, and those that appear to be spatially and temporally bounded can be deeply impacted by transnational linkages. By identifying the mutually constitutive relationship of the global-particular dynamic, it becomes possible to discern, trace, and analyze the multiple, and at times contradictory, interdependencies associated with globalization.

Recognizing the "persistence of the particular" condition poses the risk that the study of globalization will descend into the study of everything. The global can be everywhere and assume as many forms as there are different sociocultural processes scattered across time and space. To curtail the diffusion of the global into both everything and nothing, a conceptual rubric is proposed. Its three analytical vantage points capture different "moments" of the global-particular relationship. The first is the "global in the particular." It focuses on how individual sociocultural processes, to varying degrees and intensities, mediate and are transformed by transnational linkages. The global constitutes the particular, but in a way that does not dissolve the context-specific qualities of the latter. An example of this dynamic is local immigration policy "by proxy" (Varsanyi 2008). Some cities that intersect with transnational immigration flows have become sites for the enforcement and formulation of immigration policy, an area in which the United States government has traditionally held sole authority. While some urban areas have passed new laws, others have used existing city ordinances, such as those concerning trespassing and housing, as mechanisms for controlling day labor markets and their predominantly undocumented participants (Varsanyi 2008). In this example, spatially and temporally specific phenomena appear unchanged while simultaneously being constituted by global dynamics. It thus illustrates the "global in the particular" vantage point.

The second moment is the "particular in the global." It focuses on how the particular plays a critical role in the emergence and functioning of the global. Spatially and temporally specific dynamics do not simply mediate or become altered by globalization. Instead, the reach of the particular extends beyond its immediate context and becomes global in scope. Global financial flows, for instance, do not signify the "end of geography." Rather, they are produced and reproduced by networks of advanced producer services firms with their specialized labor, information, and cultures (Sassen 2001, 2006). Different nodes and expert networks, moreover, produce the interfaces of the legal and extralegal elements central to the functioning of the global economy (Nordstrom 2007). In each example specialized circuits are central to economic globalization. They thus capture the "particular in the global," or how globalized processes are dependent upon, and constituted by, particulars.

The final moment is the "global particular." It captures how the particulars producing and reproducing self-evidently global dynamics are concealed. In this guise the global appears to be a homogenizing and placeless force. The term and imagery of "global finance" provides an example. It tends to conjure images of a seamless hyperglobal web of transactions involving profit maximizing and disembedded actors (Agnes 2000). The possibility that these markets are not only located in particular locations, but deeply shaped by their context disappears. Yet, global financial markets, which are often seen to be the most disembedded, are socially, institutionally, and culturally differentiated (Agnes 2000; Cetina 2007; Cetina and Bruegger 2002; Ho 2009). Such diversity, moreover, is crucial to market functioning. Yet with the concept of "global finance," the particularities constituting the varied instantiations are concealed. The appearance of a global particular thus signals the need to recover the spatio-temporal specificity central to the emergence and functioning of globalized phenomena.

The conceptual rubric and its constituent moments are not designed to produce a better definition of globalization. Instead they are a point of departure that can be deployed by global studies to research and theorize globalization. To further illustrate the different global-particular instantiations, three case studies are used. Each represents an almost ideal-typical version of the vantage points. The first is a reactionary, rural social movement that appeared to be detached from global processes. Its constitution by multiple globalization-related dynamics, however, makes it a "global in the particular." The second is a pricing ritual that is more reminiscent of the Pax Britannica, the zenith of the nineteenth-century British Empire, than of a globalized financial market. Despite bearing deep contextual imprints, it actually constituted a transnational network of gold trading markets. It is, in other words, a "particular in the global." The final case study, the global foreign exchange market, resembles the abstract and seamless space often presumed to epitomize global financial markets. Yet its structure and daily operation were marked by temporal, spatial, and institutional specificities. The erasure of these elements made it a "global particular." Together these three phenomena illustrate the conceptual rubric and demonstrate the importance of the particular for capturing and conceptualizing global interdependencies.

THE PARTICULAR

The global-particular dynamic is a prevalent tension in three prominent approaches to globalization. "First wave" theorizing proclaimed that increasing interconnectedness created universal social, cultural, and institutional dynamics and forms (Hay and Marsh 2000; Martell 2007). These hyperglobalists argued, for instance, that the instantaneous transmission of capital through global electronic networks outside the nation-state, or the eradication of local cultures in the face of global media, was producing a compressed and homogenized space (Friedman 1999; O'Brien 1992). Identifying such trends made it possible to speak of a unified global market, civil society, culture, and governance system. In this approach, however, the particular lost its significance and disappeared. Not only did global dynamics exist outside of specific times, places, and sociocultural processes, but the latter were overcome by the former. The global, in other words, was without a particular.

Two groups of scholars responded to the hyperglobalist position by arguing for the durability of spatially and temporally specific sociocultural dynamics in an interconnected world. Drawing on this critique, the second of the three perspectives pointed to the autonomy of local, regional, and national processes and forms in the face of globalization (Hay and Marsh 2000; Martell 2007). Specific spatio-temporal phenomena could be outside, or unaffected by, global dynamics. The nation-state might be constrained, for instance, by global capital flows, but it was not powerless and remained an important, albeit altered, actor in domestic and international policy domains (Evans 1997; Hirst and Thompson 1995; Mann 1997; Weiss 1997).[2] Global forms and processes were also mediated by the various sociocultural milieus they encountered. This occurred when, for instance, globally circulating cultural forms, such as corporate brands or human rights discourses, were adapted to different institutional settings and acquired alternative meanings. They were, in other words, vernacularized (Merry 2006). Scholars working within this framework showed, to use the language of the conceptual rubric, that particulars could be detached from globalization. The global could also be mediated by the particular. The result was, at the very least, a vernacularization of the global or the continued resilience of spatio-temporally specific forms even if modified by transnational dynamics.

A third perspective built on the second, but emphasized how the particular did not simply withstand global dynamics: It was central in their emergence and functioning. Nation-states did not only retain a certain degree of autonomy, but often constructed and supported the very global processes that supposedly undermined their influence (Burn 2006; Helleiner 1995; Sassen 2006; Vogel 1996). The divergent pathways to neoliberalism showed not only the "embedded" nature of this ideology, but also that it was produced by spatio-temporally specific institutions (Brenner and Theodore 2002; Fourcade-Gourinchas and Babb 2002). The third approach thus asserted the resilience of spatio-temporally specific sociocultural processes, as well as showing how they were critical components in the emergence and operation of globalization. The global was, in other words, constituted by the particular.

While the three perspectives did not reference the global-particular tension, it is a common thread in their treatment of global dynamics. It is thus possible to partially map each perspective onto the conceptual rubric (table 9.1). The second framework loosely overlaps with two cells. The "particular without a global" references those phenomena that are either detached or minimally connected to global dynamics. This does not mean they are only "particulars." By signaling the limits to the global, it suggests that other sociocultural processes, such as the nation-state or the region, might be appropriate counterparts to the particular. The "global in the particular," on the other hand, captures how sociocultural processes rooted in specific times and places mediate or are shaped by global dynamics. At one level this results in the global being vernacularized. Yet in the case of the "global in the particular," the contextualizing of the global is contained. It remains within the bounds of the specific spatio-temporal setting and does not become global in scope. The global thus constitutes the particular, but not the other way around.

Table 9.1

	Global	Particular
Global	"Global Particular" Global without a particular *Hyperglobalist*	"Global in the Particular" Global constitutes the particular *Partial overlap with Second Framework*
Particular	"Particular in the Global" Particular constitutes the global *Third Framework*	"Particular without a Global" *Second Framework*

The third approach to globalization best aligns with the "particular in the global." This vantage point captures how national, regional, and subnational elements are critical in the creation, development, and operation of global dynamics. As a result, the reach of specific spatio-temporal dynamics becomes global. The processes and forms producing the global, however, are still contextually marked to varying degrees. In this manner the particular constitutes the global. The final vantage point, the "global particular," captures the hyperglobalist perspective. Here, the homogeneous and deterritorialized markets, cultures, civil society, and governance regimes are, like other global forms and dynamics, dependent upon the particular. The presence of such specificities is, however, "erased" so that "the global" appears to be detached from the specific temporal and spatial orders that originally gave rise to them. As a result, any effort to understand the globalized phenomena is truncated. Only by recapturing the presence of the particular is it possible to grasp the dynamics of a "global particular."

As an approach to global studies, the above conceptual rubric recognizes the importance of the global-particular tension and mobilizes it as a series of vantage points for understanding the transformative dynamics of globalization. It also can point to the limits of the global. As a result, the uneven and contingent characteristics of global processes can be recovered. To further elaborate on the rubric, three case studies will explore "the global in the particular," "the particular in the global," and the "global particular." While each represents an ideal-typical example of the distinctive moments in the conceptual rubric, they were not selected for this quality. Rather the global-particular vantage points emerged from my efforts to synthesize the different research projects; to make sense of their varied spatio-temporal specificities; and the implications of this diversity for understanding global dynamics.

THE GLOBAL IN THE PARTICULAR

My interest in globalization originally brought me to northeastern Nevada and its urban center, Elko. In the 1980s, Elko and its surrounding areas were the site of the largest gold rush in American history (Limerick 2000). The boom transformed the state of Nevada into one of the world's largest gold producers, and the area became intimately linked with, and dependent upon, the global financial markets trading physical gold and its "paper" derivatives. The extent and significance of this interconnectedness, and the area's relative economic independence from its closest regional cities (Reno, Nevada, and Salt Lake City, Utah), were revealed during the 2008 financial crisis.[3] As one of the "ground zeros" of the subprime financial crisis, Nevada's economy suffered and its unemployment rate hovered around 13 percent. Yet with gold prices being spurred higher by global economic uncertainty, the northeastern Nevada economy boomed, with Elko's unemployment rate averaging 6 percent. Given the area's position as a "hinterland" to the most important global cities, I expected to see "The Global" writ large across Elko and the region.

For every sign pointing to contemporary globalizing processes—such as the open pit gold mines or the immigrant labor from Mexico—there were phenomena that seemed detached from the global. Elko and its surrounding areas bore the imprint of a pioneering cowboy culture; cattle and sheep ranches homesteaded in the nineteenth century; and perhaps the most recognizable hallmark of the Nevada landscape, its casinos. It was within this context that I learned about a regional phenomenon that appeared to be, like much of the area, isolated from globalization: the Jarbidge Shovel Brigade. This conservative rural social movement and its struggle with the U.S. government over a remote dirt road appeared simply to be a continuation of the land disputes ubiquitous in the western United States, and, therefore, detached from the transnational processes coursing through the region. It was a particular without a global. Yet after living in Elko, attending events related to the social movement, familiarizing myself with the history of the region, and tracing the movement's development, I learned how incorrect this stance was.[4]

In 1995 a strong spring storm caused the Jarbidge River, located in Elko County, to overflow its banks and wash out the South Canyon Road running alongside it. The government agency, the United States Forest Service (USFS), managing this section of federal land, the Jarbidge Wilderness Area, made plans to reconstruct the road after conducting a preliminary environmental impact assessment. Local residents approved of this decision. Just as the report was released, however, a national conservation non-governmental organization (NGO), Trout Unlimited, challenged the ruling on the grounds that further scientific evidence was needed to demonstrate that reconstructing the road would not damage the habitat of the bull trout fish living in the Jarbidge River. In response to the NGO's objections, the USFS altered its initial plans and instead proposed installing a foot trail along the river. When the new plans were announced in 1999, many of the region's residents and local politicians were upset. In a state where 87 percent of the land is managed by the federal government, the decision was seen as yet another example of outside forces overriding local control.

Expressing their discontent with the altered plans, citizens of northeastern Nevada and the commissioners of Elko County both contested the federal government's right to make the decision. While the county officials began a legal battle in the court system over ownership and control of the road, the residents of the region engaged in various acts of civil disobedience. Showdowns with the federal government eventually garnered national attention in late 1999. In response a sawmill owner originated an effort to send 10,000 shovels to Elko County as a show of solidarity (see figure, page 190). For organizers and the supporters of Elko County and its citizens, the shovel, which became the movement's main symbol, expressed the hard, physical labor they valued. It also captured a conservationist vision of the environment which emphasized a productivist engagement and aesthetic view of nature oriented around the needs of humans. Nature was meant to be molded by humans, and the product of such interaction could result in the landscape's enhancement and beautification.

The 10,000 shovels arrived in Elko in January 2000, and took their place alongside a twenty-eight-foot-tall shovel on the courthouse lawn (see figure,

Shovels of Solidarity. Photo by Rachel Harvey.

page 191). A parade was held on the last Saturday in January to celebrate their
arrival. At this time, the mobilization became linked with discontent over
President Bill Clinton's Roadless Areas Initiative.[5] In the weeks following the
parade a social movement organization, the Jarbidge Shovel Brigade (JSB),
was created to organize a July 4 road reopening event. Despite tensions surrounding the legality of the event, and concerns about violence erupting
due to the presence of militia members and gun rights activists, the July 4
event was held. It resembled a picnic and culminated with the leveling of a
nine-hundred-foot portion of the road by hand. A large boulder used by the
USFS to block vehicular access to the road, which the protesters dubbed
"Liberty Rock," was removed. After the July 4 event the legal battles continued and, as of March 2013, were still unresolved.[6] Even though the fate of
the South Canyon Road remained uncertain, the Jarbidge Shovel Brigade's
involvement in the struggle lessened. They did not, however, completely
disappear. As the years passed the JSB was active in supporting other U.S.
rural residents' struggles with the federal government relating to resource

Giant shovel on the Elko County Courthouse lawn. Photo by Rachel Harvey.

use and environmental regulation impacting rural areas. They also inspired other movements to use similar tactics, such as the Klamath Bucket Brigade in Oregon and more recently a new "shovel brigade" in Tombstone, Arizona.

Any association with globalization appears to be absent from these actions. The Jarbidge Shovel Brigade was marked by a highly particularized historical and spatial legacy. It simply seemed to be a continuation of the ubiquitous land disputes in the rural western United States focusing on the use of, and access to, public lands and resources, such as the Sagebrush Rebellion.[7] Despite being part of this heritage, the JSB was also deeply implicated within, and a response to, three global processes. It was not a particular without a global. The globalization of food and fiber production lowered real prices for natural resources and, as a result, negatively impacted the livelihoods of Elko County residents dependent on farming and ranching. An indication of such hardship was that during the emergence and height of the JSB activities, principal farm operators with jobs unrelated to their agricultural duties increased from 81 to 89 percent between 1997 and 2002.[8] Cultural shifts related to the globalization of industrial production and the increasing importance of service sector employment in western U.S. economies were a second important factor. These economic transformations helped spark the rise of "ecologism" approaches (Mertig, Dunlap, and Morrison 2001) which valued nature for its own sake without reference to humans. With these changes the environmental politics of public lands shifted from a conservationist focus on resource management toward designing regulations that treated these lands as storehouses of environmental amenities, recreational playgrounds, or places for spiritual renewal (Sheridan 2007; Smutny and Takahashi 1999).

While the JSB was a reaction to these structural shifts, a third aspect linked the movement to globalization. Some participants and leaders viewed the protest activities as taking a stand against an emergent "New World Order." The exact contours of the "New World Order" were varied, but they revolved around fears that the United States was ceding its territorial, economic, political, and cultural sovereignty to transnational organizations. JSB participants and leaders critiqued the power of multinational corporations and "international bankers," but they were particularly focused on the role of the federal government in facilitating the ability of global processes to undermine U.S. material and cultural self-sufficiency. One concern was that the federal government was using public land as collateral for the debt owed to foreign countries and citizens. The participation of the federal government in creating "biodiversity corridors" and transnational agreements, such as the unratified Convention on Biological Diversity, were also seen as curtailing resource-based economic activities. In both of these instances certain JSB leaders and participants viewed the federal government as betraying and undermining the heritage and self-sufficiency of the United States. Thus, by participating in the JSB, protesters were taking a stand against globalization and their own economic, political, cultural, and territorial marginalization.

It is the critical role of global dynamics in a rather idiosyncratic social movement that makes the JSB a good example of the "global in the particular." Of the three case studies examined, it is perhaps the phenomenon that seems most detached from globalization. Unlike protests during the G-20 summit meetings and the Minuteman Project, designed to police the U.S.-Mexico border, the JSB appeared to be the antithesis of these self-evidently global examples of collective action. It did not operate across national boundaries and was not connected to social movements located outside the United States. Given its explicitly national focus on the federal government and U.S. environmental legislation, it appeared to simply be an extension of past struggles over the management of public lands. Despite bearing hallmarks specific to the region, however, it was deeply implicated in global dynamics. Not only was the JSB struggling against economic and cultural changes related to globalization, but for some it was identified as an opportunity to take a stand against such shifts. The movement thus both mediated and was constituted by global processes. These qualities make the JSB an almost ideal-typical example of the global in the particular.

THE PARTICULAR IN THE GLOBAL

While conducting my preliminary research on the JSB, it took only a small intellectual leap to reach the gold trading centers that established the prices determining the fate of northeastern Nevada's economies. Most of these markets took very familiar forms such as Chicago-style trading pits, or the individually negotiated, predominantly electronic, contracts traded by large financial institutions in the "over-the-counter" market. Amidst these transnational trading networks was a pricing ritual more reminiscent of the Pax Britannica than a modern global financial market. Much like the JSB, the

London Gold Fixing, as the auction was known, appeared to be a particular without a global. While constructing the history of the market from archival materials, interviews with past market participants, and an analysis of other primary and secondary sources, it quickly became evident that the auction was preserved for reasons other than nostalgia.[9] Rather, the London Gold Fixing established the world's most important gold pricing benchmark and was a critical element underpinning the transnational networks trading the precious metal. In this instance the global was dependent upon, and shaped by, the particular.

A round-the-world and round-the-clock (except on weekends) network of gold dealing centers represented a departure from the past. During the era of the Pax Britannica and the classical gold standard, London was the dominant gold trading center. Until the end of the 1800s, gold dealing in London was conducted through individually negotiated bilateral contracts, that is, it was an over-the-counter market. At the turn of the twentieth century over-the-counter dealing was joined by an auction in which all gold transactions were executed at a single price—what became known as the London Gold Fixing (GF).[10] In most cases, business in the London Gold Fixing took less than fifteen minutes. When the auction was not in session, transactions were conducted through bilateral contracts that were individually negotiated on the phone in the over-the-counter market. Since the late nineteenth century the term "London gold market" has referred to both the auction and the over-the-counter market.

During the twentieth century the dominance of the London gold market (LGM) was far from assured. It faced numerous challenges such as the decline of the British Empire and the First and Second World Wars. Factors such as the Bank of England's support and the cooperative ethos dominating the market assured that the LGM did not lose its significance (R. Harvey 2008). It remained at the core of the international financial system until the early 1970s, when gold was demonetized and national restrictions on trading the precious metal loosened. The liberalization of gold meant the LGM and the GF had to increasingly compete in the emerging network of precious metals trading centers. By the mid-1980s a global gold market had emerged in which trading no longer centered on London but was dispersed across multiple trading centers.

Despite these developments London was able to retain its position as one of the most important trading centers. Throughout this process the auction did not disappear, and despite transnational corporations becoming GF members, the practices that had emerged in the 1930s (R. Harvey 2012) did not change. At the conclusion of the twentieth century, representatives of the GF member firms still would make their way through the streets of London to the offices of N. M. Rothschild & Sons twice a day.[11] Once at the office, they would enter the wood-paneled "Gold Fixing Room" upon which paintings of the royal figures, for which N. M. Rothschild & Sons had provided financing, graced the walls. Just moments before the start of each meeting the five representatives from the bullion firms took their seats each at his own individual table. Resting on each participant's table were a telephone and a small Union Jack lying on its side. The telephones connected each representative to his trading room. The trading desks in each financial firm were linked, in turn, to their customers. In this manner, the GF was at the center of a network spanning the world like the tendrils of a spider web. Upon the commencement of trading, the representatives negotiated the price of gold based on their buy and sell orders. Unlike the rest of the trading day, they acted only as brokers and did not deal for their own account. If the process needed to be halted at any point, traders would raise their Union Jacks. Once the issue was resolved, the flag was laid on its side, and trading would proceed until a single price was determined at which the market cleared.

Even though the GF had a cloistered quality, the process was not closed. During the ritual, the different price levels tested and the final figure settled upon were transmitted electronically to trading rooms around the world. In this manner, the GF price was incorporated into the trading stream that continued while the GF was in session. Only moments after its dissemination, however, the GF price would be surpassed by a new figure. In an era of continually fluctuating prices and volatile markets, the GF represented, after all, only one price at one moment. Yet after trading moved on, the price produced by the auction continued to be used. Deals for large amounts of gold either directly referenced the GF price on a specific date or used an average price based on several of the auctions. It was also employed in the pricing of many complex gold derivatives contracts. The trust placed in this respected benchmark meant that the GF price represented a moment of fixity in the peripatetic markets of global finance. In this manner, a "particular" was an important component underpinning the functioning of the global gold market.

It is critical to note that the continued existence of the GF was not simply based on its ability to produce a price through a transparent process or because the auction simply worked well. Elements in the culture of the LGM also played an important role (R. Harvey 2008). The traders seemed to be aware, for instance, of the importance of rituals in bolstering the status or legitimacy of the GF. Participants recognized that there was a strong association between the price produced in the GF and its ritualistic procedures. In the decision to "not fix what was not broken," there was a cognizance that changing the GF might undermine the status of the auction. The recognition of the power of rituals was based, in part, on the importance attached to tradition. This was displayed in the early 1960s when N. M. Rothschild & Sons, which housed and chaired the GF, decided to replace its Victorian-era building. In the newly constructed offices, a room was designated as the "Gold Fixing Room." Along with being outfitted with a modern technological infrastructure, décor from the old building—including the wood paneling—was a central feature of the new room. The emphasis on tradition and an understanding of how ritual might serve a legitimizing function underlay the continued existence and operation of a "particular" that constituted the global gold market.

The story of the GF shares certain commonalities with the JSB case study. A phenomenon appearing to be detached from contemporary transnational connections was instead deeply intertwined with them. Despite such similarities, there is an important distinction that allows the GF to highlight a different aspect of the global-particular relationship. Unlike the JSB, the GF did not simply mediate the impact of globalizing dynamics. Rather, it actually shaped the contours of the global, and the reach of this particular became global in scope. It did so by producing a trusted benchmark that was used to price physical gold bars and derivative contracts. In addition, the preservation of the ritualistic elements of the GF was dependent, in part, upon the LGM culture. Together these reasons make the GF perhaps the ideal-typical "particular in the global."

GLOBAL PARTICULAR

Just as the gold mining in the northeastern Nevada region led me to the GF, the latter brought me to the global foreign exchange market.[12] Primary and secondary sources discussing the GF often emphasized the small and specialized quality of the LGM in comparison to the foreign exchange market.

As the largest and most liquid market in the global financial system, the "electronic herds" in the market were even portrayed as dwarfing the power of nation-states (Friedman 1999). With its supposed absence of particulars, the foreign exchange market appeared to epitomize the placeless market. It thus conformed to the hyperglobalist notions of the global. Yet this conception of the foreign exchange market was highly problematic. Instead, the global foreign exchange market was marked by important particulars that shaped its daily operation. Far from being an abstract space, it was characterized by temporal, spatial, and institutional concentration. The concealment of these particularities, however, makes this market the perfect example of a "global particular."

In the same period that the GF globalized, the foreign exchange (FX) market experienced a similar transformation. The end of the Bretton Woods international monetary system in the early 1970s yielded to a floating exchange rate regime. The resulting increased macroeconomic uncertainty, interest rate fluctuations, inflation, and the continued globalization of business produced new opportunities for speculation, profit, and, to a lesser degree, currency services for multinational corporations. Between 1977 and 1980 alone, daily turnover in the market grew from $5 billion to $100 billion. The further liberalization of financial markets in the early 1980s led to the development of a truly round-the-world, round-the-clock FX market. New currency derivatives and telecommunications developments, such as electronic dealing systems, led to even more dramatic growth in this over-the-counter market. In 1989 daily turnover was $650 billion, but it increased to $1.7 trillion in 1998, and $3.4 trillion in 2007 (Bank of International Settlements [BIS] 2004, 2010). The sheer magnitude of the market becomes even clearer when compared with the LGM, whose average daily turnover for 1998 and 2007 was $10.6 billion and $13.7 billion, respectively.[13] Given the contrast, it is perhaps little wonder that the FX market appears to be a global without a particular. Yet such a presupposition is problematic.

The round-the-world, round-the-clock aspect (except for weekends) would suggest that the FX market was characterized by an even and steady trading stream. This was, however, not the case. The FX market was marked by temporal specificities.[14] The worldwide trading week began quietly in Wellington, New Zealand, on Sunday night New York time. With the opening of Tokyo, the market would surge for several hours, but fall quiet in the early afternoon. There would be an uptick in trading around 3–4 PM in Tokyo when markets in Europe and London opened. Trading would continue at high levels until Hong Kong, Singapore, and Japan closed for the day. Dealing would become quiet once again until the opening of New York. It was here that the highest trading levels of the entire twenty-four-hour period occurred. As London closed, another quiet period would ensue until there was a spike in dealing as the Chicago currency markets wound down. At 4 PM EST the entire cycle would repeat itself when the New Zealand market began trading (or, if it was a Friday, the FX market would close for the weekend).

A spatial pattern can be detected in the trading day rhythms. The highest dealing periods coincide with the opening of particular markets or when trading in geographically dispersed markets overlap. Such trading ebbs and flows hint at spatial concentration in the FX market. Data compiled by the Bank of International Settlements (BIS) indicate this was not simply a faint trend. Since 1989 seven countries have accounted for at least 75.5 percent and as much as 79.4 percent of turnover in the FX market. In the same period trading in the United Kingdom and the United States alone increased from 41.6 percent in 1989 to 55 percent in 2010 (BIS 2001, 2004, 2007, 2010). While the BIS data are listed by country, such trading largely occurs in the main financial centers of each nation-state.

While the FX market is clearly characterized by temporal and spatial nodes, it does not necessarily follow that this leads to institutional concentration. Trading in each of the major financial centers could be characterized by many small firms. This is, however, not the case. In fact, between 1998 and 2010 institutional concentration in the FX market increased dramatically in each of the most important financial centers. In the seven top trading centers, the average number of banks accounting for 75 percent of FX turnover fell from eighteen to eight (BIS 2004, 2010). The degree of concentration is perhaps even more pronounced since in the same period the estimated daily turnover increased from $1.7 trillion to $3.9 trillion. Less than half as many firms accounted for over twice the level of daily turnover. If we further take into account that London and New York accounted on average for 45 percent of all turnover during this period, then the centrality of the market is even more pronounced. In fact, the movement of a trading desk from one city to another actually altered the trading distribution among the top financial centers (BIS 2001). Given the degree of concentration, it becomes possible for the social, cultural, and institutional arrangements constituting the FX market (Cetina 2007; J. Harvey 1993; Oberlechner 2004; Zaheer 1995) to have impacts that are global in scope (Cetina and Bruegger 2002).

Traditional understandings of the FX market treat it as a global without a particular. It thus appears to epitomize the seamless hyperglobal web attributed to all global financial markets. This image is, however, deceiving. The FX market instead is characterized by significant temporal, spatial, and institutional agglomerations. The dense nature of this most globalized market suggests, moreover, that it is highly dependent upon the particular for its emergence and daily functioning. The concealment of these qualities and their implications for understanding the FX market as a globalized entity make this case study a powerful instance of the "global particular."

FLUID MOMENTS

The three case studies are all, at one level, extreme examples. It is this quality that makes them ideal-typical instances of the different vantage points. The JSB showed how a movement that emerged from a specific dynamic in the rural western United States was both structured by, and became an explicit struggle against, globalization-related economic and cultural transformations. It was the confluence of such dynamics that made the JSB a perfect example of the "global in the particular." Unlike the JSB, the GF was not simply intertwined with global dynamics: it also constituted them. The GF became global in scope as its proceedings were followed by dealers around the world and its respected pricing benchmark was used worldwide in trading. For these reasons, the GF nicely represents the "particular in the global" moment. Finally, with its global electronic and banking networks spanning the globe, the FX market appeared to epitomize the hyperglobalist notion of globalization. Yet the data presented above indicated the strong degree to which the FX market was characterized by temporal, spatial, and institutional concentration. The contrast between the hyperglobalist vision and the structure of trading made the FX market an excellent illustration of the "global particular."

It is important to note that attention to the centrality of the particular in the global entails certain methodological presuppositions. Due to the diversity and uneven quality of transnational connections and their multi-scalar quality, some of the most critical dynamics are not easily detectable (Sassen 2006, 2007). Historical studies and ethnographies of the particular, both multi- and single-sited, are thus critical for discerning the contours of global-ization. In utilizing these approaches it becomes a question of what specific qualities of the particularities present in the field site, or historical narrative, are important for understanding globalization. Quantitative methods are also important for the study of globalization, but they must employ a multi-scalar approach (Sassen 2006, 2007). Data sets will then avoid the limits inherent in "methodological nationalism" or the assumption that the nation-state is the necessary unit of analysis (Amelina et al. 2012; Chernilo 2006). Whether qualitative or quantitative methods are utilized will depend on the research question being asked and the characteristics of the object of inquiry (Harvey and Reed 1996). It is only in combining the relative strengths of each method that the full power of the "persistence of the particular in the global" approach can be utilized in researching and theorizing globalization.

There is another crucial dimension to the conceptual rubric. It is a dy-namic system. Depending on the global-particular relationship they embody, different entities can be characterized by one or more vantage points. The alignment with a certain moment can, moreover, shift over time, resulting in phenomena transforming into another category. This dynamism is captured by the GF. In 2004, the chairman of the pricing ritual, N. M. Rothschild & Sons, decided to withdraw from the gold market. As a result the GF lost its home. Whereas in the past there had been a concerted effort to maintain the rituals of the auction, this time the decision was made to no longer have an in-person meeting. Rather, dealing would take place over the telephone. The wood-paneled room, the paintings, and the small Union Jacks all disap-peared. Chairmanship of the GF would now also rotate on a yearly basis. The pricing ritual became a placeless market in that participants needed only to inhabit a similar temporal moment. Besides indicating a shift in the LGM's culture (R. Harvey 2008), the new characteristics meant that the pricing ritual was perhaps closer to being a "global particular" than a "particular in the global." But as with any global particular, the spatio-temporal specificity did not fade. The GF was still a moment of fixity in continual, and global, price fluctuations. The shift also did not disturb the auction's role in global gold markets. It remained the legitimate global gold pricing benchmark. A ritualistic element, moreover, from its past was retained. Participants continued to use the word "flag" when they wanted to temporarily halt trading. While these elements did not disappear, as with any global particular the specificities were harder to detect.

Using the conceptual rubric to identify the relationship between an individual object of inquiry and global dynamics can lead to its occupying two different moments in the conceptual rubric. The JSB was a highly particularized phenomenon. Yet the critique of a New World Order employed by some movement leaders and supporters placed the JSB on the fringes of other reactionary anti-globalization movements, such as the Minuteman Project (Castells, Yazawa, and Koselyova 1995–1996; Castells 2004; Gallaher 2002). When the linkages or similarities in the stances toward globalization of the JSB and these other movements are identified, it is possible to understand how together they constitute "particulars in the global." In this instance, the global becomes the dispersed and not necessarily connected conservative and reactionary movements struggling against their globalization-related material, social, and cultural marginalization. In order to grasp this aspect of globalization, however, an initial excavation of the particular was required.

The conceptual rubric and its methodological presuppositions can be used to identify core characteristics and relationships of our increasingly interconnected ecological, social, cultural, and institutional world. It can reveal how transnational interdependencies shape and connect seemingly isolated forms and dynamics. Focusing on the importance of particular sociocultural processes in the emergence, development, and functioning of global forms recovers, moreover, the contingent and produced quality of globalization. Discerning how an object or process fits within the conceptual rubric is not, moreover, the sole province of either qualitative or quantitative methods. Rather, the research approach depends on the question being explored and the qualities of the phenomena being examined. Only by using a diversity of methodologies and employing a degree of fluidity in relation to the rubric is it possible to understand, map, and capture the transformative moments entailed in globalization.

NOTES

I would like to thank Hilary Kahn and Deborah Piston-Hatlen of the Center for the Study of Global Change; Janet Rabinowitch and Rebecca Tolen of Indiana University Press; Anne Griffiths, Faranak Miraftab, and the other Fellows of the Framing the Global Research and

Publication Project for their support and for fostering a vibrant intellectual environment for researching and theorizing globalization.

1. Hay and Marsh (2000) originally posited the idea that there were three waves of globalization theory. Martell (2007) delves further into this categorization and discusses the waves in more detail.

2. Spatial scales are socially and culturally constructed (Agnew 1994; Brenner 1999; Taylor 1994). They are not pre-given territorial entities.

3. "Elko, Nevada: Where the Recession Never Hit," by Richard B. Stolley. http://money.cnn.com/2009/08/17/news/economy/elko_gold_nevada.fortune/.

4. My interest in Elko began as preliminary research for a dissertation designed to explore the impact of globalization on this mining region. In the process of preparing for this study, I stumbled upon the Jarbidge Shovel Brigade, which, upon the encouragement of Professor Terry N. Clark, became the topic of my MA thesis. Data gathered on the social movement included content analysis of newspaper coverage; attending the July 4, 2000, road reopening celebration; living in Elko between October 2000 and March 2001; and analyzing oral histories housed in the library at the University of Nevada, Reno. While I ended up following the golden flows from the region to the London Gold Fixing, I have continued to follow the movement and update my data over the past decade.

5. President Clinton's Roadless Areas Initiative was a plan to provide protection for the 54 million acres of national forests that were considered to be roadless. Part of the conflict was over how to define a "roadless area."

6. *Elko Daily Free Press*, "Lawyers, Environmentalists, Continue Court Fight over Trout," March 11, 2013.

7. The Sagebrush Rebellion originated in Nevada during the 1970s, when the state assembly passed a law claiming Nevada's right to purchase the federally managed lands within its borders. Several other western states soon followed suit.

8. United States Agricultural Census, Various Years, "Table 1: County Summary Highlights." Available from http://www.agcensus.usda.gov. The figure increased dramatically in the 2007 census. At this time 94 percent of all primary operators spend time working in jobs not related to their farm.

9. The bulk of my research on the London Gold Fixing took place during a stay in London from October 2006 until May 2007. During this period I gathered materials from the Bank of England Archives; the Rothschild Archives, London; the HSBC Archives; the National Archives, UK; and the Manuscript Section of the Guildhall Library. Further archival sources were gathered at the Federal Reserve Bank of New York Archives during numerous visits during 2009–2010, when I was a post-doctoral research scholar with the Committee on Global Thought at Columbia University. The completion of the research was facilitated by an overseas dissertation research grant and the Markowitz Dissertation Fellowship.

10. London's bullion market also had a Silver Fixing that was established in the nineteenth century. Initially it appears that the GF took place within the Silver Fixing (R. Harvey 2012). Both of these markets are discrete Walrasian auctions.

11. Reflecting the significance of New York as a financial center, a second pricing ritual was added in March 1968. This occurred during a two-week closure that resulted from pressure to maintain the statutory price of gold ($35/ounce) as determined by the Bretton Woods monetary system. The events of March 1968 were a dramatic blow and signaled the end of the post–World War II financial order.

12. My research on the global foreign exchange was conducted between January 2011 and August 2012. It was part of the Center on Global Legal Transformation's Global Finance and Law Initiative, funded by the Institute for New Economic Thinking. For the initiative I explored the historical trajectories of two legal instruments in order to examine the role of law in the foreign exchange market. The completion of this project was greatly facilitated by Katharina Pistor, director of the Center for Legal Transformation, and member of the Committee on Global Thought.

13. The average daily turnover statistics were for the months of April in 1998 and 2007. This is the same month in which the Bank of International Settlements conducts its triennial survey. The London Bullion Market Association only began to publish statistics on turnover among the six clearing firms in 1996. The only other time statistics were regularly collected in the London gold market was during the 1930s, and this included only turnover in the GF.

14. This description is taken from Williams (2006).

REFERENCES

Agnes, Pierre. 2000. "The 'End of Geography' in Financial Services? Local Embeddedness and Territorialization in the Interest Rate Swaps Industry." *Economic Geography* 76(4): 347–66.

Agnew, John. 1994. "The Territorial Trap: The Geographical Assumptions of International Relations Theory." *Review of International Political Economy* 1(1): 53–80.

Amelina, Anna, Thomas Faist, Nina Glick Schiller, and Devrimsel Nergiz. 2012. "Methodological Predicaments of Cross-Border Studies." In *Beyond Methodological Nationalism,* ed. Anna Amelina, Devrimsel Nergiz, Thomas Faist, and Nina Glick Schiller, 1–19. New York: Routledge.

Bank of International Settlements (BIS). 2001. "Triennial Central Bank Survey of Foreign Exchange and Derivatives Market Activity." Basel: Bank of International Settlements.

———. 2004. "Triennial Central Bank Survey of Foreign Exchange and Derivatives Market Activity." Basel: Bank of International Settlements.

———. 2007. "Triennial Central Bank Survey of Foreign Exchange and Derivatives Market Activity." Basel: Bank of International Settlements.

———. 2010. "Triennial Central Bank Survey of Foreign Exchange and Derivatives Market Activity." Basel: Bank of International Settlements.

Brenner, Neil. 1999. "Beyond State Centrism? Space, Territoriality, and Geographical Scale in Globalization Studies." *Theory and Society* 28(1): 39–78.

Brenner, Neil, and Nik Theodore. 2002. "Cities and the Geographies of 'Actually Existing Neoliberalism.'" *Antipode* 34(3): 349–79.

Burn, Gary. 2006. *The Re-emergence of Global Finance.* Basingstoke, UK: Palgrave Macmillan.

Castells, Manuel. 2004. *The Power of Identity.* Malden, MA: Blackwell Publishing.

Castells, Manuel, Shujiro Yazawa, and Emma Kiselyova. 1995–1996. "Insurgents against the Global Order: A Comparative Analysis of the Zapatistas in Mexico, the American Militia, and Japan's AUM Shinrikyo." *Berkeley Journal of Sociology* 40: 21–59.

Cetina, Karin Knorr. 2007. "Global Markets as Global Conversations." *Text & Talk* 27(5–6): 705–34.

Cetina, Karin Knorr, and Urs Bruegger. 2002. "Global Microstructures: The Virtual Societies of Financial Markets." *American Journal of Sociology* 107(4): 905–50.

Chernilo, Daniel. 2006. "Social Theory's Methodological Nationalism: Myth and Reality."
     European Journal of Social Theory 9(1): 5–22.
Evans, Peter. 1997. "The Eclipse of the State? Reflections on Stateness in an Era of Globaliza-
     tion." *World Politics* 50: 62–87.
Fourcade-Gourinchas, Marion, and Sarah L. Babb. 2002. "The Rebirth of the Liberal Creed:
     Paths to Neoliberalism in Four Countries." *American Journal of Sociology* 108(3): 533–79.
Friedman, Thomas L. 1999. *The Lexus and the Olive Tree.* New York: Farrar, Straus, and
     Giroux.
Gallaher, Carolyn. 2002. "On the Fault Line: Race, Class, and the U.S. Patriot Movement."
     Cultural Studies 16(5): 673–703.
Harvey, David L., and Michael Reed. 1996. "Social Sciences as the Study of Complex Sys-
     tems." In *Chaos Theory in the Social Sciences,* ed. L. Douglas Kiel and Euel Elliott, 295–323.
     Ann Arbor: University of Michigan Press.
Harvey, John T. 1993. "The Institution of Foreign Exchange Trading." *Journal of Economic Is-
     sues* 27(3): 679–98.
Harvey, Rachel. 2008. "Duty to Firm and Market: The Subnational Constitution of a Global
     Finance Market, the London Gold Fixing." PhD diss., Department of Sociology, Univer-
     sity of Chicago. UMI Dissertation Publishing (2011).
———. 2012. "The Early Development of the London Gold Fixing." *Alchemist* 65: 3–6.
Hay, Colin, and David Marsh. 2000. "Introduction: Demystifying Globalization." In *Demysti-
     fying Globalization,* ed. Colin Hay and David Marsh, 1–17. New York: St. Martin's Press.
Helleiner, Eric. 1995. "Explaining the Globalization of Financial Markets: Bringing States
     Back In." *Review of International Political Economy* 2: 315–41.
Hirst, Paul, and Grahame Thompson. 1995. "Globalization and the Future of the Nation
     State." *Economy and Society* 24(3): 408–42.
Ho, Karen. 2009. *Liquidated: An Ethnography of Wall Street.* Durham, NC: Duke University
     Press.
Limerick, Patricia Nelson. 2000. *Something in the Soil: Legacies and Reckonings in the New
     West.* New York: W.W. Norton.
Mann, Michael. 1997. "Has Globalization Ended the Rise of the Nation-State?" *Review of In-
     ternational Political Economy* 4: 472–96.
Martell, Luke. 2007. "The Third Wave in Globalization Theory." *International Studies Review*
     9: 173–96.
Merry, Sally Engle. 2006. "Transnational Human Rights and Local Activism: Mapping the
     Middle." *American Anthropologist* 108(1): 38–51.
Mertig, Angela G., Riley E. Dunlap, and Denton E. Morrison. 2001. "The Environmental
     Movement in the United States." In *Handbook of Environmental Sociology,* ed. Riley E.
     Dunlap and William Michelson. Westport, CT: Greenwood Press.
Nordstrom, Carolyn. 2007. *Global Outlaws: Crime, Money, and Power in the Contemporary
     World.* Berkeley: University of California Press.
Oberlechner, Thomas. 2004. *The Psychology of the Foreign Exchange Market.* West Sussex, UK:
     John Wiley & Sons.
O'Brien, Richard. 1992. *Global Financial Integration: The End of Geography.* London: Royal
     Institute of International Affairs.
Sassen, Saskia. 2001. *The Global City: London, New York, Tokyo.* Princeton, NJ: Princeton Uni-
     versity Press.

———. 2006. *Territory, Authority, Rights: From Medieval to Global Assemblages.* Princeton, NJ: Princeton University Press.

———. 2007. "Introduction: Deciphering the Global." In *Deciphering the Global: Its Scales, Spaces, and Subjects,* ed. Saskia Sassen, 1–18. New York: Routledge.

Sheridan, Thomas E. 2007. "Embattled Ranchers, Endangered Species, and Urban Sprawl: The Political Ecology of the New American West." *Annual Review of Anthropology* 36: 121–38.

Smutny, Gayla, and Lois M. Takahashi. 1999. "Economic Change and Environmental Conflict in the Western Mountain States of the U.S.A." *Environment and Planning A* 31(6): 979–95.

Taylor, Peter J. 1994. "The State as Container: Territoriality in the Modern World-System." *Progress in Human Geography* 19: 1–15.

Van Der Bly, Martha C. E. 2005. "Globalization: A Triumph of Ambiguity." *Current Sociology* 53(6): 875–93.

Varsanyi, Monica W. 2008. "Immigration Policing through the Backdoor: City Ordinances, the 'Right to the City,' and the Exclusion of Undocumented Laborers." *Urban Geography* 29(1): 29–52.

Vogel, Steven K. 1996. *Freer Markets, More Rules: Regulatory Reform in Advanced Industrial Countries.* Ithaca, NY: Cornell University Press.

Weiss, Linda. 1997. "Globalization and the Myth of the Powerless State." *New Left Review* 225: 3–27.

Williams, Robert G. 2006. *The Money Changers.* London: Zed Books.

Wrong, Dennis H. 2005. *The Persistence of the Particular.* New Brunswick, NJ: Transaction Publishers.

Zaheer, Srilata. 1995. "Circadian Rhythms: The Effects of Global Market Integration in the Currency Trading Industry." *Journal of International Business Studies* 26(4): 699–728.

10 – RIGHTS

The Rise of Rights and Nonprofit Organizations in East African Societies

ALEX PERULLO

WHILE THE CONCEPT OF RIGHTS HAS A LONG HISTORY IN LEGAL AND cultural thought, it has increasingly become a focus of contemporary global processes and movements. In East Africa (Tanzania, Kenya, and Uganda), community organizations, religious institutions, and individuals regularly debate the tensions of justice and injustice occurring in society. There are frequent workshops, conferences, public speeches, and parliamentary sessions about the scope of rights in contemporary societies. Radio shows, musical events, and newspaper articles consistently feature explanations of and clarifications about rights-based issues. Rarely does a week pass without a public event organized by a nonprofit organization to educate the public about civil society.

In Tanzania, for instance, rights-based conversations cover a variety of themes, including the rights of women to be represented in political conversation; the rights of patients and the need for equitable standards in health care; land rights, particularly for women who may be unaware of the laws meant to protect them in situations where their husbands die and in-laws claim ownership of the land (a common occurrence in many parts of Tanzania); the rights of animals and the prevention of animal cruelty; the rights of children in society and within their own families; and legal counsel on the prevention of gender violence.[1] The abundance of topics, organizations, and rights-based dialogue in East Africa presents one of the more significant transformations in the interactions occurring within the region and also between people in the region and other parts of the world.

This profusion of opportunities to claim and protect one's rights is a central aspect of larger cultural and political transitions occurring in African societies. Through an increased focus on neoliberal policies and a surge in transnational communication, people use rights-based language and actions to establish opportunities to protect and advance their interests. More specifically, the proliferation of debate about rights, as well as institutions meant to support those debates, such as nonprofit organizations, is in response to the growing need to formally communicate social justice issues to national and international audiences. Without the establishment of rights-based or ganizations, many individuals and groups lack the capabilities to push for more political and legal representation, or to establish options in attaining access to health care, land, education, citizenship, financial compensation, or other elements considered central to a person's "basic rights." States need to formally acknowledge their positions on rights in order to remain viable players in the global economy. In short, having the ability to use rights rhetoric is a distinct advantage to those who want to advance their interests whether in small rural communities or in cosmopolitan networks of international exchange.

The increased attention to rights globally is a response to several factors, including efforts to harmonize laws and policies. The universalization of rights laws and policies incorporates the development of institutions that attempt to standardize the development and implementation of rights throughout the world. The World Intellectual Property Organization (WIPO), which was created by the United Nations in 1967, aims to normalize development of international law dealing with intellectual property rights, including patents, trademarks, and copyrights. The World Health Organization (WHO), also an agency of the United Nations, aims to promote standards in health care worldwide. Margaret Chan, director-general of WHO, notes, "This world will never become a fair place all by itself. Fairness, especially in matters of health, comes only when equity is an explicit policy objective."[2] Through creating a universal notion of health, intellectual property, or many other forms of human rights, these institutions promote the notion that everyone can and should be guaranteed equalities that are essential to all humanity.

Even though many institutions attempt to standardize rights laws and policies, many individuals and communities encounter difficulties ensuring those rights. And, more importantly, many do not share the same understanding of the meaning of human rights as international institutions or state governments. The standardization of rights presupposes a universal interpretation of personhood. Many individuals, communities, and cultural groups interpret rights in culturally or politically specific ways. The ability to promote rights has become a central means to ensure the protection of a particular vision of personhood. To promote those visions, people can use the courts or attempt to pass legislation. They can hold protests or promote their ideas through music, the media, and popular culture. However, in East Africa, one of the most common means to protect, promote, or contest particular visions of personhood is through nonprofit organizations. Nonprofit organizations become the vehicle through which people promote their ideologies, knowledge, and belief systems. Nonprofits can be used to raise money, file lawsuits, lobby legislators, or organize protests, political campaigns, or community action. Rather than promote the standardization of rights, they sustain a diverse and contested interpretation of personhood located in various communities and groups.

My argument that rights dialogue is an increasingly important form of social and political interaction is not meant to suggest that more people's rights are being protected. Rather, the rights-based dialogue has proliferated through individuals, the media, global institutions, and governments to the point where it is a vital means for people, companies, institutions, and governments to engage with one another. Familiarity with the dialogue of rights is an important skill for people to have as they negotiate concerns about their own safety, health, and well-being. Yet, there are also many barriers to protecting rights given divergent conceptions of their meanings, as well as inequalities in people's ability to protect their interests. A drug company, for instance, can defend its interests in a patent, while health-care workers argue that those who are sick have the right to less expensive drugs. The ability to protect an invention and the right to protect the health of people are both considered foundational rights even if they may conflict with one another.[3]

Understanding tensions over rights and the formation of nonprofit organizations is central to conceptualizing power in social and economic relations between peoples around the globe. In particular, the shifting landscape of many contemporary societies from violent conflict to conflict over rights provides a means to comprehend contemporary global processes. Several scholars, most notably Steven Pinker (2011), have shown that violent conflict has steadily declined in the past century. Part of the decline is due to an increasing array of legal and security measures meant to protect people's basic rights. The rise of civil rights movements has further encouraged a decline in physical conflict in favor of contestations over the meaning of basic rights. While human rights can also be used to mask violence or promote one group's interest at the expense of others (Allen 2013), it remains a potent means to avoid physical conflict and promote a particular vision of justice, equality, or personhood.

The overall movement away from violence toward rights rhetoric emphasizes the notion that claiming power over the meaning of rights has become central to participating in broader debates about the contemporary human condition. If comprehending the global requires one to be attuned to the increasing interconnectedness of human interactions, then there needs to be a means to understand the ways people, communities, and nations negotiate those interactions. Claiming the right to something—a value, belief, idea, cultural norm, or economic policy—means carving out space within an increasingly interconnected world. The rhetoric of rights and, increasingly, the values attached to them force a position into public view and create the potential for situating oneself in a protected position. To say "I have the right to something" sets up boundaries—tangible or intangible—that can force others to take notice or counter those same rights. To interpret global exchanges of ideas, values, and cultural norms requires attention to the negotiation and protection of rights among individuals, communities, and governments around the world. The conflict between the harmonization of rights globally, particularly through the formation of international institutions, and the promotion of local interests through the creation of small-scale nonprofits proves to be one of the more engaging forms of cultural production occurring in contemporary East African societies.

PERIODIZATION OF RIGHTS

In a 2011 interview on the BBC, the British prime minister David Cameron stated that "we want to see countries that receive our aid adhering to proper human rights, and that includes how people treat gay and lesbian people." He continued by stating that the treatment of homosexuality in African countries can determine British aid policy.[4] The statement caused an uproar among leaders and pundits in several African countries, including Ghana, Malawi, and Uganda. For many, Cameron's statement went against the values and cultures of African peoples. Tanzania's minister for foreign affairs, Bernard Membe, stated: "Tanzania will never accept Cameron's proposal because we have our own moral values. Homosexuality is not part of our culture and we will never legalize it. . . . We are not ready to allow any rich nation to give us aid based on unacceptable conditions simply because we are poor."[5] Others referred to the comments as a way of encouraging "weird behaviors from the Western world."[6]

The debate between the United Kingdom and many African countries revolves around the issues of basic human rights: the right to be free from discrimination regardless of sexual orientation and the right to define boundaries of morality and human decency. It also deals with the right of governments to make decisions based on cultural judgments drawn from their own society. Even though British and Tanzanian citizens may disagree with the positions of their leaders, the comments serve to reify national positions to international audiences. Many people living in East Africa, for instance, may be less familiar with the diversity of opinions on gay rights in England, just as many in England may be unfamiliar with the nonprofit organizations and community leaders that attempt to fight for those gay rights in East Africa. Through the public comments about rights, there is a political tug-of-war over the meaning and justification of fairness, justice, and, more profoundly, morals and values. Rights are not politically or morally "neutral"; rather, they "privilege certain social groups, practices, and values, while marginalizing others" (Donnelly 2002, 230). To lay claim to certain rights is to legitimate a specific cultural position and, potentially, to illegitimate others.

Conflict over rights, such as occurred between the British prime minster and African leaders, is a common occurrence in relations between these two parts of the world. Since at least the nineteenth century, disagreements have emerged and reemerged over rights to land, resources, and possessions. It has also had a profound impact on conceptions of basic human rights, particularly aspects of freedom, equality, and dignity. Given the often contentious histories between the West and Africa, it is important to realize both the divergent perspectives on rights and the point where they become forcefully intertwined. In East Africa, the rhetoric over rights can be separated into periods based on major events, including colonization, independence, and post-independence reforms. This section examines these periods in order to show the historic contentiousness of rights and the rapid growth in rights dialogue that has emerged since the late 1980s. To begin, however, I need to briefly discuss the rise of rights in the West, which became the cultural tradition enforced in many African countries during colonialism.

Even though discussions about rights date at least from the time of Aristotle, the focus on issues of political rights significantly increased during the Enlightenment period. Rights in the Enlightenment were often described as distributed equally to everyone (Edmundson 2012, 23). There were natural rights where "moral law governs human beings even in a state of nature, prior to any social contract" (Feser 2012, 27). While the notion of rights for everyone was theoretically explored, in practice a great deal of inequality existed in the application of legal and political representation for all but a few in society. For instance, slavery was commonplace in pre-colonial Africa, as well as in Europe during part of the Enlightenment. Women could not vote, run for political office, or even attain economic autonomy (Mack 1984, 9). There was heavy taxation on the poor, and prisoners often had few civil protections. Natural rights, in practice, were often limited in scope and employed only in certain conditions and among certain populations. This is not to say that some did not argue for the universal presence of natural rights. Rather, it underlines the narrow application of rights to only a small segment of Western populations.

While there is no historical equivalent to the Enlightenment in Africa, studies that took place during the colonial period discuss historic conceptions of law and jurisprudence among local populations. Max Gluckman found that the Lozi of western Zambia (formerly Northern Rhodesia) explained their law as a body of rights and justice, which has existed since time immemorial (1967, 1). The concept of rights, along with justice and truth, was flexible and allowed judges to use rights to cover a wide range of meanings in legal cases. If someone failed in his responsibilities to others, such as the need to show generosity to people, then that person could lose other rights, which could be determined by the judges depending on the severity of the wrongdoing. Gluckman notes, "The flexible generality of these concepts enables the judges to bring almost any action under the rubric of right or duty, or to define anything done against the interests of another as a wrong or injury. It enables the concepts to be expanded to contain all the customs and values, both historic and emergent, of Lozi law" (ibid., 299). The flexibility of applying rights to different situations established a dynamic system of rules that could be shaped to fit each situation.

Other scholars documented records of court cases, legal proceedings, and organized forums for dealing with legal claims. The main concern of many of these legal proceedings was over land rights, inheritance, murder, witchcraft, treason, adultery, and other similar issues. In addition, the rights that were protected varied widely by community. Among many of Tanzania's ethnic groups, particularly pastoralists, land was communally held to allow various members of the community to graze cattle or other livestock (Tenga 1992, 14–17). In other communities, individual rights existed through distinct land interests, such as gardens, homes, and family property (Mwaikusa 1993, 146). Individual rights in these areas were important for inheritance, illegal trespassing, and the passing of land to family members. Even before colonialism, ownership practices shifted due to interaction with other groups, land scarcity, or economic factors (Dobson 1954, 81). This meant that populations living in what is now Tanzania, even before colonialism, did not share a single perspective on land tenure. Land was something that could be inherited, rented, borrowed, allocated, or shared (Malcolm 1953, 50–51).

The conceptions of law and rights promoted in the Enlightenment and among African populations came forcefully into contact during the colonial period. When colonialists arrived in East Africa, they promoted Enlightenment principles, particularly notions of liberalism. There was interest in encouraging free trade, fair labor, and Christian notions of rights and values. These were ideals held by a growing British middle class, which played a primary role in the colonization of East Africa; it was interested in eliminating slavery but also in expanding the potential for trade in goods such as ivory, tea, coffee, rubber, palm oils, and sisal (Iliffe 1979).

Along with the promotion of liberal ideals and free-market capitalism, however, there was also a strong belief that Africans themselves were incapa-

ble of self-determination and self-rule. While colonialists argued for freedom
for all people, they also made clear that African populations did not possess
the knowledge, skills, and, in particular, morals to adequately fulfill notions
of freedom. This perspective played significantly into the design of colonial
law and in the administration of the new territories. In contemplating the
role of colonial administration in African societies, the British district officer
based in Moshi, Tanganyika, in 1916, Theodore Morison, wrote:

> Should we override native customs, some of which are in conflict with our Western stan-
> dard of ethics? How should a District Officer regard witchcraft? How far should he support
> the father who marries off his daughter to the highest bidder? The gift of cows and goats
> which legalise a marriage comes perilously near the price of a slave. The missionary, of
> course, has no difficulty in answering these questions. These, he says, are pagan customs,
> his duty is to destroy them and substitute a higher law. He denounces polygamy, he insists
> upon covering nakedness and preaches the superior decency of clothes. . . . In theory the
> District Officer says that his policy is the sublimation of native custom so that it may
> approximate even more nearly to what we believe to be a higher standard (Morison 1933,
> 141–42)

Rather than acknowledge the varied and flexible forms of legal structures
in African territories, colonial administrators often viewed African peoples
in essentialized ways, and local policies, values, and morals were dismissed.
The establishment of morality and law in the new colonies or protectorates
came from external forces that obfuscated local traditions and practices. In
addition, it attempted to create static and bounded notions of rights for entire
colonies, a practice that remained in place for much of the colonial period.

Changes in rights and self-determination emerged with the formation of
the United Nations and the Universal Declaration of Human Rights (UDHR)
during the 1940s. Bonny Ibhawoh writes: "The UDHR was significant in the
global anti-colonial movements of the post-war period and, specifically, the
emergence of independent states in Africa because it reinforced the rights of
self-determination" (2012, 719). Many African independence leaders articulated the move toward self-determination and self-rule through promoting
rights ideals found in the UDHR. It was a means to embrace the language
of the West in order to undermine the policies and practices of colonial rule.

Once independence arrived, the UDHR remained central to the design of
state policies, constitutions, and legal structures. After independence in Tanzania, for instance, Julius Nyerere promoted the Arusha Declaration, a state
policy document. One of the primary objectives of the Arusha Declaration
was to "safeguard the inherent dignity of the individual in accordance with

the Universal Declaration of Human Rights." In Kenya, the Bill of Rights in the independence constitution were largely drawn from the UDHR. Similar provisions were made in all East African countries during the 1960s and 1970s.

The attention to the ideals of the UDHR in the creation of constitutions and policies in East Africa did not mean these governments guaranteed the rights of the UDHR. Many exceptions were made that limited the potential for ensuring or guaranteeing rights for all citizens. James Orengo, the controversial Kenyan lawyer and former presidential candidate, states: "We borrowed the Bill of Rights from the Universal Declaration of Human Rights but added in all the exceptions to rights that were common in Stalinist countries. In short, we now have a presidency without checks, a parliament without teeth, and a Bill of Rights that reads more like a Bill of Exceptions rather than Rights."[7] While Orengo's statement is an overgeneralization, there were many instances in which the rights, borrowed from the UDHR, were ignored, reinterpreted, or redesigned. In Tanzania, for instance, the movement toward African socialism meant that there was a profound rethinking of morality and values in terms of traditional African societies. The notion of community, including the sharing of community land, resources, and knowledge, had precedent over any sense of individual claim to those same elements. The UDHR, however, is a decidedly individual-rights document. Relying on the UDHR only meant that nations borrowed the language of the global standardization of rights. In practice, many exceptions and flexible interpretations emerged to accommodate the political landscape of post-independence Africa.

The 1970s and 1980s brought a dramatic decline in the effectiveness of African governments to provide for their citizens. While several countries were able to operate stable economies during the 1960s, the decline in commodities markets, the rise in oil prices, corruption, and increasing restrictions brought on by authoritarian rule made the ensuing decades more difficult for independent countries on the continent. Zambia's economy, for instance, collapsed when the price of copper fell and the cost of oil rose. Tanzania was unable to stabilize its economy after fighting a war against Idi Amin in Uganda. Cold War activities also limited the capabilities and trade potential of countries that had previously moved toward socialism, including Tanzania, Ghana, Mozambique, and the Democratic Republic of the Congo (formerly Zaire). In many situations, the decline in the effectiveness of the government brought protests, strikes, wars, and coups d'état. Between 1956 and 2001, there were 139 reported coups d'état in sub-Saharan Africa, 80 of which were successful (McGowan 2003). The economies of all East African countries had stopped growing by 1984, when the economic crises peaked for the region (Arrighi 2002, 13).

The decline in many African economies meant that governments needed to turn toward Western institutions for support. Referred to as the Washington Consensus, institutions such as the World Bank and the International Monetary Fund (IMF) began a series of structural adjustment reforms in order to alleviate a specific country's debt, liberalize the pricing and marketing of commodities, expand the private sector, improve tax collection, and reduce government spending.[8] These efforts were meant to alleviate the debt burdens and promote growth through spurring trade. For many countries, however, the impact of these changes was an even more drastic decline in economic growth and a significant rise in corruption. In addition, it meant that African countries needed to move away from self-determination and to harmonize laws and policies with those of the West. This included sweeping changes to freedom of speech, freedom of the press, and multi-party elections. It also meant the passage of legislation meant to ensure the protection of basic rights.[9]

The decline of state services during the 1970s and 1980s meant that more people living in Africa had to search for ways to protect themselves and ensure their own social security. There was a significant shortage of basic goods, such as soap, clothes, and oil, due to the governments' lack of funds to import materials from overseas. Schools became too expensive for many individuals, especially given the cost of basic necessities, such as books and uniforms. Many countries experienced food shortages at some time during the 1980s. While the governments moved toward decentralization, people needed to be more creative in fending for themselves and finding security. This included illegal strategies, such as bribery and collusion, as well as legal strategies, such as building networks with well-connected individuals inside and outside of the country (Perullo 2011).

During this period of transition and instability, dialogue about rights became a central means to draw attention to injustices occurring on the continent. Discussion about universal human rights came from many places, including conversations among Africans living in the diaspora and on the continent about freedoms and opportunities in the West. Because many Africans were being educated in the West, there was a growing interest in establishing codes of conduct, rules, and ideology associated with Western governments. Many artists and musicians criticized government policies and ideas. Remmy Ongala, the Tanzanian musician, sang "Mnyonge Hana Haki" (The Poor Have No Rights) as a critique of the failure of government policies to ensure the rights of the poor. Local community associations mobilized and gained confidence in voicing concerns about problems they encountered.

The proliferation of dialogues about rights, including both those interpreted as universal rights for all of humanity and those enshrined in African traditions and customs, created an explosion of interest in creating governmental and community-based organizations. The language of rights allowed people to gain support from international donors, charities, and religious organizations. If individuals embraced the proper rights language, there was a sense that they could leverage support from any number of international institutions. And when it was not possible to find international support, small-scale community groups could fight for social justice locally in order to gain recognition. States even sought ways to appease international lenders by passing rights laws, while also advancing country-specific interests in adapting the interpretation of those laws. The tension over laying claim to and defining the meaning of rights became a central means to push a specific worldview and protect one's own interests.

GENERATIONS OF RIGHTS

Human rights scholars often divide rights into three generations: classical rights (first generation), welfare or socioeconomic rights (second generation), and peoples', solidarity, or developmental rights (third generation). First-generation rights focus on liberty and the ability to live securely within a society. Second-generation rights include a variety of rights related to economic, cultural, and social issues. Whereas first-generation rights focus more on the individual—an individual's right to live without interference from the government—the second generation fosters collective or group rights. These rights include the right to live without discrimination, to organize unions, to earn enough to sustain an adequate standard of living, to have rest and leisure, to participate in cultural life, and to receive an education. It also includes the ability to promote and protect intellectual property rights.

Finally, the third generation of rights, which is the most contested, focuses on the actions and behaviors of everyone in society, including the state and individuals. It includes the right to development, peace, and a healthy environment. The right to a healthy environment promotes the idea that people, companies, and governments should not negatively impact local ecosystems. Cultural heritage may also be considered a third-generation right where the traditions, customs, and beliefs of a population are widely supported and protected. In addition, there is a strong sense that third-generation rights apply most significantly to indigenous populations. The United Nations Declaration on the Rights of Indigenous Peoples, for instance, promotes indigenous peoples' rights to self-determination, which includes the right to freely determine their political status, as well as their economic, social, and cultural development. In other words, the declaration opens up the potential for alternative forms of justice and law even within an established nation-state.

Viewing the question of rights through these categories is useful for several reasons. First, it shows an important expansion in the rights dialogue that emerged in the post–World War II period. Second-generation rights were most significantly introduced in the UDHR, as well as postcolonial constitutions and the International Covenant on Economic, Social, and Cultural Rights, all documents that appeared after 1945. The growth in interest of third-generation rights has been more recent, and mirrors a growing impetus to protect indigenous populations and those living in less-developed countries. Collectively, the expanding rights dialogue has encouraged a movement toward universality in the adherence to and enforcement of moral attributes of persons since rights are often connected with cultural values and norms. State sovereignty became more tenuous as international organizations such as WIPO and WHO moved to encourage reforms to existing laws and practices, as well as to educate local populations about the rights available to them. A proliferation of nonprofit organizations and charities also emerged around the world to promote particular interpretations of these rights. According to 2012 U.S. Internal Revenue Service (IRS) records, over five thousand nonprofits existed in the United States to work on rights issues in Africa. That growth was even greater in African countries.

A second reason to categorize rights is that there is a correlating interest by international organizations and governments in protecting those rights. This has played a significant role in shaping policies and agreements between nations. The more nations move toward harmonization of national legislation, the greater the effort to enforce those standards transnationally. In 2005, a United Nations summit meeting promoted the notion of responsibility to protect (R2P), which obligates outside nations to become involved if other nations are unable or unwilling to prevent gross violations of human rights in their jurisdictions (Forsythe 2012, 4–5). While the focus of R2P is on mass atrocities and crimes against humanity, it opens the possibility for increasing disciplinary action in situations where there is cultural or political disagreement over the coverage or circumstances of rights. If a less-developed nation is unable or unwilling to protect certain rights, can they face sanctions, decreased aid, or other problems? If so, does that mean that many nations lack sovereignty in terms of deciding the moral obligations of the state and its citizens?

The contestation over homosexuality is one example of the rising tensions over the harmonization of rights. Many other conflicts have occurred in the past decade within East Africa: over water rights, held by a community for generations, when ownership was suddenly shifted to a transnational company; over ownership in traditional culture, knowledge, and music, which was not clearly or well protected under Western intellectual property regimes; and over appropriate ways to penalize violations over rights. In Uganda, for instance, the Lord's Resistance Army (LRA) has committed mass atrocities in the northern part of the country for over twenty years. In the year 2000, the Uganda Amnesty Act provided amnesty for rebels who abandoned and renounced their crimes. Close to thirteen thousand rebels received amnesty, including some high-ranking figures in the LRA.[10] In addition, the International Criminal Court (ICC) indicted five LRA leaders. Problematically, many populations affected by the LRA do not agree either with the amnesty policy or with efforts to extradite leaders of the LRA. Instead, according to Albert Gomes-Mugumya, who works on conflict resolution issues in Uganda, many people, such as the Acholi of northern Uganda, favor traditional justice mechanisms, such as *mato oput*, which "promotes community reconciliation and reasserts lost dignity" (2010, 78). The ceremony involved in *mato oput* is a nonviolent means to repair conflict within a community and push for a process of healing. Neither the amnesty nor the ICC provides the same sense of healing that many people living in northern Uganda desire.

The more focus that is placed on protecting and harmonizing rights globally, the more likely tensions are to emerge between governments, communities, and individuals over the meaning, implementation, and enforcement of those rights. From the point of view of many people in East Africa, the universal harmonization of rights occurring in the neoliberal period mimics many characteristics of neocolonialism. If neoliberalism is a move toward creating open markets, free trade, privatization, and decentralization of governments, then the ability to shape and control the outcomes of national markets, courts, and social structures becomes critical to influencing the practices that take place within a country or region. The harmonization of rights can be thought of as a move toward shaping the outcomes of neoliberal reforms. Considering the strongest influence for harmonization comes from the West, these efforts not only impinge on a nation's sovereignty but also present a perceived sense that African countries are being forced to share the same ideals, values, and norms as the West. In his discussion about restricting aid to African countries that do not protect the rights of homosexuals, David Cameron stated, "I think these countries are all on a journey, and it is up to us to help them on that journey, and that is exactly what we do."

Cameron's rhetoric is similar to that of colonial administrators. It presupposes a form of international morality, which many African nations and, by default, many African people have yet to realize. The legal and historical scholar Brian Tierney writes, "Rights language did not grow up in the West because Western people are better or wiser than others; it is just that we have had a different history. There is at least a possibility that others may choose to profit from it" (1997, 347). The notion that Western countries have a purchase on morality has the same sense of elitism of the colonial and postcolonial periods. Yet, is there some accuracy to the point that the West has some purchase on morality? Or are alternatives presented in Africa also legitimate? In the case of the LRA, the Acholi's means of attaining social justice seems to offer an alternative to that of the ICC. In addition, it provides a means for the community to heal from the wounds created by the LRA. The issue here is that the language of rights need not be something controlled by the West within a system of international morality. Rather, the dialogue of rights needs to be flexible and dynamic in order for there to be a sense of establishing fairness and justice according to various communities. To privilege one sense of morality is also to privilege one sense of justice.

One of the outcomes of having expansive conceptions of rights law, particularly that of second- and third-generation rights, is that it creates the possibility for individuals, communities, and governments to claim indigenous rights as unique and worth protecting. Through using the media, public dialogue, and the formation of nonprofit organizations, groups have learned to use rights to stake claims in their own concerns and potentially respond to injustices that they see in the world. Unlike previous historical periods in East Africa, when there were fewer opportunities to attain power through the advancement of indigenous concerns, today more people have the ability to debate their place in society and attempt to use the rhetoric of rights to advance their interests. At the same time, according to many East Africans, the protection of many types of rights remains tenuous. Even though more avenues exist to discuss rights, there are also more attempts to stifle exposure to rights violations. The conflict between protecting and preventing rights claims is a struggle that has grown more significant in East Africa.

GROWTH OF RIGHTS-BASED ORGANIZATIONS

While debates about rights provide a means to negotiate notions of self against those of others, the formation of nonprofits draws people together who share similar ideological perspectives. These nonprofits then become a means to represent the interests, desires, concerns, values, or beliefs of a community of people. They also provide a means for those same communities to build support for their causes. The more support that communities gain for their organizations, the more potential power they have in negotiating with other nonprofits, the state, local businesses, or international communities.

This potential to attain power—established through personal investment in nonprofit organizations—also creates a new set of relations that no longer depend solely on the state. Nonprofits can connect to organizations in other regions or countries to establish a stronger voice and more credibility. They can link to international organizations that can then place pressure on state governments to make changes; this occurred with copyright law in several East African countries where musicians pressured their governments by first attaining the support of WIPO. And nonprofits can use the media to further promote their interests. The growth of nonprofits points to a new set of relations in East Africa and between Africa and the West, relations that are central to comprehending global processes of movement, exchange, and negotiation.

In many African countries, nonprofit organizations provide jobs and represent anywhere from 2 to 5 percent of a country's GDP. Most significant is that these organizations educate and assist a large number of people living in Africa. If statistics about Kenya are accurate, then there is a nonprofit for every one hundred ten people living in that country. That means that many Kenyans would have relative easy access to the resources, expertise, and assistance of nonprofits. While it is not possible here to assess the quality of these organizations, the relative number of nonprofits to the number of people living in Africa makes them a powerful and significant force in people's everyday lives.

The increase in rights-based dialogue fostered the formal establishment of nonprofit organizations to assist in the implementation and protection of rights among citizens of various nations. The nonprofit sector has a variety of subsets, including volunteer and charitable organizations and non-governmental organizations, and is sometimes termed civil society, the third economy, or the social economy. Organizations in the social economy work in a variety of areas, including hospitals, schools, and libraries, and a variety of contexts, such as grassroots organizations, sports and arts clubs, and intellectual property rights organizations. The scope and breadth of these organizations is so vast in African countries that it often appears that there are few areas or issues left untouched by nonprofit organizations.

Increased academic attention to the nonprofit sector is in part due to recognition of its size, in terms of both economic activity and workforce. The Johns Hopkins Comparative Nonprofit Sector Project organized a research project in thirty-six countries that documented the "scope, structure, financing, and role of the civil society sector" (Salamon et al. 2004, 5). The project started in 1991 and covered countries around the world including both developed and developing countries, such as Kenya, Tanzania, and Uganda. In tabulating the workforce of the civil society sector, the study provides a glimpse of the involvement of nonprofit organizations in national economies. In the thirty-six countries, 45.5 million people, including volunteers, worked in the civil society sector, while only 6 million worked in utilities, 39.3 million in transportation, and 44.3 million in construction. Only manufacturing, at 105.8 million, had a larger workforce than the civil society sector.

As the authors of the Johns Hopkins study point out, however, 44 percent of the civil society workforce are volunteer, which often means they are an unpaid workforce. Nonetheless, they also note that since most volunteers actually do not work full-time, in which case they would not be counted in the civil society workforce, the actual number of people working in the social economy is estimated to be closer to 132 million or 10 percent of the adult population of these countries. The number of people working in civil society provides a sense of the needs that are not being met by other areas of society, including business and government, and also the growing desire to deliver certain services to local populations. Since many nonprofit organizations are small-scale and grass roots, they have an ability to work closely with lo-cal populations, organize around community concerns, and establish social capital. Social capital includes "bonds of trust and reciprocity that seems to be crucial for a democratic polity and a market economy to function effec-tively" (Salamon et al. 2004, 23). The large and growing workforce organized around social issues, whether human rights, advocacy, or leisure activities, presents a populace engaged in establishing rights and activities neglected by other areas of society, particularly the state and the market.

The growth of nonprofit organizations was so rapid that Lester Salomon has called it a "global associational revolution" (2004, xxi; see also Mascar-enhas, chapter 14, this volume). Since the Johns Hopkins study, the number of nonprofit organizations working in African countries has only continued to expand at a rapid pace. Problematically, it is a challenge to determine their exact number. Most countries do not have the ability and/or the in-clination to require organizations to register with the state when they start or to deregister when they stop functioning. There are also country-specific ways of identifying nonprofit organizations so that a search for just non-governmental organizations may miss cultural, youth, and social service groups that are categorized separately. Even government agencies struggle to formally identify the number of organizations operating in their country. For instance, in a November 2001 report, the vice president's office stated that three thousand local and international non-governmental organizations existed in Tanzania. This number is, even according to the report, incorrect: because of the "lack of information on who should register, inadequate information of what is an NGO and to some extent [the] cumbersome process of registration, there are Organization [*sic*] which are not registered, but which quali[fy] to be identified as NGOs."[11]

Despite the difficulty in capturing the size of civil society in Africa, many studies and reports attempt to assess the number of organizations that exist. In Rwanda, there are an estimated 37,000 informal groups and 319 registered nonprofit organizations.[12] In the early 2000s in Tanzania, 2.1 million people or 11 percent of Tanzania's adult population engaged in volunteer work, while organizations employed over 330,000 people full-time (Kiondo et al. 2004, 127–28). The estimated total number of registered organizations, including cooperative societies, cultural and arts organizations, and community-based organizations, was 58,807 (Ndumbaro and Mvungi 2007, 27). Given the significant focus on rights and community organization in Tanzania, particularly after state efforts to privatize water and electricity in the country, which led to protests by nonprofit organizations (Perullo 2011), the interest in civil society expanded significantly. Based on estimates in Tanzania, more than twice as many non-governmental organizations were registered in 2009 as compared to 2001 (around 9,000 and 3,865 respectively).[13]

The proliferation of organizations in a short time span is not unusual. In Kenya, for instance, the number of nonprofit organizations tripled between 1998 and 2005 (113,259 to 347,387). These numbers include self-help, women's, and youth groups, cooperatives, non-governmental organizations, foundations and trusts, and unions (Kanyinga, Mitullah, and Njagi 2007). In Ghana during the same time period, the number of nonprofit organizations quadrupled to 40,000.[14] The combination of local and international assistance for various social issues in these countries provides tremendous support on a variety of social and legal issues. In fact, the number of areas covered by nonprofit organizations has expanded at an equally rapid rate. Tanzania's Ministry of Community Development, Gender, and Children divides nonprofits into fifteen categories, including education, capacity building, agriculture, legal rights, and health. These categories indicate only a small portion of the spectrum of rights work being done in East Africa.

Aware of the dramatic rise in nonprofit organizations, many governments, including all of those discussed thus far, have increased restrictions on their activities, required some level of reporting, and attempted to curb problematic practices, such as corruption or the distribution of misinformation.

Some countries have also attempted to increase the registration of nonprofits in order to avoid conflict or collusion between nonprofits working on the same issue. Most African governments, however, do not have the resources to monitor the actions or statuses of nonprofit organizations. Instead, there is a cacophony of nonprofits working in African countries—run by either local or foreign interests—that aim to help those in need or spur action from anyone else. Regardless of the job, social position, political or religious beliefs, or cultural philosophies, there is a nonprofit that can support that point of view. And, if there is not, the possibility always exists to start one.

THE AGE OF RIGHTS

In his book *The Proliferation of Rights* (1999), Carl Wellman makes the point that while the dialogue of rights has spread to more areas of modern life, it has also produced increasing resistance. That resistance can be seen within East African countries, as there are frequent debates in newspapers, parliamentary sessions, songs, and conversations about the character of rights. While European liberalism brought many specific conceptions of rights, national and indigenous concerns provide a means to reshape the landscape of meaning and the significance of those debates. More debates over rights will emerge simply as a means to establish identity differences between nations and between communities. Those debates create tensions over the use of morality in daily life. Laying claim to and advancing specific moral interests can create profound shifts in relations between people and nations. The move by Cameron to insert gay rights into dialogue with Africa is one example, as is the competing response by African leaders. Both sides clearly believe that they are correct in their assessment of morality and rights. Both are willing to take risks to protect those rights. If history provides any indication, then more African countries will adapt the policies and practices coming from the West. As the role of rights continues to proliferate, however, new debates will arise to once again test relations between people, communities, and nations.

In addition to the escalation in tensions over moral concerns, the increasing attention to rights in East Africa has also led to significant shifts in everyday life. It is now common for governments to have departments dedicated to ensuring the rights of local populations. There are new laws, amendments, legal norms, and courts that hear cases about human, environmental, intellectual, or community rights. There is a vast network of nonprofit organizations and even organizations meant to survey the rights conditions of specific countries, such as the Legal and Human Rights Centre based in Tanzania. Nonprofit organizations from East Africa frequently send representatives to international meetings of the United Nations, WIPO, WHO, and other institutions. International development is no longer focused on infrastructure projects, but on issues related to rights. The law professor David Kennedy notes, "Human rights has elbowed economics aside in our development agencies, which now spend billions once allocated to dams and roadways on court reform, judicial training, and 'rule of law' injection" (2012, 20). He continues by arguing that the world of rights has created a "common vernacular of justice for a global civil society" (ibid., 20). Rights and rights dialogue are a fundamental part of people's lives in East Africa and central to understanding global processes in the establishment of notions of universality, law, justice, and personhood.

NOTES

1. All of these rights-based issues were topics of conversation in Tanzania between June and September 2012. For English-language versions of these stories see Issa Yusuf, "Need to Involve Women in Decision Making Issues," *Daily News,* 12 September 2012; Kilasa Mtambalike, "Human Rights Body Urges Dedication to Health Care," *Daily News,* 1 June 2012; Jaffar Mjasiri, "Doctors' Strike: Were the Patients' Rights Violated?" *Daily News,* 14 July 2012; Dr. Ali Mzige, "The Bill of Rights of the Patient," *Daily News,* 8 July 2012; Daily News Editors, "Violation of Animal Rights," *Daily News,* 6 July 2012; Matthew Moses, "Ngara NGOs in Gender, Land Rights Awareness Campaign," *Daily News,* 22 June 2012; Daily News Editors, "NGOs to Offer Training on Gender Violence," *Daily News,* 27 August 2012; Meddy Mulisa, "RC Wants an End to Violence against Women and Children," *Daily News,* 13 July 2012.

2. See Margaret Chan, "More Countries Move towards Universal Health Coverage," opening statement at the International Forum on Universal Health Coverage: Sustaining Universal Health Coverage: Sharing Experiences and Supporting Progress, Mexico City, 2 April 2012. http://www.who.int/dg/speeches/2012/universal_health_coverage_20120402 /en/ (accessed 21 August 2012).

3. For instance, WIPO promotes the protection of intellectual property rights, including patents, while WHO promotes equitable health care globally, by, among other things, attempting to lower the costs of medicine.

4. Cameron made comments about gay rights in Africa and foreign aid at the Commonwealth Heads of Government Meeting in Perth, Australia. See "Cameron Threat to Dock Some UK Aid to Anti-Gay Nations," BBC News, 30 October 2011. Online edition: http://www.bbc.co.uk/news/uk-15511081.

5. Richard Mbuthia, "Africa, Want Aid? Recognise Gay Rights!" *Daily News,* 26 December 2011.

6. The Citizen Reporters, "Tanzania Says NO to UK," *Citizen,* 3 November 2011.

7. The quote is from "Constitution and the Crisis of Governance in Kenya," an address given to the Kenya Community Abroad Conference, Concordia University, Minnesota, 30 June–3 July 2000. The quoted section appears in Shadrack Wanjala Nasong'o and Theodora O. Ayot, "Women in Kenya's Politics of Transition and Democratisation," in *Kenya: The Struggle for Democracy,* ed. Godwin R. Murunga and Shadrack W. Nasong'o, 164–96 (Dakar, Senegal: Codesria, 2007).

8. A great deal of academic writing has appeared discussing the policies of structural adjustment, privatization, or the types of reforms that actually emerged in African countries through liberalization efforts. For a small sample, see Ferguson 2006; Hibou 2004; Logan and Mengisteab 1993; Lugalla 1997; Briggs and Yeboah 2001; and Tripp 1997.

9. In Tanzania, this included the passage of the Commission for Human Rights and Good Governance Act of 2001 and the Basic Rights and Duties Enforcement Act of 1994 (Act No. 33 of 1994).

10. Ashley Benner, "Uganda Rules That Amnesty Can't Be Denied to LRA Leaders," *Christian Science Monitor,* 27 September 2011. http://www.csmonitor.com/World/Africa/Africa-Monitor/2011/0927/Uganda-rules-that-amnesty-can-t-be-denied-to-LRA-leaders. Accessed on 28 August 2012.

11. The United Republic of Tanzania, *The National Policy on Non-Governmental Organizations* (Dar es Salaam: Vice President's Office, November 2001).

12. The International Center for Not-for-Profit Law, "NGO Law Monitor: Rwanda," 17 December 2009. Online at http://www.africancso.org/documents/10136/0/NGO+Law+Monitor+-+Rwanda. Accessed 28 August 2012.

13. In July 2012, only 1,370 local non-governmental organizations were officially registered with the Ministry of Community Development, Gender, and Children. Part of the change is in the way that organizations report their status to the government and the government's newer requirements for registration by non-governmental organizations.

14. For data on the Ghanaian nonprofit sector in 1998, see Anheier and Salamon 1998, 31.

REFERENCES

Allen, Lori. 2013. *The Rise and Fall of Human Rights: Cynicism and Politics in Occupied Palestine.* Stanford, CA: Stanford University Press.

Anheier, Helmut K., and Lester M. Salamon. 1998. "Introduction: The Nonprofit Sector in the Developing World." In *The Nonprofit Sector in the Developing World,* ed. Helmut K. Anheier and Lester M. Salamon, 1–50. Manchester, UK: Manchester University Press.

Arrighi, Giovanni. 2002. "The African Crisis." *New Left Review* 15 (May/June): 5–36.

Briggs, John, and Ian E. A. Yeboah. 2001. "Structural Adjustment and the Contemporary Sub-Saharan African City." *Area* 33(1): 18–26.

Dobson, E. B. 1954. "Comparative Land Tenure of Ten Tanganyika Tribes." *Journal of African Administration* 6: 80–91.

Donnelly, Jack. 2002. "Human Rights, Globalizing Flows, and State Power." In *Globalization and Human Rights,* ed. Alison Brysk, 226–41. Berkeley: University of California Press.

Edmundson, William A. 2012. *An Introduction to Rights.* 2nd ed. Cambridge: Cambridge University Press.

Ferguson, James. 2006. *Global Shadows: Africa in the Neoliberal World Order.* Durham, NC: Duke University Press.

Feser, Edward. 2012. "The Metaphysical Foundations of Natural Rights." In *Handbook of Human Rights,* ed. Thomas Cushman, 23–34. London: Routledge.

Forsythe, David P. 2012. *Human Rights in International Relations.* 3rd ed. Cambridge: Cambridge University Press.

Gluckman, Max. 1967. *The Judicial Process among the Barotse of Northern Rhodesia.* Manchester, UK: Manchester University Press.

Gomes-Mugumya, Albert. 2010. "Reflections on Rights and Conflict from Uganda." In *Human Rights and Conflict Transformation: The Challenges of Just Peace,* ed. Véronique Dudouet and Beatrix Schmelzle, 75–83. Berghof Handbook Dialogue No. 9. Berlin: Berghof Conflict Research.

Hibou, Béatrice. 2004. "From Privatizing the Economy to Privatizing the State: An Analysis of the Continual Formation of the State." In *Privatizing the State,* ed. Béatrice Hibou. New York: Columbia University Press.

Ibhawoh, Bonny. 2012. "Human Rights in the African State." In *Handbook of Human Rights,* ed. Thomas Cushman, 719–32. London: Routledge.

Iliffe, John, 1979. *A Modern History of Tanganyika.* Cambridge: University of Cambridge Press.

Kanyinga, Karuti, Winnie Mitullah, and Sebastian Njagi. 2007. "The Nonprofit Sector in Kenya: What We Know and What We Don't Know." Nairobi: Institute for Development Studies (IDS).

Kennedy, David. 2012. "The International Human Rights Regime: Still Part of the Problem?" In *Examining Critical Perspectives on Human Rights,* ed. Rob Dickinson, Elena Katselli, Colin Murray, and Ole W. Pedersen, 19–34. Cambridge: Cambridge University Press.

Kiondo, Andrew, Laurean Ndumbaro, S. Wojciech Sokolowski, and Lester M. Salamon. 2004. "Tanzania." In *Global Civil Society: Dimensions of the Nonprofit Sector,* vol. 2, ed. Lester M. Salamon, S. Wojciech Sokolowski, and Associates. 126–39. Bloomfield, CT: Kumarian Press.

Logan, Bernard Ikubolajeh, and Kidane Mengisteab. 1993. "IMF—World Bank Adjustment and Structural Transformation in Sub-Saharan Africa." *Economic Geography* 69(1): 1–24.

Lugalla, Joe L. P. 1997. "Development, Change, and Poverty in the Informal Sector during the Era of Structural Adjustments in Tanzania." *Canadian Journal of African Studies/Revue Canadienne des Études Africaines* 31(3) 424–51.

Mack, Phyllis. 1984. "Women and the Enlightenment: Introduction." *Women and the Enlightenment,* ed. Margaret Hunt, Margaret Jacob, Phyllis Mack, and Ruth Perry, 1–10. Binghamton, NY: Haworth Press.

Malcolm, D. W. 1953. *Sukumaland: An African People and Their Country.* London: Oxford University Press.

McGowan, Patrick J. 2003. "African Military Coup d'Etats, 1956–2001: Frequency, Trends and Distribution." *Journal of Modern African Studies* 41(3): 339–70.

Morison, Theodore. 1933. "The Wachaga of Kilimanjaro: Reminiscences of a War-Time District Officer." *Journal of the Royal African Society* 32(127): 140–47.

Mwaikusa, J. T. 1993. "Community Rights and Land Use Policies in Tanzania: The Case of Pastoral Communities." *Journal of African Law* 37(2): 144–63.

Ndumbaro, Laurean, and Abu Mvungi. 2007. "Estimating the Size and Scope of the Nonprofit Sector in Tanzania: Employment, Membership, Revenue, and Expenditure." In *The Third Sector in Tanzania: Learning More about Civil Society Organizations, Their Capabilities, and*

Challenges, ed. Laurean Ndumbaro and Saida Yahya-Othman, 24–38. Dar es Salaam: Aga Khan Development Network.

Perullo, Alex. 2011. *Live from Dar es Salaam: Popular Music and Tanzania's Music Economy.* Bloomington: Indiana University Press.

Pinker, Steven. 2011. *The Better Angels of Our Nature: Why Violence Has Declined.* New York: Viking.

Salamon, Lester M. 2004. "Preface." In *Global Civil Society: Dimensions of the Nonprofit Sector,* vol. 2, ed. Lester M. Salamon, S. Wojciech Sokolowski, and Associates, xxi–xxiii. Bloomfield, CT: Kumarian Press.

Salamon, Lester M., S. Wojciech Sokolowski, and Associates. 2004. *Global Civil Society: Dimensions of the Nonprofit Sector,* vol. 2. Bloomfield, CT: Kumarian Press.

Tenga, R. W. 1992. *Pastoral Land Rights in Tanzania: A Review.* London: IIED Drylands Programme, Pastoral.

Tierney, Brian. 1997. *The Idea of Natural Rights: Studies on Natural Rights, Natural Law, and Church Law, 1150–1625.* Atlanta: Scholars Press.

Tripp, Aili Mari. 1997. *Changing the Rules: The Politics of Liberalization and the Urban Informal Economy in Tanzania.* Berkeley: University of California Press.

Wellman, Carl. 1999. *The Proliferation of Rights: Moral Progress or Empty Rhetoric?* Boulder, CO: Westview Press.

11 – RULES

Global Production and the Puzzle of Rules

TIM BARTLEY

TWO SEEMINGLY CONTRADICTORY IMAGES HANG WITHIN FRAMINGS of the global. On one hand, globalization appears to be an unruly phenomenon: Rapid flows of money, products, ideas, and people are difficult for governments to manage. Events in one part of the world can ripple quickly, unpredictably, and seemingly uncontrollably to other places. And complex, geographically dispersed global production networks can be both extremely dynamic and incredibly opaque. Yet there is also an image in which globalization requires and spurs the production of rules: Global capitalism depends on rules that create cross-border markets, allow participants to use common metrics, and regulate the quality and safety of products. In addition, the globalization of industries—and the controversies it has generated—has spurred a number of new rule-making projects, including attempts by activists and non-governmental organizations (NGOs) to build global rules for environmental sustainability, labor conditions, and human rights. Other global rule-making projects have been led by professional communities seeking to harmonize standards for accounting, business arbitration, and many other issues.

Both of these images have more than a grain of truth in them. Indeed, it is difficult to examine the operation of global industries without coming to the conclusion that both images are essentially accurate. In many consumer products industries—like food, clothing, electronics, and home furnishings—large retailers and "brands" nimbly move orders across different suppliers and countries, breeding intense competition among supplier companies, investment-hungry governments, and workers in different areas. The rapid, complex transactions of the global financial industry are even more unruly, as the financial crisis of 2008 made very clear. But neither global financial architectures nor global supply chains would exist were it not for rule-making projects that facilitate greater cross-border trade and coordination by powerful firms. In addition, the exposure of both financial mismanagement and exploitation in consumer products industries has fueled projects by reformers to implement better "rules of the road" and "rules of fair play" in global industries, whether through the Basel Accords for banking or by pressing brands to submit to labor codes of conduct, sustainable sourcing standards, or principles of fair trade. Of course, these proliferating standards are as often subverted as obeyed, leading to the observation that, in both senses of the term, global industries are "lousy" with rules.

This situation, in which globalization can be characterized as both unruly and rule-filled, is what I call the puzzle of rules. How can global social formations be simultaneously unruly and rule-filled? This puzzle has rarely been addressed explicitly because most scholars of globalization have tended to focus on one or the other of its components. For instance, many early analysts of globalization portrayed it as corrosive, ungovernable, and destined to lead to the decline, retreat, or eclipse of the state (Schmidt 1995; Strange 1996). Sociologists and political scientists reacted so strongly against this image (see, for instance, Evans 1997) that they constructed their own accounts of globalization and global governance with a strong emphasis on rule-making, whether done by states or by non-state actors. Unruliness largely fell out of the picture, but to develop a fuller account of global processes, it is necessary to bring it back in.

This chapter describes the puzzle of rules as a theoretical concern and illustrates the coexistence of "ruliness" and unruliness by drawing on my research on production processes and rule-making in the global apparel and forest products industries. These are cases in which NGOs and firms have constructed new systems of rules—as well as auditing, certification, and eco-/social-labeling systems to enforce them—but industry activity has remained unruly in some crucial ways. After exploring these cases, I consider several general solutions to the puzzle of rules. I argue that a promising solution comes from seeing neoliberalism—that is, the ideology and practice of privileging markets both analytically and normatively—as increasing the number but altering the character of rules.

A focus on rules can be an entry point into a variety of global social formations and scholarly endeavors, as a brief and partial genealogy of the term illustrates. While rules—that is, prescriptions and proscriptions for behavior—have obviously been a central concern of legal theorists and moral philosophers for millennia, they have also been central to several specific lines of social theory and research that inform my own approach. Theorists of social institutions conceptualize rules in two revealing ways. Some scholars, especially those influenced by rational choice theory and institutional economics, define institutions as "rules of the game," which arise out of individuals' (and organizations') attempts to secure collective goods and overcome collective action problems (North 1990; Ostrom 1990). Taking the game analogy further illustrates this account of institutions. Imagine individuals playing a game in a state of anarchy. To keep the game from self-destructing, they may develop rules and even hire referees to enforce them. Similarly, at least by a simplified version of this account, institutions of government, markets, and natural resource management are the result of this type of process. In contrast, a different set of institutional theorists—especially in organizational sociology—portray institutions as less provisional, more *constitutive* of social action, and often taken for granted (DiMaggio and Powell 1991; Douglas 1986). In this more phenomenological account, there could be no game if there were no rules to define its means, ends, and players. Despite their differences, both traditions of institutional theory have spurred large bodies of research on the evolution of rules—within communities, organizations, and nation-states, and in transnational orders. The dialogue and debate between these approaches has profoundly influenced my approach to transnational governance broadly and to the specific sets of labor and environmental standards that I have examined (Bartley 2007).

Rules are also central to socio-legal scholarship, which tries to move past the "law on the books" to study the "law in action." One product of doing so has been an analysis of "legal pluralism," that is, a situation in which societies are governed by numerous quasi-legal rules, including informal norms, customary rights, and other rules that have some authority but are not necessarily recognized by the state and formal bodies of law (Merry 1988). This basic insight of legal pluralism is increasingly being revived and pushed to the global level as scholars try to make sense of the interplay of multiple sets of rules and the construction of quasi-legal rules by private actors (Berman 2007; Parker 2008; Perez 2003; Rodríguez-Garavito 2005b). This work has led me to conceptualize the proliferation of standards for global production in part as a "layering" of new rules on top of existing legal and quasi-legal rules (Bartley 2011b). Yet questions remain regarding which sets of rules have the power, individually or as hybrids, to reshape global industries.

GLOBALIZATION AS RULE-GENERATING

While early analysts of globalization often portrayed it as destructive and "manic" (Greider 1998), nearly the opposite view has since become prominent. Increasingly, scholars have argued that globalization has spawned extensive rule-making projects, regulatory expansion, and new forms of governance. For instance, Sassen (1996) argues that "globalization has been accompanied by the creation of new legal regimes and practices and the expansion and renovation of some older forms that bypass national legal systems" (14). In part, this is because rules are always necessary to make markets—that is, to stabilize markets in the face of crises and destructive competition. As Fligstein (1996) puts it, "[C]apitalist firms could not operate without collective sets of rules governing interaction" (660). Globalization thus creates demand for new global rules for issues like accounting and technical specifications (Büthe and Mattli 2011). This type of "market-making through rule-making" can be seen clearly in studies of the development of the European Union and World Trade Organization (Eberlein and Grande 2005; Fligstein and Mara Drita 1996), as well as in markets for things like air pollution and carbon credits (Lederer 2012; Levin and Espeland 2002). Gille (chapter 8, this volume) demonstrates one way in which rule-making in the EU has had profound effects.

It is not simply that rules are generally necessary for markets, though. Scholars have pointed out several ways in which the globalization of industries can lead to the expansion and diffusion of regulation. Contesting the image of a global "race to the bottom," many scholars have shown global economic integration can foster a "ratcheting up" of regulation (Drezner 2007; Vogel and Kagan 2004), in which international trade and investment allow relatively stringent standards in some markets to be exported elsewhere (Vogel 1995). Braithwaite and Drahos's (2000) wide-ranging analysis of global business regulation finds a ratcheting up over time in most domains, often traceable to expanding "regulatory webs"—constituted not only by economic linkages but also by dialogue among policy entrepreneurs, trade associations, and international organizations.

In fact, rejecting the image of this as an era of deregulation, some scholars have called the turn of the twenty-first century the "golden era of regulation" (Levi-Faur and Jordana 2005). This image is especially inspired by studies of infrastructure industries, like telecommunications, where privatization and the breakup of national monopolies have led to the situation that Vogel (1996) described as "freer markets, more rules." Privatization has required rules to structure competition and make the market. Thus, as Levi-Faur and Jordana (2005) put it, "[F]or every regulation that in the past quarter of a century has been removed from the books, many new ones have been added. . . . Privatization, at least in some spheres, is accompanied by new sets of regulatory controls either to socialize the market or to constitute it as a competitive order" (6). Through these processes, a new model of the "regulatory state" has emerged, not only in advanced industrial countries but also in many parts of the Global South (Dubash and Morgan 2012).

The growing literature on transnational governance perhaps goes the furthest in portraying a world dense with rules. Here, the focus is not only on governmental and intergovernmental standards but on rule-making projects by private actors and resulting fields of governance that transcend the nation-state (Bartley 2007; Bernstein and Cashore 2007; Dingwerth and Pattberg 2009). NGOs have led projects to build global rules for corporations' performance in the areas of sustainability, labor conditions, and human rights, often as a way to address environmental degradation, sweatshops, and various "conflict" products (for example, diamonds, gold, and rare earth minerals). Professional communities have shaped these standards while also globalizing their own rules of conduct. As Djelic and Sahlin-Andersson (2006) summarize, "[T]he proliferation of regulatory activities, actors, networks or constellations leads to an explosion of rules and to the profound re-ordering of our world" (1)—a reordering "marked by more—not less—rule-making activity" (376). Though some actors are clearly more powerful than others, the lack of a singular global authority—like a world state—means that particular rule-making projects quickly spawn competitors and spiral into larger systems of governance—meaning rules for the rule-makers, auditing of the auditors, certification of the certifiers—as actors seek to legitimate their projects.

From all these strands of research, it is clear that whether at the level of national governments, intergovernmental relations, or transnational fields, one can see a proliferation of rule-making activity. Among many scholars, a few provocative arguments about the anarchic state of global capitalism and the supposed decline of the state spurred a counternarrative that has since become dominant: Global capitalism is both facilitated by and generative of rules. To study globalization is to study these rule-making projects.

GLOBALIZATION AS UNRULY

Yet there are warrants for reconsidering the unruly character of globalization as well. Markets need rules to function, but capitalism may also have a tendency to disrupt or undermine existing rules. New rules may be developed only to be subverted. According to some theories, disruption and instability are inherent to capitalism itself. Harvey (1982), following Marx, argues that capitalism tends toward greater accumulation but also faces endemic crisis, as rates of return on capital investment tend to decline. Schumpeter's (1942) famous analysis put innovation through "creative destruction" at the heart of capitalist enterprise. By these accounts, capitalism can never be stable, even at the national level, much less as it expands to the global level.

Regardless of whether one views unruliness as inherent to capitalism in all times and places, there are particular socio-legal and industry structures that foster unruliness in global capitalism. For one, the mobility of capital clearly puts constraints on rule enforcement by states. The strong version of the "race to the bottom" theory—which predicts that strong forms of regulation will be "competed down to the level that rules in over-populated Third

World countries" (Daly and Cobb 1994, 221)—is clearly false. But this need not lead to a rejection of the idea that the ease of moving investments across borders generates downward pressure on place-based social controls of industry. Capital mobility is neither universal across firms (Murphy 2004) nor the prime determinant of government policy, but it can still play a profound role in structuring the relationship between business, government, workers, and citizens. This is clear to scholars of organized labor, who have shown how actual and threatened movement of factories can effectively undercut worker organizing (Bronfenbrenner 2000; Cowie 1999). The threat of exit may also have a chilling effect on government regulation without necessarily spurring a full-scale race to the bottom (Lindblom 1977). In the shipping industry, for instance, international competition and cross-national harmonization projects have pushed up the lowest safety, labor, and environmental standards, but high standards have also been pulled down as governments in maritime countries have had to compete with low-cost "flag of convenience" countries (DeSombre 2006).

Many scholars have too hastily dismissed the effects of capital mobility because they have tested only a crude version of the race to the bottom theory. Studies that assess whether investment moves from strong to weak regulatory regimes (Jaffe et al. 1995) or whether investment flows to "pollution havens" (Lucas, Wheeler, and Hettige 1992) miss the possibility of chilling effects. Furthermore, arguments about capital mobility have far too often focused on competition between affluent northern and developing southern countries, which have numerous and wide differences, rather than South-South competition, where smaller (but still meaningful) differences in cost and regulation can create far more intense competition (Chan and Ross 2003). While some industries are clearly more mobile and sensitive to differences in labor or regulatory costs, the supply chain revolution—that is, the "integration of trade and disintegration of production" in a growing number of industries (Feenstra 1998)—has allowed powerful "lead firms" to move orders across borders without bearing the costs of physically moving a factory.

The financial crisis of 2008 showed how certain industry structures can turn market disruptions into spiraling crises that are difficult to rein in. When financial products were highly complex and different parts of the financial system were tightly coupled, a drop in the price of real estate and a subsequent tightening of credit rippled widely and almost uncontrollably—as theories of "normal accidents" would expect (Palmer and Maher 2010; Schneiberg and Bartley 2010). Specifically, the combination and re-combination of securitized mortgages and their derivatives led to products so complex that even sophisticated traders struggled to understand their underlying risks. A tightly coupled financial system—with millions of trans-actions flowing through a few large companies that were, in effect, insuring one another—helped the crisis to rapidly spiral out of control. Losses in the United States and Europe quickly rippled more broadly to both financial and non-financial firms in Asia and Latin America.

Beyond unruliness in formal, legally sanctioned industries, globalization has also meant an expansion of illicit and illegal markets. The boundary between legal and illegal markets can be quite blurry, and states may la-bel activities "illegal" when they lack other schemes for categorizing them (Abraham and Schendel 2005). Indeed, illicit trade is often not marginal but rather "constitute[s] a series of power grids that shape the fundamental econo-political dynamics of the world today" (Nordstrom 2007, xvii). The rise of "illegal" markets reflects not only a framing project by states but also changes in the infrastructure of the global economy, such as the expansion of global shipping, which has made it easier to transfer illicit cargo at sea (Nordstrom 2007).

It seems that scholars have often downplayed the unruly aspects of global capitalism in order to counteract simplistic and triumphant images of state-less global markets wiping away older structures—what Hirst, Thompson, and Bromley (2009) called the "breathless enthusiasm for the novel" (226). These images have been effectively countered by showing that globalization does not erode distinct national forms of industrial policy, corporate gover-nance, and welfare policy (Campbell 2004; Pierson 2004). But even some scholars in this tradition increasingly emphasize common, disruptive aspects of capitalism. Streeck (2009), for instance, argues that capitalism has pro-found disordering tendencies, driven largely by capitalists themselves, who "invent ever new ways of converting social arrangements into opportunities for profit, or subverting them where this turns out to be impossible. . . . [Capi-talists] are *fundamentally unruly*: a permanent source of disorder from the perspective of social institutions, relentlessly whacking away at social rules, continuously forcing rulers to rewrite them, and undoing them again by creatively exploiting the inevitable gap between general rules and their local enactment" (241). Similarly, Sewell (2008) highlights the common "unruly dynamics" of capitalism, which is "always churning, always self-valorizing" (526). He argues that it is not just expansion but "the *unpredictability* of the actual pattern of expansion" (524; emphasis added) that makes capitalism unruly. Overall, one does not have to subscribe to a "decline of the state" discourse to accept that states have become less effective or aggressive in the social control of industries. States may be involved in "making markets" or "steering" private governance in meaningful but minimalistic ways. Or the state may end up "incorporating the global project of its own shrinking role in regulating economic transactions" (Sassen 2002, 94).

THE PUZZLE OF RULES:
RULES AND UNRULINESS IN GLOBAL PRODUCTION

One can see how global capitalism is both rule-governed and unruly at the same time by looking at consumer products industries that have been the site of extensive projects to make and enforce rules for fair or sustainable production processes. As activists have exposed brand-name companies' complicity in exploitation and abuse, they have also forced companies to accept new kinds of scrutiny of conditions in their supply chains. The integrity and independence of the resulting standards varies widely, but in at least some cases, activists have pushed companies to accept rules made by "multi-stakeholder" initiatives, in which NGOs and sometimes unions have a seat at the table. Environmental NGOs have strongly shaped the rules of many leading sustainability certification initiatives (for example, the Forest Stewardship Council, Marine Stewardship Council, and Roundtable on Responsible Palm Oil). Yet even as these certification initiatives have grown, the industries have proven difficult to tame. For instance, sustainable seafood standards have gained a presence in the market, as well as in intergovernmental negotiations (Gulbrandsen 2010), but over the same period, global fishing yields have declined, regional ecosystems have lost biodiversity, and the rate of fisheries collapse has increased (Worm et al. 2006). Similarly, palm oil plantations are increasingly certified as sustainable for the surrounding environments and communities, but conflicts over land and the destructive clearing of natural forests for oil palm plantations remain common (Silva-Castaneda 2012).

"Ruliness" and unruliness coexist in the two main industries that I have studied, apparel and forest products, where I have conducted a number of interviews with companies, NGOs, auditors, and others. (See Bartley 2007 and 2011b for details.) Obviously, these are particular kinds of cases, in which rule-making has focused on addressing the impacts of production processes (rather than the features of the product itself) and rules have been largely voluntary (consistent with a neoliberal setting, which I will discuss in a later section). These are just one of many possible illustrations of the puzzle of rules, as the theoretical discussion suggested. Broadly similar (though not identical) dynamics might be found if one examined rule-making and regulation in the financial sector and in food safety, where the recent scandal over horsemeat in the European beef supply has raised red flags about the existing mix of public and private regulation.

Apparel Production: Racing to the Bottom and the Top at the Same Time?

In response to anti-sweatshop campaigns, nearly all large apparel brands and retailers in North America and Europe have developed codes of conduct or other ethical sourcing standards for their supply chains (Bartley 2005; Ro-dríguez-Garavito 2005a). Most also audit their suppliers for compliance, and some go beyond this by affiliating with multi-stakeholder initiatives (Fransen and Kolk 2007) or encouraging suppliers to get independently certified as complying with high standards, such as the SA8000 standard developed by Social Accountability International. Some firms face additional scrutiny from the Worker Rights Consortium, an independent and activist-oriented effort to investigate factories where alleged code of conduct violations have occurred. From companies' reporting on these activities and from much of the academic literature on corporate social responsibility (CSR), one can easily get an image of the apparel industry as transparent, rule-governed, and responsible. Furthermore, research on governmental regulation finds that respect for labor rights seems to increase with international trade (Greenhill, Mosley, and Prakash 2009) and that some countries that had been known for sweatshops have strengthened their enforcement of labor rights (Schrank 2009).

Yet many features of the industry belie the image of a more rule-governed production process. While standards have improved in some places, the apparel industry has gravitated to countries with weak labor rights and standards—not only China and Vietnam, where labor rights are heavily restricted, but also Bangladesh and Pakistan, where basic safety and working conditions are typically dire. The location of export-oriented apparel production has proven highly sensitive to increases in wages. The Mexican garment industry was largely priced out of the market by competition from China, and more recently, rising wages (and strikes) in China and Vietnam have coincided with the growth of the industry in Bangladesh and India.

Furthermore, some of the most shocking forms of labor abuse have not ceased. The Gap has earned a reputation as a leader in monitoring its suppliers, but nevertheless, bonded child labor was discovered at one of its Indian subcontractors in 2007. Bonded child labor schemes have apparently become common in segments of the Indian garment industry that produce for European and American brands (SOMO 2012). In 2012 in Pakistan, nearly three hundred workers died in a fire in a factory that, amazingly, had just been approved for SA8000 certification. A spate of factory fires in Bangladesh in 2010–2012 killed hundreds of people producing apparel for Tommy Hilfiger, Wal-Mart, C&A (a European retailer), and others. In the midst of international scrutiny over these fires, a prominent Bangladeshi labor activist was killed. In 2013, the collapse of the Rana Plaza factory in Bangladesh killed more than a thousand people who had been producing for Primark (a British retailer), Benetton, Wal-Mart, and others. In Cambodia, just after the launch of the much-celebrated "Better Work" program led by the International Labor Organization, a prominent Cambodian trade union activist was assassinated (Hughes 2007). For all the discussion of responsible production and some examples of real improvement, the global apparel industry remains an unruly and sometimes brutal place for the workers—typically young women—who staff it. Furthermore, the attention to working conditions in the apparel industry has often left other aspects of the supply chain—like water pollution by textile factories or the changing nature of cotton production (see Kumar, chapter 5, this volume)—largely unaddressed.

Forestry and the Global Timber Trade: Shadows and Sustainability

The details are different in the forest products industry, but the coexistence of rules for responsible production and practices of rapid destruction are similar. The forest products industry is dense with rules. In the early 1990s, a group of environmental NGOs, companies, foresters, and certifiers developed the Forest Stewardship Council (FSC) to oversee the certification of well-managed forests and the labeling of wood and paper products. Within a few years, "forest certification" had become a dynamic and competitive field, as industry associations and government agencies began developing their own certification initiatives (Cashore, Auld, and Newsom 2004; Meidinger 2006), which later combined into the Programme for the Endorsement of Forest Certification (PEFC). As of mid-2012, nearly 160 million hectares of forest area was FSC-certified and roughly 240 million hectares were PEFC-certified. These amount to around 7.5 percent and 11 percent, respectively, of the 2.15 billion hectares of forest worldwide designated for production or multiple use (Food and Agriculture Organization 2010).

Forest management is also embedded in extensive rules made by governments, related to both land use and management practices. In an extensive review of policies across countries, McDermott, Cashore, and Kanowski (2010) find that "the policies governing forest management, and the forest practices which they allow and require, have changed—sometimes dramatically—in most countries over the past quarter century. Typically, they have become more restrictive and more demanding, as governments have given progressively greater weight to the environmental values of forests" (5). A few policies have become remarkably similar across countries, suggesting an influence of transnational epistemic communities.

Although neither public nor private policies are always fully enforced, there have clearly been extensive rule-making projects for forest management, both national and global in scale. It is easy to get the impression of a rule-governed, orderly, and ecologically sound timber trade.

Yet even as these rule-making projects gained steam, deforestation rates in many parts of the world continued to increase at alarming rates (Food and Agriculture Organization 2006). In part, this is because rules for forest management did little to reduce large-scale clearing of forests for agricultural plantations (Gullison 2003; Nebel et al. 2005). Even those parts of the industry that are managing forests (rather than converting them) are often quite volatile and opaque (Dauvergne and Lister 2011). Sometimes, the sustainable and the shadowy coexist in the same companies. Sinoforest, a company based in Hong Kong and listed on the Toronto stock exchange, became a leader in the growth of forest certification in China when it had one of its timber holdings there FSC-certified. But in 2011, it became clear that the company had also been falsifying information about its timber holdings in China in order to drive up its stock price. Stora Enso, a Finnish firm that has supported FSC and various other corporate social responsibility initiatives, was also investing in forests in China where locals had been strong-armed or manipulated into selling at a low price (Ping and Nielsen 2010). Land grabs have become common more generally in the past five years, especially in Africa (Deininger and Byerlee 2011), and voluntary rules for forestry, agriculture, and investment have struggled to keep up.

The coexistence of rules and unruliness in the forest products industry can also be seen in the rise of illegal logging. As support for sustainable forest management was growing in the late 1990s and early 2000s, so was illegal logging and the global trade in illegal timber. While forest certification sought to improve and recognize good forest management, it had little bearing on the more shadowy—and lucrative—parts of the industry. In Indonesia, illegal logging networks grew up in the wake of the Suharto regime's demise and disastrous attempts to decentralize forest governance (McCarthy 2004). Scholars estimated that between half and three-quarters of all timber production in Indonesia in the late 1990s in Indonesia could have been illegal (Tacconi et al. 2004). Much illegal timber ultimately travels through "legitimate" supply chains, as it flows "from Russia, Africa, and Southeast Asia into China where it is turned into 'legal' products for worldwide export" (Dauvergne and Lister 2011, 122). Up to 30–40 percent of Chinese imports of raw timber materials may be illegal, and more than a quarter of the wood imported to the EU comes from illegal or suspicious sources (ibid., 121–22).

These brief sketches of the apparel and forest products industries call for an analysis of why rule-making projects have not proven especially effective and how they might be improved, which some scholars are beginning to develop. But they also call for a theoretical analysis of how rule-making and unruliness may go together—and what this means for theories of globalization. To simply note that existing rule-making projects have been too weak is insufficient.

SOLVING THE PUZZLE OF RULES

The Compensatory Account

How can the combination of globalization's rule generation and unruliness be explained? How might the tearing apart and putting together of rules coexist? One explanation is that the proliferation of rules is a direct *reaction* to the unruly, disruptive features of globalization. This "compensatory" account treats rule-making projects as attempts to tame globalization and compensate for the disruption of previous social orders. As a general framework, it is perhaps the most common way of explaining the explosion of rules and fields of transnational governance. It is inspired by Polanyi's (1944) account of the double movement of capitalism—from the dis-embedding commodification of social and natural life to an attempt to re-embed markets in social standards. The Polanyian frame can be used to some degree to explain anti-sweatshop standards and sustainability efforts, but it is especially apt for explaining the specific case of fair trade certification, in which activists have explicitly sought to re-embed production and consumption of coffee in interpersonal relationships (Guthman 2007; Raynolds 2000). It was the greater marketization of coffee prices, which followed the crumbling of the International Coffee Agreement price supports, that produced a crash in coffee prices and farmers' incomes and spurred the fair trade movement (Linton, Liou, and Shaw 2004).

However attractive the Polanyian account is as a frame for transnational governance, it is insufficient as an explanation. There is no doubt that collective action against marketization and neoliberal "market fundamentalism" is part of the story behind many rule-making projects, but this general account of resistance does not explain how and when robust collective resistance emerges. Compensatory accounts have little to say about the form that rule-making projects take—that is, as voluntary or mandatory sets of rules, public, private, or mixed. Most importantly, the compensatory account solves the puzzle of rules by positing a simple stepwise approach from market disruption to re-embedding. It has a hard time explaining the continuing coexistence of rules and unruliness, even after protective rules have been more or less institutionalized.

Decoupling

A second way of solving the puzzle of rules is to emphasize the decoupling of rules and practices. Rules may proliferate in the global economy, but they may serve primarily symbolic, legitimating purposes, while remaining decoupled from "on the ground" activities. Furthermore, the more unruly the activities, the greater is the need for symbolic structures to legitimate them. This type of argument, inspired by Meyer and Rowan's (1977) classic account of decoupling, has become a common way of making sense of the continued unruliness of globalization even as more and more standards are adopted. Hafner-Burton and Tsustui (2005) use the concept of "radical decoupling" to explain why ratification of human rights treaties is associated with *worsening* of human rights records.

There is no doubt that decoupling is rampant in global governance. But a focus on decoupling is at best a partial answer to the puzzle of rules. At worst, emphasizing decoupling is a shorthand way of recognizing contradictory dynamics without really making sense of them. In addition, like the compensatory account, theories of decoupling speak only in the broadest of terms about the nature of rule-making projects. The themes that scholars have identified as central to global legitimation—universalism, individualism, and science—can take numerous forms and inspire a wide array of different rule-making projects, but beyond invoking "myth and ceremony," the decoupling account has little to say about this.

Neoliberalism: Rules and Unruliness Cut from the Same Cloth

Consider a further solution. Whereas the previous two accounts treat rules and unruliness as separate, interacting phenomena, we may also ask if there is a common thread running through both the "ruliness" and unruliness of globalization, a singular source of these seemingly contradictory phenomena. Might the unruly and rule-generating features of globalization be "cut from the same cloth"? There are reasons to think so, and to view neoliberalism as that cloth. By neoliberalism, I mean a set of ideas stressing the power of "free markets" and an associated political project of deregulation, privatization, and the removal of other impediments to the flow of capital across borders (Fourcade-Gourinchas and Babb 2002).

The neoliberal project to make the world more like "one big market" has also, to a great extent, created the puzzle of rules. This explanation relies on two basic arguments. First, neoliberalism leads to an increase in the number of rules but also to a change in the character of rules, such that they are less likely to enforce collective social control of markets. Second, because neoliberalism is not monolithic but rather a polyvalent set of ideas and practices

(Ferguson 2009), a neoliberal order sometimes does open up paths for alternative rule-making projects (such as those that constrain rather than enable markets). I take up each of these arguments in turn.

That the neoliberal project is also a massive rule-making project is evident in the construction of the World Trade Organization (WTO), which grew out of the 1947 General Agreement on Tariffs and Trade and turned into a massive rule-making project, especially for dispute resolution (Kim 2010). The construction of the WTO is a prime example of what political scientists call the "legalization" of international institutions, that is, the development of rules that are obligatory, precise, and delegated from governments to authorized international organizations (Goldstein et al. 2000). But WTO rules are of a particular sort, privileging the expansion of markets (Chorev 2005) and the protection of private property rights, especially intellectual property (Sell 2003). WTO jurisprudence has occasionally allowed *exceptions* (DeSombre and Barkin 2002), but it has been quite wary of setting market-restricting rules.

That neoliberalism expands particular types of rules can also be seen in the analysis of "freer markets, more rules" in infrastructure industries, as described above (Levi-Faur and Jordana 2005; Vogel 1996). This type of "regulation *for* competition" may necessarily require some regulation *of* competition and even some engagement with questions of equity and rights (Chng 2012). But the authorities charged with this task have been convincingly described as fundamentally technocratic in orientation with the explicit charge to buffer markets from democratic forces (Roberts 2010).

Rules for sustainable and fair production—like those in the apparel and forest products industries—appear to contest the market, or at least to insert alternative "orders of worth" beyond price. But their mode of doing so is profoundly shaped by neoliberalism. They are voluntary rules, trumpeted by many as removing the need for coercion, binding obligation, or an omniscient central authority. (All of these have been elements of the neoliberal critique of states from Hayek (1944) onward. See Plehwe 2010). They are created and enforced by private actors (for example, coalitions of NGOs and firms) for reasons that are directly tied to neoliberalism: Because they were private, they were largely immune to WTO rules against *state* imposition of "non-tariff barriers to trade," and they received early support from governments in part for this reason (Bartley 2007). In addition, programs to certify and label fair or sustainable products invoke an image of the individual, autonomous, ethically choosing consumer as their driving force. In reality, more collectively organized forms of protest and market demand have often been behind the expansion of certification (Bartley 2011a; McNichol 2006; Seidman 2007), but the image of the autonomous consumer remains potent as a legitimating force (Maniates and Meyer 2010).

A promising attempt to theorize the character of rules under neoliberalism comes from Streeck (2009), who describes a shift from rules that enforce a shared social obligation to those that facilitate market-building and coordination. (He calls the former "Durkheimian," in reference to Émile Durkheim, the classical theorist of collective representation and solidarity, and the latter "Williamsonian," in reference to economist Oliver Williamson's work on how institutions make markets more efficient.) An expansion of rules and institutions "is fully compatible with a liberal order as long as the institutions in question either make markets possible or are driven by them, promoting competition and presumably, as a result, competitiveness and efficiency" (158). Put slightly differently, the proliferation of rules under globalization has expanded "market-making" or "market-enforcing" regulation without expanding "market-correcting" or "market-restricting" regulation. Perhaps the aphorism should not be "freer markets, more rules" but "more rules, less control," at least in the sense of collective control *of* the market by citizens.

While ruliness and unruliness may be cut from the same cloth of neoliberalism, it is important not to assume a monolithic neoliberalism. There is more variety in the shape of global rule-making projects than a strong account of neoliberal hegemony would predict. Ferguson (2009) makes this point in reflecting on "basic income" policies in South Africa that mix neoliberal arguments for "human capital investment" and against "welfare dependency" with redistributive goals that are typically thought of as anathema to neoliberalism. In some circumstances, rule-making projects that privilege markets may have elements that are not easily reconciled with the expansion of markets, or they may open up avenues for rules that do restrict markets, subjecting them to more stringent, potentially more democratic, external social control.

Consider two examples from the case of forestry standards. Forest Stewardship Council certification has grown through partnerships between its main NGO sponsor (WWF), retailers (Home Depot, B&Q, and Ikea), and the World Bank. In some ways, it has become incorporated into neoliberal governance, and it derives substantial credibility among advocates of neoliberalism for being voluntary, market-based, and consumer-driven. But some elements of the FSC standards are much harder to square with a neoliberal logic. In particular, FSC Principles 2 and 3 recognize customary communal land rights, even when these are not legally recognized. These challenging provisions have made it more difficult to expand FSC certification (Colchester, Sirait, and Wijardjo 2003), yet they have remained intact. A totalizing account of neoliberalism as the solution to the puzzle of rules would not expect such standards to exist at all, but a more nuanced view allows for market-restricting rules to exist at the margins of market-enhancing rules.

A second example from forestry illustrates how a neoliberal order can sometimes support rule-making projects that restrict international trade. In response to the problem of illegal logging described above, both the United States and European Union have passed or extended laws (the Lacey Act and EU Timber Regulation) that restrict the import of illegally harvested timber. Notably, these are binding rules that impose hard and significant penalties—confiscation of products, monetary penalties (and in the United States even possible imprisonment)—on firms that import products made in violation of forestry laws in their country of origin. The laws (especially in the EU) were designed not to run afoul of WTO rules about trade barriers, and although they are not entirely in the clear, it is plausible that they would survive WTO challenges (Brack 2009). A complex combination of factors, having to do with scrutiny, learning, and industry interests, helped to bring about this new timber legality regime (Overdevest and Zeitlin, 2012). Most important for the topic at hand is that the emerging timber legality regime suggests that there is some space, albeit constrained, within the neoliberal order for bringing global rules that restrict rather than just coordinate markets, although the construction of this around "legality" raises additional conundrums (Abraham and Schendel 2005).

In sum, being attuned to the effects of neoliberalism helps us solve the puzzle of rules by showing that much of the proliferation of rules is due to the growth of market-making or market-enhancing rules, though some market-restricting rules are also possible at the margins. If one wants to understand how globalization can be simultaneously unruly and rule-generating, then attention to neoliberalism is crucial. This analysis should not entirely replace attention to compensatory processes or to decoupling, and the three processes may intersect in revealing ways. For instance, the Polanyian double movement may be taking on a decidedly neoliberal hue as attempts to re-embed markets take on narrow market logics and get co-opted by firms (Guthman 2007). Neither do these processes cover the entire gamut of rules across different settings or at different scales, especially since subnational rules have their own complexities (see Griffiths, chapter 6 this volume) and since profound power differences make some rule-making projects appear farcical (see Mascarenhas, chapter 14 this volume). But the puzzle of rules provides an entry point into a number of salient questions about global industries, standard-setting initiatives, and the evolution of regulation.

FRAMING GLOBAL (UN)RULINESS

"The global" could not exist without rules. Rules constitute social order, facilitate exchange and cooperation, and set limits for action—defining socially constructed but practically important lines between fair and unfair, appropriate and inappropriate, and even seemingly basic distinctions like foreign and domestic. Global capitalism structures and is structured by many kinds of rules. Yet scholars have been slow to come to terms with the full relationship between rules and globalization. A first wave of research painted globalization as unruly. In reaction, a second wave painted it as founded on and generative of rules. The time has come to bring these images together and to grapple with the accuracy of both images.

To be sure, this puzzle and the solutions proposed here are stylized, ideal-typical versions. In particular domains, industries, places, and times, it may be possible to assess whether ruliness or unruliness wins out, whether the tendency of globalization to produce rules outweighs the tendency of globalization to subvert them. But in most settings, the two seem to go together. We can account for this by invoking a Polanyian double movement from commodification to decommodification or by invoking decoupling of rules and practices. But a more thoroughgoing solution comes from the analysis of neoliberalism, which shows how rules can grow in number while changing in character in ways that most often reduce collective social control of markets.

REFERENCES

Abraham, Itty, and Willem van Schendel. 2005. "Introduction: The Making of Illicitness." In *Illicit Flows and Criminal Things*, ed. Itty Abraham and Willem van Schendel, 1–37. Bloomington: Indiana University Press.

Bartley, Tim. 2005. "Corporate Accountability and the Privatization of Labor Standards: Struggles over Codes of Conduct in the Apparel Industry." *Research in Political Sociology* 12: 211–44.

———. 2007. "Institutional Emergence in an Era of Globalization: The Rise of Transnational Private Regulation of Labor and Environmental Conditions." *American Journal of Sociology* 113(2): 297–351.

———. 2011a. "Certification as a Mode of Social Regulation." In *Handbook on the Politics of Regulation*, ed. David Levi-Faur, 441–52. Northampton, MA: Edward Elgar.

———. 2011b. "Transnational Governance as the Layering of Rules: Intersections of Public and Private Standards." *Theoretical Inquiries in Law* 12(2): 25–51.

Berman, Paul Schiff. 2007. "Global Legal Pluralism." *Southern California Law Review* 80: 1155–1238.

Bernstein, Steven, and Benjamin Cashore. 2007. "Can Non-State Global Governance Be Legitimate? An Analytical Framework." *Regulation & Governance* 1(4): 347–71.

Brack, Duncan. 2009. *Combating Illegal Logging: Interaction with WTO Rules.* London: Chatham House. Briefing paper.

Braithwaite, John, and Peter Drahos. 2000. *Global Business Regulation.* New York: Cambridge University Press.

Bronfenbrenner, Kate. 2000. *Uneasy Terrain: The Impact of Capital Mobility on Workers, Wages, and Union Organizing.* Ithaca, NY: Author. Submitted to the U.S. Trade Deficit Review Commission, http://digitalcommons.ilr.cornell.edu/reports/3/.

Büthe, Tim, and Walter Mattli. 2011. *The New Global Rulers: The Privatization of Regulation in the World Economy.* Princeton, NJ: Princeton University Press.

Campbell, John L. 2004. *Institutional Change and Globalization.* Princeton, NJ: Princeton University Press.

Cashore, Benjamin, Graeme Auld, and Deanna Newsom. 2004. *Governing through Markets: Forest Certification and the Emergence of Non-State Authority.* New Haven, CT: Yale University Press.

Chan, Anita, and Robert J. S. Ross. 2003. "Racing to the Bottom: International Trade without a Social Clause." *Third World Quarterly* 24: 1011–28

Chng, Nai Rui. 2012. "Regulatory Mobilization and Service Delivery at the Edge of the Regulatory State." *Regulation & Governance* 6(3): 344–61.

Chorev, Nitsan. 2005. "The Institutional Project of Neo-Liberal Globalism: The Case of the WTO." *Theory and Society* 34: 317–55.

Colchester, Marcus, Martua Sirait, and Boedhi Wijardjo. 2003. "The Application of FSC Principles 2 and 3 in Indonesia: Obstacles and Possibilities." Report published by Wahana Lingkungan Hidup (WALHI), Aliansi Masyarakat Adat Nusantara (AMAN), and the Rainforest Foundation. Bogor, Indonesia.

Cowie, Jefferson. 1999. *Capital Moves: RCA's Seventy-Year Quest for Cheap Labor.* New York: The New Press.

Daly, Herman E., and John B. Cobb. 1994. *For the Common Good: Re-directing the Economy Toward Community, the Environment, and a Sustainable Future.* Boston: Beacon Press.

Dauvergne, Peter, and Jane Lister. 2011. *Timber.* Malden, MA: Polity Press.

Deininger, Klaus, and Derek Byerlee. 2011. "Rising Global Interest in Farmland." Washington, DC: World Bank.

DeSombre, Elizabeth R. 2006. *Flagging Standards: Globalization and Environmental, Safety, and Labor Regulations at Sea.* Cambridge, MA: MIT Press.

DeSombre, Elizabeth R., and J. Samuel Barkin. 2002. "Turtles and Trade: The WTO's Acceptance of Environmental Trade Restrictions." *Global Environmental Politics* 2(1): 12–18.

DiMaggio, Paul, and Walter W. Powell. 1991. "Introduction." In *The New Institutionalism in Organizational Analysis,* ed. Walter W. Powell and Paul DiMaggio. Chicago: University of Chicago Press.

Dingwerth, Klaus, and Philipp Pattberg. 2009. "World Politics and Organizational Fields: The Case of Transnational Sustainability Governance." *European Journal of International Relations* 15(4): 707–43.

Djelic, Marie-Laure, and Kerstin Sahlin-Andersson, eds. 2006. *Transnational Governance: Institutional Dynamics of Regulation.* New York: Cambridge University Press.

Douglas, Mary. 1986. *How Institutions Think.* Syracuse, NY: Syracuse University Press.

Drezner, Daniel W. 2007. *All Politics Is Global: Explaining International Regulatory Regimes.* Princeton, NJ: Princeton University Press.

Dubash, Navroz K., and Bronwen Morgan. 2012. "Understanding the Rise of the Regulatory State of the South." *Regulation & Governance* 6(3): 261–81.

Eberlein, Burkard, and Edgar Grande. 2005. "Beyond Delegation: Transnational Regulatory Regimes and the EU Regulatory State." *Journal of European Public Policy* 12(1): 89–112.

Evans, Peter. 1997. "The Eclipse of the State? Reflections on Stateness in an Era of Globalization." *World Politics* 50: 62–87.

Feenstra, Robert C. 1998. "Integration of Trade and Disintegration of Production in the Global Economy." *Journal of Economic Perspectives* 12(4): 31–50.

Ferguson, James. 2009. "The Uses of Neoliberalism." *Antipode* 41: 166–84.

Fligstein, Neil. 1996. "Markets as Politics: A Political-Cultural Approach to Market Institutions." *American Sociological Review* 61: 656–73.

Fligstein, Neil, and Iona Mara Drita. 1996. "How to Make a Market: Reflections on the Attempt to Create a Single Market in the European Union." *American Journal of Sociology* 102: 1–33.

Food and Agriculture Organization (FAO). 2006. "Global Forest Resources Assessment 2005." Rome: FAO.

———. 2010. "Global Forest Resources Assessment 2010." Rome: FAO.

Fourcade-Gourinchas, Marion, and Sarah L. Babb. 2002. "The Rebirth of the Liberal Creed: Paths to Neoliberalism in Four Countries." *American Journal of Sociology* 103(3): 533–79.

Fransen, Luc W., and Ans Kolk. 2007. "Global Rule-Setting for Business: A Critical Analysis of Multi-Stakeholder Standards." *Organization* 14(5): 667–84.

Goldstein, Judith, Miles Kahler, Robert O. Keohane, and Anne-Marie Slaughter. 2000. "Introduction: Legalization and World Politics." *International Organization* 54(3): 385–99.

Greenhill, Brian, Layna Mosley, and Aseem Prakash. 2009. "Trade-Based Diffusion of Labor Rights: A Panel Study." *American Political Science Review* 103(4): 169–90.

Greider, William. 1998. *One World Ready or Not: The Manic Logic of Global Capitalism.* New York: Simon & Schuster.

Gulbrandsen, Lars H. 2010. *Transnational Environmental Governance: The Emergence and Effects of the Certification of Forests and Fisheries.* Northampton, MA: Edward Elgar.

Gullison, R. E. 2003. "Does Forest Certification Conserve Biodiversity?" *Oryx* 37(2): 153–65.

Guthman, Julie. 2007. "The Polanyian Way? Voluntary Food Labels as Neoliberal Governance." *Antipode* 39(3): 456–78.

Hafner-Burton, Emilie M., and Kiyoteru Tsutsui. 2005. "Human Rights in a Globalizing World: The Paradox of Empty Promises." *American Journal of Sociology* 10: 1373–1411.

Harvey, David. 1982. *The Limits to Capital.* London: Verso.

Hayek, Friedrich von. 1944. *The Road to Serfdom.* Chicago: University of Chicago Press.

Hirst, Paul, Grahame Thompson, and Simon Bromley. 2009. *Globalization in Question.* London: Polity.

Hughes, Caroline. 2007. "Transnational Networks, International Organizations and Political Participation in Cambodia: Human Rights, Labour Rights and Common Rights." *Democratization* 14(5): 834–52.

Jaffe, Adam, Steven Peterson, Paul R. Portney, and Robert Stavins. 1995. "Environmental Regulation and the Competitiveness of U.S. Manufacturing: What Does the Evidence Tell Us?" *Journal of Economic Literature* 33: 132–63.

Kim, Soo Yeon. 2010. *Power and the Governance of Global Trade: From the GATT to the WTO.* Ithaca, NY: Cornell University Press.

Lederer, Markus. 2012. "Market Making via Regulation: The Role of the State in Carbon Markets." *Regulation & Governance* 6(4): 524–44.

Levi-Faur, David, and Jacint Jordana. 2005. "Globalizing Regulatory Capitalism." *The Annals of the American Academy of Political and Social Science* 598: 6–9.

Levin, Peter, and Wendy Nelson Espeland. 2002. "Pollution Futures: Commensuration, Commodification, and the Market for Air." In *Organizations, Policy, and the Natural Environment,* ed. Andrew J. Hoffman and Marc J. Ventresca, 119–47. Stanford, CA: Stanford University Press.

Lindblom, C. E. 1977. *Politics and Markets.* New York: Basic Books.

Linton, April, Cindy Chiayuan Liou, and Kelly Ann Shaw. 2004. "A Taste of Trade Justice: Marketing Global Social Responsibility via Fair Trade Coffee." *Globalizations* 1(2): 223–46.

Lucas, Robert E. B., David Wheeler, and Hemamala Hettige. 1992. "Economic Development, Environmental Regulation and the International Migration of Toxic Industrial Pollution, 1960–88." In *International Trade and the Environment,* ed. P. Low, 67–86. Washington, DC: World Bank Discussion Papers, no. 159.

Maniates, Michael, and John M. Meyer. 2010. *The Environmental Politics of Sacrifice.* Cambridge, MA: MIT Press.

McCarthy, John F. 2004. "Changing to Gray: Decentralization and the Emergence of Volatile Socio-Legal Configurations in Central Kalimantan, Indonesia." *World Development* 32(7): 1199–1223.

McDermott, Constance, Benjamin Cashore, and Peter Kanowski. 2010. *Global Environmental Forest Policies: An International Comparison.* London: Earthscan.

McNichol, Jason. 2006. "Transnational NGO Certification Programs as New Regulatory Forms: Lessons from the Forestry Sector." In *Transnational Governance: Institutional Dynamics of Regulation,* ed. Marie-Laure Djelic and Kerstin Sahlin-Andersson. New York: Cambridge University Press.

Meidinger, Errol. 2006. "The Administrative Law of Global Private-Public Regulation: The Case of Forestry." *European Journal of International Law* 17(1): 47–87.

Merry, Sally Engle. 1988. "Legal Pluralism." *Law & Society Review* 22(5): 869–96.

Meyer, John W., and Brian Rowan. 1977. "Institutional Organizations: Formal Structure as Myth and Ceremony." *American Journal of Sociology* 80: 340–63.

Murphy, Dale D. 2004. "The Business Dynamics of Global Regulatory Competition." In *Dynamics of Regulatory Change: How Globalization Affects National Regulatory Policies*, ed. David Vogel and Robert A. Kagan, 84–117. Berkeley: University of California Press.

Nebel, Gustav, Lincoln Quevedo, Jette Bredahl Jacobsen, and Finn Helles. 2005. "Development and Economic Significance of Forest Certification: The Case of FSC in Bolivia." *Forest Policy and Economics* 7: 175–86.

Nordstrom, Carolyn. 2007. *Global Outlaws: Crime, Money, and Power in the Contemporary World*. Berkeley: University of California Press.

North, Douglass C. 1990. *Institutions, Institutional Change and Economic Performance*. New York: Cambridge University Press.

Ostrom, Elinor. 1990. *Governing the Commons: The Evolution of Institutions for Collective Action*. New York: Cambridge University Press.

Overdevest, Christine, and Jonathan Zeitlin. 2012. "Assembling an Experimentalist Regime: Transnational Governance Interactions in the Forest Sector." *Regulation & Governance*.

Palmer, Donald, and Michael Maher. 2010. "A Normal Accident Analysis of the Mortgage Meltdown." *Research in the Sociology of Organizations* 30A: 219–56.

Parker, Christine. 2008. "The Pluralization of Regulation." *Theoretical Inquiries in Law* 9(2): 349–69.

Perez, Oren. 2003. "Normative Creativity and Global Legal Pluralism: Reflections on the Democratic Critique of Transnational Law." *Indiana Journal of Global Legal Studies* 10(2): 25–64.

Pierson, Paul. 2004. *Politics in Time: History, Institutions, and Social Analysis*. Princeton, NJ: Princeton University Press.

Ping, Li, and Robin Nielsen. 2010. "A Case Study on Large-Scale Forestland Acquisition in China: The Stora Enso Plantation Project in Hepu County, Guangxi Province." Washington, DC: Rights and Resources Initiative.

Plehwe, Dieter. 2010. "The Making of a Comprehensive Transnational Discourse Community." In *Transnational Communities: Shaping Global Economic Governance*, ed. Marie-Laure Djelic and Sigrid Quack, 305–26. Cambridge: Cambridge University Press.

Polanyi, Karl. 1944. *The Great Transformation*. Boston: Beacon Press.

Raynolds, Laura T. 2000. "Re-embedding Global Agriculture: The International Organic and Fair Trade Movements." *Agriculture and Human Values* 17: 297–309.

Roberts, Alisdair. 2010. *The Logic of Discipline: Global Capitalism and the Architecture of Government*. New York: Oxford University Press.

Rodríguez-Garavito, César A. 2005a. "Global Governance and Labor Rights: Codes of Conduct and Anti-Sweatshop Struggles in Global Apparel Factories in Mexico and Guatemala." *Politics and Society* 33(2): 203–33.

———. 2005b. "Nike's Law: The Anti-Sweatshop Movements, Transnational Corporations, and the Struggle over International Labor Rights in the Americas." In *Law and Globalization from Below: Toward a Cosmopolitan Legality*, ed. Boaventura de Sousa Santos and César A. Rodríguez Garavito, 64–91. Cambridge: Cambridge University Press.

Sassen, Saskia. 1996. *Losing Control? Sovereignty in an Age of Globalization*. New York: Columbia University Press.

———. "The State and Globalization." 2002. In *The Emergence of Private Authority in Global Governance,* ed. Rodney Bruce Hall and Thomas J. Biersteker, 91–112. New York: Cambridge University Press.

Schmidt, Vivien A. 1995. "The New World Order, Incorporated: The Rise of Business and the Decline of the Nation State." *Daedalus* 124(2): 75–106.

Schneiberg, Marc, and Tim Bartley. 2010. "Regulating or Redesigning Finance? Market Architectures, Normal Accidents, and Dilemmas of Regulatory Reform." *Research in the Sociology of Organizations* 30A: 281–307.

Schrank, Andrew. 2009. "Professionalization and Probity in a Patrimonial State: Labor Inspectors in the Dominican Republic." *Latin American Politics and Society* 51(2): 91–115.

Schumpeter, Joseph A. 1942. *Capitalism, Socialism, and Democracy.* New York: Harper.

Seidman, Gay. 2007. *Beyond the Boycott: Labor Rights, Human Rights and Transnational Activism.* New York: Russell Sage Foundation/ASA Rose Series.

Sell, Susan K. 2003. *Private Power, Public Law: The Globalization of Intellectual Property Rights.* New York: Cambridge University Press.

Sewell, William H., Jr. 2008. "The Temporalities of Capitalism." *Socio-Economic Review* 6(3): 517–37.

Silva-Castaneda, Laura. 2012. "A Forest of Evidence: Third-Party Certification and Multiple Forms of Proof; A Case Study of Oil Palm Plantations in Indonesia." *Agriculture and Human Values* 29(3): 361–70.

SOMO. 2012. "Bonded (Child) Labour in the South Indian Garment Industry." Amsterdam: Stichting Onderzoek Multinationale Ondernemingen (SOMO).

Strange, Susan. 1996. *The Retreat of the State.* Cambridge: Cambridge University Press.

Streeck, Wolfgang. 2009. *Re-forming Capitalism: Institutional Change in the German Political Economy.* Oxford: Oxford University Press.

Tacconi, Luca, Krystof Obidzinski, Joyotee Smith, Subarudi, and Iman Suramenggalac. 2004. "Can 'Legalization' of Illegal Forest Activities Reduce Illegal Logging?" *Journal of Sustainable Forestry* 19(1): 137–51.

Vogel, David. 1995. *Trading Up: Consumer and Environmental Regulation in a Global Economy.* Cambridge, MA: Harvard University Press.

Vogel, David, and Robert A. Kagan. 2004. *Dynamics of Regulatory Change: How Globalization Affects National Regulatory Policies.* Berkeley: University of California Press.

Vogel, Steven K. 1996. *Freer Markets, More Rules: Regulatory Reform in Advanced Industrial Countries.* Ithaca, NY: Cornell University Press.

Worm, Boris, Edward B. Barbier, Nicola Beaumont, J. Emmett Duffy, Carl Folke, Benjamin S. Halpern, Jeremy B. C. Jackson, Heike K. Lotze, Fiorenza Micheli, Stephen R. Palumbi, Enric Sala, Kimberley A. Selkoe, John J. Stachowicz, and Reg Watson. 2006. "Impacts of Biodiversity Loss on Ocean Ecosystem Services." *Science* 314(5800): 787–90.

12 – SCALE

Exploring the "Global '68"

DEBORAH COHEN AND LESSIE JO FRAZIER

1968: IN PARIS, CHICAGO, MEXICO CITY, PRAGUE, AND RIO, TO NAME but a few places, students took to the streets to fight entrenched powers, many declaring "Make love, not war." For scholars Giovanni Arrighi, Terence K. Hopkins, and Immanuel Wallerstein, such movements made up one of only "two *world* revolutions" (the other was 1848); '68, they argue, dramatically "transformed the *world*."[1] Longtime New Left activist George Katsiaficas wrote *A Global Analysis of 1968*. Popular historian Mark Kurlansky, in *1968: The Year That Rocked the World*, conceived of this as a "pivotal moment . . . in history." These scholars, among many, posit the scale of the '68 transformation as global.[2]

This chapter explores scale and, specifically, global scale. By scale, we invoke a concept that deals with space in philosopher Henri Lefebvre's sense of dimensions of the social: the product of interrelations, as the sphere of coexisting heterogeneity, and as always in the process of formation and never closed. As geographer Doreen Massey insists with respect to space, scale is not just place.[3] Scale refers to the arenas in which political, economic, and social processes and practices are imagined and investigated as occurring; such processes and practices are scalar. Global scale, then, is such an arena. "Globalization"—the term most conventionally associated with 1990s neo-liberal rearrangements of a global scale—actually gained currency during the late 1960s; as the global became a critical category in the Cold War (more or less 1948–1989). The exigencies of the Cold War brought about significant economic, political, and cultural rearrangements of prior colonial and impe-rial formations, rearrangements which produced the globe as a "unitary"— that is, planetary—"sphere," especially for the two superpowers, the United States and the Soviet Union.[4] This U.S. "imperial imperative," says Denis Cosgrove, enabled "the modern geopolitical imagination," which, accord-ing to geographer Neil Smith, allowed the United States to hide its "global ambitions."[5] In other words, recent scholarly and popular ideas about global scale have a historical genesis in the Cold War. Not only are these global re-arrangements the critical context for understanding the global scale of 1968; understanding scale's genesis helps explain why some phenomena, such as '68, are deemed "global" in scope in ways that usually go unexamined.

Scale as an analytical category brings into focus the scope of these rear-rangements, be that scope local, regional, national, hemispheric, or global. It delineates the scope of the rearrangements and aids in its visualization. Of import, problematizing this concept makes clear that the Cold War was not just a new set of military threats and alliances, but a profound global reimagining of the sites, agents, and spheres of critical action. Sixties student movements came out of, tapped into, and (often unintentionally) furthered this global (re)imagining.

This chapter has three aims: (1) to sketch current debates around scale and show why scale is so important to scholars; (2) to suggest a historical under-standing of the problem and use of scale in global studies; and (3) to posit that sexual intimacy and political desire in the 1960s became global in ways that further challenge how we as scholars use scale. Even as sociologist Saskia Sassen finds the global in the local, we posit a multi-directional methodol-ogy of scale where dynamics usually associated with the local are locatable as the global.[6] The global parameters of late 1960s social movements suggest the multi-scalar reorderings of the Cold War as both novel and fundamental to the attendant political, economic, and cultural changes that brought these movements to fruition.

SCHOLARLY SCALE DEBATES

Since the mid-1980s, there have been "a series of attempts to alternatively complicate and unravel the hierarchy located at the heart of scale theorizing."[7] Foundational—from the perspective of geographers Sallie Marston, John Paul Jones, and Keith Woodward—was a 1982 paper by Peter Taylor that laid out a "three-scale structure" model that mapped "the micro scale of the urban onto the domain of experience; the meso scale of the nation state onto the sphere of ideology; and the macro scale of the global onto the 'scale of reality.'"[8] What made Taylor's work critical, these geographers say, was that "he theorize[d] these levels (urban, nation, global) as separated domains, . . . trac[ing] their emergence to the expanding capitalist mode of production" and with the latter—the global—being the scale that "really matter[ed]."[9] Others, such as Neil Smith, picking up on Taylor's formulation, contended that it was necessary to recognize "a duality of spatial fixity and fluidity" such that scale is understood as "the always malleable geographic resolution of competition and cooperation."[10] These changes have implicitly conflated scale with size—as in the "horizontal measure of 'expansiveness'"—and with "level," discussed in terms of local, national, or global, making the concept, say Marston, Jones, and Woodward, of little use.[11]

Pro-scale researchers challenged their assessment, contending that a nuanced reformation of scale has benefited scholars by forcing them to resituate the nation-state, rather than making it uncritically *the* de facto unit of analysis or conflating nation with state. We see a conflation of nation and state in the tendency to use capital cities to stand in for the entire nation, while peripheries and frontiers are identified as particular or provincial; and certain specific places come to represent whole regions.[12]

Historians from the 1960s to the present have engaged in their own scalar experimentations. Sixties radicalization intensified scholars' questioning of "big man" history (primarily of nation-state leaders) to instantiate political commitments to non-elite social justice. The Annales school traced the long-term, aggregate social transformation of daily life; similarly, quantitative methods allowed the new field of demographic history to track population movements over wide swaths of time. The people's history movement collaborated with workers to produce histories of work and working-class communities. Marxist feminist and anti-imperialist scholars built on the insight that "the personal is political" to develop new methods to plumb archives for evidence of the struggles of subordinated sectors and to trace the impact of imperialism on psyches. The 1980s saw the emergence of ethnographically informed microhistory of "everyday life." Historians influenced by philosopher Michel Foucault connected the rise of modern institutions with epistemic individuation. Subaltern and then postcolonial studies pulled many of these innovations together to construct alternative histories of capitalism and empire; legacies of this move thrive in transnational history. A current experimentation is "big history," which subordinates human scale to planetary geo-temporal and deep evolutionary scales, rendering obsolescent dynamics of power, domination, and cultural variation among human populations. Cognizant of scale's messiness, we contend that the politics of its arrival as a methodological and foreign policy category is key to understanding the Cold War's spatial rearrangements that birthed student movement of the late 1960s.

RE-IMAGINING THE GLOBE:
"THE GLOBAL" AS SCALE IN HISTORICAL CONTEXT

The Cold War political imaginaries attached to the globe as the scale of action and imagination have an imperial history, and a politics of knowledge is imbricated in it. The post–World War II period culminating in the Cold War, loosely defined as beginning after World War II and continuing until the fall of the Berlin Wall in 1989, saw a major reconceptualization of the globe. "The world once divided by oceans and mountain ranges," said President Dwight D. Eisenhower in 1954, "is now split by hostile concepts of man's character and nature . . . into [two] world camps, . . . [camps] farther apart in motivation and conduct than the [Earth's] poles in space."[13] This Eisenhowerian realignment, that is, remapped divisions between people. It "affirmed the . . . spatial division" on which the Cold War was premised: the first world (the developed nation-states of Europe, the United States, and Japan); the second world (the now defunct Soviet bloc), and the third world (today often termed the Global South). More importantly, it broke down the understanding of these then supposedly developed first- and second-world countries as the center of import and action, substituting a recognition that the security of the nation was now dependent on the world's "remote corners."[14] Indeed, with the founding of the Bretton Woods institutions (International Monetary Fund, World Bank) and the United Nations, the nation-state became the required unit of polity. The scale of the nation was elided in a gendered logic with that of the household, seen to be wholly white, suburban, patriarchal, and nuclear-family, which must be defended at all costs by militaries and defense intellectuals who, in this logic, are imbued with a militarized masculinity. Terms like nation, region, globe, continent, and city, already marked as scalar (or indicating scale), had been in widespread use prior to this period, says geographer Matthew Farish, yet "the imaginative geographies that came to define the American Cold War . . . were fundamentally redefined . . . *in strategic terms.*"[15] The entire planet became what Daniel Lerner then called the "global arena of [U.S.] national action."[16] That is, though mountains had not moved and the flow of streams had not been reversed, this "profoundly imaginative reordering" made parts of the globe heretofore considered "[ir]relevant" critical to national security, especially U.S. national security.[17] Yet despite this new hierarchical reordering as first, second, and third world, "the nation" was still the operational unit for these new imaginative geographies. The change? Formerly unimportant nations (and peoples within them) now took on new significance and became sites of concern and intervention. Scale, in other words, became strategic.

One concrete outcome of Eisenhower's global reordering was that, by the late 1950s, intervention (overt and covert) became the U.S. watchword of the day. This interventionism, says historian Odd Arne Westad, "create[d] the Third World as a conceptual entity": from a U.S. state perspective, "these were areas to be intervened in;" just as important, "seen from the [Global] South, [these same] areas . . . had a common interest in resisting intervention."[18] In other words, this newly discovered arena of U.S. concern and action laid the groundwork for the dialectical relationship from which late 1960s social movements would emerge and to which they would respond, engage, and advocate.

Yet not only was the nation set in a new rendering of global schema, there was also a rethinking, by President Eisenhower, of the globe in terms of human character. While eugenics—and social Darwinism (the ideology of applying evolution to individual societies and their global rankings) before it—had hierarchized the countries of the world since after the middle of the nineteenth century based on the racialized intellectual potential of their people for progress, this post–World War II reordering was different: the body itself was considered universally problematic and an open and critical site for society's remaking. "Our problem is the brain inside the Japanese head," intoned a 1945 U.S. military instructional film. "There are seventy million of these in Japan, physically no different than any other brains in the world, actually all made from exactly the same stuff as ours. These brains, like our brains, can do good things or bad things, depending on the kind of ideas that are put inside."[19] This postwar description of the Japanese stood in marked contrast to an earlier eugenicist understanding that had seen different so-called races of human beings that comprised not just different human potentialities but different substances or at least amounts of substances. In places such as Mexico, for example, the goal had been to whiten the population through the immigration of those deemed white, who would in turn intermarry with Mexicans and give birth to a literally lightened generation. Now, however, the problem was less one of different human groups with different *biologies,* that is, of racial markings that made this differentiation knowable from the outside—as the film said, Japanese brains were "physically no different" from other brains. Rather, it was one of culture, character, and people—different *sociologies.* The goal for the United States, then, was to fill these Japanese heads (indeed the heads of *all* people) with the right "kind of ideas"—democracy and capitalism—remaking every nation in our own image. Only through this social remaking could Japan and the Japanese, in this case, be redeemed.[20]

Remaking the Japanese brain and body, like those of other human groups inhabiting places now deemed important within the U.S. strategic sphere, required the knowledge about these brains, these bodies, these places. This requirement generated the need for newly conceived area studies experts: people who could understand their culture, language, and history. Few were experts in these regions before World War II; yet postwar independence movements, supposed Communist beachheads, and other forms of Global South resistance highlighted a lack of information. The Ford Foundation, the Rockefeller Foundation, and the Carnegie Foundation, in particular, sounded the alarm. Their representatives pressured Congress about the need to fund the production of knowledge about these unruly places. Of particular need, argued these foundations, were political scientists who understood different political systems and economists who knew the economies of particular countries, as well as language specialists, anthropologists, and historians. These foundations, together with the U.S. government, established and funded programs at major universities to produce country specialists. Not only did these programs expand to meet federal demands, the need for and production of experts tied universities to the federal government in new ways at the moment when modernization theory demanded an expansion of universities themselves. While new university-government liaisons did create a coterie of scholars and practitioners essential to the production and use of this new knowledge, the suspicion and ultimate rejection of these ties provoked the backlash that inspired student movements.

The Cold War need for knowledge and experts and the university's role in their production were both the cause and effect of a spatial reordering writ large. The changes that brought into being a bipolar—United States (free) versus Soviet Union (totalitarian)—world not only left European colonial powers further weakened and discredited; it also put in play independence movements in places such as Africa and Asia. The transformation of former colonies into nation-states coincided with an emerging consensus among former colonial powers and newly dominant ones that economies would continue to be interlinked. They especially understood that all countries benefited from avoiding the kinds of dramatic boom-and-bust cycles that had culminated in the global debacle of the Great Depression. Modernization theory, with its economic, political, and social prescriptions for each then-unmodern country to become modern, would work against this past debacle. It would move these countries into the global economy and position them not as outsiders, but as critical participants.

MOVING NATIONS ONTO THE GLOBAL ECONOMY: ACCEPTING MODERNIZATION THEORY

Part of what would enable this economic repositioning and the attendant scalar reordering "in strategic terms" emerged from a shift in thinking about the racial ordering of the world and the relationship of race to governance.[21] From the second half of the nineteenth century till the end of World War II, social Darwinism, a theory that applied broad concepts from evolution to the development of human beings and governance, had been one of two widely accepted and interrelated racial ideologies; the other was eugenics, the application of evolutionary ideas to bring about supposed better breeding of individuals. Despite their differences, both mapped not just different racial groups but entire countries onto a single racial hierarchy where white (and whitish) people and, thus, the countries they inhabited occupied the highest rungs, blacks the lowest, and other classes of people were somewhere in the middle. According to these two theories, non-white countries (and their peoples) could progress, yet they would always remain less developed—"behind" in the language of the day—than predominantly white countries, or those dominated by groups environmental historian Alfred Crosby terms "neo-Europeans."[22] For eugenicists, there was always an absolute limit to the advancement of non-white countries and peoples. As such, each country's potential could always be known by looking at the racial composition of its population.

After World War II, with the discrediting of Nazism and fascism, eugenics and social Darwinism lost the scientific acceptance they had previously had. Modernization, the process of becoming modern, became the palliative of all social ills; and with it came modernization theory, a different kind of explanation of why some countries had progressed and others had not, and a roadmap for the latter to follow in emulation. Both approaches were attempted by leaders in many places, such as Mexico.[23] "For centuries the bulk of the world's population has been . . . inert. Outside America and Western Europe, and even in parts of the latter, until recently the pattern of society remained essentially fixed in the mold of low-productivity rural life centered on isolated villages. The possibility of change for most people seemed remote." Change was now possible, even likely. "We are in the midst of a great world revolution [of progress]."[24]

In contrast to earlier explanations, modernization theory ostensibly traded racial explanations for patterns of behavior. It advocated four prescriptions for progress: democracy and democratic institutions; the belief in technological and scientific advancements grounded in education; impersonal and routinized (as opposed to personal) citizen-state relations; and, no surprise here, free market capitalism. Although the United States considered itself the paragon of modern nation-states, it too embraced modernization theory. With millions of soldiers returning home to no job or job prospects (along with the specter of another depression), the federal government accelerated the focus on education and put into place a legislative package designed to follow modernization theory's prescriptions. Named the G.I. Bill, it specifically supported job training and university education for former military men (women were largely exempted; and gay men were overwhelmingly denied benefits).[25] Former soldiers saw the advantages of a college education and flocked to universities, especially publicly financed, land-grant institutions, kicking off a massive university expansion both in the hiring of more faculty and in investment in buildings, science labs, and other facilities. Young men whose parents and grandparents had not been able to partake of a university education, largely because of the cost, scarcity of seats, and class prescription, now filled college dorms and classrooms. And more women followed, albeit sometimes concerned less with access to a good job than with a "Mrs." degree, as the co-ed became established as a new, thoroughly modern gender, erotically animating the university campus.

While the United States strengthened its position by adhering to modernization theory's prescriptions, it was not the only country to do so. Many countries, especially those in Latin America, followed its recommendations, in particular expanding access to education. In Mexico, for example, the main public university in Mexico City, the Universidad Nacional Autónoma de México, grew fourfold. In 1949, it enrolled 23,192 students;[26] twenty years later, a year after the state had challenged the university's label as autonomous and police breached the campus, enrollment was over 100,000.[27]

Ultimately, modernization theory, while not an explicitly racial ideology akin to its eugenicist and social Darwinist predecessors, had racial implications. Whereas these earlier ideological tracts closely mapped a country's *national* racial composition onto a global racial hierarchy and thus its attendant possibilities of progress, modernization theory said essentially that any country of whatever racial makeup that followed its prescriptions could advance. Gone, therefore, were the explicit racial limits on progress of eugenics and social Darwinism. That is, although non-white countries might have, at that moment, been labeled as behind the white developed world in the critical components of progress, all countries, regardless of current racial makeup, could advance if they adhered to modernization theory's prescriptions and logic. A language of population management,[28] applied at a global scale, glossed the still deeply racial logic of the world order.

Thus, the new Cold War priorities and concerns of the two superpowers—the requirement for countries to align as either "Communist" or "free";

the anti-colonial struggles for independence from former colonial powers; the moves to strengthen economies—forced all players not just to see the world in a new way, but to reimagine a new *global* world. Gone was the earlier world mapping that had, for the United States, centered North America and Europe; where Latin America had been considered in need of U.S. help and guidance, and part of the proverbial U.S. backyard; and where other countries, especially those in Africa and Asia, were not the site of consequential action. All countries, and regions of countries, were now considered significant to this bipolar struggle; and it influenced the political struggles and economic changes happening in previously unimportant places. What modernization theory assured these formerly backward racialized people and their political leaders, independent of whose side in the bipolar struggle they chose, was both the promise of progress and a larger role in this reimagined world. Third world elites, who were "looking for a new concrete form for their states and societies" to progress so that they, too, could join the modern nations' club, saw the production of this world as "the duty of American social scientists"; modernization, whose bandwagon they readily joined, was that form.[29] Thus, the U.S. (and Soviet) focus on *all* countries was part of divvying up the world on a bipolar chessboard, a "[re]link[ing] of spaces" that enabled the logic and "simple geographic configuration for the Cold War."[30] That is, these Cold War reconfigurations were a significant scalar rearrangement.

U.S. Americans, as newly preeminent global imperial actors, were not automatically interested in these formerly obscure places, however; tired of World War II's rationing and hardship, they turned their attentions to home with war's end. Yet the Cold War's strategic demands, with particular governmental policies and allocation of resources, required that they care. Such affective investment was buttressed by the fundamentally gendered terms through which modernization theory intellectuals understood the world as one of feminized "traditional" societies and masculinized "modern" ones. As political scientist Catherine Scott demonstrates, modernization instantiated "the triumph of penetration, identity, and legitimation, and the subordination of tradition, nature, and the 'feminine.'"[31] After all, citizens of undeveloped countries, hungry, sick, and unschooled in democratic thought and practice, would be susceptible to communism's promises. And their leaders framed the discussion on communism in terms that would make the need for caring abundantly clear. "[W]idespread poverty and chaos [would] lead to a collapse of existing political and social structures which would inevitably invite the advance of totalitarianism into every weak and unstable area," said President John F. Kennedy.[32] These same populations, he told the U.S. listening audience, desired modernity: "The whole southern half of the world—Latin America, Africa, the Middle East, and Asia—are caught up in the adventures of asserting their independence and modernizing their old ways of life."[33] Too bad, however, that supposed leftists in Guatemala were pushing the country toward the wrong kind of modernization—communism—precipitating a U.S.-led overthrow of a democratically elected president.

The postwar period, then, saw a massive educational effort to generate awareness of, emotional attachment to, and caring about formerly insignificant places. Federally funded area study centers at universities promoted linguistic and cultural expertise vital to global security. In books, musicals, movies, magazines, and plays like *The King and I*, says American studies scholar Christina Klein, U.S. Americans were bombarded with the imperative of winning the hearts and minds of the so-called natives of those faraway places.[34] Countries such as Trinidad, Siam [Thailand], Guatemala, and Iran came to be part of the lexicon, as the U.S. government intervened, usually covertly, to bring about supposedly democratic change.[35] That is, while university students were learning the culture, language, history, and politics that would aid in the interventions in these countries, the general public was being schooled in them, too. In a much more heavy-handed way than in university area studies programs, the federal government sought to shape the knowledge U.S. voters and schoolchildren learned.

Part of the U.S. strategy to dissuade foreign leaders from communism was the carrot of U.S. aid: for example, the Marshall Plan, which enabled western Europe to rebuild, and the millions sent to Iran and Guatemala after the CIA-backed coups.[36] Secretary of State Henry Kissinger saw this aid as the road to persuading reluctant countries to follow modernization theory's prescribed capitalist development: "[D]evelopment [through modernization theory's priorities and techniques] was a matter of choice, and the model was the United States and its free enterprise [system]."[37]

The United States put modernization theory's prescriptions in place through the Peace Corps and the Alliance for Progress (AFP). "The [Kennedy] administration," said Arthur Schlesinger, "had to engineer 'a middle

class revolution where the processes of economic modernization carry the
new urban middle class into power and produce, along with it, such necessities of modern technical society as constitutional government, honest public
administration, a responsible party system, a rational land system, an efficient system of taxation.'"[38] Yet there was pushback from other U.S. agencies
and major players. Some, like John Foster Dulles, secretary of state under
Dwight Eisenhower, advocated "deterrent of massive retaliatory power," the
notion that the United States could curtail communism's appeal through un-
leashing its nuclear arsenal (on the Soviet Union) where and when it chose.[39]
The U.S. Agency for International Development, a federal division in charge
of administering non-military foreign aid, saw "successful efforts to influence
macro-economic and sectoral policies . . . a[s] likely to have greater impact
on growth than added capital and skills financed by aid."[40]

Still others saw it differently. Some imagined the goal of foreign aid was
to "contain communism *and* reduce the need for . . . access to U.S. markets"; while others saw the purpose of "global development education"—
both bringing technology and know-how to the underdeveloped world and
drawing foreigners to U.S. universities—as encouraging "the world to open
its markets," thus, ensuring the flow of private local capital.[41] Behind foreign
logic was always Success American Style, highlighted through displays of
U.S. products in overseas exhibitions. Freedom became synonymous with
and achievable through "washing machines and dishwashers, vacuum clean-
ers, automobiles, and refrigerators."[42] Regardless of whether officials pushed
U.S. aid or the threat of retaliation, federal decisions on whether or not to
award economic aid to individual countries linked individual consumer decisions to global economic models and military rearrangements. These were
ultimately scalar decisions.

While the United States was imposing key parts of modernization theory's
prescription in the non-developed world, it was also implicitly taking aspects of it and Keynesian economics to heart at home, especially through
expanding access to university education. Illustrative of the trepidation that
elites felt with respect to this expansion of social, political, and economic
life and its intrinsically destabilizing potentiality are the queer contours
of John Maynard Keynes's underlying and never-quite-realized "model for
modernity and for the postwar international economic order." This model,
critic Bill Maurer explains, entailed a transgressive "cosmopolitantism and a

perspective-shifting experimentalism" where the global institutions Keynes envisioned were built out of multiple "'parallel, intertwined and mutually reinforcing' logical chains . . . contingent and partial."[43] Keynes's models emerged organically from the Bloomsbury Group's intellectual minglings of practices of aesthetics, economics, and desires. Though the radical potential of Keynes's queer modeling of political economy remained unrealized in general, a more encapsulated model of promiscuous engagement was lived by some on university campuses around the world in '68.

1968 FROM A SCALAR PERSPECTIVE:
THE GEOPOLITICS OF MISCEGENATION AND MODERNIZATION

The 1960s culminated a dramatic shift in the dominant ideology justifying the hierarchy of nations (and of races/ethnicities within them) and the unequal global distribution of wealth; it was the heyday of modernization theory. Modernization theory, in contrast to eugenics and social Darwinism, did not explain differences in wealth in terms of biological superiority and inferiority, but instead promised that all nations could progress through technology, incubation of domestic industry, and, crucial to understanding the 1960s, expansion of education.

Around the globe, local elites, who had accrued power around the prior (biologically reproductive) racialized frame of political economy, were thrown into panic by the seismic shifts in the social order required for modernizationist "progress." For technological mechanisms to generate economic dynamism, large swaths of sectors previously excluded (by caste, gender, ethnicity, class, geographic location) from secondary and university education (a key site of elite social reproduction) were allowed into educational spaces, commingling with the children of the elite and inducing a form of sociopolitical miscegenation. National elites around the world expressed horror that these university children—*their* children!—who had directly benefited from the expansion of education called for by modernization theory, were attempting to subvert its fundamental rule—the prohibition of class and race mixing—by engaging in cross-class and -racial sex. In addition, what came to be called "hippy-ism" in places such as Mexico and Chile got its erotic charge in part from upper-class slumming, both in style and actual ludic (playful) encounters.[44] In the end, the actions and rhetoric of both elites and youth

suggest the impact of this miscegenation and, thus, the linkages between modernity, education, and the racialized erotics of '68 sociocultural movements.

This miscegenation, and the disciplining response to it, were seen in musicians borrowing from different musical genres, a borrowing we hear, for
example, in the recordings of Anglo-Irish soul singer Dusty Springfield, who
drew inspiration for vocal techniques and renderings of songs from across
racial, national, gender, and musical divides; the subsequent segregating
of the music industry curtailed her innovations.[45] While miscegenation is
clearly a term that emerges from a U.S. historical context (as do most of
our examples that follow), we invoke it here as sociopolitical miscegenation
to think about global '68. We use this term precisely because it forces us
to think about ongoing linkages between race, sex, and political economy.
Moreover, this concept can work to disrupt more dominant ideological categories that mask racialized political violence—for example, *mestizaje* in the
Mexican and Chilean contexts, and, as scholar Tavia Nyong'o has argued in
the U.S. case, notions such as "racial hybridity."[46] Thus, brought together in
university classrooms were students of different class, regional, and religious
backgrounds. Students who would not have had contact previously were
now sitting next to each other, rooming with each other, dating each other.
In this mixing, they began to recognize themselves as different from their
parents and as having common experiences, goals, ideas, and possibilities.
Their culture was youth culture; and universities were hotspots of this social
and cultural miscegenation.[47]

Elites in developing countries allied with the United States, hoping that
their sons and daughters could avail themselves of these educational possibilities both at home and at emerging nodal-points of geopolitical power.
Universities around the world opened their doors to students from abroad.[48]
While some foreign students stayed after completing their degrees, others
returned home. In this U.S. case, this would "constitute a massive resource
for the United States to draw on in its quest to influence and reform Third
World countries." Having been exposed to U.S. culture—especially youth
culture—education, and jobs, "many returning students wanted to achieve
modernity for their own countries, although not always, as it turned out, in
a form recognizable to their American mentors . . . In some cases, the visitors turned against the dominant American ideological message and began
identifying themselves with . . . critique[s] of U.S. modernity and especially

the U.S. role abroad."[49] That is, these critiques had percolated on college campuses and beyond, drawing in many—domestic students, foreigners, and often, through them and the media, youth not educated in the United States—who came into contact with it.

These foreign students garnered plenty of sympathy from U.S. progressive youth, who began to challenge authority, large and small, in places from Berkeley to Chicago, Kansas to South Carolina. They questioned the interventionist premise of the Cold War (including U.S. involvement in Vietnam), identified with anti-colonialist movements taking place in Africa and Asia and with the civil rights and black power movements at home, and were in solidarity with foreign student movements. Together they imagined themselves as part of a new physical and ideological demographic: youth. The rise and cross-connections among "youth" epitomize the ways changing geopolitical formations and technologies impelled the accelerated movement of knowledge and culture that fostered broad shared connections and undermined local authority systems in favor of national and transnational influences. That is, youth connections and their imaginings beyond the nation-state were indeed scalar in nature.

In the U.S. South, the prospect of miscegenation through educational contexts produced wholesale panic—expressed in explicitly sexual terms—among local elites whose power rested on an established racialized social order. In such places where the terms of social control were explicitly racist, the concept of manhood as entailing honor, paternal benevolence, and uplift through community "development" dominated both white supremacist and black civil rights rhetorics.[50] Indeed, developmentalist discourses were pervasive throughout the Americas.[51] In places, such as North Carolina, where elites were interested in "progress," elite panic over loss of racialized control—that is, miscegenation through desegregation—would at time manifest itself through Cold War rhetoric of invasive international "communism" and through efforts to ideologically regulate universities and prevent cross-race and cross-class mixing. At other times, elites would relinquish such efforts, persuaded that censorship would stifle a more important goal: economic progress. Modernization thus provoked both desire and fear, expressed in sexualized political discourses.[52]

In the articulation of worldviews, sex and gender are quintessential grammars of power, as scholars Ann Stoler and Joan Scott have taught us. In much the same vein, Denise Ferreira da Silva demonstrates that race, particularly with the rise of modernist social sciences in the late nineteenth century, has been the ongoing global idiom for figuring the power to define an Other available for subjugation. The racial idiom works even in ostensibly anti-racist contexts, as Jodi Melamed argues in her work on the aftermath of World War II; she sees this idiom in a transition from what she terms "white supremacist modernity" to a nominally anti-racist capitalist modernity where racial violence remains a normative frame for representations of difference.[53] Using race and sex to frame the global '68 demonstrates the gendered and sexed nature of racialized politics, and the profound social, political, and cultural transformations many of the '68 movements engendered.[54] Indeed, feminist methodologies are, in and of themselves, generative of questions of scale: the slogan emerging from the 1960s of "the personal is political," to take but one example, challenges the status quo regarding the scale at which "the political" is recognized.

Elite panic over challenges to (racialized) authority, particularly those by upper-class youth, offers a partial explanation of why sexual rebellion assumed such a prominent place in many '68 movements: their racialized erotics threatened the dominant faith in the ultimate value of modernist processes. Like the modernizationist faith in education as a means of societal betterment, sex was still key in ostensibly post-eugenic (though definitely racialist) elite imaginings of how the social order should be reproduced. Elites were particularly invested in students because universities were seen as a site of social and political reproduction and betterment for the nation at the high point of developmentalist modernization (e.g., the "Mexican miracle")—modernization itself was described as the means of national reproduction—explaining the upped ante around education as a particular privileged site. The baggage of racism and eugenicist state forms therefore helps explain the erotic impulses of student movements as they challenged the patriarchal authority of "the establishment." Indeed, '68 as a global phenomenon both emerged from and attacked the profound connections between the underlying logic of modernization, the educational programs which promoted this logic, and global racial/biological hierarchies of nations. It was also an explicit product of Cold War dynamics even as 1960s social movements used an overt break with Cold War logic as the basis for organizing international alliance and solidarity.

CROSS-FERTILIZING MOVEMENTS, SOLIDARITY,
AND RACIALIZED EROTICS

Scholars of the 1960s, such as Fredric Jamison, locate the beginnings of "first world '60s" outside the elite nation, in decolonization movements in English and French Africa and Asia. With reorganizations of old imperialist economic and political relations, geopolitical bonds were changing: Europeans lost direct control over their colonies and the United States asserted its dominance as a so-called benevolent (imperialist) power opposing the Soviet bloc and China. Global struggles over resources, like oil, copper, and rubber, increasingly centered on the role of these resources in commodities (as opposed to infrastructure and capital goods) and would be the building blocks for a forthcoming revolution in transportation and communication that enabled the global restructuring of the 1980s and 1990s. U.S. and European sixties students and peace activists similarly looked beyond the nation at various anti-colonial and anti-imperialist liberation movements in the so-called Third World, especially Vietnam, Cuba, and later Chile. They found in these movements sources of inspiration, political models, and language, as well as subjects of solidarity protests; that is, these movements became objects of intense desire onto which activists' revolutionary aspirations were projected.

The willingness of these movements to question reigning logics, to take unorthodox ideological positions, or to refuse to choose ideological sides altogether meant that many successful student organizations and movements, especially those in the United States and France, were charged with so-called ideological incoherence. The refusal to choose sides was for many activists fundamental to the appeal of participating in such organizations. They saw such a stance as directly supporting the third world's non-aligned movement, made up of countries effectively refusing to serve as passive subordinate mirrors of, and objects for, the desires of the so-called superpowers.

Sixties activists drawn to solidarity with anti-imperial, revolutionary, and non-aligned movements enacted forms of political desire that defiled the race and gender politics of the geopolitical status quo. Indeed, transnational currents of desire traveled in multiple directions, though not necessarily with the same force in each case; thus the May '68 suppression in France and the October '68 massacre in Mexico led to marches and demonstrations of solidarity and sympathy around the world. These sympathy protests evidence the degree to which movements were following news of each other, saw each other's struggles as connected to their own, and borrowed models and iconographies of struggle.

Among this cross-nation borrowing was a shared language and methodology, evident in the cross-indexing of techniques and symbols in movement art.[55] In part this cross-fertilization and borrowing of iconography and strategies came about because television and newsprint media coverage of these movements extended beyond national borders. Like the early U.S. civil rights protests and beatings before them, student demonstrations were beamed across the globe. Student leaders commented on how they came to know one another through television, a knowledge furthered by multinational gatherings, such as that which occurred in late '68 when the BBC hosted—and televised—a gathering of U.S. and European student leaders. This borrowing and exchange have at times led to charges of the "Americanization of protest," where U.S. aesthetic styles were appropriated by local activists and used in places such as Australia and Great Britain, often, ironically, by movements protesting U.S. imperialism and the penetration of U.S. capital.[56]

The global dialogue, which fed specific movements and generated a transgressive scene and sensibility, questioned the concentration of authority and power in the hands of a select few, leading students to adopt anti-authoritarianism as their mantra. Their version of dialogue and borrowing meant that no movement wholly accepted the goals of kindred struggles, but instead, enacted, in today's parlance, a global-local relationship. For many activists, '68 entailed the expansion of ideas about polity and actors.[57]

Dynamics of geopolitical desires, connecting powerful actors and subordinate ones within a given national context and transnationally, meant that '68 was not just a middle-class, ethnically and nationally privileged student phenomenon but was all about forging postcoloniality. Although some cross-national projects could not fully shed the baggage of imperialism in their engagement, as a whole, these movements established political solidarity between sectors in the so-called metropoles and former or soon-to-be-former colonies, applied such insights to the metropoles through the concept of internal colonialism, and generated the space for heightened alliances between subaltern struggles. Moreover, while geopolitical sympathies had previously been managed by unions and Cold War parties of the left across the Iron

Curtain, all of whom privileged languages of class, 1960s activists challenged this leftist sectarian discipline, drawing from a wide array of languages, logics, and methodologies.

The political miscegenation, creativity, and promiscuity known later as the New Left is precisely what made '68 so threatening to the dominant power structures, for the universities that incubated this promiscuity had been seen as sites for reproducing class privilege and future state bureaucrats. More destabilizing still, the state turned its repressive apparatus against its own children (in terms of class and ethnicity), and against more subordinate, aspiring sectors. This state reaction not only generated questions about the existence of that apparatus; it shined a light on the very architecture of the larger national project on behalf of which the state was understood to act. In this sense, '68 is an ideal moment to consider for understanding the tensions between the interests of nation-states, transnational actors, and geopolitical processes.

Given the scholarly and popular assessment of 1968 as global, here we consider phenomena already deemed as such—the social movements of 1968—and ask, "If so, how so?" Since '68 has already been deemed global by a range of scholars and movement participants, we instead examine how these movements were grounded in the kinds of broad spatial processes and transformations—scalar rearrangements—that were already recognizable and how the movements saw themselves as such. That is, we do not see '68's globalness as a series of places and events—if it's May, we must be in Paris. The answer to the problem of scale, we contend, is not a place solution, conceived of as planetary coverage or as place units such as "global cities." Instead of seeing scale as primarily a problem of place, we understand the methodological challenge of scale as a spatial one. This challenge requires that we consider the viability of processes that may have had global manifestation in micro-relations of marked intimacy. Specifically, we wonder if what may have made '68 global—such that worried governments were willing to harshly discipline even elite youth—were the ways in which the movements and cultural dynamics of the day contested the status quo dynamics between body, family, polity, and world.

Critical to decoding both the actions of rebellious youth and the elite panics that this youth activism provoked in a thoroughly racialized global arena is a transnational analysis of the global '68. This analysis looks at geopolitical processes and cross-fertilizations as part of erotic economies of power expressed in gendered and sexualized terms that called attention to a modernist project premised on the global, already racialized, hierarchization of nations and peoples.

To consider the problem of scale in global studies, we have made two analytic moves: first, we have provided a broad discussion of the question of scale in the politics of scholarship to historicize the term "global" as it has accrued particular implications, and, second, by way of a case, we have examined a phenomenon that was dubbed at the time and subsequently as "global" to suggest the crucial dimensions of '68 that made its explicitly global scale apparent. Methodological thinking about scale, then, requires awareness of the historical and geopolitical contexts of assertions about "the global."

In looking at the global '68 and asking what assertions of its globalness have meant over time and what this might reveal about the historical embeddedness of the global as a political and scholarly category, we are beginning to see the importance of asking what happens to eugenics as the modus operandi of governance in the shift to modernization theory. It is the transfiguration of racial miscegenation into a generalized fear of social miscegenation that may explain in part why the social movements of the 1960s were so threatening to "the establishment." Our decision to look at this problem through feminist methodologies further provokes a methodological interrogation of scale.

Telling the story of "global '68" is less about geographical coverage of particular spaces and places, and more about the processes of building, rupturing, and reconfiguring of institutional, social, and cultural networks. In this case, we are thinking about the racialized erotic of political economy through the rise of transnational media ventures as they intersected with and portrayed movements that saw themselves as globally constituted. Here we suggest that the reproductivist racialized logics of governance and social order of social Darwinism and eugenics did not disappear but rather morphologically expanded as a racialized erotic grammar to encompass the restructuring of political economic orders in the broadest terms. Thus, at stake in the global '68 were big frames in the sense of political and cultural worldviews and the ways in which political actors understood that the power of framing was central to changing models of political economy.

The global '68 offers an ideal case for exploring the ways in which global scale can have often surprising implications. One key implication is that a feminist analysis of '68 posits dynamics of sexuality, intimacy, and desire writ large as a thoroughly global phenomenon. Furthermore, through historical analysis, we have shown that the category of "global scale" is emergent from the very case itself, here the racialized and sexualized ideologies of Cold War capitalist modernization. Methodologically speaking, then, scholars must understand that our analytic categories have histories. Moreover, these political and intellectual histories entail ongoing ramifications for how we use categories such as global scale.

NOTES

We thank Andrea Friedman, Shane Greene, Prakash Kumar, Sean Metzger, Heather Vrana, Laura Westhoff, and Indiana University's Center for Latin American and Caribbean Studies Research Seminar for their critical feedback and insights on the various iterations of this piece. We single out Hilary Kahn, Janet Rabinowitch, and Rebecca Tolen for special mention in this regard.

1. Giovanni Arrighi, Terence K. Hopkins, and Immanuel Wallerstein, *Antisystemic Movements* (London: Verso, 1989), 97. Emphasis added.

2. Mark Kurlansky, *1968: The Year That Rocked the World* (New York: Ballantine, 2004), 263; the publisher also used this phrase to market the book (see http://www.amazon .com/1968-Year-That-Rocked-World-ebook/dp/B000FC0XWI/ref=dp_kinw_strp_1); George Katsiaficas, *The Imagination of the New Left: A Global Analysis of 1968* (Boston: South End Press, 1987). For perspectives both international and transnational, see "Forum: The International 1968, Part 1" (articles by Jeremi Suri, Timothy Brown, and William Maroth), *American Historical Review* 114(1) (2009); and "Forum: The International 1968, Part 2" (articles by Sara Evans, Jeffrey Gould, and Richard Ivan Jobs). *American Historical Review* 114(2) (2009).

3. Spatial, non-place-bound examples include Matthew Guterl, *American Mediterranean: Southern Slaveholders in the Age of Emancipation* (Cambridge, MA: Harvard University Press, 2008); Micol Siegel, Lessie Jo Frazier, and David Sartorius, "The Spatial Politics of Radical Change: An Introduction," "Revolutions and Heterotopias, a Special Forum," *Journal of Transnational American Studies* 4(2) (2012). Several articles in this special issue deal with the 1960s. On place, see Janise Hurtig, Rosario Montoya, and Lessie Jo Frazier, eds., *Gender's Place: Feminist Anthropologies of Latin America* (New York: Palgrave, 2002).

4. Matthew Farish, *The Contours of America's Cold War* (Minneapolis: University of Minnesota Press, 2010), 1.

5. Quoted in Farish, *Contours*, 1; Neil Smith, *American Empire: Roosevelt's Geographer and the Prelude to Globalization* (Berkeley: University of California Press, 2003), referenced in Seth Fein, "New Empire into Old: Making Mexican Newsreels the Cold War Way," *Diplomatic History* 28(5) (2004): 705.

6. Saskia Sassen, *Territory, Authority, Rights* (Princeton, NJ: Princeton University Press, 2006).

7. Sallie A. Marston, John Paul Jones III, and Keith Woodward, "Human Geography without Scale," *Transactions of the Institute of British Geographers,* new series, 30(4) (2005): 417.

8. Peter Taylor, "A Materialist Framework for Political Geography," *Transactions of the Institute of British Geographers,* new series, 7 (1982): 15; quoted in ibid.

9. Taylor, quoted in ibid.

10. Marston et al., "Human Geography," 418.

11. Ibid., 420.

12. Micol Siegel, "Beyond Compare: Comparative Method after the Transnational Turn," *Radical History Review* 91 (Winter 2005): 62–90; Nancy Stepan, *"The Hour of Eugenics": Race, Gender, and Nation in Latin America* (Ithaca, NY: Cornell University Press, 1996).

13. Farish, *Contours*, 3.

14. Ibid.

15. Ibid., xii. Emphasis in original.

16. Daniel Lerner, "American Wehrpolitik and the Military Elite," *New Leader* 26 (April 1954): 21; quoted in ibid., 1.

17. Ibid., 2–3.

18. Westad, *The Global Cold War* (Cambridge: Cambridge University Press, 2006), 131; also see Carl E. Pletsch, "The Three Worlds, or the Division of Social Scientific Labor, circa 1950–1975," *Comparative Studies in Society and History* 23(4) (October 1981): 565–90; and Chandra Mohanty, Lourdes Torres, and Ann Russo, *Third World Women and the Politics of Feminism* (Bloomington: Indiana University Press, 1991).

19. U.S. Army film, 1945; quoted in John W. Dower, *Embracing Defeat: Japan in the Wake of World War II* (New York: W. W. Norton, 2000), 215; quoted in Westad, *Global Cold War*, 24.

20. Westad, *Global Cold War*, 24.

21. Farish, *Contours*, xii.

22. Alfred Crosby, *Ecological Imperialism: The Biological Expansion of Europe, 900–1900* (Cambridge: Cambridge University Press, 2004), 2.

23. Stepan, *"The Hour of Eugenics"*; Deborah Cohen, *Braceros: Migrant Citizens and Transnational Subjects in Postwar United States and Mexico* (Chapel Hill: University of North Carolina Press, 2010).

24. Walter Rostow and Max Millikan, *A Proposal: Key to an Effective Foreign Policy* (New York: Greenwood Publishing Group, 1976). Quoted in Westad, *Global Cold War*, 33.

25. Margot Canaday, *The Straight State* (Princeton, NJ: Princeton University Press, 2005).

26. http://www.unam.mx/acercaunam/en/unam_tiempo/unam/1940.html (accessed November 28, 2012).

27. http://www.unam.mx/acercaunam/en/unam_tiempo/unam/1970.html (accessed November 28, 2012).

28. Matthew Connelly, *Fatal Misconception: The Struggle to Control World Population* (Cambridge, MA: Harvard University Press, 2008).

29. Westad, *Global Cold War*, 32.

30. Farish, *Contours*, xvii.

31. Catherine V. Scott, *Gender and Development: Rethinking Modernization and Dependency Theory* (Boulder, CO: Lynne Rienner, 1995), 39.

32. Westad, *Global Cold War*, 34–35.

33. Ibid.

34. Christina Klein, *Cold War Orientalism: Asia in the Middlebrow Imagination, 1945–1961* (Berkeley: University of California Press, 2003).

35. Harvey R. Neptune, *Caliban and the Yankees: Trinidad and the United States Occupation* (Chapel Hill: University of North Carolina Press, 2007).

36. http://www.americanforeignrelations.com/E-N/Foreign-Aid-The-eisenhower-administration-and-expansion-of-foreign-aid.html#b (accessed November 28, 2012).

37. Westad, *Global Cold War*, 32.

38. Arthur Schlesinger, "Memorandum from the President's Special Assistant (Schlesinger) to President Kennedy," *Foreign Relations of the United States, 1961–1963*, vol. 12, American Republics, Document 7; U.S. Department of State Office of the Historian; http://history .state.gov/historicaldocuments/frus1961-63v12/d7 (accessed May 12, 2013); quoted in Westad, *Global Cold War*, 35.

39. http://history.state.gov/departmenthistory/short-history/eisenhower (accessed November 28, 2012).

40. Dulles to CP Jackson, August 24, 1954, Jackson Papers; quoted from HW Brands, *The Specter of Neutralism: The United States and the Emergence of the Third World, 1947–1960* (New York: Columbia University Press, 1989), 108; quoted in Westad, *Global Cold War*, 32.

41. Eric Foner, *The Story of American Freedom* (New York: W. W. Norton, 1999), 271; quoted in ibid.

42. Ibid.

43. Bill Maurer, "Redecorating the International Economy: Keynes, Grant, and the Queering of Bretton Woods," in *Queer Globalizations*, ed. Arnaldo Cruz-Malavé and Martin Manalansan, 100–33 (New York: New York University Press, 2002), 126.

44. Patrick Barr-Melej, *Psychedelic Chile: Youth, Counterculture, and Politics on the Road to Socialism and Dictatorship* (Chapel Hill: University of North Carolina Press, forthcoming).

45. Annie J Randall, *Dusty! Queen of the Postmods* (Oxford: Oxford University Press, 2009).

46. Tavia Nyong'o, *The Amalgamation Waltz: Race, Performance, and the Ruses of Memory* (Minneapolis: University of Minnesota Press, 2009).

47. See Beth Bailey, *Sex in the Heartland* (Cambridge, MA: Harvard University Press, 2002).

48. Westad, *Global Cold War*, 32.

49. Ibid., 37. On the sexual implications of youth culture, see Bailey, *Sex in the Heartland*.

50. Steve Estes, *I Am a Man!* (Chapel Hill: University of North Carolina Press, 2005).

51. María Josefina Saldaña Portillo, *The Revolutionary Imagination in the Americas and the Age of Development* (Durham, NC: Duke University Press, 2003).

52. William J. Billingsley, *Communists on Campus: Race, Politics, and the Public University in the Sixties* (Athens: University of Georgia Press, 1999).

53. Denise Ferreira da Silva, *Toward a Global Idea of Race* (Minneapolis: University of Minnesota Press, 2007); Jodi Melamed, *Represent and Destroy: Rationalizing Violence in the New Racial Capitalism* (Minneapolis: University of Minnesota Press, 2011).

54. Deborah Cohen and Lessie Jo Frazier, eds., *Gender and Sexuality in 1968: Transformative Politics in the Cultural Imagination* (New York: Palgrave, 2009).

55. Daniel Sherman, Ruud van Diijk, Jasmine Alinder, and A. Aneesh, *The Long 1968: Revisions and New Perspectives* (Bloomington: Indiana University Press, 2013).

56. Julie Stephens, *Anti-Disciplinary Protest* (Cambridge: Cambridge University Press, 1998).

57. Lessie Jo Frazier and Deborah Cohen, "Mexico '68: Heroic Masculinity in the Prison and 'Women' in the Streets," in *Hispanic American Historical Review* 83(4) (2003): 617–60; Lessie Jo Frazier and Deborah Cohen, *Beyond '68: Gender and Political Culture in the 1968 Mexican Student Movement and Its Legacies* (Urbana: University of Illinois Press, forthcoming).

13 — SEASCAPE

The Chinese Atlantic

SEAN METZGER

"SEASCAPE" DOES NOT CIRCULATE AS FREQUENTLY IN DISCUSSIONS
of globalization as many of the other key words in this volume do. Seascape
generally denotes an image featuring the ocean, the watery equivalent of
landscape. Demanding attention to flow, seascapes decenter claims to authority and territory grounded in particular places. Views from and of the
ocean enable ways of seeing and knowing that emphasize not only forms
that lie on surfaces but the processes that enable and sustain those forms
as well as the ripple effects emanating from such constructions. Within existing scholarship, the perceptual shifts facilitated through seascapes have
primarily been used to register commercial networks on a regional level (for
example, Ottoman trade in the Indian Ocean, slave traffic in the Atlantic,
computer hardware in the Pacific Rim) or to reveal the precarious conditions of human connectivity on a global one (such as the threat of nuclear
contamination suggested in images of the 2011 Japanese tsunami or the consequences of climate changes captured in the photos of drowned polar bears

throughout the Arctic).[1] The circulations of these concepts, pictures, and materials demonstrate relationships between surface and depth; they indicate changes in both information and epistemology. From hand-painted canvases to satellite-generated imagery, the look of the sea and the life sustained by it serves as a means to track processes rapidly transforming the world. Far from being anachronistic or irrelevant, seascape remains a useful optic for thinking through the phenomena often cast under the rubric of globalization.

Thinking about a Chinese Atlantic seascape requires an orientation toward the movement of forms and a recognition of China's role as a major force on the global scene. Academic work in Chinese studies and Chinese diaspora studies has considered the question of global flows in terms of subjects linked through kinship to China, and a more recent turn has considered networks facilitated through Sinitic languages.[2] If ontological questions have organized the former oeuvre—what might it mean "to be" Chinese under different conditions of migration?—the latter has favored epistemological queries: how is Chineseness produced through local contexts around the world? The Chinese Atlantic seascape, however, interrogates the visuality of Chineseness without a primary emphasis on language. It provides an aperture through which Chineseness in the Atlantic may be seen and linked to a dominant power on the edge of the Pacific, thousands of miles away.

As a heuristic for global studies, seascapes demonstrate the interconnectedness of oceanic zones as physical waterways and as paradigms of knowledge. To illustrate these elements of analysis, the first section of this chapter tracks the seascape as a general concept, emphasizing a few key areas where China has entered or might enter this discourse. Because my own work uses seascape to designate an aesthetic vision and a theoretical framing, the methodologies here include formal and textual analysis as well as attention to the affective production around marine scenes. Affect moves spectators from the surface of the image to a state of feeling. The second section refines this overview to disaggregate the multiple scales involved in the social reproduction of Chineseness. In the last section, the concept of seascape frames a discussion of a small island rarely, if ever, mentioned in discussions of globalization. This discussion reveals that Chineseness is an aesthetic form that appears in surprising embodiments. The shift in scale and methodology demonstrates the elasticity that is necessary to think and write about global flows and processes. This approach helps to outline an emergent notion of a seascape, the Chinese Atlantic, by elaborating how a set of subjects animate this aesthetic in unexpected ways.

SEASCAPES AS ANALYTICS OF GLOBALIZATION

The sea has long provided a principal mechanism by which commerce moved beyond the boundaries of individual states and regions. Maritime trade has, of course, shifted with the ascendance of a capitalist system that continues to accelerate and expand along with the "denser and more extensive communicational networks" that both propel and are fueled by it (Jameson 1998, 55). In a literal sense, then, overseas trade may seem increasingly antiquated; globalization would seem to name a new feature of capitalism in which the market is unrooted, one in which the mode of production may seem unmoored and increasingly difficult to track. At the scale of that amorphous thing we might call culture, everyday life would seem to be in a state of hyperflux as unparalleled numbers of human migrants together with ever faster and more sophisticated technologies alter the ways in which people inhabit the world (Appadurai 1996).[3] As images that attempt to suggest, account for, or even briefly arrest movement, seascapes frame the fluidity of changes difficult to grasp.

The seascape provides one lens through which to look critically at processes of globalization. As a tool of analysis, seascapes isolate particular places but with the accompanying sense that any one vision is necessarily incomplete: the sea flows beyond the boundaries of a given border, suggesting that any surface appearance floats on top of a deep history. Giovanni Arrighi's last book, *Adam Smith in Beijing* (2007), provides an example that reveals some of the occluded histories of a Chinese Atlantic seascape. The theorist of global capitalism notes that seafaring expanded China's economy from the Southern Song (1127–1279) through the early Ming (1368–1644) dynasties, after which such ventures proved too costly to continue, thereby fostering China's turn inward. During the later Qing Dynasty (1644–1911) the Middle Kingdom constituted the largest market in the eighteenth-century world. However, because the Chinese state did not generally yield authority to merchants and entrepreneurs (unlike the current American system), the Chinese economic example should be considered a market economy within

a non-capitalist state. Nevertheless, protocapitalist activity continued outside of the empire's immediate oversight among *huaqiao* (Chinese overseas)
populations. And the Opium Wars in the middle of the nineteenth century
would again demonstrate how important the ocean was to establishing and
maintaining a position of international political and financial hegemony,
because China lost those conflicts at the hands of European naval powers
(Arrighi 2007, 321–50). Images of the sea and its inhabitants, therefore, can
point to the complicated relations of geopolitics and the flows of power that
render some states dominant in particular historical moments.

Arrighi's Chinese story is, in part, useful for reminding readers of the
importance of waterways in the narrative of capitalist development; history has conventionally taught us that activities within a different oceanic
zone fostered the conditions for a world economy. Perhaps nowhere have
the currents moving an emergent global economy been more crucial than in
the Atlantic slave trade, which involved the movement of an estimated 12.5
million individuals through some 35,000 sailings over approximately three
and a half centuries. The importation of low-cost labor to particular sites for
the production of goods later shipped through an extensive transnational
distribution network anticipates many of the features associated with globalization today (Davis 2010). Yet the specificities of these movements, dic-
tated as they were by "prevailing winds and ocean currents" that shaped the
Atlantic system into two distinctive trade routes, is finally mappable (Eltis
and Richardson 2010, 2). Globalization would seem to exceed such bounded
cartography. The Atlantic as a physical site might thus seem only to serve
as an antecedent for the flows that constitute the larger scale of the global.
But it is worth remembering that the etymology of "geography" suggests a
writing of the world ("Geography" 2012). As such, the Atlantic might serve
more usefully as an interpretive device constituted by the ostensible realities
of that space but also attentive to the imaginations and fantasies that render
marine discourse meaningful. This approach bridging cognitive and material maps has long been familiar to peoples whose livelihood depends on the
sea, and it is worth revisiting such worldviews to inquire into what rises to
and sinks below the notice of scholars whose work has purchase in studies
of globalization.

The particular project of using the Atlantic as a heuristic has produced a
productive focus on certain cultural streams, while deemphasizing others;

this constitutes part of the influential argument proposed by Paul Gilroy (1992) in *The Black Atlantic*. For Gilroy, "black Atlantic" names an assemblage of mobile elements that connect seemingly fixed places, sites from England to Africa to North America. His schema privileges the ship as a key term to mark mobility. The boats that motivate his discussion are not only literal ocean crafts, but also objects of discourse that surface in paintings, novels, and musical performances. Gilroy writes an intellectual trajectory to reshape British cultural studies that had, until that point, largely concerned itself with white working-class formations in England. The project shifts emphasis from these territories to a now familiar triangular model spanning from the United Kingdom through Africa to the United States. Below the sea surface (or, perhaps, the surface we can see) in Gilroy's work, another presence remains nascent that might complicate his admittedly fluid geography. This shadowy manifestation emerges in relation to one of the best-known images associated with Atlantic studies. A reinterpretation of this picture facilitates a consideration of the ways in which Chineseness might drift into view and complicate rubrics like the black Atlantic.

Gilroy discusses Joseph Mallord William Turner's painting *The Slave Ship* (1840). For Gilroy, the canvas points towards transatlantic voyages through its subject matter and its own circulation. Originally titled *Slavers Throwing Overboard the Dead and Dying, Typhoon Coming On*, the painting has been much discussed for the ways in which it demands a changing sympathy for the plight of slaves. Ian Baucom has argued that Turner's depiction is most notable for evoking an "image of what we do not see," both literally beneath the deck and the waves, and more figuratively in terms of the capital investment black bodies represent and the affective responses they elicit (2005, 275). The immediate reference for the work is the 1781 incident aboard the merchant ship *Zong*, in which the British captain ordered his slave cargo pitched overboard. The canvas itself works as something of a translation device, shifting the discourse around the ostensible subject matter from a question of inductive reasoning (such as the costs of slave traffic) to one that queries the spectator's emotive response. To gaze at the canvas is to generate feeling, sparked through formal composition: bold, clashing hues of pigment rendered through rapid brush strokes. The people in the image can be glimpsed only in fragments, most often a hand briefly escaping from the watery tomb engulfing it. This vision plays on the ways in which the

Joseph Mallord William Turner, English, 1775–1851. *Slave Ship (Slavers Throwing Overboard the Dead and Dying, Typhoon Coming On)*, 1840. Oil on canvas. 90.8 × 122.6 cm (35¾ × 48¼ in.). Museum of Fine Arts, Boston. Henry Lillie Pierce Fund, 99.22. Photograph © 2014 Museum of Fine Arts, Boston.

seascape forecasts human fortune not only in terms of the horrific fate of the imprisoned Africans left to drown, but also of the brokers who would file an insurance claim based on cargo lost.

As Baucom has suggested, the painting connotes a "repetitive presentness of the past within the present" (282). Baucom's provocation here is to consider the canvas's depiction of loss (in terms of monetary capital and human life, inexorably linked) as constitutive of the modern epoch. For Baucom, the image almost threatens to flow out from the canvas to the spectator, to immerse the onlooker in the material contradictions of a system of slavery perpetuated by the British Empire. However, the border of the painting finally contains the horror depicted. This distance between viewer and object changes the potential effects of the image. Rather than a call to action,

The Slave Ship elicits a detached interest not so much in the specific scene depicted but in an aesthetic approximation of something horrible. The sentiment created is repeatable. It relies less on the particular content of the historical events involving the *Zong* and its cargo and more on a generalized notion of slavery. The "real" event of slavery becomes a subject not so much of historical inquiry but of feelings about the past and those who have passed in the development of an industrial world (remember that Turner's lifetime witnessed the deployment of the steam engine for commercial purposes, including the shipping industry). Although not within the purview of Baucom's critical eye, this analysis of the painting as setting up a way of seeing the past within the present, of seeing a generalized notion of something horrible in relation to sea traffic and eliciting an affective response, helps to bring into relief a different laboring population also borne across the Atlantic.

From this perspective, the original title of the work allows for a geographically more expansive interpretation of Turner's *The Slave Ship*. What is connoted by the phrase "Typhoon Coming On," the often forgotten subtitle? The present participle renders the scene in process but not yet fully realized. The word "typhoon" derives from weather patterns around East and South Asia; it appears in English via translation as early as 1588.[4] By the early 1600s, English clergyman Samuel Purchas had during his travels described hearing "typhoon" as a local term to denote what Englishmen of the day would likely have called by the venerable label "tempest" (in use as early as the thirteenth century) or perhaps "hurricane," a term that apparently originated from the transliteration of a Carib word that found its way into English during the sixteenth century. Given its appropriation from indigenous inhabitants of the Caribbean islands, "hurricane" would seem perhaps most appropriate, since it signifies the Atlantic passages that were Turner's subject. Typhoon, like its mid-nineteenth-century counterpart "cyclone," emerged from locations far overseas from England and the principal waterways of slave trafficking, typhoon being linked to the Cantonese words for "big wind."

Sites like China became increasingly relevant to England and other European powers as the so-called coolie trade increased throughout the Atlantic, following moves to abolish slavery during the mid-nineteenth century. As early as 1806, English merchants had experimented with obtaining labor from Asia rather than Africa to energize the plantation system. To augment the decreased (slave) workforce, planters exploited new recruits through the coolie trade, which procured field hands from various regions, primarily in India and China.[5] While Turner's work appeared too early to register the scalar expansion of coolie importation, the painting's earlier title nevertheless opens up a history of oceanic commerce until recently occluded from narratives that would historicize globalization.[6]

If the Atlantic provides a major node for tracing an ascendant global capitalism, particularly during the nineteenth century, the Pacific has garnered increasing attention during the twentieth and twenty-first centuries as the region of capitalist acceleration. As Bruce Cumings has pointed out, this project of Pacific Rim discourse is often apprehended by "academic pundits and government policymakers" engaged in what Cumings has called "rimspeak" (1998, 54). For Cumings, who gave the first version of his article as a keynote during the early 1990s (significantly, before the 1997 Asian financial crisis), "Pacific Rim" describes the spread of emergent global cities that had experienced tremendous economic growth. The press and other institutions of public discourse used "miracle" and "dynamism" to characterize the robust economies of several Asian countries where these urban centers are located, from South Korea to Singapore. The celebratory tone of these reports after the Cold War marked a clear break in the Euro-American reception of Asia. The perceived threat of "Communist pan-Asianism" or an earlier "imperial Pan-Asianism" orchestrated by Japan had waned (Cumings 1998, 68).

However, fiscal proclamations celebrating growth in terms of business statistics eschew the realities that those numbers might conceal. Arif Dirlik's work reminds readers of the contradictions engendered by capitalism, highlighting new and continuing forms of disenfranchisement and exploitation endured by laborers throughout the Pacific Rim's constituent countries (Dirlik 1998a, 10). Along similar lines, the late Epeli Hau'ofa cautioned against the use of economic instruments as a measure of health, success, or development. Such evaluations privilege surface output, literally, because they tend to assess value in relation to a landmass (for example, gross national product). In this worldview, he argued, the smaller island nations of the Pacific tend to be seen as isolated units that hold little or no currency in the global marketplace.

Hau'ofa insisted that his theorization of island relations emerged after his initial commitment to dependency theory, which posited peripheral islands as repositories of unskilled labor for industrialized core nations (1995, 4). His

notion of Oceania responds to dissatisfaction with such explanatory models. Hauʻofa offers in its place a regional articulation to displace economic
determinism. To execute this move, Hauʻofa endorses a structure that is,
perhaps necessarily, older than capitalism, one that asserts time and space as
non-teleological and non-linear both in the imagination and in lived experience. While this theory remains a geography understood etymologically as
a writing of the world, it implies an almost limitless horizon. As expansive as
the seas and as old as the geological formations that produced and continually reshape archipelagos, Oceania counters capitalism through a totalizing
move of a different order (see Teaiwa, chapter 4, this volume). Economics
may not shape this worldview, but a faith in ecology and its effects on human subjects does. Remember, the sight of Hawaii's Mauna Loa inspires
Hauʻofa's initial shift away from the discourses of economic development.
The "remote majesty" of the volcano motivates a reflection on the sovereignty
of islands. This geothermal vent erupts, producing lava flows that materialize
into the environments people inhabit. Far from a backwater, the Pacific site
becomes an index of earthly creation. Hauʻofa's seascape—for what else is
Hauʻofa seeing but the tip of a mountain most of which extends under the
ocean?—offers a framing of islands that renders them part and parcel of the
energies that literally shape the world. The stakes of his analysis of Mauna
Loa are high indeed!

Insofar as Hauʻofa reaches for a grandiose view of Oceania that exceeds
the minor roles allotted to small islands in Pacific Rim discourse, he relies
in part on metaphors of movement; flows of lava set up the flows of kin later
in his essay. The passage of islanders across water and continents produces
an Oceania that expands beyond shores to wherever migrants might find
themselves. The agents of Oceania are, finally, its people, whose journeys
continually rewrite the world in an ever-evolving geography. This is a broad
vision, one in which the ostensible story of a region flips into that of the globe.
Yet, as a concept aimed at thwarting theories of capitalist circulation that
marginalize smaller Pacific islands, Oceania might still overlap with rhetoric
emphasizing "flow."

Stuart Rockefeller (2011) has scrutinized the uses of this term in certain anthropological literature, but his findings perhaps have a broader significance.
For Rockefeller, the increasing use of "flow" has favored large-scale analyses
that lose sight of local specificity and individual agency. Movement over-

comes fixity. Theoretical abstraction triumphs over empirical data. Such displacements finally shift focus from the often small and remote communities that for decades constituted the privileged object of anthropology—from a certain perspective. Rockefeller's critique alerts readers to the ways in which attention to macro-level phenomena (including, perhaps, concepts such as globalization) can obscure the details of how processes work themselves out on the ground. But there remains an important difference between the writings of Hau'ofa and, for example, certain cooperative projects that seek to further capitalist development. Hau'ofa finds particularity in flow; specific places not often connected in studies of globalization come into relief as a network. This set of interconnections, in turn, provides new means of evaluating the quotidian activities that occur on little islands and their possible significance in discussions of the global.

Hau'ofa's changing scales of analysis from the small isle to the ocean would seem to constitute a sort of "tidalectics" as articulated by the Barbadian writer Kamau Brathwaite (1999). Tidalectics is a riff on dialectics, but whereas the popularized notion of Hegelian dialectics posits a somewhat linear trajectory from thesis to antithesis to synthesis, Brathwaite proposes a more circular model attentive to the gravitational pull moving tides in opposing directions. The aquatic currents produced by the elementary force of gravity are further complicated by the ripple, or the small waves that occur because of local conditions including the weather and the composition of the shoreline. As elaborations of such processes, Elizabeth DeLoughrey (2010) has studied roots and routes in relation to Atlantic and Pacific literatures. As homonyms, the terms of her analysis enable a tracking of flip sides of island discourse. DeLoughrey investigates how transoceanic voyages, including those of diaspora, might be held in tension with specific territorial claims, such as those associated with nationalisms and indigeneity. In Brathwaite's case, we might think of what is at stake in claiming him a Bajan writer, a Caribbean writer, an Anglophone writer, a postcolonial writer, and so on. The sort of flows at issue here suggest that often tiny territories far removed from one another and the cultural productions that seem localized within each of those places might share surprising commonalties that would in turn help reveal and potentially unsettle larger discourses of empire and other structures of governance, today and in the past. Both Hau'ofa and DeLoughrey insist that the island cannot be thought of in isolation but as an active part of the sea.

Baucom, Brathwaite, DeLoughrey, Gilroy, and Hauʻofa introduce various conditions of possibility for globalization through islands by attending to continually shifting scales and types and levels of relations; seascapes function as literal or metaphorical manifestations that animate their theories. They often move from aesthetics and narrative to political economy. One bridge that supports this move is the often explicit but sometimes implicit production of affect. The art they discuss, whether in prose or in other forms, engages a socially produced emotional response rather than a purely subjective one. This framework suggests and can also reinforce claims of feeling black or islander even as it can complicate or undo such assertions.

If China does not explicitly enter into these conceptualizations, each writer leaves open the possibility for Chineseness to transform island spaces. Certainly one dominant modality for this process would be creolization, a dynamic long associated with island spaces, and expansively articulated by Michaeline Crichlow and Patricia Northover as "a historicized process of *selective creation and cultural struggle*" (2009, 1). To mark the particularity of the region always morphing in relation to economic and social forces that may initially seem only tangentially related to the Caribbean archipelagos, Crichlow chose as the book's frontispiece a seascape by Trinidadian artist Christopher Cozier, specifically a detail, "Castaway," from a larger project, *Tropical Nights*. The image depicts a floating humanoid silhouette, impaled by a sail on which appears the outline of a map. This subject adrift is part of an ongoing series of eight-and-a-half-by-eleven-inch drawings. The question of how to capture a dynamic process like creolization is thus rendered moot. It is the changing iterations of this ongoing progression of artistic creation that make it relevant to a study of globalization. We do not know what will come next in this string of paintings, nor do we know the order in which any individual frame may next appear, but we can say that the form of the overall work remains relatively consistent.

In the vein of maintaining a recognizable form with some continually changing features, a set of Cozier's series of works on paper have featured the stamp "Made in China." He has also rendered this text on three-dimensional boxes, which might suggest the tons of imported goods shipped from China to docks and airports around the world. The artist has noted the ubiquity of these labels in his native Trinidad as the inspiration for the project. The juxtaposition here of an explicit seascape connoting creolization and globalization with an image where the sea is only suggested, if at all, as one pathway of the box's arrival gestures to the shifting forms of Chineseness in the Atlantic. The artist compels questions about the relation of subjects to objects, of local culture to global circulation. While he has posed such questions from his avowed Trinidadian perspective, other sites in the Atlantic might pose similar questions but in markedly different ways.

THE CHINESE ATLANTIC

Seascapes, as artistic inventions that depict marine scenes and as ways of knowing the globe, provide different epistemological framings of globalization and its histories. The typhoon haunting the title of *The Slave Ship* connects the Atlantic to the Pacific. Though the Pacific region has gained critical currency in the last three decades as a zone of expanding capitalism, it has also generated responses that refute the perception of the oceanic space solely in economic terms. While all of these discourses anticipate certain features of globalization, they retain a spatially bounded unit of analysis, even if those boundaries extend across vast distances. Recent scholarship attempts to move beyond the exploration of any region in isolation, demonstrating the interconnections of far-flung locales. This foray through several paradigms of thought demonstrates the potential utility of thinking through seascapes to imagine Chineseness in particular. Recognizing that Chineseness increasingly registers as a symptom, or perhaps even a feature, of globalization, I wish to think through some particular Chinese seascapes in more detail.

Rather than place China or economic thought at the center of analysis as Arrighi has done, my ongoing project examines cultural production in the Chinese Atlantic (Metzger 2008, 2009, 2011, 2012). This neologism expresses both the insular and the interconnected qualities of islands marked by the ascent of global capitalism—with Chinese characteristics. The temporalities available through such a notion of the Chinese Atlantic tend toward the anticipatory and future-oriented because past Chinese investments tend to be forgotten or harnessed to a developmental logic (in contrast to, for example, some strains of black Atlantic studies, which work through retrospection). My emphasis on cultural production follows Jameson in recognizing that the cultural and economic blend into one another as mutually reinforcing justifications of the discourse of globalization (Jameson 1998). On a less grand

scale, the focus on a constellation of islands facilitates new ways of thinking about Chinese migration, or migrations of Chineseness, read through
specific localities, usually held apart from studies concerned with Chinese
circulations.

Arjun Appadurai ends *Modernity at Large: Cultural Dimensions of Globalization* with a reflection on the "production of locality," which he sees as "a
phenomenological property of social life, a structure of feeling that is produced by particular forms of intentional activity and that yields particular
sorts of material effects" (1996, 182). In his analysis, locality is juxtaposed
against the material lived experience of the neighborhood. And this work in
general would seem to run in an oblique relationship to the work of Henri
Lefebvre, who suggests that space generates its own rhythms that facilitate
the production of meaning (1991). In following Raymond Williams, Appadurai emphasizes what Williams called the "forming and formative processes"
that orthodox Marxists had undervalued in social organization.[7] Rather than
social institutions producing behavior (base determining superstructure),
Williams emphasizes that lived experience in the present mediates social
forms. For Appadurai, structures of feeling enable him to track the continually morphing structure of, and the shifting dispensations available through,
the neighborhood. He predicates this continual reformation on diasporic
movement, virtual and electronic communities, and nation-state power. Appadurai's provocations about the production of locality provide scaffolding
for questions that I expand in my own work.

Indeed, Appadurai's discussion cries out to be elaborated in relation to
islands because on the one hand, as he discusses, "forms of human movement
are created by the reality or lure of economic opportunity . . . In yet other
communities, the logic of movement is provided by the leisure industries . . .
The challenge to producing a neighborhood in these settings derives from the
inherent instability of social relationships, the powerful tendency for local
subjectivity itself to be commoditized, and the tendencies for nation-states,
which sometimes obtain significant revenues from such sites, to erase internal, local dynamics through externally imposed modes of regulation, creden-
tialization, and image production" (1996, 192). Chinese flows through the Atlantic have been steadily increasing for economic reasons, but this movement
has accompanied a revaluation of existing Chinese populations throughout
the region who are now being recognized (validated, celebrated, denigrated,

or otherwise complicated) because of these new currents of migration. The localization of Chineseness on individual islands throughout the Atlantic contrasts with the circulation of Chinese investment and products flowing into the region. Appadurai's work provides a set of tools for analyzing the synergies and disjunctures among different levels of Chineseness.

If the Atlantic is often perceived as the engine of modernity, obtaining regional coherence because of the transatlantic slave trade and the plantation economy writ large, the particular inflection of Chineseness on the consolidation of what is now ostensibly global capitalism draws attention to a formation called the Chinese Atlantic. On the one hand, such a formulation might return us to the structures of feeling that Appadurai takes from Williams. For Williams, we may remember, uses the example of language to illustrate his point.[8] Because we enter into a language before we can cognitively process what we are doing, language is a structure that exists before we come into existence. The life of language in the present, he argues, reveals shifts difficult to categorize. So the term "structures of feeling" indicates that unformed sense that something is happening anew. This move would seem to correlate with the recent turn to Sinophone studies, in which contingent communities emerge across national and ethnic lines based on Sinitic language use. Although my project does not foreground linguistic commonality, it overlaps with Shu-mei Shih's notion to "rethink the relationship between roots and routes by questioning the conception of roots as ancestral rather than place-based" (2007, 189–90) in order to create "not a theory of mobile citizens who disidentify from the local nation-state and disengage from local politics, but the politicization of that mobility" (190). This politicization of mobility strikes me as useful. Moreover, since Shih turns to visuality in part to mark the increasing speed of image production as communication in a globalized world, her work returns me to the implications of visuality in Appadurai's notion of scape.[9]

Shih herself cautions that the stress on language, particularly *Putonghua* (Mandarin), easily collapses Chineseness with mainland China. My analysis privileges sight and non-verbal performance rather than Chinese-language use in order to foreground how Chineseness may manifest as local through unintended signifiers. These expressions of locality may take the form of site-specific cultural productions where language may not register explicitly at all. This move emphasizes the visuality of the seascape.

"Seascape" as a term dates to the cusp of the eighteenth and nineteenth centuries, when imperialist ventures brought visions of new expanses of oceans back to the European metropole. According to the *Oxford English Dictionary* (2012), the earliest documented uses of the word are in 1799 and 1806. The latter year is rather serendipitous for my study, since the first experimental shipment of Chinese coolie labor in the New World landed in Trinidad in 1806. We might think of Arif Dirlik's query posed in relation to another seaview—"whose Pacific?"—in his exploration of the Asia-Pacific idea (1998b). Dirlik and other theorists find in the seascape a perspective laden with power relations of looking. The word also has an etymological resonance of "scape," as in escape, conjuring the different forces that have motivated the displacement of populations from greater China. Such occluded histories emerge in some unusual constellations in Trinidad and other islands that form seascapes of images and meaning.[10]

MOBILE AFFECT: TAI CHI IN MARTINIQUE

Taking a Friday ferry from Anse à l'Âne across the Bay of Fort-de-France, I spotted in the distance a group of people seemingly suspended in motion. Disembarking, I walked towards the foot of Fort St. Louis, on the eastern end of the *malecón,* catty-corner from La Savane. The image became increasingly clear and increasingly animated. This time the assemblage numbered sixteen, split into two groups according to level of ability, with an instructor in front. The most advanced group distinguished itself not only through the fluidity of motion—with deft transitions from a push to a whip to cloud hands—but also through its sartorial appearance. Several of the more proficient individuals wore a loose-fitting silk pant and shirt ensemble in white. The obvious coach in this scene sported a bright yellow version of the same pattern, which shined in the remaining shards of twilight as he jogged back and forth between the clusters of his pupils. Most of the rest of the troupe wore black sweats and white T-shirts. Together, they created an ethereal spectacle of moving bodies by the side of the sea, largely illuminated by the glow of the garrison wall. The corporeal practice of the ensemble created a seascape for the spectator.

I had arrived towards the end of a two-hour session of Martinique's tai chi club. Having participated earlier in the week, I recognized the awkward stumbling of those who, like me, were unsure of the sequence of movement.

And when, during a brief pause, the organizer and master, Michel Assouvie, handed out a series of fans, I knew to expect the increase in pace that would elevate the heart rates of everyone, leaving sweat and the endorphin-induced satisfaction of having exercised. This conclusion was Assouvie's innovation; he recognized that his students wanted to feel physical exertion in exchange for the euros they had spent to join him for the evening. This last succession of gestures and stances also marketed the club, as the noise and display of the flicking fans attracted attention from passersby.

The club's weekly visits to the site of the long-standing colonial battlements are perhaps the most sustained public exhibition of Chinese expressive culture anywhere on Martinique. Yet, no ostensible Chinese subjects are involved. Indeed, since Assouvie began the club in 2007, upon returning from a decade in the metropole, there have been almost no participants of Chinese descent. On this particular evening, the island's major constituent demographics, however, were represented: white Europeans, creoles, black Martinicans. But the absence of any Chinese participants was noticeable, because Martinique's Chinese population has significantly increased, particularly in Fort-de-France and nearby Lamentin (Dubost 2007). Earlier in the week, for example, I observed a trio of women chatting in Mandarin as they walked around La Savane, without acknowledging Assouvie or his group.

David Ho, the leader of the recently formed Chinese community organization, now estimates the Chinese population at close to a thousand of the island's more than four hundred thousand inhabitants. If this number seems minuscule as an overall percentage, a half-kilometer stroll into downtown brings the sight of restaurants, "snacks," and bazaars adorned with red lanterns, Chinese characters, and *maneki-neko* (an appropriation of Japanese kitsch) that dot the area. This is a town where the look of the urban landscape is in flux. The long-term residents often say that as soon as a local (Martinican) closes shop, a Chinese immigrant will claim the space. Such processes of change register obliquely in the seascape adjacent to the center of the city. Many of the tai chi students are engaged in language study; all of them are cognizant of the growing influence China is exerting in the world. A tension emerges between the increasingly felt presence of Chinese immigrants on Martinique and the feeling of Chineseness tapped by the tai chi club.

I came across the club during my preliminary research when I typed in "Martinique chinois" on YouTube. I had been looking for clips from a recent documentary on the subject of Chinese immigrants in Guyana and Marti-

nique. The first hit intrigued me: a business focused on maintaining an ostensibly Chinese movement practice led by a black Martinican man. I would
soon learn that this man, Michel Assouvie, had been practicing martial arts
for over thirty years. His desire to express his respect for what he saw as Chinese culture would be mitigated by the migrant Chinese population itself.
Indeed, many of Assouvie's participants would describe the Chinese community as closed, even as the Chinese entrepreneurs themselves often described
themselves as integrated. What accounts for these apparent contradictions?

The very naming and identification of the Chinese community as such is
interesting in this context. This recent wave of immigrants was being perceived by many islanders as qualitatively different from the earlier waves of
Chinese migrants, the traces of which are easy enough to find in the city. For
example, the Schoelcher Library across La Savane contains several records
documenting the nineteenth-century coolie traffic that carried the initial
Chinese population to Martinique's shores. Most of this group had died
without offspring, repatriated, or lost any clear Chinese connection through
intermarriage. The 1930s witnessed a second wave of Chinese laborers, including the arrival of one Mr. Ho Hio Hen, whose descendants continue to
run one of the largest companies in Martinique, named after the patriarch
himself. These Chinese Martinican amalgams persist today in various forms,
but they generally register as local, as a result of the dynamics of creolization.
The latest wave of immigrants, in contrast, seems to be eliciting new sentiments. Such a changing index of feelings about the Chinese, I would argue,
can be analyzed in the live seascape at the foot of Fort St. Louis. What factors
explain the participants' attachment to a certain vision of Chineseness as an
unchanging aesthetic form? How is this bodily discipline seen as markedly
different from the corporeal behaviors of newer Chinese entrepreneurs, who
are often described as *le niveau de base* (the lowest level)? What is at stake in
performing Chineseness in different contexts? How do such performances
transform or otherwise impact upon the idea of the local? In what ways might
Chineseness be rewriting the place of Martinique, the French overseas departments, or the Caribbean archipelago of which they form a part? What
does this new geography (writing of place) tell us about new flows of capital
and people from China or elsewhere?

One of my informants tells me she has pursued tai chi because she has
always felt Chinese, although she was born and continues to live in Marti-

nique. She materializes this feeling of attachment through the physical discipline of tai chi. This movement practice is, of course, about moving energy (qi) around and between us. We may remember that Jean-Luc Nancy (2000) has elaborated "being singular plural" as circulation, as everything that *se passe* between us. Tai chi is an interesting phenomenon in this regard because it is movement that does not go anywhere (there is no teleology), but this movement nevertheless brings an awareness of and creates connection. In this vein, the practitioner of tai chi does not move in place so much as move, creating place. With this formulation in mind, I would ask again what it might mean for a black Martinican woman to feel Chinese? What might we learn if we think about place, affect, and movement as an ensemble in relation to what would often be held up as an Orientalist construction?

Pursuing answers to these questions offers a new way of apprehending processes of globalization. The "Chinese Atlantic" names a formation, perhaps not yet here, not so unlike globalization. As an analytic, the Chinese Atlantic points to symptoms of some shift in the present, one for which there seems to be increasing evidence as investment capital and overseas workers flow through the oceanic region. But these movements also produce unexpected responses. An ostensibly Chinese image animated by non-Chinese bodies may denaturalize and complicate the stories of migration that we already know, of people leaving one locale for another in search of greater opportunity, of migrations imposed on the unfortunate. Seascapes demand that spectators scrutinize such pat visions in order to think differently about the framing of such narratives.

NOTES

1. On seascapes generally, see Bentley, Bridenthal, and Wigen (2007). See Dow and Downing (2011) for an investigation of waterways and risk.

2. See Shih, Tsai, and Bernards (2013), particularly Shih's opening essay.

3. My definition of culture here borrows from Williams (1983) and is attentive to Appadurai's reminder that culture should be thought of as a series of processes rather than as a thing (1996).

4. The etymological discussion in this paragraph comes from a reading of the relevant entries in the *Oxford English Dictionary*.

5. I have discussed some of the similarities and differences between coolie and slave labor in my essay "Ripples in the Seascape" (Metzger 2008).

6. On the issue of the interconnectedness of labor systems, see Lowe (2006).

7. Williams articulates his position in his chapter "Structures of Feeling" in *Marxism and Literature*.

8. See Williams, *Marxism and Literature*, 131–32.

9. In *Modernity at Large,* Appadurai discusses five dimensions that structure globalization: ethnoscape, financescape, ideoscapes, mediascapes, and technoscape. My point here
is to call attention to this lexicon and its evocation of older terms for visual production like
landscape and seascape.

10. See my essay "Incorporating: Chineseness in Chen's Trinidad" (Metzger 2012).

REFERENCES

Appadurai, Arjun. 1996. *Modernity at Large: Cultural Dimensions of Globalization.* Minneapo-
lis: University of Minnesota Press.
Arrighi, Giovanni. 2007. *Adam Smith in Beijing: Lineages of the Twenty-First Century.* New
York: Verso.
Baucom, Ian. 2005. *Specters of the Atlantic: Finance Capital, Slavery, and the Philosophy of His-
tory.* Durham, NC: Duke University Press.
Bentley, Jerry H., Renate Bridenthal, and Karen Wigen, eds. 2007. *Seascapes: Maritime Histo-
ries, Littoral Cultures, and Transoceanic Exchanges.* Honolulu: University of Hawaii Press.
Brathwaite, Kamau. 1999. *ConVERSations with Nathaniel Mackey.* Staten Island: We Press.
Crichlow, Michaeline with Patricia Northover. 2009. *Globalization and the Post-Creole Imagi-
nation: Notes on Fleeing the Plantation.* Durham, NC: Duke University Press.
Cumings, Bruce. 1998. "Rimspeak: or the Discourse of the 'Pacific Rim.'" In *What Is in a Rim?
Critical Perspectives on the Pacific Region Idea,* ed. Arif Dirlik, 53–72. Lanham, MD: Row-
man & Littlefield.
"Cyclone." 2012. *OED Online.* Oxford University Press. June. Web. 25 August 2012.
Davis, David Brion. 2010. "Foreword." In *Atlas of the Transatlantic Slave Trade,* ed. David Eltis
and David Richardson, xvii–xxii. New Haven, CT: Yale University Press.
DeLoughrey, Elizabeth M. 2010. *Routes and Roots: Navigating Caribbean and Pacific Island
Literatures.* Honolulu: University of Hawaii Press.
Dirlik, Arif. 1998a. "Introduction: Pacific Contradictions." In *What Is in a Rim? Critical
Perspectives on the Pacific Region Idea,* ed. Arif Dirlik, 3–13. Lanham, MD: Rowman &
Littlefield.
———. 1998b. "The Asia-Pacific Idea: Reality and Representation in the Invention of a Re-
gional Structure." In *What Is in a Rim? Critical Perspectives on the Pacific Region Idea,* ed.
Arif Dirlik, 15–36. Lanham, MD: Rowman & Littlefield.
Dow, Kristin, and Thomas E. Downing. 2011. *The Atlas of Climate Change: Mapping the
World's Greatest Challenge.* Berkeley: University of California Press.
Dubost, Isabelle. 2007. "Au dela de l'ethnicité: Les "Chinois" à la Martinique." In *Dynamiques
Migratoires de la Caraïbe,* ed. Calmont Andre and Cedric Audebert, 239–252. GEODE
Terres d'Amerique. Paris: Karthala.
Eltis, David, and David Richardson. 2010. *Atlas of the Transatlantic Slave Trade.* New Haven,
CT: Yale University Press.
"Geography." 2012. *OED Online.* Oxford University Press. June. Web. 25 Aug. 2012.
Gilroy, Paul. 1992. *The Black Atlantic: Modernity and Double Consciousness.* Cambridge, MA:
Harvard University Press.
Hau'ofa, Epeli. 1995. "Our Sea of Islands." In *Asia/Pacific as a Space of Cultural Production,* ed.
Rob Wilson and Arif Dirlik, 86–98. Durham, NC: Duke University Press.
"Hurricane." 2012. *OED Online.* Oxford University Press. June. Web. 25 August 2012.

Jameson, Fredric. 1998. "Notes on Globalization as a Philosophical Issue." In *The Cultures of Globalization,* ed. Fredric Jameson and Masao Miyoshi, 54–77. Durham, NC: Duke University Press.

Lefebvre, Henri. 1991. *The Production of Space.* Trans. Donald Nicholson-Smith. Malden, MA: Blackwell Publishing.

Lowe, Lisa. 2006. "The Intimacies of Four Continents." In *Haunted by Empire: Geographies of Intimacy in North American Empire,* ed. Ann Laura Stoler, 191–212. Durham, NC: Duke University Press.

Metzger, Sean. 2008. "Ripples in the Seascape: The Cuba Commission Report and the Idea of Freedom." *Afro-Hispanic Review* 27(1): 105–21.

———. 2009. "Unsettling: Towards a Chinese/Cuban Cultural Critique." *Cultural Dynamics* 21(3): 317–38.

———. 2011. "Le Rugissement du Lion: Mapping and Memory in Montreal's Chinese/Canadian Street Theater." In *New Essays in Canadian Theatre.* Vol. 1, *Asian Canadian Theatre,* ed. Nina Lee Aquino and Ric Knowles, 86–97. Toronto: Playwrights Canada Press.

———. 2012. "Incorporating: Chineseness in Chen's Trinidad." *The Global South* 6(1): 98–113.

Nancy, Jean-Luc. 2000. *Being Singular Plural.* Stanford, CA: Stanford University Press.

Rockefeller, Stuart Alexander. 2011. "Flow." *Current Anthropology* 52(4): 557–78.

Shih, Shu-mei. 2007. *Visuality and Identity: Sinophone Articulations across the Pacific.* Berkeley: University of California Press.

Shih, Shu-mei, Chien-hsin Tsai, and Brian Bernards, eds. 2013. *Sinophone Studies: A Critical Reader.* New York: Columbia University Press.

"Seascape." 2012. *OED Online.* Oxford University Press. June. Web. 25 August 2012.

"Tempest." 2012. *OED Online.* Oxford University Press. June. Web. 25 August 2012.

"Typhoon." 2012. *OED Online.* Oxford University Press. June. Web. 25 August 2012.

Williams, Raymond. 1977. *Marxism and Literature.* Oxford: Oxford University Press.

———. 1983. *Keywords: A Vocabulary of Culture and Society.* Oxford: Oxford University Press.

14 ~ SOVEREIGNTY

Crisis, Humanitarianism, and the Condition of Twenty-First-Century Sovereignty

MICHAEL MASCARENHAS

BY MOST ACCOUNTS CRISIS HAS BECOME THE PARADIGM OF MODERN government. Drought, fires, hurricanes, and tsunamis, not to mention fiscal cliffs, financial meltdowns, and regional uprisings, dominate both our attention and our institutions of government. Crisis continues to be the modus operandi for humanitarian efforts worldwide as much of the world's population still lacks access to basic human rights, such as water, food, and shelter. Increasingly, non-governmental organizations (NGOs) are leading efforts to improve access to water and other human rights. As part of this global humanitarian effort, NGOs have witnessed an unprecedented growth in recent decades. In some places they have replaced government agencies, become strategic business investments, and translated local water and sanitation needs into bureaucratic planning. The relentless expansion of NGOs on the basis of emergency has resulted in a contingent form of sovereignty, where increasingly NGOs are defining which populations to champion or "let live," and by default which populations to "let die." However, in spite of this profound decision-making authority, few scholars, with notable exceptions, have paid attention to the ways in which the policies and practices of non-governmental organizations continue to reassemble the character of modern sovereignty for the majority of the world's population. I argue that the policies and practices of NGOs represent a new form of contingent sovereignty among the world's deprived, a form of non-state sovereignty that is transnational in character, emergent in form, and flexible in practice. This new form of sovereignty, while not replacing state-based sovereignty, clearly signals the presence of a growing humanitarian apparatus that exercises sovereign power over transnational territories and populations. The goal of this chapter is to explain how particular techniques and technologies of contemporary humanitarian governance function as a new type of post-Westphalian sovereign power, and what the implications are for humanitarian and political rights for the majority of the world's population.

FROM THE POWER OF SOVEREIGNTY TO THE POWER OVER HUMANITARIAN LIFE

During his "Society Must Be Defended" (Foucault 1997) lecture series at the Collège de France from 1975 to 1976, Michel Foucault argued that one of the greatest transformations in the nineteenth century was in the new techniques and technologies of sovereignty. This transformation did not occur all at once, he argued, however; during the second half of the eighteenth century a new technology of power started to emerge that transformed sovereignty's old right "to take life and let live," and established a new sovereign power: "the right to make live and to let die" (Foucault 1997, 241). This new form of power does not replace sovereignty's old right—to take life or to let live—or its disciplinary techniques, but rather it exists at a different level, on a different scale, and makes use of different mechanisms, techniques, and technologies (Foucault 1997). For example, unlike discipline, which is addressed to bodies, the new nondisciplinary power is applied to social groups within a sovereign territory, such as the labor force, the sick, or the educated. This new technology of power, what Foucault (1977, 1994, 1997, 2008) has named biopolitics, involved "a set of processes such as the ratio of births to deaths, the rate of reproduction, the fertility of a population, and so on" to address "a whole series of related economic and political problems [associated with human development] . . . in the second half of the eighteenth century" (1997,

243). The mechanisms introduced by biopolitics, Foucault argued, included forecasts, statistical estimates, censuses, demographic surveys, and overall measures that provided extensive knowledge about the population that was deemed essential by the state to provide for the well-being of its population (1997). The great governmental apparatus that proliferated throughout the nineteenth century was found at both the state level and at the substate level, in a whole series of governmental institutions such as hospitals, prisons, schools, welfare funds, and insurance. The nature and implications of this particular biopolitical formation were based on the legitimacy of state sovereignty over a particular territory and legitimacy of the sovereign state to govern the population within that territory. By comparison, the nature of twenty-first-century sovereignty, particularly as it applies to humanitarianism, is one where sovereignty has become transnational. The role of crisis as the paradigm of modern government has provided the means for the continued global expansion of this new sovereign power.

A PERMANENT STATE OF HUMANITARIAN EMERGENCY

One enduring feature of the postcolonial condition has been, and continues to be, its spectacle of humanitarian emergencies. Consider the genocides in East Timor, Rwanda, Congo, Liberia, Sierra Leone, and the former Yugoslavia; the ongoing Israeli-Palestinian conflict; protracted conflicts in Iraq, Afghanistan, and Syria; humanitarian crises in Darfur and Sudan; the 2004 Indian Ocean tsunami; the 2010 Pakistan flood; Hurricane Katrina's inundation of New Orleans in 2005; and cyclones in Myanmar, not to mention seasonal flooding in floodplains around the world; prolonged droughts and other climate-related emergencies; and earthquakes in Haiti, China, Japan, and elsewhere. In addition to this truncated list of spectacles, however, are the endemic and more subtle crises that are features of the postcolonial condition. In this category, one might note the rising rates of both obesity and poverty in the so-called developed world, and the rapidly accelerating wealth gap throughout the postcolonial world (Domhoff 2012). Basic needs are unmet for too many: sixty years after the end of colonialism, approximately 1.1 billion people, or 18 percent of the world's population, still lack access to safe drinking water, and about 2.6 billion people, or 42 percent of the total, still lack access to basic sanitation (United Nations 2010).

These states of emergency and many more have become the rule rather than the exception, with which the postcolonial condition is realized by the majority of the world's population. Moreover, this permanent state of exception or emergency has provided the impetus to introduce a range of "supposedly necessary reforms" to the new world order (Deleuze 1992, 4). In fact, many development scholars recognize the importance of President Truman's 1949 inaugural address as a watershed moment in the inscription of a permanent state of emergency into postcolonial relations. It was here that Truman proclaimed ([1949] 1964):

> More than half the people of the world are living in conditions approaching misery. Their food is inadequate. They are victims of disease. Their economic life is primitive and stagnant. Their poverty is a handicap and a threat both to them and to more prosperous areas . . . I believe that we should make available to peace-loving peoples the benefits of our store of technical knowledge in order to help them realize their aspirations for a better life.

As a consequence of this and other humanitarian declarations, for more than sixty years this notion of a "state of exception" has provided a remarkably stable problem-space with which contemporary questions about the growing polarity of postcolonial life and its relationship to state, market, and civil society can be understood. This perspective, often referred to as the golden age of U.S. hegemony and launched by President Truman during the postwar period, pioneered an institutional reform of global proportions, one that would bring together complex interdependencies between developed and underdeveloped countries, human rights and obligations, and wealth and poverty. Since its inception, this postcolonial state of exception or humanitarian emergency has progressively become "the dominant paradigm of government in contemporary politics" in which postcolonial life and its relationship to state, market, and civil society must be understood (Agamben 2005, 2).

GOVERNING A PERMANENT STATE OF EMERGENCY

The new visibility of NGOs as international governmental actors is a subject of growing interest among international relations and development scholars (see also Perullo, chapter 10, this volume). Part of that attention has come from the rapid expansion of this newly (re)forming sector of civil society. In fact, NGOs have proliferated massively in the last two decades, while some of the more established, such as Oxfam, Save the Children Fund, CARE, and

World Vision, have expanded not only in size but also in the scope of their activities. Some reports have suggested that the not-for-profit sector might be the world's eighth-largest economy (SustainAbility 2003). In 2010, public charities in the United States, the largest component of the U.S. non-profit sector, reported $1.51 trillion in revenue, $1.45 trillion in expenses, and $2.71 trillion in assets (Blackwood, Roeger, and Pettijohn 2010). That same year the non-profit sector contributed $804.8 billion to the U.S. economy, making up 5.5 percent of the country's gross domestic product (ibid.). There are also recurring moments of legitimation crises when the practices of an NGO contradict the way it is perceived by the outside world. The tsunami of 2004 provided a striking example of the legitimation crisis that engulfed this sector, resulting in a call for more transparency and accountability with regard to donor contributions. Both its relentless growth and issues of legitimacy and representation have led to repeated and urgent calls to review, and in some cases to further evolve the NGO sector (SustainAbility 2003).

Weiss and Gordenker (1996, 18) define NGOs as "a special set of organizations that are private in their form but public in their purpose," thus distinguishing them from intergovernmental organizations (IGOs) and transnational corporations (TNCs). This characterization fails to acknowledge how both the form and the practices of NGOs have become aligned with both private and governmental interests. NGOs have become crucial to the United Nations' future and a salient phenomenon in international policy-making and execution (Weiss and Gordenker 1996), and, at the same time, they have also been at the forefront of reforming humanitarian consultancy, entrepreneurialism, and financial services (Bebbington 1997). This transition within the current contexts of humanitarian reform and economic liberalization, Michael Edwards and David Hulme (1996) argue, has resulted in some NGOs being "too close for comfort," in other words too close to their private and public donors, as they become increasingly dependent on external resources and policy agendas.

Dorothea Hilhorst has argued that there is "no single answer to what an NGO *is*, what it *wants*, and what it *does*" (Hilhorst 2003, 3). While an NGO might adopt a particular structure, in practice it is much more difficult to identify its boundaries (Hilhorst 2003). Some scholars argue that the NGO movement and activism against "big dams" over the last two decades has demonstrably shifted public opinion away from top-down, technocratic approaches and toward people-centered, bottom-up development (Phadke 2005; Khagram 2004). This activist response has developed alongside, and often in association with, important efforts by social scientists to document the deleterious environmental and social impacts of large international water development projects. On the other hand, NGOs have been accused of "flirting with the enemy," as they have transformed their identity and objectives from empowerment to service delivery (Miraftab 1997). Moreover, Jenny Pearce (2000, 20) argues, to a certain extent NGOs have "succumbed to the pressures and incentives to pick up the social cost of neo-liberal restructuring," and thus are implicated in the expansion and legitimation of market-led globalization.

The challenge to understanding the role of NGOs, in part, comes from conventional ways of thinking about globalization and development. Most macro theories of development, for example, condense all cultural developments into a single program or trajectory: the emergence of the global era. For example, modernization theory argues that over time "underdeveloped areas" of the globe will emerge from traditional societies and become modern. The causes of many of the problems associated with underdevelopment—lack of access to drinking water, poverty, and military conflict, for example—are assumed to be mostly internal to a given country, and the solutions to these social problems are seen to lie in more ties to the West. This conventional approach to theorizing the relationship between the global and the state quite often pits NGOs and other civil society groups against the incapacities of sovereign state power. However, this instrumentalist perspective continues to assume a Westphalian and/or national frame, where states are the only sovereign power over national territories and populations. In so doing, critics argue, this implicitly Westphalian perspective not only ignores long-standing traditions of domination but also fails to recognize how new forms of transnational sovereignty contribute to the continued biopolitical restructuring of the world's poor (Agamben 2005; Escobar 1995; Hardt and Negri 2001).

One purpose of this chapter is to illustrate how twenty-first-century NGOs are more assemblages (global assemblages) than conventional institutions—a product of multiple determinations that are not reducible to a single logic, such as challenging global neoliberal reforms. In making sense of them I have found Michel Foucault's notion of the apparatus particularly helpful. Foucault describes apparatus as a "heterogeneous set" of elements "consisting of discourses, institutions, architectural forms, regulatory decisions, laws, administrative measures, scientific statements, philosophical, moral, and philanthropic propositions" (1980, 194–95). He goes on to state that apparatus is "a kind of a formation . . . that at a given historical moment has as its major function the response to an urgency."

The state of urgency is particularly important in understanding the role of NGOs in development theory and practice. "Emergency," Mark Duffield (2007, 48) argues, "has provided a means of penetrating the world of peoples, ignoring existing laws, conventions or restraints." Drawing on Georgio Agamben's (1998, 2005) work on the state of exception, Duffield argues that this ability to describe and define a permanent state of exception or emergency among the world's poor has allowed NGOs to expand as non-state or petty sovereign powers. However, as Michael Hardt and Antonio Negri (2001, 39) remind us, we are dealing with a special kind of sovereignty—a discontinuous form of sovereignty, one that challenges the Westphalian notion that nation-states are the only sovereigns and that sovereignty is territorially based. Today, Nancy Fraser (2005, 2007) and other critical thinkers argue, sovereignty is being disaggregated, broken up into several distinct functions and assigned to several distinct agencies, which function at several distinct levels, some global, some regional, some local and subnational. These new transnational assemblages, most often associated with military and security functions and global economic development, are increasingly becoming the dominant institutional structure for humanitarian interventions worldwide.

But as Partha Chatterjee (2004) has carefully illustrated, this form of sovereignty does not reign over citizens, per se, but rather populations of people that are described and organized with particular conditions, such as water insecurity, ill health, or poverty. The sovereignty of NGOs over these populations lies in their endless decision-making authority concerning *how* particular humanitarian conditions are defined, *who* is to be helped, *how* to go about helping them, and, consequently, who can be left behind. These now-global humanitarian assemblages, Saskia Sassen (2006) argues, are contributing to different meanings of territory, authority, and rights in the twenty-first century. Yet in spite of what amounts to sovereign decision-making authority to give life and take it away, we know very little about how water needs are determined and communities selected, how money is raised and spent, how technology is used, how expertise is established, how water programs are supposed to work and why they usually fail. When people set out to change the water crisis conditions in most of the world, the devil is truly in the details.

The central question addressed in this chapter is how do NGOs establish and maintain legitimate sovereign authority over the state of exception, and what sort of sovereignty are they practicing? By insisting that the social and physical life of water development consists of a long labyrinth of associations, I posit that we can open up the possibility of multiple opportunities for politics directed towards social justice ends. One particularly informative sovereign feature of organizations delivering contemporary humanitarian aid has been their ability to function like state agencies. The tragic events of the South Asian tsunami illustrate this point.

THE TRANSNATIONAL HUMANITARIAN AGENCY

On December 26, 2004, people in the Northern Hemisphere watched as a massive earthquake triggered a series of devastating tsunamis that inundated the coasts of fourteen countries along the rim of the Indian Ocean, killing nearly 230,000 people, injuring tens of thousands more, and displacing more than ten million men, women, and children. In the days that followed, the South Asian tsunami became a truly global affair. Bombarded with media reporting and seduced by YouTube videos, we watched live as millions of helpless people lost their homes, livelihoods, and in some cases their lives. These horrific images combined with the seemingly arbitrariness of these people's fate provoked an outpouring of empathy and generosity of global proportions. Governments, humanitarian organizations, community groups, and individuals around the world scrambled to offer aid and technical support. And within six months, official aid and private donations raised over $13 billion for the victims of this natural[1] disaster.

However, in the weeks and months that followed another storyline started to emerge, one that questioned the role of NGOs in this and other humanitarian efforts. Reports started to emerge from the media about donations not reaching victims or donations being diverted by NGOs to other campaigns.

We were introduced to the uneasy fact that these civil society organizations not only were involved in matters of state sovereignty by effectively making decisions over who "to make live and to let die" (Foucault 1997, 241), but were doing so by advancing a particular notion of costs and benefits. It turns out that the practice of diverting donations to other projects is a usual practice of NGOs, but donors are troubled by the fact that only about half of what is donated ever reaches the poorest people affected by these disasters.[2] A new kind of sovereignty is being created by civil society organizations which are trying to control the population of the world's destitute without having to answer to anyone.

Yet, this form of sovereignty is not without its own organizing logic, which grows and stabilizes along particular lines of power relations. One particularly striking feature of contemporary humanitarian aid has been its connection to transnational finance. David Harvey has suggested that the whole history of capitalism as it has expanded over the globe has been about "radical innovations in the state-finance nexus" (Harvey 2010, 85). "Finance capital in rich industrial countries has grown at a rate that is 2.5 times that of the national product. The trade in currencies, bonds, and equities has increased at 5 times the rate of increase in the national product. . . . [M]ore and more capital is being invested in the trade of stocks, bonds, and currencies than in manufacturing, presumably because the profits are quicker and greater" (Chatterjee 2004, 88). It stands to reason, then, that finance has also profoundly transformed twenty-first-century humanitarian practice and policy. For example, as many progressive and well-intentioned NGOs continue to seek innovative ways to finance their humanitarian efforts, they are also becoming increasingly dependent on the boom-and-bust risks associated with finance capital. The concern with venture philanthropy, in practice, is that humanitarian efforts become more aligned with investment than with opportunities for social change. Moreover, in shifting their humanitarian values to align with donor-driven targets and programs, NGOs risk losing substantial funding if specific donor targets are not met or if donor programs become unfashionable. One impact of this relationship between transnational financial capital and humanitarianism is that concerns over efficiency and accountability have become one of "the hottest topics for discussion by NGO practitioners," as they demand the same performance and accountability criteria of their beneficiaries that their donors demand of them (Hilhorst 2003, 125).

FINANCING SOVEREIGNTY AND SOVEREIGN FINANCE

In an effort to secure legitimacy in this highly speculative form of sovereign power, many NGOs have taken to enrolling financiers in various practices of their humanitarian assemblages. I was first introduced to the importance of finance in humanitarian efforts during an interview with a field manager employed by the non-profit Water for People. Working in ten countries, and with revenues over $14 million, Water for People is a major player in the water aid world.

"We are now looking into bigger roles in business," the manager stressed. "We're now bringing in more folks in finance because they know this [humanitarianism and aid] better than anything, especially folks that work in international markets." This perspective that financial planners know more about humanitarianism and water aid than the agencies and institutions that have been doing humanitarian policy and practice for more than half a century signals a clear shift in how the welfare of the majority of the world's population is to be designed and managed by the non-profit sector. The repositioning of finance at the heart of humanitarian and aid policy and practice also has clear implications for sovereignty as it shifts the targets and priorities with which the life (and death) of a particular population is to be looked after. In effect, finance has changed not only the practices of humanitarian policy worldwide but also how we come to think about humanitarian values of empowering the poor, improving health, and saving lives (Redfield 2012).

Water.org, another major player in the water aid world, is also looking to financial innovation to grow and stabilize its water aid programs. An employee expanded on the importance of proper finance to its projects:

> Water.org has water credit where they loan community share households money so they can build the water project and then they pay off. We have something similar, which is sanitation loans for folks in India. They do it for folks in India, some in the slum areas, but most of them in the rural areas, and we are working our way into more densely populated areas. (personal communication)

Indeed, many NGOS are turning to financial innovation as the only legitimate means with which to both expand and legitimate their humanitarian efforts. In many ways, what sets one non-profit apart from another is its ability to achieve and secure financial independence, both for itself and for the programs it introduces.

Nowhere is this more clearly captured than in a YouTube video of Ned Breslin, current CEO of Water for People.[3] Standing (naked) in front of an improved water source project that Water for People supported in western Uganda, Breslin declares that he is "offended by the fact that this" five-month-old "project is not sustainable." He goes on to say that "the construction is spectacular," and that "the engineer... did a beautiful job." "Everything looks great," Breslin continues, "but the naked truth [the title of the video] is this project is going to fail." For Breslin, the reason for failure is simple:

> The reason is not because of the quality of the construction, it's not because of the great work that our (engineering) partner did, it's because the financing for this system is not in place. That is the story of hand pumps throughout Africa. . . . The biggest problem in Uganda is functionality. Hand pumps get put in, tariffs aren't collected, management is weak,[4] and the systems fail.

This blunt assessment is indicative of a larger sentiment by many NGOs regarding the root problems of contemporary humanitarian aid. Systems fail not because of the quality of the technology installed or the overall project development process; across Africa systems fail because of (the lack of) financial management. Equally apparent, at least to this CEO, is the solution to the problem of sustainable humanitarianism amidst a permanent state of emergency—the need for more rigid forms of financial management and control. In contrast, the technology of the pump is deemed to be perfect by Ned Breslin. He reverently describes its construction as spectacular, and claims the "the engineer . . . did a beautiful job." It functions not only as a model for water provision, but also as a "health promoting technology" (de Laet and Mol 2000, 231) when compared with other unimproved sources. However, in spite of its beauty, the functionality of hand pumps, Breslin argues, continues to be the "biggest problem in Uganda," because local governments (all over Uganda and Africa) are unable to manage the new infrastructure. The problem for Breslin is not the virtuous non-human hand pump but the people. And the solution is equally clear:

> So Water for People is monitoring its work. We have come back and we've seen that this system, though beautiful, is not sustainable. So we need to turn this around, we need to finance in different ways to support our partners, so that they can continue to work long after the project is finished, and only then will this community truly emerge from water poverty, and never have to return to unprotected waters sources ever again. That's the naked truth.

In other words, water security for the majority of the world's population rests on the tenacity of NGOs to secure their water development interventions and programs with long-term financing strategies. The emphasis on "sound financial management," then, is an effort to tie their water development interventions and programs to "global" capital. This new humanitarian regime secures its legitimacy not by the participation of citizens or local communities (in spite of what NGOs might claim on their websites) in matters of local, regional, or national water governance but rather by claiming to provide for the well-being of the population. Its mode of reasoning, however, is not deliberative openness, in part because local "management is weak," but rather an instrumental notion of costs and benefits (Chatterjee 2004). Its apparatus comes by way of an elaborate network of surveillance that provides extensive monitoring and evaluation of financial flows and other instantaneous transactions that have become the hallmark of twenty-first-century humanitarianism (Galloway 2001).

However, tying humanitarian policy and practice to finance capital has some important consequences for the character of modern sovereignty. First, the markets in financial capital are dominated by a few major institutions such as insurance companies, pension funds, and mutual funds. By tying themselves to transnational capital, NGOs may become associated with business strategies that come into direct conflict with their humanitarian principles or financial relations that work to undermine their humanitarian efforts. For example, one striking feature of Breslin's assessment is its time frame. Five months after its completion this Water for People project was considered inefficient and unsustainable by its chief executive. The fact that this "beautiful" artifact was still fully functional is dwarfed by the assertion that the local community is weak. Moreover, the ability to label this project *unsustainable* five months after its completion would suggest that this analysis seems to serve the quarterly reporting demands and efficiency interests of outside funders, rather than community interests like long-term empowerment, poverty relief, and other exemplars of social and political reform. Tying which populations to champion or "let live," and, by default, which populations to "let die," to networks of transnational finance ensures that this form of sovereignty is not only no longer unified with a particular place, territory, or state but also that this form of sovereignty is constantly being reaggregated and rescaled to fit the interstitial sensibility of transnational finance.

Second, some of the biggest profits from finance markets these days do not come from buying or selling actual things (such as houses or wheat or cars), but from the manipulation of ethereal concepts like risk and collateralized debt. Wealth flows from financial instruments that are one step away from reality (Kaufman 2012). Investing in water indexes is now more popular than ever. There are more than a hundred indexes that track and measure the value of stocks of companies in water-related businesses, such as utilities, sewage treatment, desalination, and water aid. Several offer healthy returns. As a result, the World Bank and other international lending institutions, as well as the International Monetary Fund—always on the lookout for market-based security for the billions of dollars of credit they extend—have been pushing countries to privatize their water resources (Kaufman 2012). These include the lakes, streams, reservoirs, and hand pumps throughout Africa and India. In short, Ned Breslin and other advocates of venture philanthropy are suggesting that they will guarantee the loans made by the World Bank and other lending institutions interested in investing in non-profit water and sanitation programs throughout the world. In this instance, sovereignty comes from the constant work of translating business principles into charity undertakings. Program legitimacy depends on the active enrollment of supporters, including lending institutions and other potential investors, as well as governments and the so-called "beneficiaries." It requires taking risks (with people's lives), many venture philanthropists would argue, because the upside, it is argued, is to do massive public good.

THE MODERN HUMANITARIAN ASSEMBLAGE

Given the changing nature of contemporary humanitarian crises and a growing humanitarian caseload, NGOs, international agencies, and even sovereign states—the United Kingdom recently cut all aid to India—continue to rethink and restructure their institutional efforts (Labbe 2012). Like most NGOs, Water for People has steadily grown in number of projects and areas of influence. Water for People is currently operating in eleven countries (Honduras, Guatemala, Nicaragua, Dominican Republic, Bolivia, Peru, Ecuador, Malawi, Rwanda, Uganda, and India) and claims to have worked in

Table 14.1. Water for People Global Corporate Sponsors (donated between $100,000 and $999,999)

Sponsor	Type of business	Additional ties to WfP
CDM Smith	A private consulting, engineering, construction, and operations firm in water, environment, transportation, energy, and facilities	Senior vice president—member of WfP board of directors
AECOM Technology Corporation	A public company providing technical and management support services to a broad range of markets, including transportation, facilities, environmental, energy, water, and government	
American Water	The largest public water and wastewater utility company in the U.S.	
American Water Works Association	A non-profit organization that provides water quality and supply information, and other water industry resources to its membership	Founded Water for People in 1991
CH2M HILL	Engineering consulting and service provider	Managing director—member of WfP board of directors. Employees "volunteer" in the regional operations.
Green Mountain Coffee Roasters, Inc.	Producer of coffee and coffee-brewing devices	
Nalco Company	A public company involved in water treatment and process improvement services	Chief marketing officer and VP of sales, Americas—member of WfP board of directors. Employees "volunteer" in the regional operations.
Xylem	A public company involved in water and wastewater treatment and process improvement services	

some capacity in over forty different countries in the past. Offices of Water for People are located in nine cities across the globe. Balancing out the centers of "bureaucratic" activity has kept a distributed power base at the global level as well as a sense of agility in responding to local emergencies, such as the South Asian tsunami in 2004. This global local presence ensures that Water for People is well positioned to serve (control) local water crises and to transport its local expertise and experiences to other places.

However, the tension of having to be in multiple places at once has also been a concern for many NGOs that struggle to secure their presence during a permanent state of humanitarian emergency. One strategy to weather the crisis-driven demands of humanitarianism has been to reach out to the private sector. For example, corporate support to Water for People has been instrumental in helping them achieve financial independence. Currently, they have eight "global sponsors" who have donated between $100,000 to $999,999 each (see table 14.1). All except one of the global sponsors (Green Mountain Coffee Roasters, Inc.) are involved in the water services sector. Water for People is also supported by five "continental sponsors" who have donated between $50,000 and $99,999, over fifty "country sponsors" who have donated between $10,000 and $49,999, and numerous other smaller donors. Total revenue for 2011 was $14,328,110.[5]

In addition to their financial aid, many corporate donors have chosen to support the efforts of NGOs in other ways. For example, of the eight "global sponsors," three have executives who are also members of Water for People's board of directors. Similarly, executives from two of the five "continental sponsors" are members of Water for People's board. Many on Water for People's board of directors, in fact, are board members, CEOs, and presidents of large companies with a hand in water technology, facilities management, and engineering and consulting. Some corporate donors also supply the volunteer labor force required by NGOs to carry out their programmatic work. For example, in a baseline assessment in Rwanda, in which I was a participant, the project manager was an engineer from CH2M HILL. He was intensely involved in the planning, data gathering, and reporting phases of the project. The three water quality technicians for the baseline assessment were also employees of Nalco, one of the five "continental sponsors," and their two-week participation in the project was paid for by their employer.

Support from foundations has also helped Water for People secure financial independence. In 2010 Water for People received a $5.6 million grant from the Bill & Melinda Gates Foundation to support their Sanitation as a Business program. The goal of this program is to introduce profit incentives into the improvement of sanitation in households and schools in "developing" countries. According to Water for People, this program will transform "unsustainable, subsidy-based sanitation programs" into "sustainable, profitable sanitation services" by "merging business principles of market research and segmentation" with community involvement and program monitoring (Water for People 2010). This grant, according to an employee, has put Water for People "on the map." "That just lifts us to a whole new category of non-profit." "People [subsistence farmers] in developing countries," a Water for People employee explains, "understand composting, they just don't know [or] understand the business side of it. So, what Water for People is trying to do is branch out of sanitation and make it lucrative for business." Financial security for some NGOs has resulted not only in a shift in development practice but also in a transformation in what it means to do "development" in the twenty-first century. An employee of another non-profit informed me, "We in water and sanitation are moving away from specific projects to long-term programs that employ new methods, and modes of analysis and evaluation." "Once we do that," she continued, "then I think there is going to be a bigger hope . . . not only to meet development goals, but also [to] go further, and think about development on a larger scale, not just in the community level."[6]

That transnational "thinking" about development has, in part, been facilitated by the strategic use of what has become the material epitome of the global assemblage—the World Wide Web. In effect, the Internet has been a formidable ally for NGOs, providing a medium to communicate extensive monitoring and evaluation criteria required by their donors and trustees while at the same time providing invaluable networking potential to people from outside the "development" world. For example, in 2010 Water for People introduced Field Level Operations Watch (FLOW) as part of its commitment to self-sustained long-term water coverage. The FLOW Internet site allows browsers to monitor Water for People's projects for up to ten years after their completion date. The data are displayed on an open-source platform called the Dashboard, indicating the state of projects (functioning, functioning with problems, no improved system, and broken) as well as the type of project that is being evaluated (water access point, school, or public institution). FLOW, according to Water for People, will provide a new kind of transparency that is lacking in most other NGOs, non-profits, and volunteer groups. This information, Water for People claims, will hold them accountable for their work, pushing them to make informed investments and data-driven decisions in order to invoke sustainable impacts within communities.[7] FLOW has been described by an employee of Water for People as a "game changer" in water development. FLOW uses remote data acquired through Android cell phone technology and Google Earth software to provide information to practitioners and donors. The irony is that these technologies are entirely foreign to the majority of the people in need of water and sanitation. As a result, the collection tool becomes a one-sided solution, because community participants are unable to understand or engage with these technologies.

Aside from the virtual technology that FLOW utilizes as a monitoring and social advocacy tool, Water for People uses various forms of social media to spread its mission and work in "developing countries." Facebook, Twitter, MySpace, and LinkedIn, as well as E-Cards and e-newsletters, act as resources in order to inform, educate, and motivate others towards Water for People's vision for safe drinking water and sanitation throughout the "Global South." Water for People also created its own social networking site, called the TAP Portal, which creates collaborative websites to allow a large variety of groups to have deeper conversations about the global water crisis and other relevant topics. Joining the individual sites that are linked within the TAP Portal allows one to discuss topics, interact, and comment on postings, hear news updates, and RSVP for events. Supporters, committees, and staff are expected to communicate with the public through this forum, ensuring that the organization remains committed to learning through a transparent display of information and collaboration.[8]

In effect, the use of the World Wide Web allows for the simultaneous communication of programs to current supporters and the active enrollment of potential supporters, including lending institutions and governments. As in finance, the constant flow of digital measures requires a certain amount of institutional tenacity, not to mention resource allocation, but the upside, it is argued, is not only "to do" but also "to communicate" massive public good.

THE NEW SOVEREIGNS

The power of contemporary humanitarian institutions is embedded in both the practices and technologies that have come to influence decisions regarding which populations to champion or "let live," and by default which populations to "let die." These institutions seek to address not only the symptoms but the causes of humanitarian crises. Their strategies involve various types of intervention, including trading of armed forces, advocating for the enactment of international law in domestic legislation, human rights reform, and strengthening domestic justice systems (Labbe 2012). To these ends, NGOs are becoming integral parts of a transnational decision-making apparatus. For example, over 1,500 NGOs have consultative status with the United Nations, and this number continues to grow. "Many UN agencies now hold periodic consultations with NGOs on substantive policy and programme strategies, and the governing body of at least one agency, UNAIDS, has five seats for NGO representatives" (Opoku-Mensah 2001, 2). Moreover, in 1997 the NGO Working Group was established as part of the UN Security Council. This thirty-member consultation group meets regularly with government delegations to collaborate on issues that pertain to local, regional, national, and international security. In a similar fashion the transnational networks of NGOs are increasingly gaining access to other multilateral organizations like the World Bank, the World Trade Organization, and the World Economic Forums (Opoku-Mensah 2001).

The relentless expansion of NGOs on the basis of emergency, facilitated by new forms of humanitarian intervention—financial, transnational, and digital, to name only three important features—has resulted in a new and contingent form of sovereignty, where increasingly NGOs are defining and deciding on the state of exception for the world's poor. This new form of sovereignty, I argue, is more global assemblage (Ong and Collier 2005) than conventional nation-state—a product of multiple determinations that are not reducible to a single logic or space—like providing humanitarian water aid or even challenging global neoliberal reforms. Increasingly, NGOs are embedded in a transnational, if not exactly global, space. These flows of knowledge, expertise, and finance move within the liminal spaces and apparatuses of control that are constitutive of "the 'non-place' of Empire" (Galloway 2001, 82; Hardt and Negri 2001). The goal of this global studies analysis is to make these largely invisible lines and assemblages theoretically coherent and informative. In effect, the rise of NGOs is evidence of an "associational revolution" that might prove to be as important to matters of life and death in the latter part of the twenty-first century as the rise of the nation-state was to matters of sovereignty in the late nineteenth century. Making visible the multiple contradictory dynamics of this transnational assemblage may also open the possibility for meaningful social change with regards to poverty and inequality throughout the world.

NOTES

1. Although highly selective, some research has pointed to the removal of coral reefs for marine traffic and development as having added to the devastation from the tsunami.

2. Max Lawson of the charity Oxfam told CBC Radio that when Hurricane Mitch ravaged Central America in 1998, only a third of the money promised got to the people of Nicaragua and Honduras (retrieved from http://www.cbc.ca/news/background/asia_earthquake/how-charities-spend.html).

3. See http://www.youtube.com/watch?v=EJmnFEkZDRs.

4. I am particularly intrigued by the use of the word "weak." Here we have a partially naked white man referring to local water management systems, which are typically collectively managed and also have a women's constituency or presence, as "weak," in need, I suppose, of making it more competitive, and masculine, of course. This reproduces the stereotype that competition is an essential feature of good (strong) governance.

5. http://www.waterforpeople.org/about/financials/.

6. Personal communication 2010.

7. http://www.waterforpeople.org/programs/field-level-operations-watch.html.

8. http://www.waterforpeople.org/programs/field-level-operations-watch.html.

REFERENCES

Agamben, Giorgio. 1998. *Homo Sacer: Sovereign Power and Bare Life*. Stanford, CA: Stanford University Press.

———. 2005. *State of Exception*. Chicago: University of Chicago Press.

Bebbington, Anthony. 1997. "New States, New NGOs? Crises and Transitions among Rural Development NGOs in the Andean Region." *World Development* 25: 1755–65.

Blackwood, Amy S., Katie L. Roeger, and Sarah L. Pettijohn. 2010. "The Non-Profit Sector in Brief: Public Charities, Giving, and Volunteering, 2012." Washington, DC: Urban Institute.

Chatterjee, Partha. 2004. *The Politics of the Governed: Reflections on Popular Politics in Most of the World*. New York: Columbia University Press.

de Laet, Marianne, and Annemarie Mol. 2000. "The Zimbabwe Bush Pump: Mechanics of a Fluid Technology." *Social Studies of Science* 30: 225–63.

Deleuze, Gilles. 1992. "Postscript on the Societies of Control." *October* 59: 3–7.

Domhoff, G. William. 2012. "Wealth, Income, and Power." In *WhoRulesAmerica.net*. Online at http://www2.ucsc.edu/whorulesamerica/power/wealth.html. Accessed February 18, 2013.

Duffield, Mark. 2007. *Development, Security and Unending War: Governing the World of Peoples*. Cambridge, UK: Polity Press.

Edwards, Michael, and David Hulme. 1996. "Too Close for Comfort? The Impact of Official Aid on Nongovernmental Organizations." *World Development* 24: 961–73.

Escobar, Arturo. 1995. *Encountering Development: The Making and the Unmaking of the Third World*. Princeton, NJ: Princeton University Press.

Foucault, Michel. 1977. *Discipline and Punish: The Birth of the Prison*. New York: Vintage.

———. 1980. *Power/Knowledge: Selected Interviews and Other Writings 1972–1977*. Edited by C. Gordon. New York: Pantheon Books.

———. 1994. *Michel Foucault: Power–The Essential Works of Foucault, 1954–1984*. Vol. 3, ed. J. D. Faubion. New York: New York Press.

———. 1997. *Michel Foucault: "Society Must Be Defended." Lectures at the Collège de France, 1975–1976*. Edited by M. Bertani and A. Fontana. Translated by D. Macey. New York: Picador.

———. 2008. *The Birth of Biopolitics. Lectures at the Collège de France, 1978–79*. New York: Palgrave Macmillan.

Fraser, Nancy. 2005. "Transnationalizing the Public Sphere." *Re Public Art*. Online at http://www.republicart.net/disc/publicum/fraser01_en.htm. Accessed December 5, 2012.

———. 2007. "Transnationalizing the Public Sphere: On the Legitimacy and Efficacy of Public Opinion in a Post-Westphalian World." *Theory, Culture & Society* 24: 7–30.

Galloway, Alex. 2001. "Protocol, or, How Control Exists after Decentralization." *Rethinking Marxism* 13: 81–88.

Hardt, Michael, and Antonio Negri. 2001. *Empire*. Cambridge, MA: Harvard University Press.

Harvey, David. 2010. *The Enigma of Capital and the Crises of Capitalism*. New York: Profile Books.

Hilhorst, Dorothea. 2003. *The Real World of NGOs: Discourses, Diversity, and Development*. New York: Zed Books.

Kaufman, Frederick. 2012. "Wall Street's Thirst for Water." *Nature* 490: 469–71.

Khagram, Sanjeev. 2004. *Dams and Development: Transnational Struggles for Water and Power*. Ithaca, NY: Cornell University Press.

Labbe, Jeremie. 2012. *Rethinking Humanitarianism: Adapting to 21st Century Challenges*. New York: International Peace Institute.

Miraftab, Faranak. 1997. "Flirting with the Enemy." *Habitat International* 21: 361–75.

Ong, Aihwa, and Stephen Collier, eds. 2005. *Global Assemblages: Technology, Politics, and Ethics as Anthropological Problems*. Oxford, UK: Blackwell Publishing.

Opoku-Mensah, Paul. 2001. "The Rise and Rise of NGOs: Implications for Research." Online at http://www.svt.ntnu.no/iss/issa/0101/010109.shtml. Accessed June 15, 2013.

Pearce, Jenny. 2000. "Development, NGOs, and Civil Society: The Debate and Its Future." In *Development, NGOs, and Civil Society: Selected Essays from Development in Practice*, ed. D. Eade, 15–43. Oxford, UK: Oxfam GB.

Phadke, Roopali. 2005. "People's Science in Action: The Politics of Protest and Knowledge Brokering in India." *Society and Natural Resources* 18: 363–75.

Redfield, Peter. 2012. "Beyond the Bush Pump: Microworlds of Humanitarian Design." In *Workshop on Relocating Science and Technology*. Max Planck Institute of Social Anthropology, Halle, Germany. July 18–20.

Sassen, Saskia. 2006. *Territory, Authority, Rights*. Princeton, NJ: Princeton University Press.

SustainAbility. 2003. "The 21st Century NGO in the Market for Change." London, UK. Retrieved from http://www.sustainability.com/library/the-21st-century-ngo.

Truman, Harry. [1949] 1964. *Public Papers of the Presidents of the United States: Harry Truman.* Washington, DC: U.S. Government Printing Office.

United Nations. 2010. "Water for Life, 2005–2015." Online at http://www.un.org/waterforlifedecade/. Accessed March 5, 2011.

Water for People. 2010. "Water for People Receives Funding for Sanitation as a Business Program. http://www.waterforpeople.org/media-center/press-release/sanitation-as-a-business-funding.html." Denver, CO: Water for People.

Weiss, Thomas G., and Leon Gordenker, eds. 1996. *NGOs, the UN, and Global Governance.* Boulder, CO: Lynne Rienner Publishers.

CONTRIBUTORS

TIM BARTLEY is Associate Professor of Sociology at The Ohio State University.

MANUELA CIOTTI is Assistant Professor, Department of History and Area Studies, Aarhus University.

DEBORAH COHEN is Associate Professor of History at the University of Missouri at St. Louis and author of *Braceros: Migrant Citizens and Transnational Subjects in Postwar United States and Mexico*.

STEPHANIE DEBOER is Assistant Professor, Department of Communication and Culture, Indiana University. She is author of *Co-producing Asia: Locating Japanese-Chinese Regional Film and Media*.

LESSIE JO FRAZIER is Associate Professor of American Studies and Gender Studies, Indiana University. She is the author of *Salt in the Sand: Memory, Violence and the Nation-State in Chile, 1890–Present* and co-editor of *Gender's Place: Feminist Anthropologies of Latin America* and *Gender and Sexuality in 1968: Transformative Politics in the Cultural Imagination*.

ZSUZSA GILLE is Associate Professor of Sociology at the University of Illinois and author of *From the Cult of Waste to the Trash Heap of History: The Politics of Waste in Socialist and Postsocialist Hungary* (IUP, 2007).

ANNE GRIFFITHS is Professor of Anthropology of Law, University of Edinburgh School of Law. Her publications include *In the Shadow of Marriage: Gender and Justice in an African Community; Family Law (Scotland)* (with Lilian Edwards), and *Mobile People, Mobile Law: Expanding Legal*

Relations in a Contracting World (co-edited with Franz and Keebet von Benda-Beckmann).

RACHEL HARVEY is Postdoctoral Research Scholar, Center on Global Legal Transformation, Columbia University Law School.

HILARY E. KAHN is director of the Center for the Study of Global Change in the School for Global and International Studies at Indiana University. She is author of *Seeing and Being Seen: The Q'eqchi' Maya of Livingston, Guatemala, and Beyond.*

PRAKASH KUMAR is Associate Professor of History at Colorado State University and author of *Indigo Plantations and Science in Colonial India.*

MICHAEL MASCARENHAS is Associate Professor, Department of Science and Technology Studies, Rensselaer Polytechnic Institute. He is author of *Where the Waters Divide: Neoliberalism, White Privilege, and Environmental Racism in Canada.*

DEIRDRE McKAY is Senior Lecturer, Department of Social Geography and Environmental Politics, Keele University. She is author of *Global Filipinos: Migrants' Lives in the Virtual Village* (IUP, 2012).

SEAN METZGER is Assistant Professor of Performance Studies in the UCLA School of Theater, Film, and Television. He is author of *Chinese Looks: Fashion, Performance, Race* (IUP, 2014) and editor (with Olivia Khoo) of *Futures of Chinese Cinema: Technologies and Temporalities in Chinese Screen Cultures* and (with Gina Masequesmay) of *Embodying Asian/ American Sexualities.*

FARANAK MIRAFTAB is Professor of Urban and Regional Planning at the University of Illinois.

ALEX PERULLO is Associate Professor of Anthropology and African Studies at Bryant University. He is author of *Live from Dar es Salaam: Popular Music and Tanzania's Music Economy* (IUP, 2011) and *Hip Hop Africa: New African Music in a Globalizing World* (IUP, 2012).

KATERINA MARTINA TEAIWA is Co-Convener of Pacific Studies in the School of Culture, History, and Language, Australian National University.

INDEX

Page numbers followed by *f* indicate a figure; those followed by *t* indicate a table.